AF352495

THE CHILDREN OF SALVATION

THE CHILDREN OF SALVATION

Ritual Struggle in a Liberian Aladura Church

Samuel Irving Britt

THE UNIVERSITY OF SOUTH CAROLINA PRESS

Published by the University of South Carolina Press
Columbia, South Carolina 29208

www.sc.edu/uscpress

Manufactured in the United States of America

21 20 19 18 17 16 15 14 13 12
10 9 8 7 6 5 4 3 2 1

Library of Congress Cataloging-in-Publication Data
Britt, Samuel Irving.
  The children of salvation : ritual struggle in a Liberian Aladura
church / Samuel Irving Britt.
     p. cm. — (Studies in comparative religion)
  Includes bibliographical references and index.
  ISBN 978-1-61117-102-0 (cloth : alk. paper)
  1. Christianity—Liberia—Customs and practices. 2. Christian sects—
Liberia. 3. Ritual—Liberia. 4. Struggle—Religious aspects—Christianity.
5. Healing—Religious aspects—Christianity. 6. Prophecy—Christianity.
I. Title. II. Series: Studies in comparative religion (Columbia, S.C.)
  BR1463.L7B75 2012
  280.09662—dc23
                         2012017699

For my mother,
Rugie Virginia Hall Britt

CONTENTS

Illustrations viii
Preface ix
Acknowledgments xvii

Introduction 1

1 The Field of Prophecy 14

2 Person and Power in Liberia 47

3 The Prophet: The Paragon of Struggle 78

4 The Circularity of Signs 109

5 The Faith Home: Focused Space 138

6 Mount Tabborrar: The Sacred Passage 168

Conclusion 202

Notes 207
Select Bibliography 223
Index 237

ILLUSTRATIONS

Map of Liberia with key places, roads, and ethnic groups xi

Paynesville City: Churches, prayer groups, and Tabborrar mounts 24

Apostle Samuel Olu leading Divine Worship shouts 33

Faith Home ministers at St. Peter's 86

St. Peter's Faith Home compound 142

Prophets performing spiritual exercises during beach struggle 163

Faith Home dwellers during beach struggle 163

The sacred enclosure of Mount Tabborrar 174

Members preparing for the march to Mount Tabborrar 187

Ministers on Mount Tabborrar waiting to receive members 187

From 1983 to 1985 I lived in Paynesville City, near Monrovia, in the Republic of Liberia. I taught courses at Liberia Baptist Theological Seminary, which was jointly supported by the Liberia Baptist Convention and the Southern Baptist Mission Board. Teaching at the seminary provided me with income, valuable connections, and abiding encouragement as I pursued a special research interest: the study of healing rituals among the ubiquitous Aladura churches. That research became the basis for my dissertation, completed at the University of Virginia in 1992. This work liberally draws from that research but develops further a theological trope that I call ritual struggle. Here I explore its relevance also for understanding events and trends of the last twenty years: the Liberian Civil War, the impact of occult cosmologies or discourse, the new Liberian and Aladura diasporas, and the emergence of the global Pentecostal mission.

The Aladura churches originated in western Nigeria in the 1920s and eventually fanned throughout anglophone West Africa. They have been in Liberia since the late 1940s and are one of the best known of the African Initiated Churches (AIC).[1] The initialism AIC has been used to refer to churches that trace their spiritual or institutional lineage to the founding work of charismatic individuals often described as prophets or prophetesses. The Holy Spirit has been a dominant theological concept operative in the practice of most AIC: through the Spirit one receives visions, interprets dreams, and heals the sick. This doctrinal theme has made the recent global networking and even convergence between AIC and Pentecostal groups somewhat predictable.

The Aladura disclose narratives about sin, loss, futility; about battling nefarious spirits, experiencing God's helping hand, facing temptations, and struggling in the faith. The Aladura interlocutor (like the Southern Baptist) may circumvent theological abstractions, but she will always be forthcoming with stories about the church's power to solve problems, to heal the body, and to celebrate the presence of the Spirit. Consequently fieldwork often relayed stories of conversion and acts of testimony. Rebecca Chopp describes testimony in Foucauldian terms as "discourse that refers to a reality outside the ordinary order of things" (2001, 61). In the Aladura world, "reality" can cover a wide range of persons, forces, and experiences: the Holy Spirit, African signs, *jina*, angels, affliction, and transformation. Furthermore "reality" becomes inscribed in the order of things and leaves its traces in everyday experience.

In terms of Christopher Chesnek's description of encounter, the Aladura call forth "a creative dialogue with the world" and so produce "valuable insights by *doing* their religious activities and *living* religious lives" (2002, 59–60). Fieldwork among these "religious lives" inevitably linked theology and ritual practice. In this work I will discuss the major patterns, themes, and values that motivate and sustain a particular religious community. Ritual praxis became the primary way I entered into the Aladura world and this often dovetailed discursive accounts about encounter and elicited commitment and response. While the researcher may try to keep a detached stare, the interpretive cycle that involves the process of fieldwork (especially), the ethnographic engagement, and the writing up of "thick descriptions" often blurs the line between religious studies and theology, between "outsider" and "insider" perspectives. I have written this work as a historian of religions; however, I have also proceeded with the theological reader over my shoulder.

The nation of Liberia was founded in 1822 through the efforts of the American Colonization Society. It was recognized as a republic in 1847 and thereafter claimed to be Africa's first independent nation. From 1822 to 1867 more than twelve thousand settlers came to Liberia. They included free African Americans, recently manumitted slaves, immigrants from Barbados, and "re-captives" from intercepted slave trips. Always a small minority, the descendants of these "first families," who came to be known as Americo-Liberians, Congos, or settlers, maintained political, military, economic, and religious power for more than 120 years until the 1980 coup and the beginning of the Second Republic of Samuel Kanyon Doe.

The Second Republic was marred by corruption, failed policies, economic decline, decaying infrastructure, and ethnic conflict. In 1989 Charles Taylor, a former member of Doe's cabinet, led a rebellion that sent the country into a seemingly unending whirlwind of violence and terror. For fourteen years Liberia endured a cataclysm that left shattered bodies and scorched land in its wake. The images of child soldiers, killer gunmen in dresses and wigs and stories about ritual executions and cannibal war rites confounded and saddened anyone with a conscience, especially those with close Liberian ties.[2] These horrors, not surprisingly, became media-churned and fresh fodder for the "New Barbarism" theorists who continue to assume a reductionist dichotomy between an archaic African culture and a Western progressive one.[3] From the Aladura perspective, however, the frightening images and stories were not to be interpreted simply as evidence of cultural traits or political collapse, but as signs (with universal relevance) pointing to the temptation of secret power, the fallibility of the human subject, and the need for transcendence.

This work explores the religious culture of the Liberian world in the early to middle 1980s, in the wake of Doe's coup and just before that world began to fall

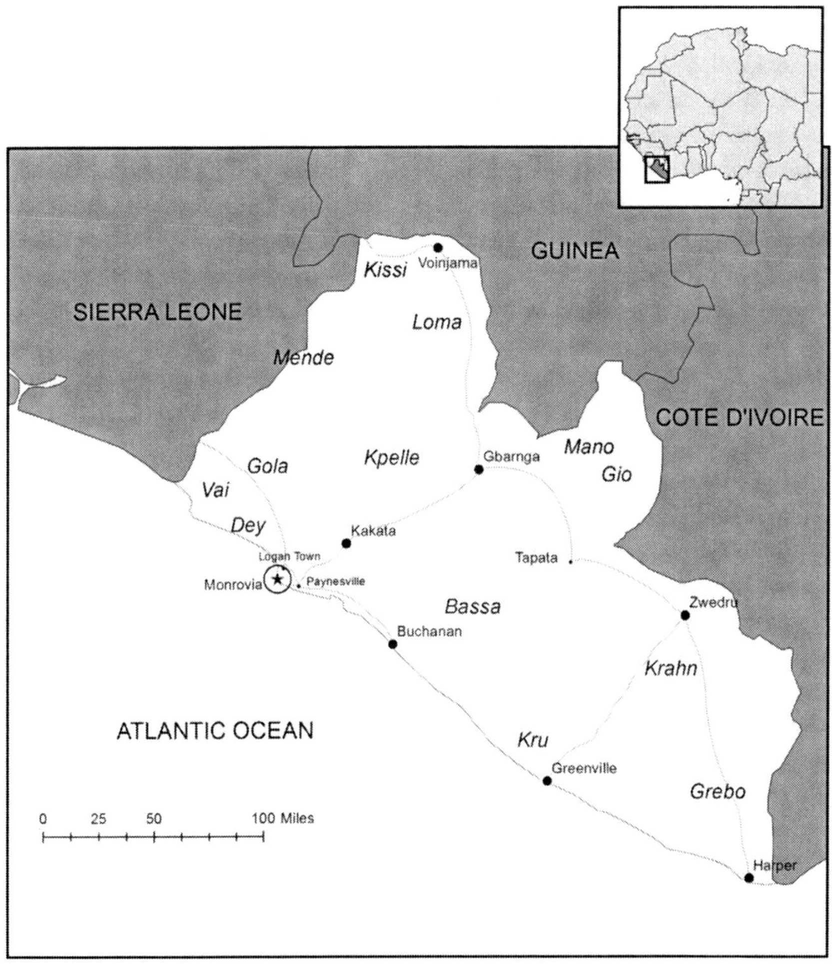

Map of Liberia with key places, roads, and ethnic groups. Boundary of Liberia from ERSI 2009, CD-Rom. Prepared by Mike Winiski.

apart. My period of fieldwork in Liberia preceded Paul Gifford's research on Liberian churches (including Mission, Mainline, AIC, and Pentecostal) and his study of the relation (and response) of these churches to Doe's regime. His work *Christianity and Politics in Doe's Liberia* (1993) attempts to describe the general character of Liberian Christianity; in the process he strongly criticizes the church's complicity with the Doe regime. Later I will comment further on Gifford's critique; for now I simply wish to underline the relevance of his work for our understanding of the networking of Liberian AIC and the impact from the burgeoning global rise of Pentecostal and evangelical groups that has occurred over the last three decades.

My focus on a church called St. Peter's United Church of the Lord Aladura and on other AIC churches in Paynesville makes for one of the strongest differences between Gifford's work and my own. In contrast to Gifford's larger canvas, I explore the theology and practice of a particular group within an old Liberia settlement. The Paynesville settlement was marked by its two crossroads, or "junctures," with their traffic of moving vendors, waiting taxis and money buses, open-air preachers, market ladies, transient workers, and unavoidable strangers. For the Aladura churches the crossroad represented an ambiguous site posing both new possibilities and dreaded dangers. It also became an appropriate metaphor for how the church came to see its role as it faced new directions. By concentrating on a particular Aladura church in Paynesville, we can gain a nuanced view of the church's role within the cultural order and its involvement in local and translocal spiritual economies.

Studies on new African diaspora churches such as the Aladura have focused on churches in Europe and the United States (Harris 2006; Adogame 2007; Crumbley 2008). However, one must also take into account trans-African adaptations, of which St. Peter's provides a meaningful example. Its diaspora experience has unfolded in two stages. First, St. Peter's stemmed from Aladura churches with Nigerian and Yoruba roots. In the 1980s the Nigerian character of St. Peter's remained notable: its founder, Prophet Samuel Olu Shoniyin (hereafter Olu), was Yoruba and many of the church's leading members were Nigerian. At the same time, by the mid-1980s St. Peter's had clearly become a Liberian church. Indeed negotiations between Nigerian and Liberian factions had been a theme in the adaptation of Aladura churches since the arrival the Church of the Lord Aladura (CLA) in Liberia. When I lived in Liberia this continued to be played out, with Liberian Aladura gaining more traction.

In the late 1980s St. Peter's began a second diaspora stage when it established a prayer group among expatriate West Africans in the Washington, D.C., area. The church's efforts to gain a foothold in the United States came after it affiliated with an African American self-described "Spiritual Church." As Gifford has shown, in the late 1980s the transatlantic networking among AIC and American churches (especially among the variety of Pentecostal and evangelical churches) had become fairly widespread.[4] Gifford has argued that the AIC lost ground with the ascendance of Pentecostal-Charismatic Churches, which have absorbed many AIC. Undoubtedly the recent influence of Pentecostal-Charismatic Churches on African churches has necessitated rethinking typologies (Meyer 2004). The extent and nature of Pentecostal influence, however, should be evaluated on a case by case basis. While the Aladura are kin to Pentecostal-Charismatic Churches, the former continue to assert their distinctive character in West Africa, Europe, and the United States. The initialism AIC, then, remains a useful category for describing these churches.

These institutional links, trajectories, and phases provide paths for the navigation of Aladura theology and practice. At the heart of their theology and practice is ritual struggle. Through a variety of ritual strategies and social practices, ritual struggle marks the commitment to make present the work of the Spirit. In terms of theology, it teaches the importance of divine-human collaboration in offsetting the powers and principalities of the world, as expressed in perceived forms of witchcraft. Ritual struggle entails an agonistic experience of the world that collapses the boundaries between natural and supernatural, visible and invisible worlds. This theme then begs discussion of the so-called witchcraft discourses (Nyamnjoh 2001; Geschiere 2006) or occult cosmologies (West and Sanders 2003) that, since Jean Comaroff and John Comaroff's seminal *Modernity and Its Malcontents* (1993), have emerged as a major topic of interest for students of sub-Saharan African religion.

The matter of occult cosmologies has relevance for analysis of the recent civil war. Among recent works on Liberia, Stephen Ellis's remarkable *The Mask of Anarchy* (2006) has been the most insightful and provocative in its claims about the impact of traditional ideas about occult power and ritual transactions on the behavior of political leaders and war combatants. In Mary Moran's words, Ellis "follows a long scholarly tradition of emphasizing the occult, the cosmological aspects of Liberian politics" (2006, 7).[5] He sees war atrocities, human sacrifice, and cannibalism, when they involve occult power, as related to a "psychology of transformation" embedded in traditional cosmologies. In the past the elders and *zoes* (traditional spiritual experts) managed and distributed invisible power for punitive and beneficial purposes. The war, however, produced terrifying bands of young men in drag who disrespected the authority of old men but found ways to mimic their use of power (Ellis 2006, 245–80).

Ellis, however, lays too much blame for the conduct of soldiers in the recent war on the influence of traditional religious or occult concepts. As Paul Richards notes, he fails to recognize the indigenous Liberian critique of the spurious expressions of occult power, such as secret executions and cannibal deeds, and to evaluate the Liberian case in relation to the "wider anthropological literature on witchcraft" (2001, 167–68). Ellis's (and Gifford's) moral critique, however, serves to sharpen our understanding of the complex relation between social, political, and religious forces that have shaped Liberia's tragic history and implicates the ethical responsibility of religious lives amid the uncertainties and mistakes of the postcolonial order.

Though the causal connection Ellis makes between supernatural power and bizarre war atrocities is overdrawn, the evocation of Liberian anxieties about hidden sources of malice is not. Many Aladura would see in his account a confirmation of their ongoing concern about the dangerous temptations of occult power on human decisions, desires, and behavior. Ellis's study simply echoes the Aladura tracing of visible/invisible disruptive powers, or what is, in the Comaroffs' terms, "a metaphysics of *dis*order" (2006, 293).[6] From the Aladura perspective, human crimes sign a theological motif, an unending contest between good and evil, and a mandate for ritual struggle. The strategies of power, both seen and unseen, that foment disorder and distrust cut across regions, peoples, and histories. Whether we talk about failed states, civil wars, shifting economies, or flourishing democracies, the problems of human frailty and malice persist. With this dualist backdrop, ritual struggle provides a notion of agency in which spiritual triumph remains coupled with conflict. This conundrum, however, empowers testimony, the urgency to share experiences about triumph over human failure and sorrow. Amid the unending strife, the Aladura uphold a theme of deliverance, a "discourse of transcendence" (Chopp 2001, 67).

Shortly before I left Liberia, I heard an Aladura prophet deliver a startling vision: he saw a band of soldiers enter a church and begin shooting at the worshippers inside. He reported that those of little faith quickly fell, but those who were resolute in their struggle—the ones he called the Children of Salvation—they remained standing, protected by a shield of faith. Now, many years later, the vision's eschatological calling seems clear: while it augured blood and terror, it also heralded possibility of deliverance, then as well as now. Such performances call to mind Ellis's caution in an earlier essay concerning the Liberian crisis: that construction of a viable political order requires "a spiritual register," an understanding of Liberian spirituality (1995, 196–97). Despite repeated allusions to a dissolute and violent world, the Aladura forms in Liberia express an "ontology of peace" (Robbins 2006, 291) and the expectations for a restored community.

Among AIC near Paynesville I interviewed more than fifty ministers, most of whom members referred to as prophets or prophetesses. About twenty of these ministers belonged to St. Peter's. I met most of them at services, at healing ceremonies, or while passing time at a Faith Home, a special location for healing rites. Some ministers had been ordained for several years, having first worked with the CLA or another Aladura church before joining St. Peter's; others had only recently become ordained. I knew two when they were patients, months before they pursued a ministerial track, and two others who would eventually give up the "prophet business." With a couple of exceptions, the ministers with whom I had the most regular contact were male junior ministers and "ministers-in-training," the initiates often referred to as *followers*. At St. Peter's I came to know about twelve such ministers; three became close friends. One, the Reverend

Kennedy Sandy, was eventually commissioned to direct the church's work in Washington, D.C.

The junior ministers and followers provided me with invaluable insights about Aladura doctrine and practice; thus, at times, their voices are the most pronounced in this work. While the junior minister was in the process of learning official doctrine and becoming a means for its public presentation, he also became privy to doctrines and practices known only by word of mouth, passed along from one prophet (or prophetess) to another. As such he became a viable link between the oral and literate levels of Aladura life. Among church members he was the one most immersed in the daily healing praxis, often serving as a go-between among patients, members, and senior prophets, and thus became a valuable source of information about specific rituals and treatments.

In my dual roles as a seminarian teaching courses in theology and comparative religion and an ethnographer exploring healing rites among Aladura churches, understandable conflicts emerged. But, by and large, I perceived tremendous support from the seminary community (which included students, professors, and missionaries) for my interest in Aladura churches and disarming hospitality from AIC members despite my denominational, cultural, and racial difference.

Fieldwork involved being ready for the unexpected, such as suddenly being asked to receive a prophet's vision or to go before the altar for a blessing. At one service, which I had arranged with church members to be videotaped, a young prophetess, under the direction of the Spirit, pulled me toward the altar, instructed me to kneel, and then directed members to dance around me. I had assumed the camera would create distance, but was reminded that everyday exchanges (including ritual) involved a play between distance and embrace: at one moment, the observer outside the circle, at the next the subject within. Though pen, notebook, camera, and recorder are necessary ethnographic tools, fieldwork always involves role-affecting choices and readiness to cross a boundary and enter the circle.

Fieldwork also involved accepting the mundane, what appeared uneventful. For instance, when I drove to Faith Home sites, hoping to do interviews or observe ceremonies, occasionally individuals asked me to drive them somewhere—to a store, to their home, to the hospital. At first such requests annoyed me, since they took me from doing work on the site and carrying out my agenda for that day. But I also realized the irony in this: that instead of truly entering the Aladura way, at those hesitating moments I became more the "outsider" trying to control the object of my study. Fortunately I came to realize the arbitrariness of my distinction between the eventful and mundane. I also came to see that providing a ride home—like making a pledge at a church rally, offering gifts of rice to the

Faith Home, or helping ministers on healing rounds—was an expected form of service.

Except in chapter 1, where I give attention to the history of Liberian AIC, I use pseudonyms for my informants. Among St. Peter's members the major exceptions are Apostle Samuel Olu, who died in the early 1990s, and the Reverend Kennedy Sandy, who started the church in D.C. I have endeavored to establish some consistency with name replacements, however. Americo-Liberian names replace Americo-Liberian names; biblical, biblical; Kpelle, Kpelle; and so on. For instance, the name Harmon might replace Johnson; Ezekial, Isaiah; and Bemah, Mulbah. When shifting from the particular to the general, gender designations present a challenge for any ethnographer. Since most ministers or prophets were male, I use more often the personal pronoun *he* or *his* when making observations about what a minister may think, believe, or do. Since most patients (and members) were female, I use more often the personal pronoun *she* or *her*. The leaders of the various Aladura churches often used the terms *prophet* and *spiritual* to describe their churches. However, the term Aladura was the most commonly shared among them. The reader should assume that my references to the Aladura way imply St. Peter's unless I indicate otherwise.

Bible verses quoted in this study are taken from the King James Version (KJV). This is the version common among Liberian Aladura churches.

I owe thanks to many individuals and groups who contributed to the completion of this project. I am enormously grateful for the kindness and hospitality I received from the late Apostle Samuel Olu, founder of St. Peter's. He provided me with a "home church," which became the focus of this monograph. I hold in fond memory his steadfast support and warm friendship. Many members at St. Peter's assisted me in understanding church doctrine and practice, including Esther Olu, James Mulbah, Eugene Flahn, and David Ishikwene. No one has assisted me more than the Reverend Kennedy Sandy; from Liberia to America he has been a devoted friend. I am overwhelmingly grateful for his charitable interest and encouragement.

Other AIC congregations in Liberia also extended gracious invitations to worship with them and study their teachings and practices. I am deeply appreciative for the goodwill I received from Apostle Moses Mayson and Prophetess Miatta Tagoe of the Church of the Lord Aladura; from my friend Amos Kueh; and from Bishop Alpha Omega Bundu of the United Church of Salvation. I also wish to thank Primate E. J. Fofana of the Church of Salvation for inviting me to his home in Bo, Sierra Leone, and the gracious hospitality I received. I owe special thanks for the generosity extended to me from members Wilmet Nelson and the late Samuel Norman.

For my stay in Liberia, I am very appreciative of the faithful support I received from Pleasant Grove Baptist Church in Barboursville, Virginia, and Hagood Baptist Church in Barnwell.

In Liberia students and faculty at Liberia Baptist Theological Seminary befriended me in numerous ways. The Southern Baptist Mission in Liberia provided me with work, an auto, a home, and the constancy of friendship while I earned my keep teaching courses in theology and world religions at the seminary. I am grateful for the countless expressions of support I received from former colleagues Jim Parks, Felix Greer, Lawrence Hardy, Bruce Davidson, Joseph Harris and John Carpenter. At the Southern Baptist Mission I wish to thank especially Oren Robinson, Martha Spangler, Pat Bellinger, Robert Bellinger, Alice Hardy, and Robert Woods. I am also grateful for shepherding offered from students. I especially render thanks to William Kollue, who took me to my first Aladura service, and to Enoch David, Peter Evande, and Richard Stryker, who did class projects on local AIC. My travels with Enoch David to his Bassa home and our late-night talks about Bassa culture remain enduring memories.

My work among the Bassa AIC in Paynesville would not have been nearly as productive without the assistance of Willis Modee. He helped me in gathering information about local Bassa and Aladura churches and occasionally served as an interpreter during interviews with ministers, members and patients.

I doubt this project would have ever been completed without Benjamin Ray's steady heartening push—from fieldwork through dissertation to the production of this monograph. My interest in the Aladura churches began more than thirty years ago when I first read his *African Religions.* Ben's mentoring as teacher and scholar most helped me to appreciate the connections between ritual, symbol, and community. Also I am indebted to the late Ed Winter for his council about fieldwork: first, begin with what you see; second, never forget that ethnography always involves ethics. I am thankful for the interest shown and the conversations over the years from other scholars of African religions: Jacob Olupona, Rosalind Hackett, Anthony Ephirim-Donkor, Brian Siegel, and Cynthia Hoehler-Fatton and Edith Turner.

In Charlottesville, Virginia, I owe heartfelt thanks to Innisfree Village, to its former director Heinz Kramp, and to the late Charlie Feigelson. The moral support and unexpected friendship they lent when I returned from Liberia was immeasurable.

Through generous summer grants, Furman University enabled me to carry out research projects among Aladura churches in the Washington, D.C., area. My last sabbatical (with extra encouragement from David Rutledge) allowed me time to make crucial headway with research and writing. Furman has been for me an incomparable community of care and learning. Through the years my colleagues in the Departments of Religion and Asian Studies have granted me time and patience. Students have also shown avid and thoughtful interest in Aladura churches. In this regard I wish to thank particularly Leanne Kittrel Diakov, who assisted me with research in Washington.

Several individuals have assisted with the general layout of the book. First I would like to thank Anne Barrington for the close reading and editorial revisions that significantly improved the original draft. Claude Stulting, Helen Lee Turner, and Bryan Bibb also helped edit portions, for which I am grateful. A thank you goes to Amanda Pruitt for work on the bibliography, to Catherine Culbertson for assistance with the index, to Jen Haldaman for help in formatting the photographs, to Mike Winiski for preparing the map of Liberia, and to my colleague Peter Valdina for his help in drafting illustrations and preparing the manuscript. I have also benefited enormously from the always reliable assistance of Sharon Dilworth. I am very appreciative of the editorial guidance received from Karen Beidel and Bill Adams of the University of South Carolina Press.

Notes of personal appreciation go to Clark Brittain, Juan Pastor, and Ban Poh. Each is a dear friend who, along the way, was an engaged listener.

I am extremely grateful to Jim Denton for the confidence he expressed in this project and the guidance he provided. I wish to thank the two external reviewers for their scrupulous readings. Both offered key suggestions that improved the text's outline and argument.

Last, I am deeply indebted to members of my South Carolina and Virginia families, but especially to my wife, Sarah, and our daughters, Julia and Virginia. Without their patience, love, and laughter, I could never have finished this project.

THE CHILDREN OF SALVATION

Introduction

It was a warm, damp Liberian afternoon in August 1984. After interviewing patients, I decided to take a short rest in the chapel. I put away pen, notebook, and recorder. Patients staying at the church for treatments began pulling out their bedding in order to catch a nap before three o'clock prayers. Some stretched out on benches. It was Tabborrar season, when church prophets secluded themselves within a forest camp for special fasting and prayers. The two male ministers assigned to the Faith Home (the church's healing clinic) were away: Flomo had gone to receive messages from the mount prophets and Isaiah was making house calls. Through the window I noticed Sister Annie, who held the office of cross bearer, lead a patient, a Krahn woman who was carrying her sick infant, into the Mercy Ground. I returned to my reverie, thankful for a few moments to myself.

Then suddenly, from the Mercy Ground, Sister Annie's fierce screeching disturbed the quiet. Dwellers got up and looked into the yard. We also heard the Krahn woman crying. I saw her dash from the Mercy Ground and run toward the chapel door. Jittery, sweaty, a book of psalms in hand, she reached toward me, handed me the psalms, and pulled at my arm. Reluctantly I followed her to the Mercy Ground, where I saw Sister Annie kneeling before a cross. The infant had been placed on the ground. Sister Annie shrieked words, often indecipherable, suggesting pain and horror. She was having a vision, a vision that included images of an open yard, a deep hole, an infant being placed in the hole, a woman with Dragon (a secret power that takes the form of a snake) leering from above.

Sister Annie instructed me to kneel and to read psalms over the infant while she continued to pray. The praying lasted for about ten minutes. The cross bearer modulated her frenzy, occasionally moving her torso with violent contortions, striking her chest, and pressing her head against the Mercy Ground. After the prayer she collapsed. The Krahn woman, weeping and clutching her child, hardly noticed me as I left. I reentered the chapel. Shaken and confused, I took a few minutes to calm myself and rest.

This study explores the relation between worldview and ritual action in an Aladura church in Liberia. Its starting point is my dissertation (1992), which emphasized the emergence of a "prophet cosmology" in the Liberian cultural landscape in the 1980s. In this book I continue to note the valuable role that the religious authority (such as the prophet) plays in Liberian religious experience. I have, however, reexamined this role in relation to the so-called occult cosmologies as described by Harry G. West and Todd Sanders that have collapsed the lines between "global and local, between modernity and traditional, and between rationality and conviction" (2003, 6). Occult cosmologies are easily encompassed by the Aladura vision of reality. They are systems of belief in a world animated by secret, mysterious, and unseen powers. Occult cosmologies suggest that there is more to what happens in the world than meets the eye—that reality is anything but "transparent." More specifically they claim that power operates in two separate but related realms, one visible, the other invisible; between these two realms, however, there exist causal links, meaning that invisible powers sometimes produce invisible results. Developing this idea merges with the so-called witchcraft discourse. The word *discourse* refers to both the description and way of talking about something; it involves the range of verbal exchanges among informants (or interlocutors).[1] Here I do not see discourse in the Foucauldian sense as "a medium through which power relations produce speaking subjects" (Hammoudi 2009, 51), but as a rubric for engagement, a dialectic of experience and interpretation. Discourse, though, assumes bodily as well as verbal exchanges: how ideas and values become inscribed in ritual and behavior and, in turn, help reproduce them. The phrase *witchcraft discourse* refers to the ways of talking about the ideas, the rituals, and the behaviors that implicate ideas about witchcraft and "occult power" (Moran 1990, 36–40).

In Liberia a term frequently used to suggest the notion of occult power was *African science.* In itself it referred to something that was morally neutral; it became good or bad depending on its use. The application of this knowledge became known as "placing African signs." Though Liberian Aladura parlance indicated ambivalence about this knowledge and power, and that it should not be reduced to witchcraft, the Aladura prophets were clearly cautionary about interest from members. They stressed the opposition between virtue, or spiritual power, and other forms of mysterious, hidden unauthorized power, including African science. In this context terms such as *witchcraft* and *African science* obtained polemical value, as when one prophet used them to accuse another of undermining his work.

Through this work I elaborate the concept of ritual struggle, which describes the strategies of ritual action, ethical behavior, and predispositions toward the world consistently expressed in Aladura churches. The word *struggle* was frequently used to refer to a category of rituals, such as beach struggles, but it might also be used to denote other symbolic rites, personal trials, or dramatic encounters. Ritual struggle always assumed a dualistic backdrop, which makes the matter of cosmology especially relevant. The cross bearer's vision described above presents images of terror: the child in the hole, the evocation of the Dragon power. But these were countered by her emphatic gestures and forceful prayers signaling hope.

The Aladura Churches

The Yoruba term *Aladura* (*aladua*) means the praying ones, or owner of prayer. In Nigeria the term has been used to refer specifically to four major institutional groups—the Cherubim and Seraphim Society (C&S), the Christ Apostolic Church, the Church of the Lord Aladura (CLA), and the Celestial Church of Christ. Over time, however, the term has become more general. As the Aladura churches spread throughout southern Nigeria and into other parts of West Africa, *Aladura* came to describe a type of church that emphasized prophetic healing (Adogame 2004, 493). An analysis of this church involves an appreciation of the prophet's role, the complex of forces and relations in which he worked, his domestic responsibilities, and his governance of ritual space and time. In the Aladura world the person known as the prophet mirrored popular concepts of self and power, two concepts critical to understanding the Aladura way. The term *prophet* referred to one who received "revealed knowledge" and who mediated this through a specific ritual praxis that most often involved healing. Thus, for Aladura participants, being in the Aladura way implied confidence in the prophet's words and deeds, which, according to church doctrine, revealed the working of the Holy Spirit.[2]

Despite this guiding normative rule, the perception of the prophet involved ambivalence about his use of mystical power but, ironically, advanced his status in the church. The prophet embodied a "struggling self" in the sense that he constantly faced the temptation to misuse power, to promote his own welfare over that of others. However, the Aladura understood that the very persistence of such temptation and the resolve to overcome it actually strengthened a resolute prophet. The notion of a struggling self effectively reverberated what the Aladura identified as basic divides of human experience—male-female, senior-junior, village-bush, desire-control, good-evil, dream-waking, front-back, and tied-loosed. Awareness of such dualities created moral and social tensions that were played out in the ritual and social space, often testing the prophet's power. The notion of self, then, follows Sherry Ortner's description of agency as project, which takes into account a person's "culturally constituted intentions, desires, and goals" (2006, 151). The idea of ritual struggle assumed personal agency but involved managing circumstances "embedded in webs of relations." In this context self-identity and power became negotiated concepts.

The notion of a struggling self became articulated in the very person and work of a founder. A former CLA minister, Prophet Samuel Olu Shoniyin founded St. Peter's in 1980 and led the new church until his violent death during the Liberian Civil War. Based in Nigeria, the CLA was always the most dominant and influential of the African Initiated Churches (AIC) in Liberia. Throughout the 1970s Olu had been among the CLA's most gifted healers and effective evangelists. In my conversations with CLA leaders, they spoke about the prophet with mixed admiration and disappointment; they considered him an inspired minister but also a misguided son of the church. Olu and his followers, however, always insisted that his leaving the CLA came from a divine mandate and, in response to his detractors, that St. Peter's represented an authentic Aladura church. According to Olu, the St. Peter's way was the Aladura way. Olu claimed, furthermore, that St. Peter's descended from the C&S, with which he had been involved as a young man in Nigeria.[3]

Before the mid-1980s the Aladura churches in Nigeria had been the topic of three lengthy monographs: Harold Turner's *History of an African Independent Church* (1967), a theological evaluation of the CLA's beliefs and practices; J. D. Y. Peel's *Aladura: A Religious Movement among the Yoruba* (1968), a sociological analysis of the development of the Christ Apostolic Church and the C&S; and Akim Omoyajowa's *Cherubim and Seraphim: The History of an African Independent Church* (1982), a theological evaluation of C&S. Turner and Omoyajowa address the matter of the theological "authenticity" of Aladura churches. In both works the authors discuss the churches' official line on doctrine and practice. They base their evaluations mainly on their review of church literature and on the perspectives of church leaders. While Turner's and Omoyajowa's studies illuminate theological traits and historical trends, both authors largely overlook the oral traditions and the forms of knowledge mediated through such strategies as dreams, visions, and healing rituals, which also disseminated doctrine (Probst 1989, 488–90).

In giving more attention to the social context of the Aladura movement, Peel complements the theological analyses of Turner and Omoyajowa. According to Peel, Aladura success was related to the ability of church leaders to provide an explanation of misfortune and a rational program for its control.[4] Peel elucidates the links between Aladura theodicy and Yoruba cultural experience, but, unlike

Turner and Omoyajowa, he neither privileges written and official sources nor does he slight the impact of symbolic and ritual dimensions.

In the last thirty years other historians of religions and anthropologists have also deepened our understanding of Aladura ritual and its relation to communal experience. Articles by Rosalind Hackett (1980), Jacob Olupona (1987), Peter Probst (1989), Diedra Crumbley (1992, 2003, 2006, 2008), Benjamin Ray (1993), and Afe Adogame (2000, 2004), and the recent monographs by Hermione Harris (2006) and Crumbley (2008) have further indicated significant links between cultural and theological forms. These studies have also added to our knowledge about the variety of Aladura groups while bringing to light common patterns emerging from the interface between Yoruba culture and Christianity.[5]

The Nigerian and Yoruba traditions continued to play a role in the shaping of the character of the Aladura church in Liberia. Indeed, St. Peter's maintained strong links with Nigerian sources. But in the 1980s St. Peter's, as well as other Aladura churches in Liberia, encouraged a process of indigenization. Thus, in Liberia the Nigerian or Yoruba threads became interwoven into the tapestry of Liberian cultural experience. At the same time, Aladura churches developed new affiliations abroad and tested the waters of the new emerging Pentecostalism. The works of Peel, Adogame, Harris, and Crumbley have given valuable attention to both the Yoruba and Nigerian background of new AIC and to the impact of the global cultural and religious forces, such as Pentecostal and evangelical churches, on the theology and practice of diaspora Aladura. In the case of Liberian churches, the disruption caused by the recent civil war facilitated new interactions between Aladura and Pentecostal groups, both in and beyond Liberia.

Though seldom cited in this study, Harold Turner's *History of an African Independent Church* proved the most useful reference during my fieldwork in Liberia. In the 1980s CLA authorities in Liberia held Turner and his work in high esteem. During my first audience with Apostle Moses Mayson, then head of the Liberian diocese, he encouraged me to read Turner's work if I wanted to learn about Aladura theology and practice. Fortunately a Baptist missionary couple gave me their copy of Turner's two-volume study, which they had purchased in Nigeria. It provided a useful compendium of information and complemented my research on the nonliterate and ritual aspects of Aladura practice. Turner's work proved invaluable for another reason. His chapter on the Aladura church in Liberia was then the most thorough account of the early history of any independent church in Liberia. Covering the first two decades of Aladura history in Liberia, Turner's study concludes with the death of the legendary apostle Samuel Oduwole in 1965. In the 1980s Oduwole remained the most revered figure in the history of Aladura churches in Liberia. Even among "schismatic" churches, his name continued to be invoked to legitimate their authenticity and authority.

Unfortunately Turner gives limited attention to the role of ritual praxis in the Aladura church's early development. One cannot understand the expansion and the steady work of the Aladura churches without appreciating this dimension. These churches accentuate the praxis of ritual struggle, which assumed an agonistic vision about the world and a call to specific ritual action and ethical behavior. Despite an ameliorative role, Aladura ritual implicated the menacing presence of evil powers, and with that an anxiety about defilement and the loss of power. Taking the Aladura way, embracing its specific ritual praxis, therefore meant "to be in struggle." It is possible to see this idea of struggle in light of the Yoruba proverb *"aye lajo,"* meaning "Life is a journey," which, as Adogame notes, evokes a world marked by "uncertainties, unpredictability in human relations, failures at self-actualizing, conflict in relations, insecurity and fear derived from power" (2000, 3). The fray and fracas of life provide the context for ritual and moral action; they generate the temptations that we are called to subdue and through which the self becomes empowered.

Ritual struggle enabled the self, but it also implicated self-denial or renunciation. Paul Gifford's claim that ascetic values are not African would not apply to the Aladura churches in Liberia.[6] Authentic struggling required the renunciation of self-interest, and the most effective struggles always involved fasting. For the Aladura prophet, fasting entailed an act of renunciation, or self-sacrifice. Indeed, only through the diminishment of the self did one obtain "virtue." The Aladura prophet provided a model for and of asceticism, which, in L. William Countryman's terms, is *"a relatively demanding bodily praxis, voluntarily undertaken, that sets those who adopt it apart from and, in the view of some, above the ordinary run of people in the world"* (1999, 371).

Radical self-denial, however, can also be goal focused. As Pamela Eisenbaum notes, ascetic "practices make up a disciplinary technology that allows one to achieve a higher goal. . . . Asceticism is a form of goal oriented behavior" (1999, 333). In the Aladura way the practice of self-sacrifice was not an end in itself but related to the ongoing praxis of problem solving. Though the value of self-sacrifice appeared to contradict the instrumental aspect of Aladura ritual, where ritual functioned primarily to help subjects obtain blessings here and now, the contradiction became resolved, in Ward Keeler's view, through a homology between desire renounced and desire obtained.[7] One attained the longed-for goal only by putting aside self-interest.

An evaluation of the prophet's exemplary role in the healing process is critical to understanding the Aladura way. The relation between models of the holy person and indigenous cosmology has been well explored in anthropological literature. For understanding this relation I have found especially useful Stanley

Tambiah's discussion of a Buddhist healing cult in Thailand, in which he locates the cult leader, the *achan* (teacher), within Thai cosmology. Tambiah contends that the meaning of Thai healing and the appreciation of the role of the *achan,* "the extraordinary person," is best illuminated through reference to both cosmological and performative axes. Rituals work both to "translate and create the cosmology" and to transform the involved participants. Through certain performative acts[8]—sacred words, gestures, use of special materials—beliefs and values are communicated and persons affected.

The analysis of the character, role, and expectations of the Liberian prophet helps clarify the understanding of the Aladura cosmology and provides an evocation of Liberian culture in the 1980s. This has relevance as well for appreciating the relation between prophetic mastery and ritual/communal praxis in today's translocal contexts. The Liberian prophet created, or, rather, re-created, cosmology fundamentally through a complex of sacred techniques that were understood to mediate spiritual power and to transform participants and their situations. It is important to speak about Aladura cosmology, however, in terms of the Aladura way, since this phrase, aside from its indigenous basis, effectively evokes the perceived unity between knowledge and experience about the world, as well as the processual nature of church life. To know the Aladura way was to experience it, which happened most vigorously through ritual struggle.

Theology and Christian Culture

Though I have written this work from the perspective of a historian of religions, I have done so with relevance for the theological discourse. For this task I have found especially helpful studies that explore the interface between theology and anthropology (Driver 1991; Thomas 1999; Davies 2002; Brown 2001; Robbins 2004, 2006, 2007) and stress the value of seeing doctrine in relation to everyday material practice (Keane 2007; Coleman 2006). This approach also has implications for appreciating the link between theology and religious studies (Davaney 2001, 3–16).

Theology, in Robert Orsi's words, "is the reflection upon the thought and practice of religious tradition by its adherents" (2005, 192). In this work I do not distinguish between kinds of theology, and I reject the divide between a "first order discourse" of faith and experience and a "second order discourse" of reflection. As John Milbank notes, "every Christian is a theologian, because faith is always *somewhat* reflective, albeit in the mode of symbol, ritual, and narrative" (2004, 14). Christian theology (whether folk, confessional, or academic) can evaluate the experiential claims made about God and the spiritual dimension and study how these become embodied and emplaced in everyday practice. Depending on the person and the particular tradition recognized (for instance, Roman

Catholic, Lutheran, Baptist, or Pentecostal), theology can begin at one of numerous points along a spectrum—from simply "thinking about God" on one end to "everyday practice" on the other. When I began fieldwork I gave special attention to what I saw, heard, smelled, tasted, and touched, in part because the anthropological wisdom I had received counseled attention to the visible and material dimension. At the same time, I was theologically predisposed to study personal experiences and narratives, a tendency that I have little doubt, for good or bad, came from my Southern Baptist baggage. In terms of personal theology my approach entailed looking closely at the embodied material forms and at the personal stories. Here *story* refers not only to the narrative about hardship and transformation that the interlocutor may share, but also to dramas that unfold in the context of social and spatial relations, which also include the ethnographer as performer.

In the discussion about the interface between theology and anthropology, the hermeneutical approach of Hans Frei has relevance. Following Paul Ricoeur, Frei criticizes explanatory interpretations that see religion primarily as "ideology" and as something that escapes the insider/informant's awareness. As opposed to this "hermeneutics of suspicion," he advocates a "hermeneutics of restoration" that finds a good anthropological complement in Clifford Geertz's model of "thick description." Frei notes that "rather than *explaining* the culture that one looks at, one tries to *describe* it. Culture is a kind of natural convention, and studying it is called ethnography. It's a way really of finding our footing with a group of strangers who have a common sign system, verbal but perhaps also ritual—a semiotic system within which we try then to orient ourselves" (1992, 12–13). Frei's approach supports the idea that theology should be more about narrative than about explanation or understanding. (See also Hauerwas 2004, 145.) Ironically, when Frei wrote the passage cited above, anthropology had for many years been engaged in a self-critique about its role in the construction of culture and of the praxis of power and "difference" created between researcher and informant. In any case Frei's approach appears especially useful for "picturing" an Aladura culture where theology and praxis converge. On this point I find compelling Delwin Brown's proposal to rework theology (or theology-cum-ethnography) as "theography." Here Brown is reconfiguring academic theology as an "ethnography of religious belief," which, if I understand Brown correctly, would implicate also ritual and social praxis and make room for folk as well as official theology (2001, 51). This approach encourages theology to be more mindful of the ritual and embodied forms of religious life.

If theologians have neglected the embodied forms of belief and doctrine, anthropologists have undervalued the theological or doctrinal claims and expressions of Christian communities. The recent works of Joel Robbins (2004), Web Keane (2007), Matthew Engelke (2007), and contributors to Fenella Cannell's

Anthropology of Christianity (2006), however, demonstrate a different trend. These studies explore Asian, Melanesian, and African Christian groups, churches, and communities as "Christian cultures," while they also critique the slighting by anthropologists of colonial and postcolonial Christian subjects. What follows is a brief discussion of the approaches of Keane and Robbins and how they can contribute to our appreciation of an "Aladura culture."

Keane's work indicates an appreciation of how practice relates to theology and to the meaning of soteriological models. In *Christian Moderns* (2007) he contends that one cannot understand Sumbanese Christian culture in Indonesia, in which he did fieldwork, without examining the Calvinist doctrines mediated by Dutch missionaries. Building on the work of Bruno Latour (1993), Keane stresses a key theme in Western thought that shouldered modernity—the "work of purification." According to Latour, this work was reflected in the modern agenda to separate sign from thing, culture from nature, humans from non-humans, and idea from body in a manner that diminishes the value of the second member of each pair. Reformation thought had affinity with this "work" in the growing separation it made between belief and ritual, symbol and presence, and private experience and public performance. Missionaries continued this project, Keane notes, as they made "some of the core assumptions of their Euro-American world visible" (2007, 23–24).

This approach was also linked to a new understanding of material forms. From Luther to Calvin to the left-wing reformers, one observes a progressive iconoclasm, an attempt to abolish image, ritual, and liturgy. The Protestant experiment devalued material forms and privileged scripture and words. In pushing forth their critique, however, Protestant missionaries underestimated the materiality and power of texts and words. Their strategy often took an ironic turn. As Keane notes, "agents continually constitute themselves through semiotic practices that contain an irreducibly material dimension." This indeed leads to tension between the model of purification and the "inescapability of material and social mediations" that Keane calls the "modern subject's anxious transcendence" (2006, 322).

Keane seems to suggest that the experiences of conversion in non-Western Christian communities have made problematic the reliance on modern dichotomies in the study of religion. In looking at AIC, such as the Aladura churches, one immediately faces the fact of materiality—both in terms of material objects, which manifest the spiritual, and in terms of words, names, and texts, which become empowered objects. The importance of the translation of scripture for the beginnings of AIC has been well noted (Sanneh 1994; West and Dube 2000). But more can be said about how African reformers discovered both the use and reading of scripture as the basis for a new materiality, an appreciation for things and bodies, verbal and imagined forms. The Aladura culture, for instance, speaks of holy materials, feeding the Spirit, spiritual exercises, spiritual bathrooms, food for fasting, African signs, holy names and words, mercy grounds, faith homes, and beach struggles—terms, names, and phrases implying the rejection of modern dichotomies between idea and form, sign and signified. They press for the value and reality of material forms and embodied power. At the same time, the Aladura ministers I knew would insist that holy materials, such as candle and water, and ritual struggles, such as beach struggles, had no power without the subject's genuine faith. But, though one can still observe the "anxious transcendence" described by Keane, on this point they differ significantly from Pentecostal-Charismatic Churches, which more fully embrace the Protestant critique of materiality.[9]

In his study *Becoming Sinners* (2004), about a Christian community among the Urapmin people of Papua New Guinea, Joel Robbins claims that anthropologists have ignored the study of Christian groups in places like New Guinea or Africa because their "hybridity" compromised the notion of the intact, well-defined group. They do not constitute the kinds of "cultures" that anthropologists preferred to study.[10] But, as Robbins shows, Urapmin Christianity constitutes a culture, which, like any other, generates a world of meaning and values. The form of Christianity that the Urapmin embraced was Pentecostal-Charismatic, which came directly to them through the work of native-born missionaries. Robbins explores why the Urapmin accepted the Pentecostal-Charismatic form rather than other Christian forms, which were also available (27–34, 332–33).

Robbins's approach in *Becoming Sinners* very much stresses how the study of theology helps us appreciate the formative impact of doctrinal ideas on culture. Theology, in this sense, is studied primarily as "data" for our research, which also characterizes Keane's approach. In a more recent article (2006), however, Robbins challenges anthropology to engage theology in a way that goes beyond simply appreciating its social and historical relevance or looking at it as data. Anthropology also needs to become open to the theological critique and reevaluation of social theories. Robbins is responding in particular to theologian John Milbank's *Theology and Social Theory* (1990), in which Milbank interprets modern social theory as "a breakdown product of a decaying theology" (Robbins 2006, 289). Milbank's principal interest is the restoration of theology as social science and the refutation of modern theory's ontology of difference and violence. Theology, by contrast, should present an ontology of peace; one in which the experience of the world and the descriptions of the structures and patterns of community are not reduced to discourses on power. Robbins sees this as a good rule for doing anthropology as well.

The study of a Christian culture, then, can use theology and anthropology as complementary approaches. Fieldwork circumstances make some form of theologizing unavoidable; it becomes part of day-to-day activities and discussions. If writing up and interpreting the fieldwork has created some distance (in both time and space) from my initial work, it has not lessened the importance of listening to and learning from theological voices, African and Western. The coupling of theology and anthropology, which involves researching and writing about Aladura as culture, inevitably creates, in the Ricoerian sense, a "testimony," a presentation or performance of "speech acts," of the Aladura way and its specific interface with Spirit.

Disordered States and Aladura Signs

In my effort to identify patterns, influences, and metaphors that arise in the Aladura experience in Liberia and have relevance for understanding the church in the postwar, global, and diaspora context, it has not been my intent to present the vast array of symbols, signs, and rites as part of a systematic whole. A symbolic analysis may enable us to understand components of cosmology better, but it often assumes that particular symbols, rites, and structures will reveal a coherent whole. This approach easily obfuscates our understanding of an Aladura church as a living community. I stayed in Liberia at a time that now could be described as the apprehensive calm between a roaring tempest and a cyclonic onslaught. When I arrived in Liberia in August 1983, Samuel Kanyon Doe had been in power for more than three years. He had weathered much of the bad repute created from the ruthlessness of the 1980 coup. I knew individuals and families devastated by the coup who were also glad to let bygones be bygones and give the man a chance. Still, there were voices of discontent and, occasionally, the alarming civil clash. The Nimba event of December 1983, when Krahn soldiers killed Mano policemen, and the University of Liberia massacre of August 1984 augured for many the eventual collapse of the Doe regime. Still, the most pessimistic prognosis of political observers hardly foresaw the delirious descent into the mayhem of the next two decades.

Paul Gifford's important work *Christianity and Politics in Doe's Liberia* (1993) gives extensive study to the role of churches during Doe's regime. Gifford critiques churches of all stripes for their capitulation to the political order. He believes that had the churches embraced a "theology of liberation" they could have created a more effective foil to the brutality of Doe's regime. Undoubtedly many churches shamelessly accommodated the government, and, regrettably, few Christian leaders openly challenged its policies, but Gifford's evaluation overlooks the extent to which churches were already suffering and the indirect, subtle forms that the spirit of opposition often assumed. His expectation for human agency privileges a "domination/resistance" model that sets the bar high for a political subject's overt resistance to oppression.[11] In facing oppressive conditions, though, people most often work "on the margins," developing projects and playing with strategies that are not always fully apparent, and which, according to Sherry Ortner, "are often invisible in anthropologies that remain at the level of large-scale political formations—colonialism, the state, etc—and do not as it were touch the ground" (2006, 151).

At Liberia Baptist Theological Seminary, for instance, students and teachers constantly discussed, debated, and argued over issues about Christian responsibility for social action. They knew, however, that flagrant denunciations faced the barrel of a gun. Even then risks were taken. During the University of Liberia massacre a seminary board member was among those protesting the arrest of Amos Sawyer, a vocal critic of the Doe regime. When troops entered the campus, beating and shooting protesters, the board member and about twenty students hid themselves in a small room for several hours, managing to slip away after dark. In December 1984, at the seminary's matriculation, the guest speaker, the late Mary Brown Antoinette Sherman, bravely condemned the corruption and injustice of state regimes. She named no names, but all knew of whom she spoke.

At Aladura churches the discontent and protest were not expressed in overt confrontations. But they were expressed. Carl Jung once commented that his patients' dreams in the 1920s prepared him for the Nazi atrocities to come. Similarly the Aladura therapeutic process, which involved specific narrative constructions, such as reported dreams, visions, and sermons, offered intimations of conflict and of the breakdown of a moral order. Sometimes these came through the images of visions and dreams: cruel soldiers shooting in churches, a neighbor burying a bottle, a husband morphing into a snake, or stranger grabbing a child. In vision after vision, sermon after sermon, ministers reported "signs" of contagious vice, of radical distrust, and of swirling collapse. Aladura discourse navigated the streams of contesting forces, seeking a safe landing. In the process it offered commentary for present social and political challenges. The frightening images and signs about occult power and the other world might have tapped into centuries-old memories of slave raids and ethnic wars, but this Christian culture saw such images and signs primarily in terms of contemporary maladies.[12]

The horrendous civil war from 1989 to 1997 and the turbulent years of Charles Taylor's rule that ended with his removal from power in 2003 resulted in the deaths of hundreds of thousands. More than half of the population became displaced refugees or exiles. During the war Paynesville became a strategically important place. The highways that linked the eastern, western, and northern parts of Liberia converged there. The coastal highway to Buchanan passed the nation's major airport. Paynesville had two radio stations, one located at a missionary campus, which also provided one of the best equipped medical facilities in Liberia. Predictably, on different occasions the town became a major battleground between government and rebel factions, especially during the first (1990) and the second (1992) battles of Monrovia. Businesses were looted, houses burned, churches damaged, and schools pillaged. At different times the Baptist seminary became an encampment for refugees and rebels. Many Paynesville residents were mistreated, interned, even killed. Friends and acquaintances, some who appear in this study, met with such misfortunes. My reveries on life in Liberia then often prompt feelings of grief and loss.

Undoubtedly the travesties of political violence call for, in Arthur Kleinman's terms, "a phenomenology of desperate failure" or "the ethnography of disordered states" (1995, 205), but this work does not endeavor to do so. Though my contacts over the last twenty years have proved invaluable in maintaining a kind of co-temporality (Fabian 2002) with the Liberia crisis, I do not intend to dwell on failures or disorders. The correspondences with friends and the staggered work with migrants and Aladura members in the Washington area have produced stories of faith and recovery as well as of loss and horror. Thus, what I hope will become clear are the Aladura signs and strategies for dealing with "desperate failure" or "disordered states," which were meaningful in the mid-1980s and continued to be so through war, postwar, and diaspora. These resources and strategies press forth an unremitting critique of self-interest, jealousy, and hatred and uphold models of recovery and restoration.

1 ——

The Field of Prophecy

In Liberia in the 1980s the models of the prophet as holy person and of prophecy as a spiritual function had wide acceptance. Among the Aladura the models of prophet and prophecy were tied to known geographies—even to specific buildings and grounds, such as Faith Homes and sacred mounts. These locations, however, were part of a diversified and changing landscape. Richard Werbner's discussion of regional analysis can help us appreciate the prophet's work in relation to place. Werbner contends that a regional analysis "presumes no box, no single or unitary cultural code within which all the flow of discourse must be contained. Instead, regional analysis recognizes the translation of culture by the people themselves, and takes as problematic their switching from code to code. Its utility is perhaps greatest where the transcendence of boundaries is most salient—in the conditions that are increasingly a major subject of research by anthropologists. The implication is not that 'the little community' needs to be forgotten; rather, it must be brought into focus as one point to and from which people, goods, services and ideas flow" (1989, 244). The prophet was the major conduit for affecting the flow of Aladura persons, goods, services, and ideas. This happened especially through his relation to clients and the work of healing. The Aladura minister provided strategies and services that became widely known and shared within the "little community" (Paynesville) and beyond.

The historical development of the Aladura and prophet churches in Liberia in general and the work of St. Peter's in Paynesville in particular is examined here. We will see how these churches supported the prophet paradigm and the dissemination of the healing praxis. Along with the contacts, exchanges, and associations among these churches, there were also obstructions, controls, and divisions. Churches appeared that foreswore the Aladura label and its healing methods. Some churches also resorted to rhetoric that dismissed competitors, asserting that another church had "too much witchcraft" or that its prophets used inappropriate and dangerous forms of hidden power.

Pentecostal influence also complicated Aladura identity. In her work on Ghanaian Pentecostals, Birgit Meyer notes how Pentecostals insisted on the "rupture" with the traditional past and how on the grassroots level members took umbrage with the idea that an authentic African church signaled a recovery of the traditional values and customs (1998, 316–18, 339–40). In Liberia one could indeed observe what Meyer calls a Pentecostal critique of "temporalization" often directed toward the AIC, which was seen as incorporating too much of the "African past." At the same time, the distinctions between Spiritual, Prophet, Aladura, and Pentecostal churches were actually quite tenuous. In one context an Aladura minister might call his church Pentecostal, in another context, Spiritual, or Prophet. Members of a Bassa Pentecostal church might readily refer to their church as a Spiritual Church and not take offense at being confused with Aladura.

Although the focus of this work is on Paynesville Aladura churches in the mid-1980s, it is important to consider the diaspora churches in the Washington, D.C., area and the relevance of the prophecy paradigm and ritual struggle for understanding their work in the context of translocal flows. In the 1980s exchanges were taking place that linked local and translocal groups. Its expansive dimension notwithstanding, the Aladura church's mission was grounded in a specific praxis and concrete notions of place. Though the images of home and village did provide a kind of "virtual reality" (van Binsbergen 2001, 220–25), they were also tied to the very palpable context of ritual struggle, a strategy that enabled people to find some sense of security in a world of change and uncertainty.

"A Christian Nation"

In the 1980s Liberia offered a religiously heterogeneous environment. Christianity of course was the most public of all traditions. Its impact on the formation of the Liberian nation and on the evolution of dominant cultural patterns has been well substantiated. Free African American settlers from slave-holding states introduced Christianity to Liberia. Thomas Hendrix has stressed the influence of the southern evangelical tradition on Americo-Liberian Christianity, as expressed in its revivalist piety, the language of personal salvation, the notion of divine providence, and an idea of sufficient grace. Hendrix also notes that Jeffersonian and Jacksonian principles of political and economic liberalism shaped the Americo-Liberian ethos, involving an ironic transposition of the Old South master-slave paradigm onto the settler's relationship with the indigenous population (1994, 260–271). Gifford similarly sees in modern Liberian Christianity the legacy of antebellum "slave religion" with its "emphasis on experience, conversion, revivals and the lack of social concern" (1993, 50). Though undoubtedly these patterns prevailed, Liberian evangelical culture also represented the continuation of an expansive pietistic tradition that integrated individual and communal needs.

From the arrival of settlers in 1822 until Liberia's recognition as a republic in 1847, various denominations were introduced and established. Baptist and Methodist settlers started branches in 1823, Episcopal in 1836, and Presbyterian in 1833. These groups would play a key role in giving form to a unique "Liberian Christianity" that synthesized religious and national values. In ensuing decades Lutheran and Roman Catholic churches were introduced, though it would be well into the twentieth century before these gained a solid footing (Gifford 1993, 47–57). Pentecostal missions also began arriving in the first decade of the twentieth century: the Assemblies of God came in 1907. The incremental effects of Pentecostalism could be observed early on in the rise of Bassa independent churches; but it would not be until the second half of the century that its enduring impact on Liberian spirituality would become fully apparent. When I lived in Liberia, Pentecostal churches were gaining impressive momentum, in part, because of increased symbiosis with AIC. Along with the more mainline groups, certain other church groups, often dismissed by missionaries as "cults," had created missions in the Monrovia area—the Seventh-Day Adventists (1927), the Jehovah's Witnesses (1947), and the Unification Church (1975).

The Muslim population grew steadily with each decade after World War II, particularly during the 1980s. In his discussions with religious leaders in the Monrovia area, Gifford notes, "There was some agreement that Monrovia's mosques admitted altogether about 25 new members each Friday. The growth was most apparent on Fridays at the time of midday prayer when, by 1989, traffic was obstructed around the central Monrovia mosque by a crowd which spilled over half the road along the whole block" (1993, 287). New developments in urbanization, transportation, and commerce brought greater exposure to Muslim Mandingo and Fulani merchants. Islam had also grown stronger in western and northern counties, especially among the Gola, Gbande, Vai, and Kissi. Indian and Lebanese merchants, who could be found in remote backwaters as well as in major cities and towns, had also begun to influence the spread of Islam. The majority of Lebanese were probably Marionite Christians, but Shiite Muslims and Druize comprised significant minorities (Winder 1962, 302, 305).

Hindus and Sikhs were also active in Monrovia. By the 1980s Indian immigrants had established a Hindu temple and a Sikh gurdwara in the Watertown market area. The storefront Hindu temple included many converted Liberians, among them an Americo-Liberian man who served as its president, although Gujaratis from northwest India comprised the majority of its membership. The gurdwara was also a storefront, just a few blocks from the temple. On Sunday mornings about forty people attended services. In 1984 Indira Gandhi, India's prime minister, was assassinated by Sikh bodyguards. In India tension built between Hindus and Sikhs, but, in Liberia at least, the conciliatory gestures between the parties were apparent. Shortly after Gandhi's death, I attended a Sikh prayer service at which several Hindus were also in attendance.

In Congo Town, a suburb of Monrovia, the Baha'is ran a center started by an African American couple from Chicago. One of the newest of the so-called world religions, the Baha'i faith had been in Liberia since the 1950s. When I visited the center, leaders claimed to have only about two hundred members nationwide, but five years later Gifford notes that leaders had claimed recent "phenomenal growth" (1993, 287).

Despite the nation's religious heterogeneity and the "minority" status of Christianity, Liberian authorities waved the banner of Christian identity. Since the republic's founding in 1847, the government had recognized Christianity as the state religion. Furthermore, Americo-Liberians came to see it as an attribute of the "civilized" man, distinguishing him from the tribal, indigenous "country" man. This cultural ideal, however, involved significant paradoxes (Liebenow 1987, 1–7). Though the settlers proclaimed Liberia to be a "Christian nation," most Liberians remained non-Christian. Furthermore, there were times when the missionary expansion of Christianity among indigenous Liberians appeared to collide with the established religion. The "tribal" acceptance of Christianity undoubtedly challenged the security of many among the ruling elite (81–82). However, by and large, mainline churches acquiesced to the reigning cultural model.

A greater challenge to the cultural hegemony of the "civilized" elite came from independent churches. The success of these churches corresponded to major changes that occurred in Liberia following World War II. The open-door policy begun during the Tubman era marshaled in a general integration of indigenous groups into the cultural and economic mainstream. The plan for bringing economic growth and development to the hinterland was bolstered by the construction of a new road system, a national educational program, and a system of indirect control that established a hierarchy of chiefdoms (Bledsoe 1980, 20–23). The road system, especially, enabled increased communication and commerce between Monrovia and the interior. From the 1950s Liberians migrated steadily from the interior to Monrovia and to the new industrial and agricultural sites, such as Bong Mine and the Firestone Rubber Plantation.

In response to drastic demographic changes, established and mission churches searched for effective ways to evangelize both interior and urban indigenous populations. In the 1970s and 1980s different denominations targeted specific ethnic groups. Lutherans enjoyed success among the Kpelle and Loma, Baptists among the Bassa and Gola, Assemblies of God among Krahn and Kissi, and Methodists among the Kpelle (Singler 1990, 108–26). The older churches, however, would have to share the spotlight with the new AIC and Pentecostal churches, especially in urban areas where the latter were often more responsive to the immediate needs of the new arrivals. The effectiveness of AIC, in particular, was undoubtedly related to the perception that they were "problem-solving" churches. Also, throughout the Tolbert and Doe eras, these churches made impressive gains through association with the more global evangelical and the so-called Prosperity Gospel movements (see Gifford 1993). Among the churches I worked with in the mid-1980s, American evangelists such as Oral Roberts and Jim Bakker (both with Pentecostal backgrounds) were highly regarded. It was not unusual to find literature from their organizations being used within the branches or to find dwellers watching syndicated programs of the Praise the Lord (PTL) Club on the Faith Home TV. The rapid growth of the Pentecostal movement throughout West Africa in the mid-1990s came as no surprise to anyone who had studied grassroots churches the decade before.

Our knowledge about the development of AIC in Liberia before the Aladura church's arrival in 1947 remains rather sketchy. William Wade Harris was one of the first great figures in the West African Christian prophetic tradition. He was a Grebo man from southeast Liberia, most of whose documented successes were outside Liberia, in Côte d'Ivoire and Ghana.[1] However, in his research on independent churches in southeast Liberia, Werner Korte learned stories about "prophets" working among the Grebo, Kru, and Bassa in the 1930s and 1940s, who claimed spiritual descent from the prophet Harris (1971, 82–85). Gifford reports that in Sinoe County a Fanti fisherman had started a branch of the Church of the Twelve Apostles (1993, 193), one of the most popular Harrist churches in Ivory Coast and Ghana. In Monrovia one also found Kru and Grebo churches that claimed Harris as their founder. Whether the links were real or constructed, among southeastern Liberians, Harris became an esteemed figure whose apocryphal legacy intriguingly informed the lineages of various churches. I knew one Aladura minister with Grebo descent who insisted that the prophet Harris was the true founder of the Aladura movement. He believed that Josiah Oshitelu, the founder of the CLA, had received his commission through a dream revelation from Harris.

AIC founded in the 1920s and 1930s presented alternatives to established missionary Christianity, which for many appeared to kowtow to the established culture. Among these were the Bassa Community Church and the Lighthouse Full Gospel (Fraenkel 1964, 87, 167–69; Gifford 1993, 126–27). The Bassa Community Church was founded by an African American Baptist minister as "a place where his predominately Bassa congregation could live together" (Fraenkel 1964, 87). The community included residences, a church, an elementary school, a courtroom, and a maternity ward. Merran Fraenkel refers to the Lighthouse Full Gospel as "Pentecostal." The church was founded in 1936 by an African American woman named Sister Leila January, who introduced "the Baptism of the Holy Ghost to the Americo-Liberian element in Monrovia." In the late 1950s the church was headed by a Kru woman named Sister Blatch. According to Fraenkel, the church then ministered to mostly "low caste" Americo-Liberians, who, on the one hand, were looked down on by the more privileged settler families and, on the other hand, lacked the kind of kinship connections that indigenous migrants could always fall back on. Though these churches did not have formal affiliation with mission or mainline churches, they evidenced the kind of American and Pentecostal influences that by the 1980s became typical for many AIC. The most noticeable similarity between these churches and the Aladura, however, would be the presentation of the church as a new community for transplants.

The rise of Bassa independent churches that networked between Buchanan and Monrovia also deserves mention. Buchanan was a port city about fifty miles southeast of Monrovia. In the early twentieth century a movement began in Buchanan that came to be known as the Holy Ghost Movement. It was founded through the work of a charismatic Bassa minister/prophet named Henry Neor, who formerly belonged to the African Methodist Episcopal Church.[2] His work spawned a series of "independent" churches, most with a Pentecostal flavor though often self-described as Baptist or Methodist. Between the 1940s and 1980s Buchanan became home to dozens such churches. Some of these churches eventually established branches in the Monrovia area, mainly among Bassa migrants (Scheffers 1987, 62–93). In Paynesville these included the Little Meggido, Holy Ghost Mount Zion, and the African Glory Pentecostal Church. Like the Aladura churches, these independent churches emphasized charismatic leadership and spiritual gifts and provided a communal praxis that appealed to Liberians from the lowest echelons of urban society (see Fraenkel 1964, 157–58, 167–69).

The Church of the Lord Aladura: "For All Liberians"

The Church of the Lord Aladura (CLA) arrived in Monrovia in 1947 and became the most successful new African church in Liberia. The Aladura movement began in southwestern Nigeria in the 1920s. The Yoruba name *Aladura* meant "the praying ones" and came to refer to a group of churches that emphasized reliance on "spiritual prayer" as the best means for solving problems and curing illnesses. The CLA was founded by a former catechist of the Anglican mission named Josiah Oshitelu, who remained the spiritual and administrative head of the church until his death in 1966.[3] Primate Oshitelu created the church's headquarters and its most important holy site, Mount Tabborrar (Tabieorar), in Ogere, Nigeria. Eventually the city became a major pilgrimage destination for the Aladura faithful, who sought the presence of the primate and the power of the mount.

The CLA was established in Liberia mainly through the labors of a Nigerian missionary named Prophet Samuel Oduwole. Among Liberians, Oduwole attained legendary stature. Many spoke of him as the church's greatest prophet. An extremely charismatic and strong-willed leader, he became known as a fair-minded but demanding authority. Church leaders contended that Oduwole did not ingratiate himself with any one social group. He was well respected by expatriate Nigerians and Ghanaians—who early on represented an influential faction in the church—by the Americo-Liberians, and by indigenous ethnic groups. In the beginning the church drew heavy support from Americo-Liberians, who were among its first members; but their participation declined over the first decade, as the CLA began to attract more people from indigenous groups. Undoubtedly the portrayal of Aladura as an "African church" contradicted the presentations of the "civilized" (often referred to as *kwi* culture[4]) and contributed to this trend. As Harold Turner notes concerning the Americo-Liberian reactions to certain Aladura customs: "They disliked the removal of shoes for worship, for these were one of the marks of 'the civilized' in Liberia; for similar reasons they objected to the washings before entering the church, and the introduction of the Yoruba custom of kneeling before the prophet, and of the prostrations in prayer; nor could they be happy about the refusal to 'church the corpse' at a funeral, and the admission of 'the uncivilized' to the activities of the congregation" (1967, 1:141).

The mandate that an Americo-Liberian layperson must kneel before a prophet who might be of tribal, or "uncivilized," origin struck at the heart of kwi ethos. During fieldwork Aladura members repeatedly stressed that their church rejected the distinctions between tribe and class. A Kissi Aladura prophetess once told me that her church had a "humble" nature and did not observe the "worldly" distinctions created by the settlers. On this matter members mentioned a story about Oduwole's arrest by police when he walked past the executive mansion carrying luggage on his head. The prophet had brazenly performed an African custom, which kwi culture had strongly discouraged. The church's insistence on its African or Liberian character, however, did not entail an uncritical embrace of African customs and values. In fact, like the Ghanaian Pentecostals in Meyer's study (1998), members also tended to "temporalize" many traditional African beliefs and practices as best left behind.

The majority of Monrovia's post–World War II population was from indigenous groups. For many migrants kinship and regional ties remained significant. However, life in the urban world often involved participation with groups, associations, clubs, and churches that offered new forms of identity (Fraenkel 1964). Undoubtedly the Aladura church's communal life appealed to the new urban stranger. Also it was largely through the conversion of migrants that the church was able to begin expanding into the interior. When they returned to their villages, migrants often introduced the Aladura practice and planted the seeds for developing new churches.

From the church's headquarters at the Center Street branch, where Oduwole and his family lived, the prophet maintained a tight hold on the administrative and spiritual affairs of the church. During his tenure occasional dissent occurred, but it had little impact on the overall direction of the church. Oduwole himself became involved in the founding and organization of other branches in both urban and interior areas. Significantly he encouraged the ministerial training of indigenous Liberians, on which the further success of the church depended.

Oduwole's sudden death marked a turning point in the history of the Liberian church. In 1965 he was killed in an axe attack by a man he had been treating for several months. Many church members considered his death martyrdom, not murder. One high authority, who at the time was a young minister assigned to Center Street, claimed Oduwole knew his death was imminent. He even interpreted the prophet's death as an act of Providence. An apocryphal story about the incident circulated among Liberian Aladura: Oduwole had received the axe blow to his head while he prayed over a pregnant woman. Later, when ministers delivered her baby, the baby had a birthmark in the same spot.

While he was in charge, as the narrative goes, the church remained united and centralized, but after his death it became disturbed by dissent and major secessions. The most consequential dissent came from Bishop David Fyneah, who had served as senior warden of the Monrovia Cathedral under Oduwole. Shortly before his death, Oduwole had appointed Fyneah to be his successor. But six months after Fyneah took office, the authorities in Ogere replaced him with a Nigerian. A disappointed Fyneah left the church, and about fifty members followed him. He started a new church named the United Church of the Lord Aladura (UCL), setting up headquarters in Logan Town, a suburb of Monrovia. Fyneah remained in Logan Town until his death in 1980, always claiming to be the true successor of Oduwole. I talked with several of Fyneah's supporters who insisted that the Nigerians had opposed his appointment because he was Liberian. This claim, however, overlooked the involvement of Liberian officials, who, dissatisfied with what they had judged to be Fyneah's ineffective leadership, had first gone to Ogere and requested his removal.[5]

The UCL eventually started branches in other cities and villages. While I was in Liberia, I visited several branches of the UCL, which were located in Logan Town, Synkor, and Paynesville. The Synkor branch offers a useful example of how the UCL and other Aladura churches expanded. The church's leader was a senior prophetess named Hannah Williams, who had been serving the branch in that capacity since 1976. Her mother had been a noted prophetess in the CLA, among the fifty or so members who joined Bishop Fyneah when he left the church. Serving the church early on as a cross bearer, Sister Williams never considered herself an especially dedicated member. Not long after joining the UCL, however, she had an experience that dramatically changed her life. One day she suddenly became ill and collapsed into a coma. Her family thought she would surely die, but after three days she "returned to life." She came to see her illness as a clear sign that God had called her to become a prophetess. Soon afterward she began a prayer group in Synkor and gained some reputation as a healer. Indeed it was after the successful treatment of a small child that the child's family insisted on building a small chapel for the prayer group, which eventually became a chartered branch of the UCL.

According to CLA officials, Fyneah's departure presented a special challenge to the church because at the time he was the highest-ranking Liberian in the church, and many prominent members had left with him. Fyneah also challenged the church's ritual authority when he inaugurated an observance of the Mount Tabborrar rite. As one CLA authority put it to me, "there could be only one Tabborrar in Liberia." Fyneah's church, however, would never attain the success of the mother church. CLA supporters contended this was a consequence of "the Bishop's disobedience." One church official told me that Oduwole's appointment of Fyneah was actually part of the divine scheme of things. He claimed that at the first Tabborrar after his death, Oduwole came to the mount prophets in a vision and told them that Fyneah's appointment had been a test, but now it was time for his removal. As long as he led the church, it would never be successful. Obviously UCL members rejected such claims about Fyneah, who in their minds was Oduwole's legitimate successor and a true saint. And even among dismayed CLA opponents, the mention of Fyneah's name brought as many comments of admiration as reproach.

In response to the "breakaway" church, the CLA began to specify more clearly the parameters of doctrine and practice. Also it became more attentive to the issue of "Liberianization." The 1970s and 1980s marked a period of major expansion for the CLA throughout Liberia. It had considerable success among migrants in interior cities, such as Gbarnga and Harper, and at plantation and industrial sites, such as Firestone, Bong Mine, and Bomi Hills. The church also started more branches in predominately Kpelle, Kru, Kissi, Grebo, and Krahn towns. In 1962 the Aladura church had twelve branches; twenty years later there were more than fifty.[6] In 1984 Bishop Moses Mayson became the first Liberian ever ordained an apostle in the Aladura church. His ordination took place in Ogere and was conducted by the church's primate. At the same time, five other Liberian churchmen were made bishops and commissioned to head separate dioceses in the Liberian See. The promotions undoubtedly represented a major step in the strengthening of the church in Liberia. The continued expansion paralleled that of other Aladura and prophet churches, which increasingly made problematic the matter of church identity. During several discussions I had with CLA leaders, they stressed that many churches pretended to be Aladura: they had adapted the church's doctrines and practices, but in effect had "stolen our doctrine." Leaders saw the Oduwole days as an era of unity and stability. Ironically this idealization was not restricted to the CLA. Other churches would also speak of the Nigerian prophet as their spiritual ancestor and claim an institutional link.

PAYNESVILLE CITY: A SOCIOHISTORICAL SKETCH

In Paynesville City in the mid-1980s there were always about fifteen to twenty church branches or prayer groups that could be described as AIC. About half of these were Aladura groups. Four branches belonged to the CLA. Other AIC groups evidenced Aladura influence but preferred to emphasize a distinctive identity. Most AIC in Paynesville stressed the role of the prophet or prophetess and sponsored a complex healing praxis. More than any other function, prophetic healing generated the flow of persons, goods, ideas, and services. To a great extent the effectiveness of this flow related to how churches (and prophets) addressed the matter of occult power. Before we explore more closely the various interactions between Aladura and prophet churches in Paynesville and indicate how these interactions contributed to an emergent prophet cosmology, it will be necessary to give a sociohistorical sketch of Paynesville.

Paynesville grew as Monrovia expanded after World War II. When I lived there, it numbered about ten thousand inhabitants. Though chartered as a separate municipality, it was often regarded as a suburb of the capital city (Hasselman 1979, 174). Located about ten miles southeast of Monrovia, it was linked to the capital by Tubman Boulevard, one of the most traveled highways in Liberia. The hub of Paynesville life was found between two crossroads, or red-light "junctures," located about two miles apart. The first crossroads connected Tubman Boulevard with Scheiffelin Road, which led to the Robertsfield Airport and beyond to the port city of Buchanan. About three miles from the crossroads, along Scheiffelin Road, was the Baptist seminary where I taught. Several small communities or compounds, all within the Paynesville City district, were located between the crossroads and the seminary—the King Gray Bassa fishing village; the Sudan Interior Mission, a Christian mission that ran a small hospital and the radio station ELWA (an acronym for Eternal Love Working in Africa); the Carver Bible College, which was founded in the 1950s by an African American Baptist mission; a quiet recreational and residential area named Sugar Beach; and the Kenema Cultural Center.

At the second crossroads Tubman Boulevard met Somali Drive, a road that circumvented Monrovia and joined, in Logan Town, the main highway into western Liberia and Sierra Leone. From this crossroad also began the Kakata Road, the main road to central Liberia—to the cities of Gbarnga, Ganta, and Zwedru.

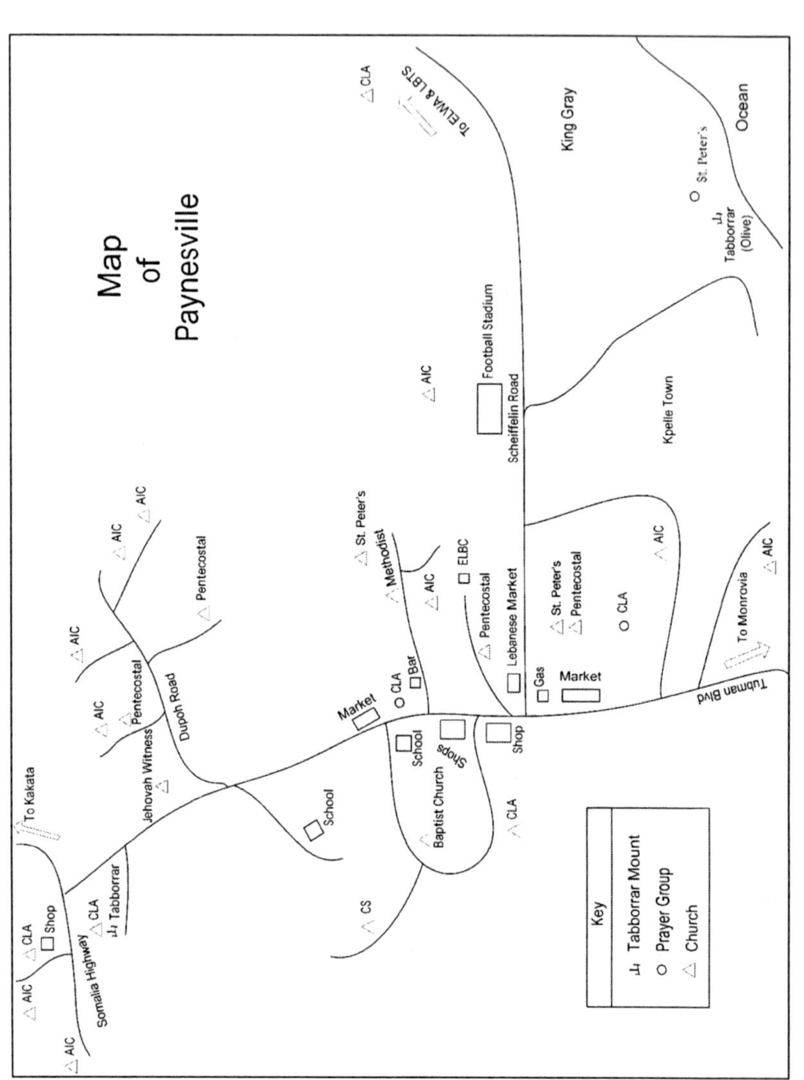

Paynesville City: Churches, prayer groups, and Tabborrar mounts. Prepared by Peter Valdina, not to scale.

Being located along such heavily traveled routes, Paynesville understandably received many migrants. Most migrants eventually made their way to Monrovia, but many remained in the suburb, sometimes finding hospice in a nearby church. Paynesville was a predominately residential area, but established along its main thoroughfare were numerous family businesses, small companies, food shops, and churches. The majority of Aladura or prophet churches I worked with were located within a three-mile radius, not far from one of the junctures, along an adjacent street or a dirt road.

The original inhabitants of the Paynesville area were known as the Mamba Bassa. Americo-Liberians and "Congo" people would later settle there. The name *Congo* referred to people whom the British rescued from captured slave ships and sent to Monrovia. Many Congos settled on the outskirts of Monrovia. They were more prepared than the American settlers for the rugged, rural life and within a couple decades emerged as powerful landowners with successful sugar plantations. By the end of the nineteenth century, Bassa and Kpelle from the interior began arriving in large numbers, often finding work as servants and farm laborers for Americo-Liberians and Congos. Farming and animal husbandry continued to be the mainstay of Paynesville's economy into the 1970s. After World War II new developments also created a demand for more unskilled laborers. These included industrial projects, such as profitable rock- and cement-crushing enterprises and the construction and maintenance of roads. Migrants came from all over Liberia, creating a diverse labor pool: Gola, Mende, and Kissi from the west; Loma, Mano, and Kpelle from the north; Bassa, Kru, and Grebo from the east.

In the 1950s two important medical facilities were set up in Paynesville— the ELWA Hospital, supported by the Sudan Interior Mission, and the Catherine Mills Rehabilitation Center, which provided psychiatric care. With the provision of electricity in the mid-1960s, other businesses set up shop in Paynesville. In the 1970s Lebanese merchants arrived and established small businesses. Throughout the next ten years, increasing numbers of trained artisans and businessmen from Nigeria and Sierra Leone moved to the Paynesville vicinity. In 1979 the city became the chosen site for the construction of a national football stadium funded by the Chinese government, a project that attracted even more laborers to the area. The site was located about a quarter of a mile from St. Peter's, which received frequent visits from migrant laborers seeking the church's assistance.

Women also ventured to the city. They migrated to places like Paynesville to escape the restrictions of village life, make money, obtain an education, visit family, or look for suitors. In her study of Loma migrations to Monrovia, Jeanette Carter indicates that among the Loma, young women were the most mobile, frequently traveling between Monrovia and the interior in pursuit of "money and men" (1970, 148). One source of income was "making market" by selling goods brought from an interior farm or extra crops from local subsistence farming. In Paynesville in the 1970s this trend was supported by the opening of two large country markets, both near the Scheiffelin juncture. "Market ladies" were well represented among members and clientele at St. Peter's and at other Aladura churches in the area.

With the flux of migrants in Paynesville, many types of household configuration developed. Though Liberia's indigenous groups were mostly patrilineal, patrilocal, and exogamous in social structure, there were always variations. Concerning the Bassa, W. Penn Handwerker notes that kinship was "not tightly structured" and that "residential alignment" usually influenced the kinds of activities and associations a person developed (1973b, 184). Among the new household configurations were those that emerged within the Faith Homes of Aladura and prophet churches, which we will explore further in chapter 5.

Christian churches existed in Paynesville almost since its founding. By the 1880s Americo-Liberian and Congo groups had established Baptist and Methodist churches, which over the next several decades became the most influential in the area. After World War II other groups started branches and established various ministries. Several other Pentecostal and fundamentalist churches started branches throughout the 1950s and 1960s, some licensed to operate elementary schools. During the 1960s and 1970s the mainline Christian groups also became more responsive to the population growth. In 1962 the Southern Baptist Mission, which had worked in Liberia during the mid–nineteenth century, was invited back by Liberian Baptists to open a new mission. By the late 1970s Southern Baptist missionaries were extensively involved with the town's Congo and Bassa groups. In 1976 the Liberian Baptist Convention, with the support of the Southern Baptist Mission, opened the Liberia Baptist Theological Seminary. From the early 1970s to the mid-1980s Roman Catholic, Episcopal, Methodist, and Jehovah's Witness groups arrived in town and founded new branches.

Despite their significant role in the religious life of Paynesville in the two decades before the recent civil war, these churches soon faced notable competition from Aladura and prophet churches, especially in their appeal to new migrants. Aladura churches also became increasingly adaptive in their relations with overseas Pentecostal and evangelical groups, seeking affiliation with American church groups that might offer effective strategies for growth. As Gifford notes, the U.S. network increased the influence from American evangelism through revivals, workshops, literature, and cassettes, a process he calls "Americanization" of the independent churches (1993, 197–225). While it alerts us to the very real transatlantic flows and exchanges, this characterization overstates the American influence and understates the agency of AIC. Indeed, Gifford shows that in the cases of the Christian Nation Church and First Church of Love and Faith the search for affiliation was a trial-and-error process that brought disappointment as often as reward. Such developments should be understood in relation to what Adogame, speaking about Aladura churches, describes as the endeavor to "work out strategies for a further insertion into global religious maps" (2004, 501).

THE NEW CHURCHES: ALADURA AND PROPHET BRANCHES

The interactions among Aladura and prophet churches demonstrated an emergent field of prophecy where cosmological constructs were generated by experiences of visionary revelations, spiritual healing, and the network of consociate relations. For many Paynesville residents, especially for members and clients, the Aladura churches informed their everyday habitus. The CLA had played a critical role in the development of prophet cosmology or discourse, but by the late 1980s it was simply one player among many. "Breakaway" churches and other AIC, such as the Bassa prophet and the Pentecostal churches, became popular among both locals and migrants. The CLA breakaway label, of course, implied a normative Aladura model that churches such as St. Peter's clearly challenged; but it also gainsays the forms of positive interaction that took place between them.[7] Indeed, in this "little community" denominational identities were frequently compromised or negotiated in both the local and translocal exchanges between members, ideas, and commerce.

The CLA branches in Paynesville obviously played key roles in this dissemination. The church had four branches in the town, as well as several prayer groups or prayer homes. A prayer group was usually led by a cross bearer or elder in the church. It met in her home, where a room was set aside with an altar table for services or prayers. With the approval of church authorities, a cross bearer might perform healing rites at her residence, but these were almost always seen as supplementing (and not replacing) the rituals that took place at the Faith Home.

A senior prophetess named Miatta Tagoe, a Kissi woman, supervised the main CLA branch. She had joined the Aladura church in the early 1960s and had received her training at Center Street. Apostle Mayson spoke of Tagoe as among the church's most dedicated clergy and effective healers. The church assigned her to the Paynesville branch in 1980. Her four daughters, three of whom were cross bearers, and her grandchildren stayed with her in the Faith Home. Tagoe also supervised four junior ministers, one male and three female. The male junior minister, who was Tagoe's primary assistant, had worked under her at a branch in Harper County. After her appointment to the Paynesville church, Tagoe requested his transfer as well. Eventually he became a rod holder, one authorized to use the holy rod, a sign of a prophet's authority. The junior minister also served as the headmaster of an elementary school in the compound.

Before Prophetess Tagoe's arrival, the Paynesville branch had been inactive for several years. The building lay in considerable ruin and was covered by bush.

Tagoe and the ministers spent several weeks removing garbage, clearing away shrubs and vines, and making repairs to the structure. During the refurbishing, nesting snakes presented a major problem. But even after the church grounds had been pruned and the building rendered safe for services, snakes continued to enter the complex. The ministers interpreted this as the witchwork of neighbors who opposed the church's reopening. Once the ministers had effectively dealt with the problem, the church opened its Faith Home. It began to experience steady growth, especially among women. Among all the churches I attended, Tagoe's branch had the highest percentage of female patients and members. At Sunday services, which averaged about sixty participants, there were usually only six or seven men. Tagoe's patrons came from a variety of ethnic backgrounds—mostly Kissi, but also Mende, Gola, Mano, and Kpelle. Occasionally Americo-Liberian or Congo individuals, who had known Tagoe since her early days at Center Street, would come to the Faith Home for treatments.

The second CLA branch, in the Kenema vicinity, was located at the private residence of a former bishop of the Liberian See who had recently been transferred to another country. The bishop had built the home in the late 1970s. When he and his family first arrived, neighbors and friends began showing up for special treatments and prayers. After the bishop's transfer, his wife, who was also a high-ranking minister, continued performing special treatments and began leading services in the house's small chapel on the first floor. Eventually CLA had the church chartered as an official branch and assigned a junior minister to assist the bishop's wife. Other family members also lived at the branch, including an adult son who one evening talked with me at great length about the work of local prophets in fighting witchcraft. He insisted that the Aladura church's success had much to do with its ability to expose it. The branch also attracted peoples of diverse backgrounds—generally more women than men and more Bassa than any other ethnic group.

The third branch, near the Somali Drive juncture, was led by a senior prophet and also attracted a large female clientele. The branch was too far away for my walking tours. The one time I visited the site, the ministers were absent. In the end I would rely on the information about the church gathered by my friend and occasional assistant Willis Modee. I had better luck with the branch at the Mount Tabborrar site. When I first visited the site in April 1984, it was being used mainly as a spiritual retreat for male ministers. By the end of the year CLA had decided to obtain property for a new Tabborrar site and had started converting the old mount into a regular branch with a Faith Home.

Despite CLA's respectable success in Paynesville, it competed with other prophet churches that also established branches in the 1970s and 1980s. Among the AIC in Paynesville were the United Healing Temple of Christ, Faith Healing Church of God, United Listeners of Christ, Universal Faith Healing Church,

Little Meggido, Christ Apostle Church, Israel Christian Church, New Jerusalem Faith Healing Church, and the United Church of Salvation. My research on St. Peter's and Aladura branches inevitably took pathways that led to each of these churches. The extensive networking among them happened through individual and social means: for instance, a minister's personal narrative of conversion, a patient's search for a cure, a shared tarry[8] between churches, a healer's referral, an August Tabborrar struggle, the diagnosis of a minister's madness and new institutional alignments. While the sharing between churches was common, the competitions were also apparent and not infrequently led to conflict and even accusations of witchcraft. For instance, just before I left Liberia, the prophet at one AIC branch died unexpectedly. His family members claimed his death had been caused by the prophet at a neighboring AIC who was envious of the branch's success.

Appreciating the importance of the exchange and control of goods, persons, services, and ideas that occurred among the churches will help us understand the context for the work of St. Peter's. In most churches the Aladura influence was apparent, if not in its doctrine and practice, certainly in the personal histories of ministers and members. The patients, in turn, seldom made firm distinctions between the churches. Though most churches strongly discouraged the practice, it was commonplace for patients to seek out healers from other churches while they were undergoing an authorized treatment within another.

The flow and interface that persisted among these churches also involved the historic mainline mission groups. The founders and ministers of all the AIC mentioned above had experience with other churches, whether Methodist, Baptist, Episcopal, or Pentecostal. Also, many of their patients continued to belong to mainline churches. Ethnographies on AIC have said too little about the connections between AIC and main line groups, often seeing the former as more "authentically African" and the latter as more Western (Meyer 2004). But despite their being rooted in locality, AIC in Liberia always insisted on their "universal" mission: they worked for the non-African as well as the African.

The emergence of African-based evangelism and the prodigious growth of Pentecostal-Charismatic Churches in the last three decades make clear the importance of looking at the crosscurrents of ideas and practices that have always been a part of new African churches. As Gifford notes, among AIC one could find "every kind of permutation and combination of characteristics," which makes problematic any hard typology (1993, 196). At the same time, our ability to discern the flow between churches depends greatly on our knowledge of distinguishable traits. While a historical review can bring out the expansive character of these churches, we should not take for granted their "planting" within an immediately known world; whether through images grounded in everyday experience or through the construction of new spaces that play between village and forest, between neighbor and the stranger, between husband and wife, between healer and client. Even those churches that pitched strong global messages continued to find ways to ground their work in "local rituals and spaces" (Hackett 1998, 272).

Among prophets and prophetesses in Paynesville perhaps the two most successful were Samuel Olu Shoniyin, founder of St. Peter's Church of the Lord, and Alpha Omega Bundu, head of the United Church of Salvation. Both men had once worked with the CLA, so their churches continued to demonstrate Aladura traces. Both were relatively new on the scene, having started their churches about 1980. Olu originally came from Nigeria; he had resided in Liberia since the late 1960s and had managed to create an effective network of clients and supporters throughout Liberia. Bundu came from Sierra Leone; though he was a more recent arrival, he had quickly become well known throughout the area. Both men were effective in attracting people of diverse backgrounds. They appeared equally successful among Paynesville's long-term residents and new migrants from the interior. While I lived in Liberia, both prophets made journeys overseas—Olu went twice to the United States and Bundu made one long tour to Amsterdam, London, and New York—in order to start prayer groups among diaspora West Africans.

Prophet Samuel Olu: The Founder

I had lived in Liberia for six months before I met Prophet Samuel Olu. My fieldwork had focused on the CLA branches, but I started to turn my attention to the breakaway churches. I had heard many stories about the Nigerian prophet. The son of one Aladura minister had described Olu as "the powerful prophet who lived near the red light juncture." One Saturday about twilight, I drove onto the church compound. A group of men seated on benches outside the chapel warmly received me, and one among them, a tall man dressed in a white leisure suit and with ritual facial scars introduced himself: he was Olu. That evening we talked for at least an hour. Before I left for home, Olu insisted that I return in the morning for the Sunday Divine Worship.

The next morning I arrived thirty minutes before the service. A young minister led me to the prayer room, where ministers, cross bearers, and choir members were assembled, preparing for the morning processional. Olu requested that I join them and sit with the junior ministers and deacons in the low altar area. About eighty people attended the service, mostly women. During "shouts" (an extended phase of songs and dance), Olu left the altar and moved freely among participants, placing his hands on as many as possible. Later a minister brought him a cup of holy water, which he offered as if administering communion to all who approached him. After shouts, standing above in the high altar, he delivered a series of visions, first for the church, then for groups, and last for individuals.

Eventually Olu turned my way and called aloud, "Brother Sam." I had already prepared myself, so immediately I knelt and prepared to receive my vision.

Olu was born in 1932 in western Nigeria. His parents were members of an Anglican mission church. They were wealthy enough to finance his primary and secondary education and his training at a technology school. In 1950 he graduated from high school ready for a career in agriculture. Shortly after graduation, however, he met a prophet who gave him an ominous message: that sometime in the near future he would experience a misfortune that would prevent him from pursuing this career. Olu did not take the message seriously; but two years later, after he had started working for an agricultural firm, he became inexplicably blind.

In 1950 the Aladura movement was already thirty years old and had significantly impacted Yoruba and West Nigerian culture. An encounter with such a prophet—Aladura or otherwise—would not have been an unusual event. At first Olu's parents dismissed the prophet's prediction as coincidence and sought help from Western-trained doctors for their son. Later, when this proved fruitless, they took Olu to traditional healers, but the results were the same. The search for a cure continued for five years, until finally, through the recommendation of friends, Olu's parents took him to a noted healer at a nearby Aladura church. The prophet divined that relatives envious of their son's success had caused the blindness through witchcraft. For two months Olu received spiritual treatments with holy water applied to his eyes. Eventually his vision improved, and he decided to join the church. Soon he began having a series of dreams and visions in which he saw himself healing people. Church authorities interpreted these experiences as signs that God was calling him into service. The young man became an active member of the church and soon he rose to the rank of Army of Jesus, which involved responsibilities of ushering services and helping ministers with the administration of healing rites. In time Olu had come to see his experience with blindness and recovery as a sign of God's call; but it would take several more years for this to become reality. During this time he would attend other Aladura churches, including one that claimed descent from Moses Orimolade, the founder of C&S. Along the way he would also pursue a career as an agricultural technician.

In 1960 Olu accepted a position with a farming company in Liberia. In this unfamiliar land he neglected religious advice and lived "the worldly life." In the 1960s the CLA had a growing presence in Liberia, but Olu chose to keep his distance. One day, however, a blind man (interestingly enough named Prophet Harris) told Olu that he should leave his job and serve only God. If he did not, blindness would return. The prophet's warning distressed Olu: he liked his job and felt committed to his employers, but he feared the "anger of God." Eventually he traveled to Kakata, where he decided to take a bush struggle. He thought this might help him understand more clearly the will of God. The first two days of his struggle nothing happened. On the third day, though, he received a vision in which a person—whom he described as "an Angel or Christ himself"—gave Olu "the Rod of Moses" and said to him: "Follow me." After the struggle he went to an Aladura branch in Kakata and told the ministers about his experience. He resigned from his job, joined the church, and decided to take up the call. Later a Kakata minister recommended him to the Center Street branch, where Olu became a follower, or minister-in-training.

During this period of training Olu gained a wide reputation as a capable healer and interpreter of dreams. Recognizing his abilities as an effective evangelist, the Aladura church appointed Olu to a series of interior posts. He established new branches in the Gbarnga area, some in remote Kpelle villages. While serving in Gbarnga, he married a young Kpelle woman, who had been raised by her Aladura relatives in Monrovia, educated at the elementary school of the Center Street Church, and considered herself to be a "daughter of the church." Though a "city girl," his wife had strong ties with her country relatives and, undoubtedly, such social contacts proved invaluable for Olu in his efforts to start new branches in Kpelle villages.

At the same time, Olu and his supporters always insisted on a narrative about church growth that stressed prophetic gifts rather than family connections. It generally went as follows: once individuals realized that Olu, a prophet, had arrived in town, they brought to him a person sick from blindness, paralysis, or insanity. After he cured the person, proving the power of his work, other sick and disabled persons were brought to him. Treatments involved exposing the witchcraft or exorcizing the bad spirits that caused problems. Such "signs and wonders" became the basis for a prayer group centered on solving problems through spiritually directed techniques. The prayer group eventually evolved into a church. A healed individual or family member (who might or might not join) sometimes became patron of the group and helped it obtain land for a new church.

Founding St. Peter's

In 1978 Olu left the CLA and moved to Paynesville. In my conversations with him about his departure from the CLA, he always insisted there was "no confusion." He expressed respect and admiration for the church. His leaving was "God's choice," discerned through a series of dreams and visions. In Paynesville, Olu began treating patients, organized a prayer group, and in 1980 founded St. Peter's. He derived the name from a Nigerian church that had been a spin-off of the C&S in Nigeria. St. Peter's never had formal ties with the Nigerian church, but Olu insisted on the importance of its lineage. Like the C&S, St. Peter's had a spiritual lineage that was traced back to Moses Orimolade. This further served to distinguish St. Peter's from the CLA, which had stressed the originary work of Josiah Oshitelu.

Apostle Samuel Olu ringing the altar bell during Divine Worship shouts. Photograph by author.

Soon after founding the church, Olu raised funds for a chapel and Faith Home. Paynesville residents begin hearing more about the Nigerian prophet and his remarkable visionary gifts. The 1980 coup occasioned an event that added to Olu's growing reputation as a healer, miracle worker, and powerful prophet. The coup took place just a month after the church's first conference. According to informants, enemies of the church reported to the new authorities that Olu had denounced the coup. One afternoon soldiers arrived at the compound and arrested him. As they prepared to leave, Olu told the soldiers they would be unable to start their truck; and so it happened. The soldiers straightway released the prophet.

The new church attracted people of diverse backgrounds, Aladura and non-Aladura alike, longtime Paynesville residents and recent arrivals. Others traveled from downtown Monrovia and the suburbs of Synkor and Logan Town. Middle-class Nigerians of both Yoruba and Igbo backgrounds joined the church, along with a few young professional Sierra Leoneans. The Paynesville church's greatest success, however, was among people who belonged to indigenous groups—local Bassa from nearby King Gray and Kpelle from Kpelle Town. The church also attracted Bassa, Kpelle, Kru, and Mano newly arrived from interior counties. Soon St. Peter's started other branches in Paynesville, Buchanan, the Firestone Rubber Plantation, Gbarnga, and Zwedru. By 1984 it had opened fifteen branches. The first Paynesville branch, where Olu normally resided, served as headquarters.[9]

Alpha Omega Bundu and the United Church of Salvation

Among Paynesville prophets, the Sierra Leonean Alpha Omega Bundu gave Olu his greatest competition. Bundu was born into a Temne Muslim family near Freetown. At fifteen he suffered an illness that seemed incurable until he was taken to a Nigerian prophet who prayed over him and divined that Bundu had been afflicted by the Holy Spirit, which the prophet interpreted as a call. But it would be several years before Bundu converted to Christianity. His story, like Olu's, involves a series of mishaps, experiencing the Spirit's continual presence and further signs from God until finally, after a successful treatment, he joins a prophet church. Bundu would continue to attend various churches, but eventually he became a member of a church named the Church of Salvation,[10] which would later play a significant role in his work in Liberia. When he moved to Liberia, he started attending an Aladura church.

Bundu and his family came to Paynesville in 1980. They resided at a former Pentecostal mission compound where he opened an elementary school. There Bundu and his wife, who were both former Aladura cross bearers, began holding prayer meetings, which attracted Paynesville locals, especially people with Congo background. Eventually the prayer group became chartered as the United Church of Salvation, a name inspired by Bundu's former affiliation. At first, Congo residents represented the majority membership; but Sierra Leoneans from surrounding suburbs began attending and over time they came to outnumber the Congo members.

Early on, Bundu's church courted good relations with St. Peter's. The two churches frequently observed joint events, such as Sunday Divine Worship services and midnight struggles. In August 1982, on the occasion of St. Peter's third observance of Tabborrar, Olu invited Bundu to take the struggle with him. They secluded themselves within a temporary bush enclosure, while junior ministers from both churches underwent the thirteen-day struggle in the Faith Homes. After Tabborrar, Olu gave Bundu a consecrated holy rod, an auspicious event for an Aladura prophet. The following year the two prophets again shared the retreat. This time Olu ordained Bundu as an archdeacon. Among AIC churches, such acts of bestowal and ordination were clear examples of the flow of doctrines and practices. Though Bundu would eventually pursue a separate course, his relationship with Olu played a key part in the validation of his new church.

In 1984 Bundu's church sought a new direction that would eventually lead to discarding its Aladura identity. Through the influence of its Sierra Leonean contingent, the church began exploring affiliation with the Church of Salvation, Bundu's former church in Sierra Leone. A merger was accomplished in spring 1984. The Paynesville branch became headquarters of the Liberia diocese and Bundu was appointed as its head. This new affiliation entailed changes in Aladura practice, such as giving up use of the holy rod and wearing white gowns in public. Ministers could use only the hand-held wooden cross, which the Church of Salvation did not consider distinctively Aladura. The most significant change concerned their policy regarding the relation between spiritual treatments and membership. A new rule was introduced: patients must be members. The ministers could pray over nonmembers, but only members (or associate members) could undergo the more elaborate spiritual treatments. Among AIC, including Aladura churches, the policy regarding membership was unique.[11]

The United Church of Salvation ceased having joint functions with St. Peter's. Olu's and Bundu's paths crossed less and less frequently. Indeed, for a period of several months I served as a rather awkward conduit between the two prophets. Olu, on his part, continued to show keen interest in Bundu's work and frequently asked me about new developments at the United Church of Salvation. Despite the competition among prophet churches, Olu actually encouraged me to explore different churches but would gently chide me if I stayed away too long from St. Peter's. Bundu rarely asked me about my work at St. Peter's.

Before I left Liberia, Bundu would travel abroad to Amsterdam, London, and New York, where he met with expatriate West Africans interested in forming prayer groups. After a successful tour, he returned to resume leadership of the Paynesville church. Under the auspices of the Church of Salvation, it continued to grow; however, in 1988 Bundu led a breakaway faction, formed a new congregation, and reclaimed the Liberian church's former United Church of Salvation name. During the civil war the prophet left for New York, where he lived for several years. In the late 1990s he returned to Sierra Leone. After the civil war the church he founded in Paynesville would eventually become affiliated with a new Pentecostal Prophet church based in London.

St. Peter's Merger with David Fyneah's Church

The year 1984 marked an important time for St. Peter's. In February the church began exploring a merger with David Fyneah's UCL. Olu had always regarded Fyneah as his "Spiritual Father." The older minister had directed him when he trained at Center Street, and the two men continued to be steadfast friends. While he remained at CLA, Olu never saw Fyneah as one who had betrayed the church. Like others, he had hoped the Liberian bishop would eventually return to the fold. After Olu left the CLA in 1978, the two prophets sought one another's company and support. They would occasionally observe common services and refer patients. Their close friendship eventually affected the direction of both churches. According to Olu, not long after his ordination as a bishop, Fyneah met with him and asked him to take over the UCL. Olu rejected the offer. Soon after their meeting Fyneah died, and Olu came to see the older prophet's proposal as foretelling his death. In 1983 the leading authority in a Ghanaian branch of the UCL reported that Fyneah had appeared to him in a dream and told him that the UCL and St. Peter's should become one church with Olu as its leader. UCL authorities in Liberia initially rejected this idea, but eventually they agreed to the merger.

In spring 1984 the two churches held a joint conference and made the merger official. All branches became chartered under the name of St. Peter's United Church of the Lord and were encouraged to recognize Olu's authority. The merger also received a supportive boost with the announcement of a new alliance formed with an American church. In June, Olu and an associate had made a trip to Washington, D.C., where they organized a prayer group among expatriate West Africans and met with officials of the Christian Community Churches of Christ, an African American Spiritual Church.[12] The Washington church agreed to help St. Peter's financially, including the donation of a school bus, and to lend support in starting new prayer groups or branches among West Africans in the D.C. area.

With the merger set in motion, the church's energies turned toward preparation for the coming August Tabborrar. It was hoped that a shared Tabborrar would strengthen the bond between St. Peter's and the former UCL. The event indeed segued into a period of goodwill between the factions, steady enthusiasm about recent successes, and optimism about the immediate future. Other AIC in the area began applying for membership with St. Peter's, and some were accepted on a trial basis. Some members, however, had criticized churches that "joined the party" out of their own interest. St. Peter's most effective growth during this period came through the creation of new prayer groups. Using the Paynesville headquarters as a base, young ministers and cross bearers began an intensive campaign of open-air preaching and working with prayer groups in King Gray and at the army barracks on Scheiffelin Road.

The euphoria between the St. Peter's and UCL parties promised by the Tabborrar celebration lasted for only about two months. After Tabborrar, Olu appointed a newly ordained archdeacon to lead the Logan Town branch. Though the archdeacon had UCL background, some branch members had opposed his appointment and continued to begrudge him support. Several members of the faction left and joined a branch in Garnersville, which had always had the strongest reservations about the merger with St. Peter's. The faction grew increasingly unhappy with it, but leaders of the Christian Community Churches of Christ were finally able to broker an understanding, albeit a temporary one, between the groups.

Civil Collapse and Olu's Last Days

In late 1985 a tragedy befell St. Peter's that augured coming hardships. As social and economic turmoil increased in Liberia, a disaffected general led a failed coup that resulted in the deaths of hundreds of citizens. In the aftermath of this event, soldiers executed one of the church's leading lay members, the chief warden, after someone had accused him of celebrating the revolt. Also, during the same troubled period a board member and major financier of the church, learning of death threats to him and his family, left Paynesville and returned to his native Sierra Leone. These misfortunes, however, did not impede the church's steady growth and its efforts to network with other churches. St. Peter's also periodically became involved with Pentecostal and evangelical projects. In the late 1980s the church sent ministers to the Monrovia Bible Training Center, an interdenominational evangelical seminary, and provided ministers as counselors for a Liberia for Christ crusade supported by a Canadian mission (Gifford 1993, 216–23). Also, encouraged by its new relations with the Christian Community Churches of Christ, the church commissioned the young minister Kennedy Sandy to travel to America to work with prayer groups in the D.C. area.

The outbreak of civil war in 1989 brought on many more challenges for St. Peter's and other churches in Paynesville. During the first battle of Monrovia in 1990, rebel forces fought ECOMOG (Economic Community of West African States Cease-fire Monitoring Group) forces, which included many Nigerian soldiers. Consequently the rebel faction began to target Nigerian expatriates as enemies. When they overtook Paynesville, they interned Olu and other Nigerians, some of whom had belonged to Olu's church. In the early 1990s one story circulated among expatriate members about Olu's capture: he was scheduled for execution when a rebel soldier, who had once been treated for an illness by Olu, recognized the prophet and spoke on his behalf. The rebel officers spared his life. They then transported Olu to Gbarnga in central Liberia, a rebel stronghold for Charles Taylor's forces. Some reports had it that he remained a prisoner but continued to minister to the sick and the needy, to rebel soldiers and civilians alike. Later it was reported that sometime in 1992 or 1993 Olu had met the misfortune that came to many hapless Nigerians—he had been executed. Now he had become, like the Nigerian prophet Oduwole before him, a martyr for the church.

THE FLOW OF VIRTUE

In the 1980s the institutional alignments between various AIC in Paynesville appeared fragile and uncertain. If the organizational links were weak, continuity through ritual ceremony and the healing praxis remained firm and ongoing. In Aladura churches institutional boundaries and identities were often made irrelevant by shared practices and personnel. The emergence of diaspora churches and of translocal exchanges also contributed to this trend. The good case in point involves the Reverend Kennedy Sandy, the evangelist commissioned by Olu in 1987 to work with the Washington prayer groups. In the summer of 1999 Reverend Sandy returned to Liberia for the church's August Tabborrar. During the trip he became ordained as bishop and as the general overseer for international operations. He received ordination from Apostle Lewis Thomas, a semiretired minister in the CLA who led the Liberian diocese in the early 1970s. Kennedy's spiritual lineage now included authorities from both the CLA and UCL, churches with competing claims of succession.

The Aladura church provided the theological, ritual, and social backdrop for the general emergence of prophet cosmology and for the growing appeal of Pentecostal-Charismatic Churches. The dissemination of Aladura doctrine happened as much through the experiences of individual ministers, members, and patients as through the work of collective groups. The prophets especially were effective through the kinds of services they offered—the ability to identify the sources of misfortune, to expose witchcraft, to interpret dreams and give visions, to solve problems, and to nurture belonging. For the most part these services centered on the healing praxis, which reflected the central importance of the healer-patient relationship. Since Aladura churches did not require membership for healing services, the healing process became an initiation, a threshold for many patients who convalesced for weeks, even months, before converting. Many never converted but continued to go from church to church, from one healer to another. Nonetheless, in Catherine Bell's terms (1992), they participated in a praxis that actualized them as ritualized bodies producing a ritual environment.

Among the AIC that I worked with, the United Church of Salvation had the most guarded membership and healing policy. Requiring new patients to register as church members did not preclude their membership in a mainline church—Baptist, Methodist, or Roman Catholic. The United Church of Salvation (and the Church of Salvation), however, strongly discouraged membership with any church it identified as Aladura or prophet, since these churches offered a healing praxis the church perceived as competing with their own. This approach worked well with Congos and expatriate Sierra Leoneans, many of whom also belonged to Baptist, Methodist, or Roman Catholic churches. It became more of a challenge in working with the indigenous migrants, who attended other AIC and liked the freedom to shop around.

The United Church of Salvation, however, understood that prophetic healing defied absolute control and impermeable boundaries. Ultimately virtue was free and spontaneous. Aladura hagiographies attested to the creative force of virtue.

Though mediated principally through given institutions, virtue was not confined to them and could inspire change and reinterpretation. In examining the Aladura way, one is constantly faced with this paradox—virtue served both as the basis of and as a disrupter of the cultural order. The model of the prophet and his relationships with clients illustrates this paradoxical dimension of virtue. Healing rituals offered a major testing ground for determining the authenticity of a prophet's virtue, which also led to competition over patients. When one prophet lost a patient to another, or if his clinic experienced greater growth than one nearby, jealousies and accusations of sorcery arose.

In the Aladura healer-patient relationship, obedience was axiomatic. Prophets criticized members and patients when they consulted other healers on the sly. Such conduct challenged the authority of the prophet and raised questions about his virtue. But the prophets knew that no one could claim a monopoly on virtue and understood why a patient, discontented with his or her progress, might seek other options. Despite alarms about shopping around, referrals and collaborations between prophets were commonplace. The field of prophecy revealed the dialectic between flow and control among the churches. The field, the complex of forces, influenced the attitudes, expectations, and actions of individuals and groups. The movement of persons, such as prophets and patients; the availability of services, such as spiritual healing; the flow of goods, such as the material transactions between prophet and patient; and the dissemination of ideas, such as the understanding of Spirit as the source of prophetic revelation, became forces generating cultural experience.

Among Paynesville churches St. Peter's remained one of the most inclusive and relaxed in its relations with others. Like the United Church of Salvation, it attempted to create a unique mission, but unlike that church it did not discourage association with other Aladura churches. Indeed the church courted such relationships. Ministers and members from other churches frequently attended the Paynesville branch headquarters. The church's membership and clientele represented perhaps the most ethnically eclectic in the area, though certain majorities emerged from time to time, often depending on the ethnicity of the ministers.

Undoubtedly St. Peter's appeal had much to do with Prophet Samuel Olu's broad background, his meaningful ties with other prophets, and his expansive spirit. Olu's story also followed a common paradigm of Aladura hagiographies: he enters a village, preaches the word, and heals the afflicted. Along the way he arouses fervent opposition from elders and *zoes* (traditional spiritual experts). He is attacked by enemies and witches, but through God's virtue brings them low, finds support, and starts a church. This demonstration of spiritual power through "signs and wonders" confirmed the truth of the prophet's message and, for the Aladura, characterized the founder's model. Benjamin Ray, in his analysis of the Aladura church in Nigeria, shows how the concept of the founder drew from both Yoruba and biblical patterns. In Yoruba religion the *orisha* (supernatural power) commissions a cultic priest, whose shrine attracts a new following, a pattern that takes hold in the Aladura understanding of biblical calling and founding (1993, 2).

In traditional Liberian cosmology one kind of call came through contact with the *jina*, the bush spirit, who enabled the subject to acquire supernatural knowledge and expertise. In the Aladura discourse, however, the jina liaison, like the orisha, became suspect and discouraged. Still the extraordinary person's association with the forest, the wild, the uninhabitable, undomesticated domain (the jina's domain) where one obtained supernatural knowledge and power through "struggling" with the resident spirit, remained a meaningful trope. In keeping with this pattern the Aladura assimilated the unfriendly, even hostile, alien town into the category of the bush, the uninhabitable wilderness, which provided an image of temptation and struggle. Still, despite the indigenous motifs in the Liberian Aladura cosmology, it was clear that the biblical paradigm for prophecy prevailed. When Aladura thought of the forest, the wilderness, or the town as a place of struggle, it was in terms of how Moses, John the Baptist, and Jesus endured in the wilderness. These associations helped confirm the church's mission in Africa and its continuity with a historic tradition.[13] They also helped manage spatial and temporal orientations for obtaining an experience that synthesized a Christian and African self.

In Paynesville City the field of prophecy encompassed multiple associations and encounters. This involved ongoing exchanges between Aladura, Pentecostal, Bassa, mission, and mainline churches. Life in the city brought significant encounters between settler families, new migrants, and Nigerian and Sierra Leonean expatriates. In the search for healing, Liberians engaged Western-trained physicians, Aladura ministers, prophet healers, and country doctors (traditional healers). Individuals and groups participated in the exchange of goods, doctrines, and services that contributed to an "argument of images" (Fernandez 1982, 562–64) in the quest for spiritual power, whether in its public or private form. The contest of prophecy and the management of spiritual goods and services would also address the disruptions caused by political instability, civil war, and dislocation.

Through Faith Home praxis and episodic events such as Tabborrar, the Paynesville AIC reinscribed onto ritual bodies various traditional and Christian paradigms. Their effect on local epistemologies included commentaries on occult desire. In Paynesville in the 1980s the *zo* (the traditional spiritual expert) played a minimal role in the public order; increasingly the prophetic discourse had begun to take hold. Bishop Bundu once informed me that President Doe visited him on several occasions to receive dream interpretations, spiritual treatments, and prognostications about his future. The prophet, however, warned the president that unless he joined the church, came out in the open, the consultations would end. The prophet discourse sought transparency in the public realm, but this did not entail advocating an ideal political order. Indeed, in Liberia the representations of power (visible and invisible) became increasingly contested. In this setting the praxis of ritual struggle—so unremittingly expressed in Faith Home praxis and Tabborrar rites—ultimately suggested a notion of renewal that implicated the crisis of occult desire. There were no allusions to a hegemonic cultural order (whether settler, Yoruba, indigenous, or state). Undoubtedly the Aladura journey from Nigeria to Liberia had already dislodged links between the political and religious realms. At the same time, the church continued to affirm the vibrancy of its signs and wonders across West Africa and its relevancy for redressing social disorder.

In her discussion of Jean Comaroff's work on South African Zionists, Catherine Bell notes that, for Comaroff, "ritual, by focusing on the making and remaking of the body, reproduces the sociopolitical context in which it takes place while also attempting to transform it" (1992, 209). In the postcolonial world the healing praxis, with its attention to the afflicted body, expresses a form of protest. The hegemonic context for that protest was all too clear in the case of South Africa. In the postcolonial world of the Doe regime and the civil war that followed, the social and political sources of oppression were obvious as well, but the expression of a hegemonic link was not. In this context the prophet churches sought to make and remake ritual bodies prepared to offset occult desire and the spurious designs they saw in the lesions of the social body. As we shall see, this making and remaking of ritual bodies continues to be an indispensable dimension of the AIC in the diaspora.

The Church in Diaspora

On an August evening in 1993, we drove from the Reverend Kennedy Sandy's Columbia Road apartment over to Alexandria, Virginia, to begin the second phase of a couple's spiritual treatment—a three-day consecration performed for the husband's protection. On the drive over, Sandy told me their story. The couple came from Sierra Leone. She worked in a nearby hospital, while he was a part-time custodian in their apartment building. The husband had recently returned from Sierra Leone, and since his return he had become sexually impotent. They had been referred to Sandy by friends who were members of St. Peter's. During the spiritual interview Sandy learned that, on his trip to Sierra Leone, the husband had an affair with another man's wife. The prophet revealed that the wronged man had "placed signs" against the husband.

When we arrived at the apartment, Sandy set up candles on window sills and in doorways. He took a cup of water he had blessed the day before and began sprinkling it throughout the apartment. Then he fumigated it with incense. His interest then turned to the husband's holy bath. The man knelt before Sandy to receive his prayers. Sandy asked me to read a psalm while he prayed over the husband and waved a cluster of burning candles around his thin body. He then placed the candles on the floor and told the man to straddle them. After he did this, the husband took the bucket of water with him to bathe.

While we waited for the husband to finish, Sandy had a private talk with the wife. The husband returned and knelt before Sandy to receive closing prayers. The prophet inserted the end of the holy rod into a bottle of olive oil and prayed. He poured oil into the husband's open palm and told him to rub it on his face, neck, and arms and throughout his hair. Then Sandy gave a closing revelation: by God's grace, and the husband's repentance, their prayers would be answered. The hold of African signs was weakening. But the couple needed to continue "strong prayers." As we were leaving, Sandy warned the couple not to extinguish the candles: "Let them burn down!"

When Sandy came to the United States in 1987, he had been an ordained minister since August 1984. Olu had appointed him as mount secretary for the Tabborrar ritual, a significant position since he became responsible for recording Olu's divine messages. He had received further training at the headquarters and eventually became its Faith Home supervisor. Sandy rose quickly in the ministerial ranks as the church grew throughout the Paynesville area. During this time Olu became increasingly concerned about St. Peter's work in the United States, which had started in 1984. The church's assigned missionary had neglected correspondence with the church in Liberia, and the relationship with the Christian Community Churches of Christ had become more strained. Olu decided to send Sandy, his "spiritual son," to the United States. He had confidence in the young minister's commitment to St. Peter's and believed that he would not take for granted the church's relationship with its sponsor. When Sandy arrived in D.C., he reconnected with the missionary. The two would have a good working relationship, but the older minister would eventually leave St. Peter's. Also, shortly after Sandy's arrival, the Christian Community Churches of Christ severed ties with the Liberian church for reasons that were never clear. When the civil war broke out in Liberia in 1989, Sandy was advised not to return to his native land. He belonged to an ethnic group whose members had suffered violent reprisals from rebels. In any event, he found that the growing Aladura flock in Washington required his services. His apartment on Columbia Road began to serve as a Faith Home.

Throughout the early 1990s Reverend Sandy's D.C. prayer group held meetings in several locations—usually rented spaces in a storefront, a school, or a church. In 1993 the prayer group became an officially chartered church, with about one hundred members. Most members were Liberian, Sierra Leonean, and

Nigerian. After 1991, when U.S. immigration authorities had granted Liberians civilian amnesty status, thousands began migrating to Minnesota, Rhode Island, New York, Philadelphia, and the Washington, D.C., area. By 2007 the District of Columbia had become home to about five thousand expatriate Liberians. During this period of growth, demands for Sandy's healing services kept increasing. As had been the case in Liberia, most of his patients were nonmembers who belonged to other denominations, such as Methodist, Baptist, and Pentecostal. Sandy's 1993 Faith Home logbook listed more than four hundred patients he had treated in just five months, a rate that remained constant throughout the decade. His work also included countless "house calls," which often took him away from the Washington area, to Baltimore, New York, and Atlanta. In subsequent years he has traveled to Akron, Ohio, and to Southern California to work with prayer groups and individual clients.

In 1994 Reverend Sandy married a Sierra Leone woman, a staff employee at a local university. They moved to an apartment in Silver Spring, Maryland, and in the same building the church rented a basement apartment for its Faith Home. His wife, a cross bearer, also assisted him with treatments. The location served as the church's "station" for the next four years. In 1998 the church moved to Hyattsville, Maryland, where it had purchased an abandoned U.S. Postal Service building, renovating it as a multiservice facility with a Faith Home, worship center, apartments, and offices. In the last decade Hyattsville has attracted increasing numbers of migrants from West Africa and the Caribbean, many who have found in St. Peter's a familiar resource.

The Hyattsville area had also become home to other AIC and to new Pentecostal churches, which attracted many West African expatriates. Grocery shops in the area were well stocked with items made available for use as holy materials: candles, incense, Florida water (a cologne manufactured in New Jersey), the blue crystals needed for blue incense and devil's incense, and bottles of water and perfume water imported from Nigeria and consecrated in Aladura sacred spaces. They also sold Aladura religious tracts and texts. And frequently in demand were low-production videos from Nigeria and Ghana, which offered seedy soap opera–style stories about deceit and revenge, about witchcraft and salvation.

Among the new AIC in Hyattsville was the Universal Church of God, which was founded in London in 2001 by Bishop Daniel Browne, a former minister in the Church of Salvation with Paynesville connections. The Universal Church of God described itself as a "Pentecostal Prophetic Church." The church's title coupled with this self-description denoted its doctrinal perspective, historical basis, and global mission (Britt 2008, 22–24). In recent decades many AIC, especially those fostering Pentecostal or evangelical links, have played down the African denotation. Indeed the diaspora AIC have emerged as agents in the emerging translocal spiritual economy, demonstrating a crosscurrent of African, American,

Caribbean, European, Pentecostal, evangelical, and therapeutic elements. At the same time, in their transatlantic travels from Africa to Europe to America, Aladura migrants have found in religious identity a form of belonging that has helped offset the experience of dislocation. As Rijk van Dijk observes in his study on Ghanians in the Netherlands, global Pentecostalism has enabled migrants to cope effectively with "the *meaning of the stranger* in an intercontinental perspective" (1997, 136–37).

The Pentecostal and evangelical impact on diaspora AIC notwithstanding, African churches, such as St. Peter's and the Universal Church of God, still maintain a specific bodily praxis, a strategy of ritual struggle, that in the "condition of translocality" (137) helps situate subjects in the present and to provide them with a meaningful spiritual narrative. Among West Africans, dislocation and separation have been especially poignant for Liberians and Sierra Leoneans. Moran has observed the intense identification that diaspora Liberians keep with their homeland (2005, 457–64). She speaks of this mostly in terms of the time and interest that exiled politicians and academics have given to political developments in Liberia. I can attest to similar interest among my Aladura friends and informants in Washington, but I would contend that many have also found in ritual struggle a meaningful strategy for living within an emergent translocal cosmology.

Like the C&S congregations in London that Harris has studied, Washington-area churches are increasingly challenged by the more contemporary Pentecostal churches, by evangelical missions, and Born Agains strategies,[14] which the younger generation perceives as being more stylish and less encumbered by old customs. As noted above, the churches in Liberia have had a history of facing such challenges. The attention to self-identity in relation to the networking with Pentecostal and evangelical groups began before the diaspora. Members at St. Peter's and the Universal Church of God acknowledge that they have overlapping interests and share common approaches with Pentecostals and Born Agains, though they continue to insist on their distinctiveness.

From its inception in Liberia, St. Peter's nurtured ties with Pentecostal and evangelical groups. During the first month I attended the church in Paynesville, the church held a revival that featured a Ghanaian Pentecostal evangelist, and throughout the year visiting Baptist, Methodist, and Pentecostal pastors offered prayers and preached sermons. The war years facilitated even more interaction among Pentecostals and AIC, much of this by necessity. The boundaries that separated groups became less significant than the doctrines they shared. Prayer bands increasingly attracted people across denominational lines. Pentecostal megameetings of the postwar era continue this pattern, attracting many Aladura. While emerging Pentecostal groups may disassociate themselves with AIC, the latter have found ways of appropriating styles from both. In Liberia, St. Peter's has in fact developed a strategy of coexistence and accommodation inspired by the work of the American branch.

In August 2009 Reverend Sandy traveled to Liberia for Tabborrar and remained for another six months. During this period he influenced several changes. St. Peter's began to sponsor a Divine Worship at the Paynesville City town hall, which could accommodate hundreds of worshippers. Sandy persuaded the church to appoint Baptist and Pentecostal ministers to assist in the service. Worshippers were not expected to remove shoes or to wear white gowns, though many Aladura continued to do so. Ministers and worship leaders were as likely to wear suits as the traditional prophet's garb. At local branches, however, Faith Home praxis and the role of ritual struggle would continue as before: insisting on the importance of fasting, holy baths, menstrual customs, praying with psalms, and attention to prescribed body decorum within an ordered sacred space.

The dualistic backdrop of the Aladura way has not lessened its imaginative hold so much as it has been reworked within the intercontinental context of "transsubjectivity" (van Dijk 1997, 137). Sermons, testimonies, dream interpretations, and vision narrations continue to refer to the temptations of occult power, witchcraft, and jina liaisons, as they do to drugs, urban strife, racism, unemployment, and the horrors of war. The traditional images, however, frequently take on a translocal, migratory form. In Liberia the "traveling" of secret signs happened through regional migrations to and from city and country. In the diaspora settings such signs navigate the global network of the Internet, the spiraling proliferation of new goods, and video productions. Among the urban diaspora, Ghanaian and Nigerian films have also become popular for reasons related to the features or themes identified by Meyer in her study of Ghanaian videos: the influence of unseen powers, the concern for domestic space, the husband-wife relationship as the film's point of departure, and a kind of wary desire for urban life (2003, 211–13). Even American films about domestic strife can assume a kind of magical dimension. Many years ago, when I lived in Charlottesville, an Aladura friend and I watched the film *Fatal Attraction* on HBO. For my friend, the Glenn Close vixen evoked Mami Wata, a dangerous she-devil capable of causing irrevocable harm to domestic life.

During a recent visit to St. Peter's Faith Home in Hyattsville, I met a Nigerian man who had lived in the United States for twenty years. At one time he worked as a consultant on Nigerian affairs for the CIA. The man, however, had fallen on hard times. At the Faith Home he was being treated for acute blindness. He had lost money and his wife had left him. When he became blind, he was treated at Johns Hopkins. But doctors were unable to treat his affliction effectively. Some friends then referred him to St. Peter's, whose ministers diagnosed his blindness to be an "African sickness" caused by witchcraft. They claimed that, on a recent trip the man's wife had made to Nigeria, she had received dangerous magic from her mother. One night after she returned, she placed signs by blowing a powder on her husband's eyelids as he slept. Now estranged from his wife, the Nigerian man had started a series of spiritual treatments in the Faith Home. These involved fasting, holy baths, and incense treatments. Like the previous vignette about the unfaithful Sierra Leonean husband, the Nigerian's case reminds us of the translocal capacity of the discourse of signs and powers and the reciprocity of cultural idioms. As Meyer notes, magic and modernity are not opposites, but can be mutually reinforcing (2003). In this context ritual struggle continues to be a valuable strategy for creating a ritual environment and for remaking the self. The two cases that frame this section reveal an undesired effect traversing the Atlantic, an affliction to be removed. Both cases show the church's emphasis on strategies—holy materials, bodily postures and gestures, and spatial orientations—that it considers equal to the task.

2

Person and Power in Liberia

Aladura cosmology can be fruitfully explored through two basic theoretical concepts: person and power. In any religious culture the notion of self or person plays a key role in shaping its values and order. What one identifies as the self's intrinsic and acquired qualities, present circumstances, and conceivable goals helps create the character of a community. The same applies to power. How one understands its source, nature, structure, and effects can instill expectations and influence actions. In the Aladura way the concepts of self and power converged most clearly in the model of the prophet. This created a paradox, because the prophet was a boundary figure: he moved between worlds—waking and dreaming, town and bush, this side and that side—which marked him as the "powerful person." Such movement also expressed the dialectic between hidden and transparent realities (Sanders and West 2003). The prophet's persona became formidably presented through ritual actions and behavior, and as such, he became the paragon of ritual struggle. As an exemplary subject the prophet embodied Aladura virtue, a term with both moral and metaphysical meaning. Among Liberian subjects, he most poignantly evoked the Aladura understanding of self, which always implied a context of relationships and the encounter with power.

Since I have referred to the Aladura way as a cosmology, I need to comment further on my understanding of the term. In his work on a Thai healing cult, Stanley Tambiah defines cosmology as "the body of conceptions that enumerate and classify the phenomena that compose the universe as an ordered whole and the norms and processes that govern it" (1986, 131). These conceptions provide the basis for theodicy, the explanation of misfortune, and the understanding of the meaning of experience. Rituals, in particular, "translate and create cosmology." For Tambiah, then, ascertaining the relationship of ritual to certain pivotal Buddhist concepts about the world, human nature, evil, and salvation can illuminate the meaning of Thai healing rituals (88–89). Making these links can also help us understand the roles and expectations that a community has of the diviner/prophet/healer.

Following Tambiah's lead, Aladura healing rituals can be tied to the "body of conceptions" that inform, explain, affect, and motivate everyday experience. This also entails seeing the Aladura way more in terms of its transformative potential, as an emergent reality (Fernandez 1982), than as a representational model or a closed system. For instance, the Aladura healing praxis revealed a cosmology, a worldview[1] that was constantly being challenged by other influences—Western, Aladura, Yoruba, Liberian, and Christian. And, as the works of Adogame (2004) and Harris (2006) have shown, Aladura cosmology continues to "emerge" through new global and diaspora contexts. I see cosmology very much as a culture that generates values, categories, symbols, rites, and relationships with which participants make sense of the world (Robbins 2004, 6). Indeed, Aladura cosmology involves ongoing interfacing and networking with a plurality of worldviews, cosmologies, and discourses.

The emergent, processual character of cosmology produces a dialectical play between subjective experience and objective orders. In his study of the Kuranko of Sierra Leone, Michael Jackson notes the Kuranko seldom understood culture as a given, objective order. One expected the Kuranko person "to be a subject who acts upon and transforms the world. This world to which he relates is not a static or closed order, a given reality which man must accept and to which he must adjust; rather, it is a problem to be worked on and solved" (1977, 237; 1989). Jackson's words can apply as well to the Aladura way in Liberia. It represented a world that revealed an oscillation between subjective and objective orders of experience, articulated in consociate relationships and specific encounters between persons—between God and prophet, prophet and patient, patient and jina, and so on—and effectively mediated through ritual performance.

The Aladura church's understanding of itself as a "problem-solving" church, as expressed through Faith Home praxis and the Aladura meaning of struggle, accentuated this dynamic quality. New misfortunes, afflictions, and dilemmas required creative responses. They offered fresh grist for the ritual mill and, consequently, participants reshaped Aladura relations, views, and values. The Aladura way created a context, in James Fernandez's words, for an "argument of images" (1982, 562–64) where the world became known and experienced through the exposure to and adaptation of an ever-expanding field of symbols, metaphors, words, and rites. In this field the Aladura prophet was a key player in the church's ongoing encounter with the known, changing world. The prophet manipulated traditional images of home, field, and body, but he also transformed these in adapting them to new technologies, journeys, pedagogies, markets, and pathologies. The image of the road frequently evoked in dreams and visions, for instance, carried variants in meaning that cut across regions and generations. The road represented new horizons, possibilities, and networking with distant places; it also denoted something foreboding. It was an obvious reminder of the daily danger of auto or bus travel. Also, the Paynesville junctures, where the highways met, made routine exchanges with the traveling stranger dangerous encounters. Roads and byways, too, evoked, however dimly, the "memoryscape" of roads as "menacing spaces" (Shaw 2002, 49), once traveled by warriors and slave traders and, more recently, by sweeping bands of soldiers, rebels, and bandits.

BEING A PERSON THE ALADURA WAY

Cheryl Mattingly notes that in "one way or another, most discussions about the Western Self presume a division between a public self, identified by roles, institutions or public symbols, and a private self, an internal experiential essence which is mysterious and unknowable" (1998, 105). Such models generally embrace the Maussian idea of the individual and of the "inner self" contrasted—indeed, in conflict with—the social self. An African notion of self, however, begins with the importance of relationality. In his work on the Kabre of Togo, Charles Piot contends that we should understand the African person as one "composed of, and constituted by, relationships, rather than as situated in them. Persons here do not 'have' relations; they 'are' relations" (1999, 18). Piot also notes that Western theories have neglected the "diffuse, fluid" understanding of self so apparent in African cosmologies. Here the self is "multiple and permeable, and infused with the presence of others, both human and nonhuman"(19).

These notions of the self are applicable to the Aladura understanding. Being a person the Aladura way,[2] becoming a "Child of Salvation," involved a specific interface between self and world, an acknowledged tension between public and private selves, but this tension did not betray a romantic drive for sovereign autonomy; instead it arose from the perceived duality (or multiplicity) of ontic experience, an awareness of the self as an aggregate of multiple forces. The Aladura accepted an internal entity called a soul, or spirit, but, in Mattingly's words, it was "mysterious and unknowable," even to one's self. The Aladura healer often spoke of solving a problem in terms of the patient "coming to himself." Sometimes the witch was spoken of in terms of someone "not knowing himself." The church's duty was to bring him to his senses and help him confess. The elusive, enigmatic character of the self prompted urgent questions: How can the church enable a person to know herself? How can someone gain the trust of others? How do we know the person we see is trustworthy? How can a friend today be an enemy tomorrow? The answers to such questions needed time, and, fortunately, God had plenty available.

Studies by Ray (1993), Adogame (2000, 2004), Harris (2006), and Crumbley (2008) convincingly show the Yoruba character of Aladura Christianity. During the first decades of Aladura's adaptation in Liberia, the Yoruba element continued to be evident and helped shape its distinctive character. Many of its leaders were Yoruba, including Samuel Oduwole. However, the church's adaptation involved a "second-order" transformation in which Liberian indigenous concepts and practices increasingly helped form the character of the church. Elements that Ray identifies as representing Yoruba culture, such as "belief in invisible spiritual powers, especially malevolent spiritual powers, and the belief in the efficacy of ritual action" (1993, 268), also surfaced in Liberia's indigenous groups, though their influence perhaps worked in a less systematic fashion.

Ascertaining the Aladura idea of person in Liberia involves identifying the major categories of personhood inherited from indigenous perspectives, such as language, ethnicity, kinship, gender, age, and life cycles (Moran 1990, 15–40). In looking at these categories in the postmodern, postcolonial, and translocal setting, we need to realize also that efforts to distinguish an African notion from a Western notion of the person have become increasingly problematic. The Aladura notion of the self in the Liberian context must be interpreted in terms of hybrid identities and experiences. At the same time, the church enabled a convergence of Christian and African ideas of selfhood.

Scholars generally identify among the indigenous population three major language groups, referred to as Mande, Mel, and Kwa, that cut across about sixteen ethnic groups or "tribes." Personal identity could be shaped by social and spiritual associations as much as by lineage or language. For most groups, patrilineal ties played a major role, but family ties were often negotiated through multiple associations. Researchers therefore have underappreciated the fluidity of tribal identity: dual ethnicities were not uncommon. As Moran notes, in many cases "local histories point to more evidence of conflict within than between ethnic categories" (2006, 4). Here I should note that my exposure to indigenous notions of ethnicity and identity was filtered primarily through Aladura experience. In their first forty years in Liberia, Aladura churches reached every major ethnic group, becoming especially successful among the Kpelle, Kru, Grebo, and Kissi. The churches I worked with in Paynesville betrayed a fluid ethnic makeup. Though in certain branches one or another ethnic group might predominate, membership was usually quite mixed. Also, from one month to another a church might experience a dramatic change in ethnic makeup because of turnovers in the Faith Home staff, success among new migrants, and networking among families.

By and large the Aladura played down tribal distinctions; rather, they emphasized the church's identity as an authentic African, Nigerian, or Liberian church that promoted unity among ethnic groups. Also, in Liberia the Aladura discourse on African authenticity reflected the conventional contrast between things considered "civilized" (*kwi*) and things considered "country," or uncivilized. The former term traditionally characterized the Americo-Liberian, or settler's, way of life, which other segments of society approximated in varying degrees but could never fully represent. The settler culture becomes evident in place names, such as Monrovia, Buchanan, Harper, Greenville, Georgia, and Mississippi—cities, towns, rivers, and counties named for American presidents and places in the southern United States. The settlers embodied traits associated with the civilized way: Western culture, mission-based churches, "the way of whites, use of machines, the hygienic habits, and rejection of superstition" (Tonkin 1981, 322). The term *country* was used to refer to people of the indigenous majority, the "uncivilized" ethnic groups traditionally excluded from the world of status and privilege (Fraenkel 1964; Hlophe 1979; Liebenow 1987). According to Moran, this dichotomy was "used unselfconsciously throughout Liberia" (1990, 1–2). Indeed the model of civilization had perhaps greater currency in Liberia than in any other part of West Africa.

Elizabeth Tonkin, however, emphasizes that these terms should not be understood in terms of reified opposites. Rather they simply represented "different domains of knowledge, power, and expertise" (1981, 322). Moran concurs with this interpretation, insisting that the country or native way referred to "an alternative path to success" (1990, 2–3).[3] Also, among indigenous Liberians one person could embrace and demonstrate equal facility in both domains, depending on context. Beryl Bellman indicates that though *kwi meni* ("civilized business") and *zo meni* ("society business") designated different orders of experience and knowledge, they were not mutually exclusive; the Kpelle simply recognized that there were different forms and ways of obtaining power (1975, 135–37).[4]

Though Americo-Liberians helped introduce the CLA to Liberians and in Monrovia played an instrumental role in its early growth, their influence notably declined as the church increasingly attracted individuals from indigenous groups. Among the Aladura churches that I attended I rarely met an individual who openly referred to himself as an Americo-Liberian or admitted settler background. Undoubtedly the 1980 coup, which brought a loss of prestige and hardship to many Americo-Liberians, made for greater reticence in doing so. But it should also be noted that Aladura identity implied a rejection of the conventional dichotomy of civilized versus country and the ideas of privilege and exclusion associated with it. As I was told, the Children of Salvation should reject those divisions promoted by cultural convention, whether African or Western, black or white.

However, Aladura informants recognized inevitable fundamental divisions within the worldly order. To begin with, the Children of Salvation refers to a community that contrasted with the world about them. Indeed, according to some informants, members wore white apparel to be recognized and clearly distinguished from nonmembers. By donning white gowns, the Liberian Aladura devalued the Western attire embraced by "civilized" Christians. Male members would especially stand out, since civilized attire—shoes, suit, tie, and hat—was more accepted among Liberian men. Also, as in the Zionist churches in South

Africa (Comaroff 1985, 220–21), the Aladura custom of wearing gowns served to blur gender distinctions, at least in some contexts. Aside from this social or political value, the act of wearing the white gown carried a ritual significance. In her analysis of dress custom among South African Nazarites, Carol Ann Muller asserts that ritual attire became "symbols of purification and resistance to outside defilement" (1999, 85). Similarly, for the Aladura the white gown became a marker of self-identity and of spiritual separateness. In the Aladura case, however, the challenge to civilized propriety and the separation from the profane world did not carry the radical political significance it did among South African Nazarites and Zionists, who confronted a systematic form of racial oppression.

The Aladura criticized "traditional" cultural forms as well as *kwi* and missionary cultural forms. Informants often spoke disparagingly of traditional cultural groups, such as Medicine and Initiation Societies. Ministers warned new members about former society associations and advised them to renounce them. Informants proudly described the Aladura church as an African church, but they did not see this in terms of the recovery of traditional forms. Any notion of recovery was discussed in terms of the biblical witness that came through God's special revelation to the African. Indeed the church insisted strongly on its connection with historic mainline and missionary churches. It may have been in deference to my feelings, but I never heard a minister or member attack mainline churches, though attacks on other prophet churches were not uncommon. They believed the mainline churches were simply unable to address the kind of spiritual problems that afflicted African subjects. Members or patients who already belonged to mainline churches were allowed dual membership. Clergy, however, were expected to be single-mindedly Aladura.

The most critical division, established by "divine authority," was found in its internal structure, in the hierarchical order and the rule of obedience articulated through a series of consociate relationships: senior prophet–junior minister, prophet-prophetess, prophet–cross bearer, healer-patient, dwellers-members, and so on. Though in many churches the term *senior prophet* or *senior prophetess* referred to a specific office, it also had a relational use. In this study I use the term metaphorically and relationally to apply to a minister who held one of the following spiritual offices: founder, apostle, bishop, senior archdeacon, archdeacon, evangelist; or who held the highest position within a church compound, a Faith Home supervisor, for instance, who might be only a junior minister but in such a context obtained seniority. The senior-junior dichotomy as applied to ministerial roles became the model for Aladura relations involving gender roles, healing, and interaction with the outside world. Being a person the Aladura way entailed obedience since virtue, or spiritual power, was mediated through a chain of command. A minister's (or patient's) trust and obedience in his or her senior was the precondition for any successful struggle or treatment.

Liberian ethnographic literature illustrates the importance of age in the matters of authority (Murphy 1980; Bledsoe 1984; Moran 1990). Here age means more than physical longevity. Moran states, "It is therefore not possible to determine the exact age at which someone becomes an elder, or even an adult. Because of the different cycles of birth and death with each family, the status of each individual must be considered on its own basis" (1990, 30). Age also refers to the prestige, the power, and the quality of knowledge one obtained through initiation into secret societies, such as the male Poro Society and the female Sande Society.[5] Discussions about age implicate gender. More recently Moran shows how the Glebo of southeastern Liberia "use relative age as a metaphor to describe the hierarchical relationship *between* the genders." The Glebo understand that men and women age differently; indeed, a Glebo saying goes, "men are always older than women" (2000, 37). In any conventional context, however, the elder, whether male or female, arouses respect and fear. One does not become old or prestigious unless he or she has access to certain occult powers, considered dangerous to the noninitiated, the young, and the outsider (37–39). Undoubtedly this indigenous idea of the relation between seniority and knowledge informed the Liberian's understanding of Aladura hierarchy. Whatever meaning these values obtained for participants, they became assimilated, transformed, or adapted within an Aladura "system of prestige" (38).

Every Aladura church I worked with had a spiritual mother, the wife of a prophet of high rank (archdeacon, bishop, or apostle). She was usually considered a powerful prophetess in her own right. When a senior prophet died, his wife continued to be held in such regard. Occasionally this term was used to refer to any woman married to any minister assigned to a branch or Faith Home. A spiritual mother had specific responsibilities and, in certain ritual contexts, was considered senior to other ranking male ministers. Most spiritual mothers I knew were over thirty-five, but younger women also assumed that role through marriage to a prophet; and in all likelihood they had already earned some reputation as prophetesses or healers. In such cases the spiritual mother remained subordinate to her husband. However, contested claims about who had the greatest authority did arise between a spiritual mother and male ministers. At one Aladura branch, for instance, a spiritual mother refused to submit to the authority of another senior prophet who had been temporarily appointed as the supervisor of the church's Faith Home. She regarded the minister as less advanced in the spiritual arts and strongly disagreed with how he treated some cases, especially those that involved children.

The Aladura prophetess/healer who led a branch was usually an older woman. The majority of her patients would be women and children. In the cases of three Aladura branches in Paynesville and nearby Congo Town, the prophetess received primary help from an assistant male minister, who, like the senior prophetess, was also a rod holder. The holy rod, a two-and-one-half-foot iron rod with a looped end, represented the primary emblem of the prophetic office, used in orchestrating daily ritual struggles. Being a rod holder enabled one "to control the altar." The advantage in having a male rod holder as an assistant was that he could take care of altar duties during the prophetess's menses. If she were postmenopausal, a qualified male minister afforded more ritual flexibility since younger female apprentices were limited by menstrual laws. A woman's monthly cycle restricted her participation in ritual activities and her movement in sacred space (Crumbley 2006; 2008).

Aladura informants openly discussed menstruation, which differed from some indigenous settings. In his study of the Gola of eastern Liberia, Warren d'Azevedo notes their reticence in speaking about menstruation in a mixed-gender context, seeing such talk as strictly a woman's matter, even as potentially unlucky for men to hear (1994, 353–54). For the Aladura, however, the acknowledged potency of menstruation made it an ongoing and public concern. It represented a power that could be used to subvert the desired order of things. In keeping with biblical law and continuous with indigenous models, the Aladura considered menstrual blood "spoiling" to holy materials, sacred areas, spiritual exercises, and ritual struggles. Though some informants did refer to menstruation as "pollution," it represented more a power than a substance; it simply needed to be controlled or contained. And, ironically, its recognition as such enhanced rather than diminished the role of women, a matter we revisit in chapter 5.

At the Aladura churches I attended, including St. Peter's, probably the most well represented religious office among women was the cross bearer. The cross bearer was so called because she used a small, handheld wooden cross. This officer, with the cross always in her possession, frequently assisted the prophet with prayers, services, and healings. Quite often she worked independently, organizing prayer groups, open-air preaching, and healing ceremonies. The cross bearer exhibited the gift of visions and prophecy, but, as we shall see, this became circumscribed within certain contexts, especially when submission to a senior prophet was expected. I met cross bearers who claimed the wooden cross was a more effective healing instrument than the iron rod. On occasion I heard debates between ministers and members on this matter. But by and large the claim for the superiority of the cross was the exception that made the rule.

In the everyday life of the church, the senior minister–junior minister relationship (which expressed a principle of obedience) became the model of social exchange, but the prophet-patient relationship provided the basis. For self-making in the Aladura way the process of remediation, of "problem solving," of being a patient became the most commonly shared experience. At one time or another everyone, including the prophet, has been a patient, has submitted him- or herself to a prophet's care, and the experience of being a patient has specifically shaped the Aladura understanding of self. Being a patient, of course, implied a notion of sickness. On this topic, Robert A. Hahn's definition of sickness, with some qualification, can be useful: "I propose that *sicknesses are unwanted conditions of self, or substantial threats of unwanted conditions of self.* Unwanted conditions may include states of any part of the person—body, mind, experience, or relationships. Unwantedness comes in degrees, and individuals may have different thresholds regarding just how seriously unwanted a condition must be in order to qualify as sickness" (1995, 22). This description works because it covers a gamut of disorders, seeing sickness as more than physical malady. Most Aladura cases involved physical malady, but these were often seen as symptomatic of a different sort of problem. Hahn's description, however, does not account for an understanding of sickness in relation to a theodicy of purpose. With further reflection, with new revelations, even an "unwanted condition" could be seen as necessary. The sickness or problem became a sign by which "God is showing you the way."

Most Aladura church members joined the community at some point during the process of affliction, treatment, and cure. A prophet discerned that the affliction was really spiritual and that the person afflicted should remain in the Faith Home for a period of time undergoing special treatments. But beyond this social process, healing entailed faith in a theological vision that brought new knowledge of God and acceptance into a new familial order that reflected the divine. This faith became embodied in practice. Spiritual healing initiated the subject into an order of experience that, in effect, helped the patient "come to her self." In a meaningful way the process involved a reconstitution of the self with a new title. Healing was the mark of adoption whereby one became a Child of Salvation. Being a patient always remained essential to one's identity as a member. Members regularly expected from ministers revelations about their spiritual and physical condition. Some expressed disappointment if, after they attended many prayers or services, the prophet had not received a vision about them. Retelling your dreams to the prophet, whether privately or publicly, was one of the most constant and trusted methods for obtaining knowledge about the state of one's soul and body. Informants/interlocutors claimed that the Aladura way offered protection from the evil intents of other members, family, neighbors, and strangers.

For all the church's emphasis on virtue, on being able to conquer temptation and infirmity, it was also clear that acknowledgment of one's limitations, acts of contrition and confession, were crucial to self-identity. These emotive and cognitive moments became coupled with decisive bodily praxis. The experience of the body, or embodiment, became the most immediate and poignant way of gaining knowledge of self and of others. Liberians at the Faith Home frequently greeted one another with "How is the body?" A common reply was "I am trying." This simple exchange alerts us both to the complex notion of self as body and to the principle of struggle involved with everyday life and daily praxis.

TRAVELING BETWEEN "THIS SIDE" AND "THAT SIDE"

Aladura cosmology assumed a division between "this side" and "that side": between the waking and dreaming, visible and invisible worlds. In the same way, Aladura anthropology betrayed two fundamental aspects: the ordinary, waking self and the invisible, dream self or soul. This dichotomy was assumed in the diagnosis and treatment of affliction, in the narration and interpretation of dreams, and in the work of the prophet. Aladura informants contended that each person has an invisible dimension, what I describe here as a dream soul, a spiritual or metaphysical side that moved in step, or at odds, with one's waking self. It represented the receptor of dreams and visions, the link with the other world, and moved freely throughout "that side," causing both health and harm for self and others. Though the traditional Christian idea of the soul informed the Aladura metaphysics of the self, it had also been influenced by a variety of ethnic sources processed in a meaningful, but not necessarily systematic, fashion. Of course, Aladura cosmology showed continuity, in Adogame's words, with the Yoruba "duality of cosmic space, though intricately intertwined" (2004, 503). Adogame, Olupona (1987), and Ray (1993) have noted the importance of the basic division between heavenly and earthly realms. Adogame indicates the Aladura reflect the Yoruba dividing of the "cosmos into *orun* (heaven/sky as the abode of the spiritual entities) and *aye* (the world/earth of human habitation). In fact, *aye* is a sacral entity because it serves as a centre for the dramatization of spirit beings" (2004, 503).[6]

When members referred to afterlife appearances, these usually involved the recently departed spirits of prophets and family members. For instance, in one minister's dream the spirit of a deceased prophet commissioned him to found a church; in a patient's dream his father's spirit directed him to join the church. Significantly the church was not greatly concerned with the ritual appeasement of ancestors. Though affliction from a spirit was a common diagnosis, I did not know of a single church case involving an ancestor. A minister once noted to me that a "true ancestor" did not cause problems. Undoubtedly the extent to which ancestors actually continued to play a role, whether negative or positive, in the lives of members and patients varied from individual to individual. In any case the traditional role that ancestors played as moral guardians receded in the life of the church, a trend identified by both Bond (2001) in his work of Yombe Christians in Zambia and Kiernan (1990) in his work on Zulu Zionists in South African.

More relevant for understanding human affliction are the indigenous ideas about the soul's "supernatural" capacities,[7] such as being able to travel apart from the body. Especially during sleep the soul can leave the body, contact other spirits, and enter the dreams of others. Informants believed such peregrinations frequently led to acts of witchcraft: the wanderer becomes enticed by a hidden power and knowledge potentially harmful to himself and to others. The nocturnal traveler changes into animals, birds, or snakes in order to harm others. All people have dream souls or spirits, but some exceptionable people, such as zoes, twins, and country doctors (traditional healers), have dream souls that are more active and dexterous than others. Through dreams they obtain special skills and knowledge. Some ethnographers speak of such people as having "two brains" or "four eyes": metaphoric descriptions that denote the subject's mystical ability to know and to see the other side (Bellman 1975, 145; compare Shaw 1985, 287; 1992, 37–41). This ability also relates to what informants referred to as the "doubling" character of powerful persons. Through such magic a person appeared in two different places at once—a gift that enabled trickery and deception.

Exceptionable people were often described as having "spirit familiars" or "spirit friends" that helped them obtain artistic skills and mystical knowledge. This liaison affected the subject's personality and interactions with others. According to William Murphy, the Kpelle spirit familiar could be "a particular animal, plant, or inanimate phenomenon often associated with a person from birth and serving as a powerful, hidden force of good or bad fortune" (1981, 669). D'Azevedo, commenting on the Gola, claims that relationships with spirit friends were established mainly in the dream world. They were actually a type of jina, a nonhuman spirit that "got behind" the person, affecting his thoughts and actions, often causing abnormal behavior. Ironically such jina liaisons were considered vital for the welfare of society: human creativity and production depended on jina-inspired individuals. But, at the same time, jina liaisons entailed risk and danger: the jina tempted the subject with power, wealth, and fame through strategies harmful to the subject as well as others (1966, 17–19).

Generally speaking, Aladura prophets regarded jina liaisons negatively: they caused more problems than they solved. Prophets portrayed the jina liaison as an unhealthy relationship that obscured the understanding of one's true self: captive to the jina's caprice, the dream soul alienates body and spirit. This alienation can be interpreted according to certain notable contrasts that reverberated in indigenous and Aladura worlds: public-private, front-back, outside-inside, and loose-tied (see Murphy 1981, 669). The public self conveyed the frontal, exterior aspects of personality, the self presented openly in everyday transactions and performances. In the ritual setting it was the self honestly exposed to others. This public self, however, was oftentimes superficial; it became a front for hidden thoughts and motives, for the secretive use of mystical power. The "back" and the "inside" denoted what is secret, powerful, and also dangerous: the Kpelle, for instance, would say the *zo* had a "deep abdomen," a mysterious power within.[8]

In various public contexts the Aladura valued what was out front, exterior, open: members were urged to narrate dreams, confess, and testify; prophets delivered visions that exposed the deviously secret. As in traditional contexts, zoes, country doctors, and twins were relegated to the secret and dangerous. Indeed they might be described as people who had abnormal amounts of spirit. Thus they were effective technicians of the unseen, but their magic was shady and harmful. Paradoxically, though, the Aladura spoke also about the prophet's supernatural abilities in terms that closely resembled those of the traditional zo. Indeed the prophet often aroused ambivalence within the community about his use of mystical power. Like the zo's, his dream soul moved freely and effectively from this side to that side, obtaining useful but secret and potentially dangerous power. And precisely because of this spiritual dexterity, he stimulated suspicion as well as admiration. In the best of circumstances, the Aladura saw total "transparency" as an impossible condition—and perhaps one not even always desirable (West and Sanders 2003).

However, the Aladura notion of the dream soul or spirit should not be understood as a disembodied, autonomous entity. My insistence on the relational aspect of personhood already makes such autonomy problematic. The very material terms that Aladura informants used to speak about a person's health and sickness, or success and misfortune, also informed the notion of the soul. The body became a sign of the soul. In their stories about witchcraft people often spoke about a person's affliction, especially when seen in the enervation and disease of the body, in terms of an idiom of eating. A person's soul or spirit was being fed to and consumed by a society of witches, by the witch who uses the Dragon power, or by jina (Ellis 2006; Schmoll 1993).

THE PROPHET: "SOLDIERS OF THE LORD"

As the image of the extraordinary man (or woman), the prophet effectively influenced the Aladura view of the human person and the idea of spiritual power. The life stories of prophets, whether oral or literary, provided models of behavior and action. The prophet's sermons and anecdotes about encounters with the unseen world, with "that side," and about personal transformation provided lessons for others. In various ritual settings he demonstrated his command of spiritual power through the confident interpretation of dreams, the stirring pronouncement of visions, the prodigious observance of fasting, the vigorous performance of dancing, and the careful administration of treatments. Through such performances the prophet managed the church's discourses on self, power, and salvation.

The biblical paradigm of the prophet figure informed the Aladura understanding of the holy man. The figures Moses, Samuel, Elijah, and John the Baptist were mentioned most often as inspiring models of prophecy. The Aladura prophet saw himself representing a continuous line with the Hebrew prophets. As one minister put it, they were "Soldiers of the Lord." This continuity marked the church's difference from historic mission groups, which the Aladura said neglected the prophet's divinatory and predictive functions. As such, the word *prophet* became an "elemental image" for the Aladura view of the person. The figure in a white gown with the "rod of Moses" represented the church and became the critical player in the making of each Child of Salvation.

The common perception of the prophet, however, diverged from the biblical discourse in ascribing to him an element of moral ambiguity. Indeed we might see the prophet as a new indigenous conception for the extraordinary person, such as the artist, the person of rare genius, the blacksmith, the diviner/healer, and the person known as the zo (who might combine any of these roles). In Liberia these individuals mediated mystical power, which could be used for good or for bad. The prophet also had these capacities; he could curse as well as bless. Other interpreters have also noted the common link concerning such ambiguity between traditional healers and the new prophets.[9]

A prophet's demonstration of virtue, or spiritual power, created both confidence and mistrust. Access to virtue enabled the church to carry out its healing function, which brought honor among other churches. But, unfortunately, prophets used this power to break down one another. Criticisms customarily made about the zo, that he sought profit and performed nefarious deeds in secrecy, also applied to the prophet. The Aladura spoke about the prophet's duality in terms of the open-hidden distinction. Virtue must be open and public, not hidden and private. A prophet's greatest challenge came in the temptation to convert something intended for the common good into a weapon for personal gain. In a sermon a minister once stressed that evil spirits were always curious about the prophet's secrets and might approach him with temptations. But temptations also came from within. Evil spirits could not make him do evil. The prophet might succumb to their entreaties because he desired to keep the "secrets of God" to himself. He would no longer share virtue with the church but tried to use it for his own gain.

This interpretation of the "prophet discourse" can be seen in terms of the "witchcraft discourse" as discussed by Geschiere in his study of the *nganga* healer/diviner. Geschiere notes that informants stress the "practical difficulties in keeping witch and healer apart" (2006, 227). Both draw their skill and strength from invisible sources that can bring both good and evil. The healer, like the witch, attests to a sense of "metaphysical disorder" that challenges contemporary modern (or postmodern) notions of societal equilibrium. Through faith and practice (especially ritual preparations) the prophet resisted temptation; yet the possibility of his subversion of spiritual power undoubtedly contributed to his aura as the extraordinary person in the Aladura world. Ironically this perception also helped to base the prophet church's presentation of authority. As a minister once put it to me, others would kneel before the prophet since he revealed secrets received directly from God.

Virtue: "A Certain Swear"

St. Peter's acknowledged a spiritual force or power that affected both visible and invisible worlds. Ministers commonly called this power virtue. They based usage of this word on Mark 5:25–34 (KJV), which tells of an episode in which a woman with "an issue of blood twelve years" became healed when she touched Jesus's garment. Verse 30 says that Jesus immediately knew "virtue had gone out from him." Though the Aladura considered virtue to be an unseen power, it also became objectified in words, things, persons, rituals, and places. Of course one could find this model of power in Yoruba cosmology, which became translated to Liberian experience through Nigerian missionaries and their texts. Harris's comments about the meaning of power in the C&S are applicable here to our understanding of the Liberian Aladura: "Power carries a multitude of meanings, which blur distinctions between metaphysics and materiality. The contrasts maintained in Western dualistic philosophy between body and mind, matter and spirit were foreign to Yoruba indigenous thought, and are blurred in the way that C&S understand their world. . . . In popular Yoruba discourse, secular and spiritual still elide, with activity in the unseen sphere affecting visible relations, and quotidian events impacting upon hidden forces" (2006, 62).

Benjamin Ray indicates how the Aladura notion of power was related to the Yoruba concept of *ase,* a term that literally meant "the authority or power of command." It represented the power of the Creator God Oludumare. In the beginning Oludumare created the world through ase, which continues to be made known through the words and actions of Oludumare's priests (1993, 279). Henry John Drewal and Margaret Thompson Drewal also insist on the creative force of ase, which they contend cannot be spoken of as good or evil. This power was morally neutral; but, depending on context and use, it could produce either positive or negative effects. The authors stress that ase "is absolute power and potential present in all things—rocks, hills, streams, mountains, leaves, animals, sculpture, ancestors and gods—and in utterances—prayers, songs, curses, and even everyday speech" (1990, 5). It was ase that could be expressed through spectacle and ritual.

Though it would be inaccurate to speak of Aladura virtue as morally neutral, it does resemble ase in terms of its conceived sacred origin, its creative potential, and its expression through ritual. The prophet's virtue, however, was always seen as ultimately beneficial. Virtue came from God, through the Holy Spirit, and was mediated through the prophet's work. In his study of the CLA, Harold Turner makes clear the significance of the Holy Spirit, the third person of the Christian Trinity, in Aladura theology (1967). More recently Caleb Oluremi Oladipo has emphasized the general importance of the Holy Spirit as a source of power for West African Christians (1996, 46–47). St. Peter's, like other Aladura churches, can also be described as presenting a theology of the Holy Spirit for which a distinction between ritual praxis and exegetical doctrine became arbitrary. Through virtue, prophets received visions, interpreted dreams, consecrated elements, purified places, and healed patients. The prophet indeed legitimized his authority through such demonstrations of virtue. The operation of virtue, however, extended beyond those who served as prophets: cross bearers, Army of Jesus ushers, and even patients might become channels of virtue, depending on their faith and commitment. The prophet, though, remained the paradigm of virtue.

In certain contexts the word *virtue* was used to denote a mystical power that authenticated the prophet's status. It set him apart from ordinary people. More often ministers spoke of virtue in terms of "power from God," which they mediated. One minister described virtue as "a certain swear," which produced powerful effects. He referred to the passage in Mark and emphasized the prophet's capacity to affect things in a positive or negative way. The prophet's ability to bring about blessings was a clear and predictable function. But the virtue could also be used to cause misfortune. Ministers cited another episode in the Gospel of Mark (11:12–21) where Jesus cursed a fig tree causing it to die and wither away.[10] Members shared stories about how Aladura prophets had performed similar acts. One story involved Apostle Samuel Oduwole. The wife of a high Aladura official once argued with the apostle. During the exchange she threw her soiled sanitary napkin at him. Oduwole then "cast his virtue" on the woman by cursing her womb. The woman sought Oduwole's forgiveness, which she received, but she remained barren throughout her life. Even the woman's husband, who had "opened the wombs" of countless women, was unable to remove Oduwole's swear. Ultimately, however, the curse of virtue brought benefit, even to the cursed; it represented a judgment, a punishment, intended to bring the misguided closer to God.

The Holy Spirit marked the prophet with virtue, but this did not happen without ritual struggle. The prophet's obtainment of virtue always entailed battles with negative, unseen forces. The Spirit of God, the Holy Spirit,[11] became known through invisible mediums such as angels and the spirits of deceased founders and prophets. Two primary types of invisible forces opposed them: witchcraft and jina. The prophet obtained spiritual strength through facing such forces directly and conquering them: the evocation of Satan's temptation of Jesus in the desert served as a meaningful model. Unlike Jesus's episodic moment, the Aladura prophet's bout with temptation was never so decisive: virtue could be lost and a prophet fall from grace if he succumbed to the allure of secret power. A prophet was obliged always to struggle—performing spiritual exercises, fasting, meditating, reading scripture, praying, and consecrating—to hold his position in the battle between good and evil.

HOLY MATERIALS

The Aladura commonly used holy names and texts to highlight the role of physical objects that they regarded as holy materials. They used these powers or forces to mediate virtue in their services, prayers, healing performances, and struggles, which were understood to weaken the power of negative forces and promote well-being. Informants often referred to ritual events, sacred space, and holy objects as batteries, storage cells of spiritual energy or electricity that empowered the church.[12] This metaphor was especially used in talking about the Tabborrar observance.

The use of holy materials always involved a ritual reckoning with time and numbers. The Aladura recognized the special quality of certain numbers—1, 3, 7, 13, and 21—and used these numbers when arranging a constellation of holy objects. Why one prayed with seven candles and not eight or read three psalms at midnight and not two implied the difference between what was understood to work and what did not. But aside from the pragmatic value, the attention to numbers expressed a kind of sacred numerology (Schimmel 1993). The numbers were derived from traditional or biblical sources: the holy Trinity, days of Creation, and days of the Tabborrar season. I once heard a prophet invoke Daniel 10:2–3 ("In those days I Daniel was mourning for three weeks. I ate no pleasant bread, neither came flesh or wine in my mouth, neither did I anoint myself at all, till three weeks were fulfilled") in order to justify a twenty-one-day fast. This numerology bracketed the appropriate time for ritual struggle. The periods of time for a holy bath, fasting, beach struggle, consecration, and incense treatment were always set according to holy numbers. The numbers signaled the sacred parameters of an event and the value of ritual objects and reminded participants of their obligation to follow through with the performance. In a broader sense the variously identified time sequences provided more structure and rhythm to communal life.

They were not described as holy materials, but in their use and impact sacred texts, such as the Psalms, and holy names, such as Ajubbah, gained a kind of material force. For the Aladura power resided in a word or name: it was not simply a form with meaning, but a force, an "independent power," (Coleman 2006, 168) that could transform persons and objects. Certain words had the value of "performative utterances": words, names, and sounds that, when used, in effect changed experience and reality.[13] Through sermons, prayers, blessings, dream interpretations, and vision narrations, the prophet's words were understood to have a transformative effect on participants. The prophet's words usually enhanced a subject's well-being, while the sorcerer's damaged it. Several members told me that one should take great care over sharing one's name with another person. That person could harm you by "placing it with African signs." Members also warned against reading the fabled text known as the *Sixth and Seventh Books of Moses:* its names, words, and symbols had a power that could derange the mind of the reader.

In healing settings a prophet repeatedly pronounced familiar English words such as *power, joy, victory,* and *blessing* in the same persuasive, forceful way he voiced holy names. It was understood that such performative utterances obtained ritual value primarily through the prophet's demonstrations. As he blessed a kneeling patient, for instance, he shouted over and over, "Victory": the energetic, repetitive pronouncement made it so. As Simon Coleman notes in his study of Pentecostals, "it is sometimes argued that sufficient repetition of a word or phrase accumulates the force of the word, for instance *joy* or *success*" (168). Thomas J. Csordas observes in cases of glossolalia that "the gestural meaning of language" can also have effects (2002, 80). The gravity and power of words, however, could also be balanced by an element of play. At the conclusion of every Divine Worship, Olu faced the altar table and led the congregation in reciting a series of auspicious words, such as *power* and *blessing,* and then turned toward audience, raised his arms, and shouted, "Laugh!" Everyone, including Olu, would then begin laughing and clapping. Informants offered various interpretations for the laughing: this holy laughter, as it were, was directed at Satan; it expressed joy in one's victory over troubles, or it simply summed up a morning service well done. Crumbley notes how the CLA in Nigeria listed the laughs among spiritual exercises, which also included rolling, jumping, running, "Amens," and "Hosannas" (2008, 74). The exercise metaphor and the bodily associations also alert us to the perceived physical quality of names and words. Like running, the shouting or laughing strengthened the subject in faith and in the capacity to resist evil.

Ministers memorized Oshitelu's holy names during their formal training. A minister might be introduced through the study of Aladura texts, such as Oshitelu's extremely popular *The Book of Prayer with Uses and Power of Psalms and Precious Treasures Hidden Therein.* The text explains how to use each psalm in healing rituals and for protection against evil spirits. In terms of its practical value, many Aladura ministers regarded the Oshitelu text as second only to the Bible. Junior ministers at St. Peter's were intrigued to learn that I had a copy and enormously grateful for the photocopies I made for them.

Oshitelu's text on the use of the psalms provides a good example of how the Aladura recognize magical value in words and names. In his work Oshitelu specified the proper use and context for each psalm. Thus Psalm 82 could be used in prayers for success in business; Psalm 91, for protection against smallpox; Psalm

98, for resolving domestic conflict, and so on. Certain psalms had special use for consecrating ritual elements and for undertaking certain struggles, such as fasting and daily prayers. An Aladura church always tried to keep a good supply of paperback copies of the Psalms, usually obtained at the Methodist bookstore in Monrovia; indeed in some churches the Psalms were more available than the Bible, the New Testament, or an Aladura hymnbook. Prophets and cross bearers almost always read from the Psalms during healing ceremonies. Simply reading a psalm over a sick person, even if that sick person knew no English, could have efficacious value; it placed virtue upon her.[14]

Ministers also learned holy names by special instruction from senior prophets, who represented a link in a chain of orally transmitted words. Many holy names were special names for God. Some names were commonly used by all. By and large, however, the use of holy names remained the privilege of prophets. Some informants claimed that they should never be voiced except when the Holy Spirit was deemed present. Though the meaning of a holy name was sometimes given, this was secondary to how it demonstrated and implemented the power of God. Usually a minister could not give the meaning of holy names that had been revealed during prayers or shouts: they were simply untranslatable. Indeed, in most cases ministers could not repeat the name since they had received it in a different state of consciousness. Also, some holy names were never causally spoken out loud. Senior prophets warned young ministers that an inappropriate use of holy names caused more harm than good (Harris 2006, 196–97).[15]

Holy materials referred to the arsenal of things or objects endowed with virtue. These included iron rods, wooden crosses, water, palm leaves, candles, incense, olive oil, honey, salt, white buckets, drums, and white gowns. These objects represented the standard fare in most Aladura churches. With their interest in holy materials, it can be argued that the Aladura have implemented a retransformation of the relation between sign and object, a challenge to the modern dichotomy between representations and acts carried forth in the mainline and missionary Christian discourse. In Keane's terms the missionary discourse transforms material objects into "forms of symbolic expression rather than media through which actions are performed; they become more representation than action" (2007, 247). The Aladura, in a different vein, have confirmed the power of the object and the efficacy of performance. In general they find a biblical paradigm for using a holy object: the iron rod, for instance, represents the staff of Moses; the Psalms provide ample support for the use of incense during services; and the Epistle of James instructs apostles to heal with olive oil. To my knowledge St. Peter's did not distinguish between "powers" with temporary potency and "specifics" with permanent, as Kiernan indicates for Zulu Zionists (1990, 105–6). The ministers in the church claimed that certain materials, such as salt water and palm leaves, did have a natural power, a kind of inherent potency, but materials became holy and powerful at the same time, and were made useful in healing contexts, through the performative acts of purifying and consecrating.

Holy materials were the "working instruments" of the prophet's trade with which he obtained spiritual power and through which he demonstrated his knowledge and use of technology. In the scheme of things, application itself entailed reproducing virtue. The prophet became spiritually stronger and his "weapons" were made more effective through constant use. In the context of ritual struggle such diligence was necessary for an Aladura defense against and victory over evil. The instrumental value of holy materials was realized also through the "argument of images" (Fernandez 1982, 562–64): they became visual, aural, olfactory, and tactile markers of Aladura self-identity and of one's relationship with the world. Wearing the white gown, bathing with holy water, consecrating homes with incense, beating the drum, rolling on the beach, and brandishing a staff or cross in a crowded market embodied Aladura experience and testified to its power.

Instruments of Virtue

Among church objects, the holy rod and wooden cross were the most crucial for effective services, prayers, and healings. The holy rod was regarded as the most effective instrument for the consecration of holy materials, battling witchcraft, and healing patients. It served as the primary symbol of the prophetic office. In liturgical and healing contexts the prophet always kept the rod close by, since it signified and enhanced his ability to bless materials, places, and persons. Among the Yoruba, rods and staffs have been emblems of an orisha's power and authority (McKenzie 1997, 69–77). Undoubtedly the traditional symbolism continued to inform the prophetic significance ascribed to the rod for the early Aladura. In Liberia it became so strongly identified with the Aladura way that churches seeking to spurn the Aladura label forbade ministers from using rods. The hand-held wooden cross signified a lesser power than the rod, but it was more widely used. Cross bearers, in particular, undertook measures to protect the sanctity of the cross; otherwise it lost its power and became useless in ritual contexts. Both objects had provisional, temporary power: only through an initial consecration by authorized figures, in an appropriate location, and within a circumscribed period of time did the objects obtain virtue, and only through further care and continued use did these materials keep their power.

For almost all Aladura rituals, participants used candles and incense: they were indispensable for services, prayers, and holy treatments. Informants referred to candles and incense as signs or symbols of the Spirit's presence, describing the fire and the smoke as "holy." They represented the link between heaven and earth, between invisible and visible worlds. Like the rod and wooden cross, these were regarded by the prophets as effective instruments for healings and conse-crations. I witnessed prayers and healing ceremonies during which a healer made gestures and motions with candles and incense that he normally did with rods and crosses. Using a candle, he might carefully sign a cross over a patient's head or before a door. As he recited psalms or holy names, the healer might flamboy-antly wave incense throughout a patient's home and yard. These were instru-ments of virtue that offered protection and also effectively changed the condition of the patient and other materials and objects that came within their reach. Some healing ceremonies required patients to sleep within a circle of candles or beside a canister of smoking incense: the fire and smoke protected the patient from the effects of witchcraft by creating a kind of "holy screen."

The Aladura were aware of the ambiguity connected with rods, crosses, and holy materials. The materials they used could also become the property of the unscrupulous prophet, who subverted their intended meaning and purpose. The Aladura insistence on the value of holy materials makes for an interesting con-trast with the Masowe Christians in Zimbabwe, as studied by Matthew Engelke. The Masowe stress the tension between materiality and immateriality. They resolve this tension with a "project of immateriality" (2005, 119) that entails dis-missing use of the physical text of the Bible. The Aladura concern about imma-teriality never involved the notion that "things do not matter." They believed that certain material objects did have sacred value and use; indeed the constant reference to "holy materials" made this clear, though the Aladura did acknowl-edge that some forms were more controversial than others.

Devil's Incense

For treating problems, Aladura churches used a variety of incense techniques. Burning incense sticks offered protection against witchcraft. In the Faith Home they were kept in constant supply. Members also kept incense in their homes for prayer and protection purposes. Blue incense was made from a solvent blue crys-tal, which was usually obtained at a country market. The ministers dissolved bits of the crystal in a bottle of cologne water called Murray & Lanman Florida Water (now manufactured in New Jersey by Lanman and Kemp-Barclay and Com-pany), which they bought at a Lebanese market near the Scheiffelin Road junc-ture. (A few years ago I bought a small plastic bag of the crystals and a bottle of Florida water at a West African shop in Hyattsville, Maryland.) Ministers used blue incense mainly for stomach disorders caused by either jina or witchcraft. They administered it by mouth or by enema. The vomiting and "runny tummy" that it brought on helped remove the stomach or intestinal infection caused by the evil spirit.

When a patient suffered from both mental and stomach problems, he might also be prescribed blue incense combined with a potion called devil's incense. The ministers considered devil's incense to be the most powerful form of incense: an instrument needed in fighting the minions and powers of the Devil, "that old man," as one minister described him. I had heard about devil's incense for several months before I learned about its contents. It was a mixture of six ingredients ground into a fine powder and burned during treatments for patients who suffered from disorders caused by witches and jina. Like ordinary incense sticks, it was used for purification and consecration purposes, but it had special value for healing rituals. Used correctly, it created an effective screen between the patient and the evil spirit. A senior prophet at St. Peter's told me that knowledge about devil's incense was privileged. He said that he had been a minister for many years before he learned how to make it. When we first discussed it, he had just started instructing junior ministers at the Faith Home on how to make devil's incense and on its proper use. Despite the usual secrecy, the senior prophet invited me to join their sessions and, surprisingly, encouraged me to take notes, insisting that God's knowledge and ways should not be secret. I found the use of devil's incense so fascinating, in part, because it revealed the crosscurrents of Aladura healing: Yoruba, Liberian, Christian, and Western medical and consumer products.

The ministers always made devil's incense in the church's prayer room, where other holy materials were frequently placed for consecration. The first ingredient was camphor provided by mothballs, usually no more than four. To my knowledge these were not used in any other healing rites. The camphor ball's effectiveness was related to its ability to repel insects, which metaphorically suggests, for the purposes of healing, its ability to drive away disease. This tendency to establish relationship through a kind of "mimetic representation" (Bourdieu 1977, 116) commonly informed why certain objects and techniques were deemed effective in Aladura healing. The second ingredient was country spur, described to me as "a hot seed in the form of beans found near the riverside." Devil's incense required about two cups' worth. Informants claimed country spurs were an effective medicine for two common maladies—malaria and intestinal parasites. Similarly the third ingredient, alligator peppers, was seen to have medicinal benefits. They were described as "small brown balls found near the riverside." Yoruba healers and diviners recommended alligator peppers for offerings made to the orisha (supernatural powers) Ogun and Shaponna (Simpson 1980, 30, 43). One minister compared its use to aspirin, a "pain tablet for the aching body." Alligator peppers were sometimes mixed with Florida water for treating open mole[16] by rubbing the mixture on the patient's head. Also, during house consecrations ministers fortified devil's incense with extra alligator peppers.

The fourth element was sasswood bark, which one minister claimed came from "an African tree planted by God for witchcraft." Devil's incense called for one piece of bark, which cost about four dollars in the country market. Liberian and Sierra Leonean diviners used the bark to determine an accused witch's guilt or innocence. Ruth E. Dennis and Ira E. Harrison give the following description of a sasswood trial: "The accused mounts a platform and sits before those assembled to pass judgement. He then undergoes the sasswood ordeal which consists of drinking varying amounts of a heavy tea brewed from bark of the sasswood tree.... The folk belief is that if the accused is innocent he will vomit up the fluid and if guilty he is unable to vomit, becomes ill, and frequently dies" (1979, 83). William E. Welmers notes that the Kpelle referred to sasswood as a "whip" that "points to the guilty clan, family, and individual, and finally whips the guilty person without apparent control by the handler" (1949, 220).

Aladura ministers also ascribed this traditional function to sasswood. One minister commented: "Sasswood is put into burning incense because it will help examine. In a house consecration, in which it is believed an evil spirit has defiled the house, it will examine the residents of the house, the people who pretend to be good. Within three days they will confess because the burning incense will make them sick." So effective did ministers consider sasswood bark for fighting witchcraft that they sometimes combined it with ordinary burning incense. During a house consecration, for example, the minister might place sasswood bark in a canister of stick incense placed inside the house. Informants claimed that before the canister burned out, the guilty person would have confessed. Some Aladura ministers also used sasswood in treating cases involving twin children. It was believed that twins were born with supernatural gifts and that one of them had the "witch nature." In some Faith Homes ministers made small cross necklaces from sasswood bark for the twins to wear. The twin with the witch nature would then become sick and the ministers could treat him accordingly.

The fifth and sixth elements were also widely used in church practices. In devil's incense, incense sticks—the fifth element—were ground up into two cups of powder and added to the potion. The senior prophet claimed that incense "draws the sickness together that comes from the deeper part of the body to the outer, the skin." Once the sickness surfaced the healer could more effectively treat the patient with water and oil. This technique expressed the inner-outer, back-front dichotomies so prevalent in the Aladura understanding of how witchcraft worked: the incense, in effect, helped localize and make external the diffused and obscure properties of spiritual sickness.

After the first five elements were mixed together, a minister slowly poured seven drops of Florida water, the sixth element, into the powder and stirred it with a spoon. Ministers emphasized the curative qualities of Florida water, frequently using it in holy baths and consecrations. Like incense sticks, Florida water strengthened the subject against the effects of witchcraft or jina. And like incense, it had a sweet and "holy" fragrance that repelled evil spirits. For this reason ministers routinely rubbed Florida water on neck, face, and head. Once the devil's incense mixture was made, ministers placed portions on white sheets of paper, white being the "color of consecration." They folded the paper, wrapped it with string, and placed it on the church's high altar or in the prayer room for three days of consecration. A good supply was always kept on hand, since situations always arose in which it would be needed.

Holy Water and the "Victory Leaf"

As we have seen, water and the palm leaf were regarded as having inherent power; that is, they presented a kind of invisible energy that resided in these materials by nature, apart from consecration. Some informants claimed that water had an ambiguous quality: it represented an enabling power but also danger and fear. One minister described water as "temptation": what the children of Israel experienced when they faced the Red Sea. But by and large the Aladura spoke of water in terms of its positive quality. They insisted that the prophet's virtue and ritual techniques activate the dormant power of water.[17] The Aladura theologian David Ogungbile has stressed the continuity between Yoruba and Aladura notions about the sacred quality of water. The Yoruba linked water with female spirits, notably the Osun. Ogungbile notes how the early Aladura prophets, such as Joseph Babalola, recognized the efficacious agency of water, which they claimed scripture supported (1997, 24–30). St. Peter's recognized a variety of purposes for water—primarily cleansing or purification ceremonies, holy baths, and consecrations. In most contexts the source and kind of water mattered: whether it came from a well, a spigot, a stream, a lagoon, or the ocean. In general, running water was considered more powerful, and thus more effective for certain problems, than well water; salt water was more powerful than fresh. Churches frequently authorized beach struggles—special prayers and services that took place on an ocean beach—because sea water was considered to have a special potency. Because some considered salt to be a useful weapon against witchcraft, ocean water was frequently prescribed for spiritual disorders. The church used ocean water for house consecrations to remove the presence of evil spirits. Beach struggles obtained power in part because of exposure to ocean water. Several ministers told me they regularly underwent personal beach struggles and bathed with sea water in order to obtain blessings, overcome sickness, and secure protection from witchcraft.

Ministers used the palm leaf during consecration and healing ceremonies. They stressed its association with Jesus's entry into Jerusalem, but, more significantly, it symbolized and imparted life, power, strength and victory. Harold Turner notes that the palm leaf had a similar meaning in traditional Yoruba thought (1967, 2:109). Ogungbile reports that the leaf was called *Ida Isegan*, "the Sword of Victory." Liberian Aladura simply called the palm leaf a "victory leaf," but the weapon trope was certainly implied. Informants claimed that its remedial value was suggested by the leaf's being "hard to die." Prophets routinely placed palm leafs in buckets and bottles of water and oil to strengthen the contents. Junior ministers, in particular, made frequent trips to the beach to replenish the church's supply of palm leaves. A faded palm leaf lost its power and always needed to be replaced.

Finally, among holy materials, oils—olive and coconut—were important additives for spiritual treatments. As one prophet remarked, olive oil represented the "Virtue of God "and consequently had an appropriate usage during ordination ceremonies when the senior official rubbed it on the initiate's crown or forehead. The most common use, however, came during healing rituals: prophets frequently added olive oil to water being consecrated, and patients rubbed it on themselves for protection after taking a bath. Olive oil, coconut oil, and blue incense were routinely used as purgatives—given by mouth, nose, or anus to help rid the patient of insidious internal agents that invaded the body through "placing African signs."

How holy materials were used by the prophet or prophetess made all the difference for the effectiveness of a liturgy, prayer, and healing rite. Though the Aladura emphasized the quality of the prophet's and the patient's inward state, they gave special attention to maintaining the proper condition and use of these materials. Beyond their use in liturgical and healing contexts, holy materials assisted in the subject's transformation through their pedagogical value. They signified the conscious parameters, the necessary movements, spatial orientations, and unavoidable interpersonal contacts of the Aladura world and referred to the ongoing application of ritual struggle, which served to integrate the bodily, emotive, and cognitive levels of experience.

Virtue also became authenticated through the idea of holy place, a concept to be explored in greater depth later. A place became holy through an event or ritual act. Prophets set aside special locations based on miracles or healings that had occurred there or on the revelation of a divine figure, such as a deceased prophet, who appeared in a dream or vision. Informants stressed that certain locations, such as a church compound or a site for struggles, generated sacred power that automatically, and radically, marked them off from their environs. They called the church compound, which included the chapel and Faith Home, the "holy ground" and described it as "too strong" for witches and evil spirits. The compound itself empowered prophets, renewed members, and sheltered patients. The churches generally recognized graduated areas of holiness within a church compound—the low and high altars, prayer room, and Mercy Ground— that served as special locations for consecrations and healings. For example, the prayer room provided an effective space for consecrating holy materials, and the Mercy Ground helped to expose witchcraft and to bring out confessions. In Jonathan Z. Smith's terms, the Faith Home became a "focusing lens" for ritual struggle; and Faith Home praxis always evidenced tension between the ideal and the real (1987, 109–11). Sacred space was never thus absolutely inviolate, a theme we revisit in coming chapters.

Town and Forest

For the Aladura in Paynesville, the streets, homes, markets, and traffic beyond the church compound presented great uncertainty and numerous perils. The country migrant, the visitor from Monrovia, or the resident from an old settler family likely encountered the stranger as often as the familiar face or kin. The town provided major material resources and opportunities for personal advancement. But the Aladura also saw it as populated by agents who posed numerous temptations, diversions, and hazards. Like the bush, the town became a place of ambiguous power; a person could either benefit or suffer from its resources. The church understood itself as providing services that enabled victory over the ineluctable difficulties of daily town life.

The relation between village and bush has been a major theme in the indigenous cosmologies of Liberia and Sierra Leone. The village represents the domestic, conventional realm, the bush the undomesticated place of spirits. Commenting on Mende cosmology, Anthony Gittins notes that they stress the relation between Ngewo, the Creator God, and his wife Mando (Earth Mother), who is always associated with the bush. The name for bush is *ndo-gboi*, which means "Mando swallowed it": "Hence the 'bush' is that part (of the earth) that 'earth mother' swallowed, and the Mende explain this by saying that the bush is the place of big trees and thick vegetation which has been 'caught' or 'swallowed' by *Mando*, so that it is fixed, immovable, caught in the earth by its roots. Within the bush are animals which are also 'fixed' to the habitat. People, however live in a town (*ta*, nest, receptacle) which is movable and of their own making" (59). This image demonstrates respect for the forest as a source of special sacred power. In traditional cultures the spiritual authorities, such as the zo or blacksmith, had intimate contact with the forest, from which they obtained their power and learned technologies for the benefit of society.

Similarly the Aladura saw the forest or bush as a place for struggle and spiritual transformation. This can be seen in the emphasis placed on bush struggles—special prayers and fasting undertaken, usually by a minister, in an isolated, uninhabited place where, it was believed, contact with the other world was immediate and intense. A prophet prayed for visions; but in the forest he might expose himself to jina as well as angels. The spiritual dualism, then, caused the retreat to become a "struggle." What also figures strongly here is the trope of temptation: one did not obtain virtue without facing an opponent who offered an alternate power and material gain, as happened with Jesus in the wilderness.

The archetypal Aladura rite, the Mount Tabborrar season, continued this line with its emphasis on the prophets' prayers within a secluded, isolated, and "wild" place, coming face to face with the other side, with other presences. A prophet's virtue went hand in hand with his ability to identify the unknown, to harness the untamed and feral.

With the emergence of the new urban community, the Aladura reworked the traditional village-town and forest dialectic. Here the typology developed by Joel Robbins in his reading of Marshall Sahlin's work can be useful (2004, 6–11). In Robbins's terms, the Aladura have provided a "transformative reproduction" of the dialectic. They have reinterpreted the relation between categories (village-bush) and their meaning. The security formerly found in the village became replaced by the Faith Home, while the locales of village, town, city, and country became subsumed by the category of bush or forest. And as in former days, the bush represented a place of power, of spirits, and of necessary resources, so also, in the new transformed cosmology, the town (or the reimaged bush) became a place for encounter with spirits and for obtaining new forms of power. This new understanding emphasized the bush-town as context for obtaining power. It provided an arena of struggle for receiving a kind of secret, deterritorialized power that ultimately transcended locations.

This dialectic can be applied also with respect to movement from the Faith Home to the traditional village in the back country, the place of zoes and elders, of powerful men and women who have access to forms of power that can bring dreadful harm to others. Many, if not most, of my Aladura informants had country backgrounds. Ties with relatives remained strong, so familial responsibilities often beckoned them home. But such journeys also necessitated caution; thus travelers to country homes often received special prayers for protection from witchcraft and African signs. Many informants insisted that "country magic" was stronger than city magic. The urban character of the Aladura church undoubtedly reinforced this image. Wim van Binsbergen contends that in contemporary Africa, the village no longer exists in the old sense. It prevails as a "virtual village," reinterpreted with a new meaning (2001, 220–25). Changes in infrastructure, mass migrations, media innovations, capital investments, new modes of production, and civil conflicts have undermined the hold of old kinships, rituals, authorities, and livelihoods. In the contemporary urban setting, new communities have emerged creating new kinships, rituals, authorities, and livelihoods. The new urban dweller found himself caught between worlds: on the one hand, he continued to fear the elders back home; on the other, he faced new allurements and obstacles in an urban world of strife and competition. In either context the idiom of witchcraft helped him make sense of contemporary circumstances.

When examining the meaning of village and forest, one must also consider the influence on the Aladura of the Yoruba notion of the world as marketplace. An old urban culture, the Yoruba developed the trope of the marketplace as a basic mediating space between the earthly world and the metaphysical world. As Henry John Drewal and Margaret Thompson Drewal state, "the market as a metaphor for the world evokes an image of a place one merely visits, whereas home or the afterworld is a permanent residence" (1990, 2). The Yoruba marketplace can be described as a transitory, worldly, liminal crossroads, a place where one might meet mysterious strangers and unknown spirits (10–11).

This representation of the marketplace and crossroads can also apply to Liberia. If Paynesville itself promised entanglements and misdirection, the Faith Home offered protection, security, and a well-guided pathway in an unstable world. It effectively tapped into both traditional and contemporary concerns for one's vulnerability, entrapment, and rescue. In her analysis of the Sierra Leone memoryscape, Rosalind Shaw indicates how the images of the bush, the road, and precarious exchanges with spirits suggest memories of the violence of slave wars and raiding: "The violence of the slave-trade eras is . . . evoked not only in the dangers of a memoryscape populated by marauding spirits but also in forms of ritual protection through which habitable human spaces are created and maintained" (2002, 56). The Faith Home (the reimagined village) offered the Aladura a new ritual closure, a safe haven from marauding spirits.

Secret Signs and Hidden Powers

Liberian Aladura interlocutors often spoke about the secret power and occult knowledge known as African science. All power came from God. This included African science, which represented natural but hidden power. A morally neutral power, it became detrimental when used for selfish purposes. In his essay about the Liberian Civil War and occult power, Stephen Ellis stresses the close association between the terms *African science, sorcery, juju,* and *witchcraft.* They were "applied rather indiscriminately to the use of perceived mystical powers which are supposed to have some grounding in indigenous Liberian religious belief (as opposed to Islam and Christianity, both of which are quite widespread in Liberia) and which are considered to have some sort of powerful application often associated with violence, such as in the business of making war" (2001, 223).

The Aladura sometimes used the terms *African science* and *witchcraft* interchangeably, but at other times they strongly distinguished between the two. They compared African science to Western science; both could be harnessed for good or bad purposes. The former, however, referred mainly to an invisible power, often misused by those who were able to access it. When someone used African science to promote self-interest at another person's expense, then it could be understood in terms of witchcraft.

The ambiguity of mystical or occult power (Moran 1990, 36–40) was well supported in indigenous cosmologies. The Methodist missionary George Way Harley claimed the Mano of northern Liberia spoke about a mystical power they called *nye*. They described it as a substance or object that contained power, which could be used to benefit or harm others (Ellis 2001, 227). According to Gittins, the Mende referred to a force called *halei*, a "metaphysical power" that came from God (*Ngewo*). This power could be invested in certain "fetish-like" objects or medicines. Traditional "societies" had access to this power, which they used for common good. While the knowledge about *halei* was transmitted institutionally, Mende informants stressed the role that dream experiences had in legitimating its use (1987, 103–9). This power was considered a source for promoting the moral good and for securing benefits, but its use by inexperienced and calculating individuals could bring harm to others.

African science was seen as a "magic" that one might use to produce food, find a job, or pass an exam. One minister told me the story of a man who used African science to win an eating competition: "He was able to eat thirty times what his opponents ate, and not get full; but they became full before they had eaten anything. He was not witching them, just competing." The church, however, warned members about using it, even for benign purposes. Informants spoke cautiously, and often pejoratively, about African science. This view also informed the church's position concerning medicine. In general the Aladura churches forbade members to see country doctors (traditional healers). However, they did not prohibit the use of Western medicine, for instance, taking aspirin, malaria tablets, vaccines, or visiting a missionary clinic: this type of medicine usually did not represent a moral threat. The problem with Western medicine was not an ethical one, but its inadequacy in dealing with what were ultimately spiritual maladies. It might help in treating a symptom, but not in dealing with its source.[18]

Interlocutors referred to the witch as one who placed signs by using the discarded hair, nails, spittle, garments, or possessions of the targeted victim and mixing them in a bottle or box with animal fats, body parts, vermin, worms, special herbs, or barks.[19] The witch then buried the bottle or box in the victim's yard. From it issued a poison or cancerous substance that made the homestead toxic, bringing on sickness and even death. Some witches used Dragon, a "power" in the form of a rope that they wore around the waist: they animated it through secret words and a magical ointment and sent it into their victim's home. Informants claimed a witch might assume an animal form, such as a snake, dog, or cat, in order to enter the victim's house. Revelations about such intrusions required house consecrations, during which the prophets located the bottle's "invisible form" and sought to weaken and contain its power.

The Aladura believed that the witch used not only secret and potent signs, but also sought to use the prophet's virtue in an inappropriate way. Both witches and jina were constantly curious about the prophet's power. For this reason references to witchcraft within the church were not infrequent. In fact specific accusations involved members or dwellers more often than people outside the church. As I noted, even the prophet was not beyond suspicion: he often provided the most startling example of discreditable subterfuge, which poignantly reversed usual expectations. The untrustworthy prophet prayed alone, using a black pot and black candles. He wrote the name of his victim in the sand and rolled over it, a movement that weakened the victim. In talking about witchcraft within the church, such images of inversion found ample use. Witches were said to attend worship and healing services. They might be prophets, members, patients, or visitors. They might appear to be praying, but actually, "on the spiritual side," the witch danced with naked buttocks facing the altar or took the "witch form" of an animal and defecated on the holy ground.

Along with witchcraft, jina were identified as major sources and explanations for disorder. Though jina were traditionally associated with the bush, they also attached themselves to humans in urban settings. In traditional cosmologies the jina were not by nature malevolent toward humans; they became so when humans trespassed their domain, violated its laws, and betrayed its trust. In traditional settings jina liaisons, properly managed, contributed to artistic creativity and social cohesion. In the Aladura world, however, jina liaisons represented obstacles to life in the Spirit and sources of disorder. At best, the church regarded jina liaisons in members as maladies, like a mental illness, that required special care, and which, it was hoped, life in the Spirit might someday cure. By and large the jina liaison served no good and was regarded typically as a source of misfortune and uncertainty. The jina became assimilated into the "field of evil" (Kiernan 1990) furrowed by the enemies of God. They now populated towns, crossroads, markets, workplaces, and schools. At the same time, the jina, whom one prophet called "the Great Witch," provided a compelling image for the uncertainty and danger of a rapidly changing world. New circumstances have collapsed boundaries between witch and jina; the latter (formerly more territorial) has become migratory and more easily confused with the witch.

Thus terms such as *African signs, witchcraft,* and *jina* are laden with ambiguous associations. Their popular use relates to practical strategies for living in a new, exciting, but threatening world. As van Binsbergen puts it concerning the viability of witchcraft beliefs, they "offered the modern African an idiom to articulate what otherwise could not be articulated: contradictions between power and meaning, between morality and primitive accumulation, between community and death, between community and the state" (2001, 255). The witchcraft concept does not provide a totalistic explanation for why things happen, especially why bad things happen inexplicably to good people, any more than karma explains this completely for the devout Hindu or Jain, but an appreciation of this idiom for the grip of this language on the Liberian imagination is critical for understanding the Aladura cosmology or discourse.

What became apparent in many discussions about occult power, witchcraft, and jina relations was the concern for sacrifice. You cannot gain something for nothing. This involves the exchange of one life for another. Open conventional exchanges in traditional settings often required the sacrificial use of sheep, goats, or chickens. These practices were used in transactions implicating occult power, but the Aladura claimed that tragically these also led to actual human sacrifices by unsavory groups. Aside from questions about its reality, the motif of sacrifice and the idiom of eating have also obtained wide currency as a poignant commentary on the "consuming" work of exchanges and statist power in the postcolonial global world. The global economy has created new "intermediary spaces" wherein the concept of witchcraft demonstrates remarkable fluidity (Geschiere 1999, 231). Despite its strong associations with kin and locality, the notion of witchcraft has proven tremendously adaptable as a translocal concept.

STRUGGLE AS BODILY PRAXIS

The Aladura recognized a fundamental dichotomy between an individual's visible self and dream or spirit self. In the public sphere they idealized harmony between these. To know the self entailed overcoming the divided self. In living according to the Spirit, one committed oneself to the physical and material well-being of others. Unfortunately the mysterious and elusive "dream self" or "dream soul" often succumbed to the sway of temptation, becoming vulnerable to the power of mystical arts, witchcraft, or the jina's overtures. This caused a person to become more private, possessive, and estranged from others and consequently prevented him from knowing his true self.

Because power also became manifest as a dual reality, it strongly affected how the Aladura understood personhood. They saw the realization of self identity in ethical agonistic terms: it happened only through moral contest, a process that the term *struggle* was intended to express. The meaning they ascribed to the term goes beyond the indigenous association with self-development or social empowerment that Caroline Bledsoe describes[20] and the series of "commands" that Harold Turner indicates.[21] In order to obtain virtue, to solve one's problem, to "come to oneself," one must struggle—internally with self-doubt and externally with other forces, with Satan. Struggle also attested to the generative work of ritual. Divine Worship services, daily prayers, beach struggles, holy baths, Mercy Ground prayers and supplications, and the like were referred to as struggles, which served as a kind of root metaphor or grounded image working to integrate notions of self, power, and community.

Ritual was at the center of the Aladura praxis. From its beginnings among the Yoruba to its spread throughout West Africa and beyond to Europe and America, Aladura ritual negotiated conflicts, resolved problems, and shaped personal identity. Adogame notes that "Aladura liturgical tradition is thus a highly expressive action characterized by a heavy dose of rituals enacted to resolve individual and collective existential problems. Each segment of the ritual worship is seen by members to be full of religious symbolism and meaning. Although they vary in matters of specific ritual details, the Aladura are perpetually engaged in rituals" (2004, 504). Adogame's description alerts us to both the functional and communicative dimensions of Aladura ritual, to its variability and constancy of purpose. Becoming a person the Aladura way was concretely realized through ritual struggle, as subjects with varying motives, unique bodily experiences, and shifting dispositions interfaced with a world marked by temptation. The psychological and spiritual aspects of struggle found expression in the workings of symbolic words and actions, in the assemblage of Aladura signs.

Ritual assumes "the other," in this case the nemesis that must be challenged and exposed. Whatever the meanings embedded in any particular Aladura performance, this was one of the most commonly understood.[22] The exegesis of the ritual must be understood in relation to the participants' "knowledge of the body" (Jackson 1989, 117–24)—demonstrated through the resolve to put oneself to the test physically.[23] An assortment of Aladura rituals—spiritual exercises, holy baths, fasting, midnight struggles, and beach struggles—often mandatory and decisive for the patient, authenticated the bodily experience of misfortune, treatment, and recovery. In Csordas's terms, being a person the Aladura way, being engaged in everyday praxis of ritual struggle, "collapse[d] the dualities of mind-body and sign-significance" (2002, 62). At the same time, it assumed sets of ritual contrasts (high-low, back-front, left-right, standing-kneeling, and so on) that became expressed and generated through the ritual body. Indeed the struggle continually articulated the connections between body, rite, and place. Through this discourse the prophets became active producers, in Bell's terms, of a ritualized environment. This became articulated in the specific praxis of the Faith Home and implied connections between body and place (Bell 1992, 109–10).

Through ritual struggle the church expressed the notion of an Aladura self and its interface with forms of power. In the next chapter we will look more closely at the model of the prophet, the symbols of his office, and his role as mediating figure. The discussion of cosmological features such as the composite self, the indeterminacy of contested power, the materiality of powers, and the village-forest dialectic has prepared the reader for further consideration of the prophet's movement within and across boundaries.

3

The Prophet

THE PARAGON OF STRUGGLE

In the Aladura way the minister as prophet/healer became the exemplary model of and for human experience and action. In cosmological terms ritual struggle demonstrated the locative role of the prophet. While the models of prophecy in African churches obviously were influenced by biblical paradigms, there were important variations in how this became evident. For many AIC, such as Aladura churches, the prophet as diviner and healer took on even more significance. More than fifty years ago Christian Baeta called prophetism "a perennial phenomenon of African life" and the work of persons who heal, divine, reveal, bless, and curse "facts of life" (1962, 6–7). The AIC prophet represented a continuation of the traditional religious authority. J. Kwabena Asamoah-Gyadu has more recently emphasized this model of religious authority in the "indigenous re-appropriations of Christianity," such as AIC and Pentecostal-Charismatic churches. According to Asamoah-Gyadu, these churches have sustained "the centrality of the prophet and his ability to heal, underpinned by the African belief in mystical causality" (2005, 96).

The Aladura prophet's gift as a healer depended on the perceived ability to move between visible and invisible worlds, a shamanic trait often minimized in Protestant representations of classical Hebrew prophets.[1] This gift informed the image of the prophet as a boundary person. As God's emissary he had special access to spiritual power, but his calling required him to know the sullied margins of human experience. The minister's home, the Faith Home, was considered a holy place, but it is best to understand this in terms of an oscillation between the conditions of purity and pollution, of being "cleansed" and being "spoiled." As a holy place it stood apart from the ordinary world, but the Faith Home also attracted elements that defiled. Misfortune or sickness almost always implied the presence of such forces. Remediation within the Faith Home, therefore, evoked the struggle between the agents of virtue who promoted spiritual/physical health and the agents of negative power who undermined it. An idea of sacred place did not imply the absolute purity of the holy ground, and the Aladura did not see the prophet as an untainted person. His necessary contact with the sources and conditions of misfortune precluded that.

As ritual performance, ritual struggle demonstrated the mediating capacities of the prophet through events, such as the Mount Tabborrar rite, and regular practices, such as fasting. The instrumental function of ritual struggle depended on the virtue of the prophet, which, in turn, he obtained through ritual performance. The prophet worked through the separate but related conditions of affliction and strength. Personal experience with affliction as well as his understanding of the suffering of others undoubtedly enhanced his reputation as a "go-between for patients and family, for dwellers and members. In the healing process he specified the conditions for healing, the expectations of patient and family, the kinds of involvement required from members, and the ways for managing encounter with invisible realities that affected the outcome of treatment. Struggles became "temptations" that tested the prophet's commitment to Aladura doctrine. A ritual struggle always presented difficulties; indeed the spiritual strength it produced was considered proportionate to the ritual's length and the degree of self-denial expected from the performer. The most demanding fasts, such as a three-day dry fast, which totally proscribed food and water, produced more spiritual benefits than the three-day white fast, which allowed for the consumption of fruit and grains after evening prayers. Completing an easier fast was, however, preferable to failing to finish a more difficult one. Inability to complete a fast only showed the prophet's spiritual weakness and lack of resolve and therefore undermined his ability to mediate virtue for others. Through ritual struggle he built up virtue and broke down negative forces, but he also risked failure and shame.

The Aladura churches expressed great concern about prophets who succumbed to the temptation of negative power and misused the "ministerial secrets." They were said to work alone, outside the ambit of church authority, and for personal material gain. They lost sight of spiritual goals. The Aladura described the wayward prophet with images of inversion: on the invisible side he danced on his hands, prayed alone with black candles, assumed animal forms, and urinated into holy water. These descriptions were used not just as metaphors but referred as well to real people who were believed to be subversive prophets. Churches talked about the property or goods that correct living and doctrine produced and did not hesitate to criticize ministers for "selling their services."

James Kiernan describes the South African Zionist prophet's work in terms of constituting and allocating roles. Through the function of preaching, which had didactic value, the prophet constitutes spiritual values; through the function of healing, he allocates spiritual power. Different individuals carry out these functions, but within the church context they work interdependently. As such, the

Zionist church provides an ethical model for the use and distribution of spiritual goods. The prophet who neglects the constitutive influence and communal relations of the church causes great concern. As Kiernan states, "The prophet who practices pure allocation is independent, he is secretive, he is mercenary, he lacks public spirit and, in Zionist opinion, he is anti-social. On all these counts, he is opposed to everything that the Zionist band stands for, i.e., the management of spiritual forces for the attainment of group goals. He is therefore denounced as an upstart and an outcast. Zionists will say of him: 'He is not one of us; he is one of those "new" Zionists; we are "Christian" Zionists'" (1990, 163).

Similarly Aladura and other AIC churches in Liberia understood the prophet's work: it should involve interdependence and balance between constituting and allocating roles. It was seldom the case, however, that the functions of healing and preaching were assigned to different individuals. In the Aladura churches I worked with, every minister preached and healed; furthermore, it can be said that preaching could allocate virtue and healing could constitute it. A prophet's sermons supplied knowledge that was "power"; his healing rituals represented "doctrine." His very words could be efficacious. Of course, the context for this interdependence was the Aladura community of faith. Outside that context healing was considered spurious and dangerous; in Kiernan's words, it was "purely allocative work" (165). Doctrine and ritual obtained true power and value only in the context of community.

The constituting and allocating roles of the prophet were most conspicuously expressed through the Faith Home habitus and the Mount Tabborrar struggle. In the Faith Home the responsibility of making sure dwellers understood and followed the rules and regulations rested primarily with the prophet. He played a didactic role essential to the church's capacity to change individuals and to maintain community. The Faith Home also provided a necessary location and structure for the allocation of virtue. A patient's healing was almost impossible without involvement in the Faith Home. It provided immediate access to the prophet's virtue that was necessary for recovery. Along with undergoing prescribed personal treatment, the subject became integrated into both structured and improvised Faith Home performances—from Divine Worship to daily prayers, from midnight struggles to church consecrations, from beach struggles to Tabborrar rites.

The constituting and allocating roles of the church were perhaps most clearly expressed during its annual Mount Tabborrar ritual. While Tabborrar disrupted the regular routines of Faith Home life for two weeks, it was seen to help reconstitute the life and mission of the church. As members repeatedly stressed, an Aladura church could not exist without the Tabborrar observance. The event produced the virtue needed for ritual healing and prophecy. As members often put it, Tabborrar was the battery needed to run the church.

If Tabborrar was the battery of the church, the prophet was the technician who provided the skill to use it. His mediation, however, always implied the context of communal values and interdependence of constituting and allocating roles. As Kiernan suggests, this model makes problematic the use of the classical Weberian model of charisma (1990, 157–59).[2] In the Aladura world virtue, or spiritual power, came to a person through God's call, but it was strengthened through ritual struggle and always referred to the "web of interdependency" (Fox-Genovese 1988, 87) expressed in communal life.

INITIATION INTO PROPHECY

The constitution and bylaws of St. Peter's contain the following description of a prophet's call: it was "always personal and mysterious" and marked by "unusual signs"; furthermore, "people concerned would wonder at his [the minister's] behavior." The experience of the call often involved encounters with sickness and misfortune, as the accounts earlier indicate. In Olu's story blindness and depression were interpreted as signs of being called. The call was seldom a one-shot affair; it was often realized through a series of events that might occur over several years. In many cases a calling relied on the input of other prophets, diviners, and healers who helped identify God's design for a person's life. These interpretations shaped experiences and created stories that can be understood, in Cheryl Mattingly's terms, as models of "narrative time": they become marked off from ordinary linear time by an ascribed significance and dramatic import (1998, 84–85).

Among St. Peter's ministers, stories about experiencing a call through sickness and healing or misfortune and reward were commonplace.[3] (Pseudonyms are used for ministers and cross bearers featured in this chapter.) One of the first junior ministers who talked to me about his call was James Flomo, a Kpelle man in his late twenties. He told me that when he lived in Bong County he use to be "so poor and dry in the flesh." His employer showed pity and took him to an Aladura church, where he stayed for three weeks. His health improved and he joined the church. Later he moved to Monrovia where he found work with a trading company. When rogues stole from the company house, he became a suspect and was arrested and imprisoned. While in prison, an Aladura minister visited him and prayed for his release. When he received his release he began to place "trust in the Lord to be a minister." Flomo told me that he came to see the misfortune of illness and the incarceration as signs from God.

Flomo's account demonstrates a standard two-step process in realizing one's Aladura identity and purpose in life. The first step involved the experience of affliction or deprivation, finding a solution, and joining the church, something that he shared with most Aladura members. The second step established the difference between the minister and a regular member. After Flomo joined the church, he found a job that brought him some short-term success. The job, however, came to be seen as only a stage in a larger design. Aladura informants insisted that if God has chosen an individual to be his servant, worldly success will always be impermanent. True success would come only through single-minded interest in God's virtue, in obtaining God's "spiritual goods." Worldly occupations and commonplace interests could only distract the subject from this goal.

Another account of a call or commission experience came from David Modee, a Bassa minister also in his late twenties. Modee joined an Aladura church during a period of multiple experiences with hardship, depression, and misfortune. During this time he received several "call" dreams. In one dream he heard the voice of his father, which a prophetess interpreted as God "trying to show power to me." In another dream he appeared dressed in a church gown, also a sign of divine calling. He eventually was anointed as a minister-in-training in David Fyneah's UCL, which assigned him work under a senior prophetess. Worldly temptations, however, continued to remain strong. Eventually he and the senior prophetess had a falling out, and he decided to look for other work. After working briefly as a houseboy, he left Monrovia and moved to Buchanan, where he remained in poverty and despair. He told me that he might have committed suicide except that he decided to visit an Aladura church, where the members took care of him and where he eventually resumed working as a minister.

But Modee again neglected the call. After serving in Buchanan for nine months, he returned to Monrovia, began attending the University of Liberia, and found work as a tariff clerk with the National Port Authority. One day, almost inexplicably he was dismissed from his job. He was preparing to challenge his former employers when he had a significant dream. In the dream he encountered a woman who pointed to the back of a man. The man was his father. Modee interpreted the dream as another indication (again his father representing an auspicious sign) that he needed to return to the church. Like Flomo, he came to realize the futility of success in a conventional workplace. In other conversations Modee would insist that God often "proved Himself" to people through problems and deprivation. He believed that God did this especially through his prophets, who were expected to endure sufferings for others.

I often met a Faith Home dweller whose affliction the ministers interpreted as a sign of being called. During St. Peter's Tabborrar ritual a young Bassa man with Baptist background was admitted into the Faith Home with stomach problems. Ministers determined that the ailment was caused by witchcraft. The Bassa man received a successful treatment, but remained in the Faith Home for a longer period than originally anticipated. A Faith Home minister reported a dream in which he saw the patient kneeling before an altar. The ministers insisted that the Bassa man's sickness and treatment had prepared him for a more important mission. When I talked to the patient about his situation he said that he was not altogether convinced that God had called him; but, nonetheless, he was pleased with his recovery, saw it as a clear sign of God's favor. He also promised to remain open to the ministers' dreams and visions and their interpretations about his personal destiny.

Another patient who came to the Faith Home after Tabborrar also considered the interpretation of dreams as crucial for understanding a call. Like the Bassa man, his "problems had brought" him to the Faith Home; in his case the problems were financial. He did not consider that his difficulties were caused by witchcraft or jina, but he believed that they happened by the will of God. As he put it, "God Himself wanted me to experience something negative. For the first time in my life I have nothing under me and can only look to Him." Along with this experience of deprivation, he believed his dreams had special meaning. In one dream he saw himself sitting in a building facing a wall when a light passed through the wall and enveloped him. Then within the penumbra of light he saw himself preaching to a congregation. According to the Faith Home ministers, the meaning of the dream was obvious: God had called the patient to be a prophet.

I knew prophets and prophetesses who claimed that when they were children they had the ability to see the "witch forms" of certain people and jina spirits invisible to normal humans. Informants believed that some individuals were endowed with power from God even before they became Christians; but even these gifted individuals needed proper training in the doctrine of the church. Without such education, without being "churched," the gifted person might be tempted to use spiritual talents for evil purposes. The call was something that held for life. Once accepted, a minister could not rescind it without bringing misfortune onto himself and his family. A senior minister at St. Peter's once left the church and joined a Baptist congregation. Soon afterward, according to one minister, he became "crazy." My informant claimed the wayward minister would not regain his sanity unless he returned to the church and resumed his former role.

At St. Peter's, once a person accepted a call and became assigned to the Faith Home of a branch, he took on the title of follower, or minister-in-training. The follower was simply an initiate. One informant spoke of the follower as one who "tried to become a minister" in the face of unending difficulties and formidable temptations. A trial period in the Faith Home tested the initiate's compliance with the rule of submission to senior authorities, his or her willingness to be "humbled." Like the patient, the initiate was "under observation" by senior officials and expected to perform readily and assiduously the Faith Home chores and rituals. Initiates assisted senior prophets with special healing cases and often were assigned simpler cases. At some point a senior prophet might require the initiate to accompany him on a bush struggle, during which he might instruct him in ministerial secrets. On a routine basis senior prophets required initiates to fast: this tested their resolve and strengthened their character. The minister-in-training's embrace of Faith Home laws and habits—such as fasting, spiritual exercises, consecrations, and cleansing rites—worked to separate him (or her) from the world outside. His training distanced him from the distractions of family, friends, job, and school. When his seniors judged the initiate to be spiritually stronger, they granted him more freedom to mingle with former associates.

Signs of Virtue

An important event in a young minister's life was his first ordination. After an extended period of apprenticeship under a senior prophet, the initiate might be judged ready for ordination as a junior minister. In most Aladura churches the initial training period took from one to three years. In the early days of the movement in Liberia, a three-year training period was common. I came to know several ministers who received their training at Center Street before 1970. Most claimed that they had been ministers-in-training for three years. Recently a shorter period of training had become more common. At St. Peters most junior ministers had been followers for at least one year before they received ordination, but I knew one minister who became ordained after only a few months of training.

Ordination took place at the Sunday Divine Worship service. The initiate, dressed in a white gown, entered the low altar area, where he knelt before a senior prophet, usually a bishop or an apostle. The senior prophet bestowed upon him four objects denoting his new ministerial status: the cross (or in rare cases, the holy rod), the Bible, a palm leaf, and a bell. Before the event these objects were consecrated at a holy place within the compound, such as the high altar or the prayer room. If the ordination occurred soon after Tabborrar, the objects had likely been consecrated on the sacred mount. The cross and the holy rod were the two most important instruments used by ministers during services and healing rituals. Anon I will say more about the meanings and uses of these instruments. For now I want to highlight their use and meaning as emblems, or seals, of the young minister's new role and authority.

The small (three or four inches) wood emblem of the cross marked the follower's distinction from ordinary members. When he received the cross, he was recognized as someone with authority to pray and heal. Though ministers deeply valued this object, they aspired more to receive the holy rod. Without the rod, they were more easily confused with cross bearers. But rarely did junior ministers become rod holders at their first ordination. This customarily happened years after one's first ordination, and it usually occasioned the junior minister's promotion to the position of an evangelist, a Faith Home supervisor, or a branch director. Also, it was commonly the case that a junior minister received his rod only after completing his first struggle within a Mount Tabborrar enclosure.

The second ceremonial gift was the Bible. In the ceremony itself the leaders stressed that receiving the Bible authorized the initiate to go forth from the church and preach the Gospel. Of course, long before ordination followers committed themselves to study the Bible and frequently used the text in ritual settings, such as praying over patients and pressing the text against the patient's body. During open-air preaching both cross bearers and ministers-in-training were expected to take along Bibles, usually provided by the church. At the ordination ceremony the initiates were given their own Bibles. I attended Aladura ceremonies, however, when the performers used the same Bible for each ordination, since the church had not yet been able to buy personal copies for the ordinands. In some cases, when the senior minister handed the Bible to the initiate, he or she immediately exhibited convulsive movements and entered trance, an act that clearly "embodied" the Bible's ritual power and use.

The palm leaf that the minister received at ordination referred to his ability to triumph over temptation. Often referred to as the victory leaf, it was among the most ubiquitous symbols in the church, used routinely during services and in healing rituals. One minister described the palm leaf as "hard to die," a reason why he believed it appropriate for using in treatments. Ministers routinely placed leaves in bottles and buckets of water for consecrating purposes. At the first Divine Worship of the month, which was called Cleansing Sunday, ministers distributed palm leafs to the congregation: the leaves symbolized success for the coming month. Also, notably, at the conclusion of the Tabborrar retreat the mount ministers tied palm leaves around their foreheads as a sign of their success.

The fourth object the initiate received, the bell, represented the minister's special mission to bring people into the church. For the ordination ceremony the ministers used as a proxy a bell always kept on an altar table. Senior prophets used this bell to announce stages of Divine Worship. During shouts, they would rhythmically ring it as they danced among the throng. This ceremonial object also evoked the church bell in the compound yard. For the latter, churches often hung a tire rim from a wood frame, which ministers rang to announce the beginning of services and prayers. The bell represented the small hand bells that ministers and cross bearers used during open-air preaching and healing. The bell, then, denoted the dual movement of the church's work: calling people in and sending them out.

Facing Temptations

After ordination the minister became invested with greater authority and responsibility. The recipient of mediated virtue, he was judged more capable of taking on serious tasks. His patient load and liturgical responsibilities increased. Still, the church considered the newly ordained minister to be extremely vulnerable to temptation. Though invested with a new level of virtue, he was considered inexperienced in its use and an easy prey for those who sought to undermine the work of the church. A junior minister's progress still required guidance from a senior prophet or prophetess. He always lacked specific "trained" knowledge that only more instruction and experience could bring. Also, as we have seen, it was commonly understood that until the minister "ascended" Tabborrar, he would be withheld from learning some ministerial secrets. The church considered it a precarious thing to entrust a Faith Home to the sole care of a junior prophet, especially over an extended period of time. Once, at an Aladura branch a mother brought her young son to the Faith Home for treatments of an affliction that ministers there diagnosed as caused by witchcraft. During the child's treatment the senior prophet traveled to another branch and left the child's care to the junior ministers. The boy died and family members laid some of the blame for his death on the inexperience of the young ministers.

Faith Home ministers from St. Peter's before a morning service. Photograph by author.

Only after a junior minister had studied for an extensive period with a senior prophet or prophetess did the church commission him to evangelize, to start a new branch, or to be the sole pastor at an established one. These assignments were an opportunity for the minister to prove himself in the face of new temptations, often personified as those who sought "to bring down" the church. A junior minister who had served at the St. Peter's headquarters for almost three years once was given full leadership of another branch in Paynesville. He had been there a month when attendance began to decline, which he blamed on witches and evil spirits. He claimed that "one old man," who lived near the church, kept an evil spirit in a latrine. When people visited the church or when services began, the old man released the spirit, which emitted a noxious odor and caused people to leave. Another neighbor kept a Dragon spirit. At nighttime the Dragon cried continuously, keeping the Faith Home dwellers from sleeping. The minister saw these attacks as challenging his virtue, but he also realized these were inevitable encounters. Of course, even more experienced ministers faced such challenges. One senior prophet informed me that in the process of constructing a church in Bong Mine, he and his wife, along with a follower, stayed in a small hut on the compound. For two months, until the chapel was finally built, they prayed, fasted, and "beat the drum" in order to protect the grounds from nearby opponents who worked against them. Such narratives were commonplace. Every senior prophet or prophetess I knew told "founding" stories about how their churches were besieged by snakes, witches, and jina.

The challenges the junior minister faced also came from within the church (Douglas 1973, 137–52). Junior ministers who were promoted and given more responsibilities often expressed concern about the envy and suspicion of other ministers and members. Church authorities frequently warned against competition among ministers and coveting another's position. They cautioned about praying for promotion, since this led to unhealthy competition with others. Competition became a context for ministers "praying against one another," which was one way of describing witchcraft. Jealousy, mistrust, rivalry, and accusations of witchcraft occurred even within a peer group of ministers who had taken Tabborrar together. At one Paynesville branch such a situation occurred between two young ministers. They had taken Tabborrar together and had developed a close relationship, but after working together for about four months distrust developed between them. One minister claimed that in his dream he had seen the other minister take the form of a snake and enter his bed. A senior prophet mediated the conflict. He interpreted the dream as a sign of conflict and jealousy but downplayed the possibility of witchcraft. He told the accusing minister that sometimes "a snake is just a snake, a dream is just a dream." He reprimanded both ministers for their lack of faith and for their self-interest and put them both on dry fasts. They had competed too strongly for the favor of the senior prophets.

FASTING AS RITUAL STRUGGLE

Among the many church practices a minister was called to perform fasting most often. The prophet could not obtain virtue and the patient could not have his or her problem solved without fasting. Any Faith Home convalescence required fasting, either by the client, a family member, or the prophet. On occasion, for maximum results all parties involved had to fast. When fasting was necessary but a patient or family member was unable to perform it, the task fell to the minister. Substitutionary fasting by the minister became commonplace and as much as any other regular struggle came to represent his call to sacrifice. One minister told me that if a minister was overweight you knew he was not doing his work. Fasting, then, provided a form of Aladura testimony.

St. Peter's ministers identified six kinds of fasts: ordinary, white, fruit, water, dry, and a fast of silence, which Bassa prophets called borbor. Fasts were observed over one, three, seven, thirteen, twenty-one, or fifty-one days. When individuals fasted, they abstained from sex and contact with menstruating women. They should not fast if they needed to attend a funeral or had any contact with a corpse. Breaking these rules automatically ruined the fast. For instance, a transgression in just the last hour of a seven-day fast canceled out whatever virtue the performer had obtained before. The ordinary fast was the most widely practiced. It entailed fasting from midnight until after six o'clock evening prayers. Cross bearers and Army of Jesus members routinely observed it every Wednesday and Friday. Usually there were no stipulations on what food one needed to eat for breaking the fast. For the white fast subjects ate fruit, cassava, groundnuts, and dry rice; no oils, soups, or condiments for the rice were allowed. The food stuffs represented fertility, wealth, and productivity and were frequently prescribed for patients and family. One minister noted concerning this fast: "During the white fast you suffer the body for the soul's survival. You break down the rich meal for the poor meal." As the name indicates, the fruit fast prescribed only fruit. Ministers considered it to be stronger than the white fast because it did not involve cooking: the food came "straight from God." Ministers performed the fruit fast more often than did dwellers or members. One minister told me it was good for "getting closer to God" and for "hearing voices and seeing visions."

The water fast and the dry fast forbade solid food altogether. The water fast allowed drinking holy water after 6:00 P.M. prayers, whereas the dry fast did not. A member or patient might occasionally be asked to undertake these fasts, but ministers took them routinely. Informants repeatedly insisted that the dry fast was the most important fast for ministers to perform. As a method for renewing virtue, as a kind of recharging instrument, St. Peter's ministers took a one- or three-day dry fast at the end of every month. Dry fasting became the surest defense against the malevolent intents of an enemy. As one minister put it, the dry fast "is a judge. Like you go to court and the judge causes you no more to go up or to go down. If you have a case and it is strong for you and your enemy is fighting you, put yourself in a dry fast and it will bring the enemy down."

The sixth fast involved a vow of silence and was carried out by the more advanced prophets. The practice of silence was coupled with abstinence from food and water. The Bassa prophets special word for the fast—*borbor*—means "to be silent," "not to talk." Most Aladura prophets, however, simply referred to the practice as taking silence. When this fast was undertaken the prophet secluded himself within a room of the Faith Home or stayed in a place where social contact was minimal. During the fast the minister communicated with pen and paper if he needed to make special requests, give instructions, or convey the divine messages he received while fasting. Throughout the year CLA ministers performed this fast at Mount Tabborrar when they retreated there for a special time of prayer. In fact, the first time I visited the mount, Apostle Mayson happened to be there undergoing the fast of silence. Not realizing this, I tried to talk with him as he came walking toward the Faith Home veranda. A junior minister quickly interceded, telling me about the apostle's fast, and asked me to return another time.

The practice of fasting reinforced prophetic authority and its relation to ritual struggle. Indeed fasting was a form of ritual struggle. Regularly a minister fasted for virtue in order to heal and to prophesy. He participated in communal fasts, he fasted for individual patients, and he fasted for himself. Also, particular ritual struggles underlined the role of the prophet's fasting. The bush struggle, which a senior prophet was expected to observe periodically, always involved fasting. Fasting was such an important part of the August Tabborrar ritual that ministers referred to it as "the fast."

How fasting related to the prophet's prestige can be further appreciated by analyzing the categories of fast with the culture-nature paradigm. The power obtained through fasting was proportionate to the degree that fasting was seen as "natural" and as "straight from God." The ordinary fast and the white fast, then, were less powerful than the fruit fast or dry fast. Cooked food compromised what came "straight from God." Also, cooked food involved more risk. For instance, the ordinary fast concluded with meals prepared by family members at home. Beyond the Faith Home it was more difficult to monitor the process of cooking and prevent food from being witched. In the Faith Home appropriate measures could be taken: a meal prepared by a trusted cross bearer using the proper utensils in a location considered holy. Yet even meals ritually prepared in the Faith Home involved the risk of pollution. Consequently fasts that did not entail cooking were more reliable. The fruit fast prescribed a diet of only fruit and nuts, the raw produce from trees, bushes, and ground. In the culture-nature continuum it became the midpoint between cooking and total abstinence. With the dry fast cooking itself became spiritualized, realized through the subject's more radical self-denial. The performer's only food was spiritual food, heavenly nourishment mediated by de-cultured fasting. And yet the cooking symbolism was not absent: for instance, ministers claimed that the dry fast produced a kind of heat that broke down all obstacles.

There was some debate among ministers about which fast—the dry fast or the fast of silence—was the more powerful. On the one hand, in performing the latter one eliminated the risk of speaking in anger, saying unsavory things, or using profanity. In a sense one took the renunciation of culture (which involved language) one step further. Wrong speech, just like eating prohibited food, immediately spoiled a fast. On the other hand, the fast of silence entailed excusing oneself from certain ritual actions that the church deemed vital to its well-being, such as the recitation of psalms and holy names. When considering the basic needs of the Faith Home, the dry fast appeared more useful. The minister remained more available to church members and Faith Home dwellers. Still, the prophet's renunciation of speech supported the crucial paradigm of struggle, in which individual and communal concerns were never totally separate. Whatever fast he performed, the devoted prophet did so for the well-being of his patients and for strengthening of the church, and not from self-interest.

Looking at the role of heat symbols in other Aladura ritual contexts helps us to appreciate how cooking became transformed through fasting. Fire and smoke symbols were important in candle consecrations, incense treatments, and sacrifices of cooked and burnt offerings. They represented the virtue of the Lord necessary for destroying evil. In consecrations and treatments the smoke and fire shielded the subject from the enemy. In sacrifices the fire consumed the offering and the smoke carried it to heaven, creating a link between this world and the other world. In Liberia the presence of fire, of heat, evoked associations that prevailed in traditional life. R. S. Leopold (1983) indicates the importance of fired clay as a cultural medium. It was used in building homes, for making pots, and for the blacksmith's furnace. In ritual contexts, white clay denoted a process of transformation, as during the Poro and Sande initiations when subjects smeared themselves daily with white clay. Just as making a clay pot, a cultural artifact, required heating, so did changing children into adults: the initiates were being "cooked" into social beings. Analogically speaking, Aladura fasting strategies cooked initiates into Aladura selves.

Finally, the culture-nature scheme was also operative in how the Aladura saw the relation between gender and fasting. Women were strongly associated with the cultural order through domestic chores such as collecting and cooking food.[4] Though regarded in a positive way, the domestic realm also became the context for witchcraft accusations: women were frequently accused of placing African signs in the food of their victims. They played a paradoxical role in the social world of the Faith Home. On the one hand, they supported its domestic character: the Faith Home was often regarded as a woman's domain. On the other hand, women had a "natural" capacity to subvert the social order if they turned to witchcraft. Thus, rituals performed away from the Faith Home, such as a bush struggle or Tabborrar, became vehicles for obtaining a kind of "undomesticated" spiritual power. Within the Faith Home dry fasting also enabled the performer to transcend more capably the domestic realm: he became less dependent on the cultural medium of cooking and on provisions from women.

Fasting also implicated rules of menstruation, which, in turn, would appear to privilege the male minister, since, as we have seen, the Aladura regarded female menstruation as a potential element of subversion. A person fasting must avoid menstruating women. Also, female ministers, members, or patients having their menses did not fast. Though fasting represented the paradigmatic struggle for all ministers, the rule about menstruation restricted the female minister. It limited her from performing the kind of extended fasting that male ministers could do. Given the expectations for the longer and more arduous fasts, the female minister or prophetess already had the cards stacked against her. But menstrual blood was also generally recognized as the natural power of women. If it spoiled a rite or sacred space, this had more to do with its being "out of place" than with its being a polluting essence. Of course, the postmenopausal prophetess or spiritual mother represented a major exception. But even in her case fasting was not as crucial in her exercise of power as her demonstration of other gifts: falling in Spirit, delivering visions, interpreting dreams, and improvising healing rites. I attended many services at which a young female minister or cross bearer confined to "behind the tent" fell in Spirit; and, on very rare occasions, delivered prophecies.

RODS AND CROSSES

In the ritual struggles he performed the prophet drew from an assortment of holy materials to mediate spiritual power—candles, incense, the Bible, consecrated water, olive oil, and palm leaves. By far, the holy rod and the small handheld wooden cross were the religious objects used most often for such purposes. Ministers who "held the rod" almost always considered it the most effective instrument for mediating spiritual power. The rod had a set form: about two-and-one-half-feet long, pointed on one end, looped on the other. Junior ministers who used only the wood cross still generally insisted on the rod's superiority. When I asked members about the basis for the rod's use, they frequently referred to biblical passages, such as Exodus 14 in which Moses uses his staff to open the Red Sea and drown the Egyptians. A minister once told me that Aladura prophets used the rod because Hebrew prophets used it to heal and to prophesy.

The welder commissioned to make the rods usually belonged to the church. At St. Peter's an elder in the church usually performed the task. He would deliver rods to the headquarters where they would be consecrated in the Faith Home's prayer room for three months. A special order was always made before Tabborrar, when the rods, placed in buckets, would be consecrated within the mount's altar. Informants noted that the rods then received the "power of Tabborrar." The services after Tabborrar occasioned many promotions when ministers received their first rods. Discussion sometimes arose about the proper allocation of rods. At a meeting that preceded St. Peter's 1984 Tabborrar observance, members complained that at former Tabborrars some ministers had received the rod but no longer affiliated with the church, as was the case with Bishop Bundu. Members advised using more caution, especially with the newer, less tested recruits. In effect, individuals who received the rod and then left the church took its power with them. Or, as some CLA authorities put it, they "stole our doctrine."

Certain rules, which every minister was expected to learn, governed the use of the rod. The rod should never touch the ground or any dirty surface. During prayers and services prostrating ministers cradled the rod so that it pointed upward and did not touch the ground or floor. Such contact could diminish the rod's power. Some ministers, as Harold Turner indicates, kept their rods safe in leather sheaths (1967, 2:105). The rod must always be cleaned, polished, and ready for use. A rusty rod, as Modee once noted, was proof that a minister neglected his work. Furthermore, if it lay disused for long, the rod could lose its virtue. Daily use, such as during services, prayers, and healing ceremonies, reconsecrated the rod, or, as it were, recharged its power. Informants also insisted that the effectiveness of the rod depended mostly on the moral character of its owner. They stressed a kind of identity between the minister and the rod that began with ordination and became expressed in use in prayers and healing rituals. When one received a rod, it was consecrated in one's own name. Therefore, a minister did not loan his rod to others, nor would he ask to use one consecrated in another person's name. The physical condition of a rod was seen as a reflection on the spiritual and moral state of its owner. The well-oiled, shiny rod indicated a minister's earnest and disciplined work, while a dull, rusty one indicated negligence. With regard to understanding one's personal struggles, rod images in dreams had considerable didactic and practical value. As one minister told me, "If you dream of a rod being bent, then you need to strengthen your path. If you dream of that rod breaking or bursting, then this means you are beset by enemies."

Ministers generally considered the wooden hand-held cross as the second most important religious object used for ritual functions. The image of the cross was certainly the most frequently used in the church. Turner notes that the image was "found on mercy grounds, buildings, and altars, chalked on the door of the minister's faith home or embroidered on his vestments, planted in the water for

baptism, signed on the new born, and given into the hand of the Cross-bearers"
(106). Almost every ritual function required the minister to sign "invisible
crosses" with his hand, the holy rod, or with the wooden cross that at one time
had been ceremonially placed in the hand of the cross bearer. Ministers usually
received the cross before they received the rod. Many ministers had once served
as cross bearers before receiving higher ordination. Though there was a strong
association between the cross and the cross bearer, there was not a rule regarding personal identification, such as between the holy rod and rod holder. For
instance, cross bearers might often share crosses, which rod holders never did
with the rods. Unlike the prophet's holy rod, the wooden cross was not consecrated in a person's name. But this did not preclude the cross bearer's keeping a
personal cross. Many cross bearers made strong claims about their "personal"
cross, which they preferred not to loan or give up.

Samuel Oduwole's pamphlet *The Cross Bearer and Rules of the Cross* circulated
widely among Aladura churches in Liberia. In the text he insists that the hand-
held cross represents both the "power of God" and the "sign of Jesus" (4). At
ordinations, when the senior prophet placed the cross in the initiate's hand, she
might quickly fall in Spirit. She usually received a cross that was consecrated for
an auspicious period of time in the prayer room or high altar or on Mount Tabborrar. Because cross bearers might be expected to share their crosses, during
services or healing ceremonies a cross bearer might be asked to surrender the
cross for general use in a healing ritual or for reconsecration. During shouts at a
CLA services, a senior prophetess ordered the cross bearers, who all happened to
be women, to place their crosses in a bucket of holy water. They began dancing
counterclockwise around the bucket, which lasted for about five minutes. When
they had finished, each cross bearer randomly retrieved a cross.

As with the holy rod, there were clear rules on how to use the cross, many
taken from Oduwole's handbook. Cross bearers were encouraged to set up small
altar tables in their homes where they could place the cross and other holy materials. Some ministers suggested wrapping the cross with clean white paper when
it was not being used. Cross bearers were warned not to take their crosses into
bathrooms and to remove it from bedrooms when having sex with a spouse. The
cross should not be touched by menstruating women, nor used by a female cross
bearer during her menses. Cross bearers were also warned not to take the cross
to funeral homes or to let it come into contact with a corpse. When a cross bearer
made love, attended a funeral home, or came into contact with a corpse, she was
expected to bathe before handling the cross again. If she did not and authorities
learned about it, the church could suspend the cross bearer and reclaim her
cross, a scenario with potential controversy.

For the cross bearer, cross images in dreams or visions had special significance, and so she needed to be able to interpret the meaning of these. Again

Oduwole's pamphlet became a valuable resource for learning interpretations (11–12). On the one hand, an image of the cross dividing into two, growing larger, turning the color gold, talking, or yielding water had auspicious meanings: victory, virtue, joy, elevation and blessings. On the other hand, images of the cross shrinking, being dropped, damaged, burned, misplaced, or found in unseemly places had inauspicious meanings: sin, danger, loss, and pollution. These images revealed something about the subject's situation or status. Ministers used these to comment on the work and intentions of an individual or a group of cross bearers. For instance, a damaged or misplaced cross image might signal negligence and irresponsibility and the need for fasting or a beach struggle.

THE JUNIOR PROPHET AND THE CROSS BEARER

On occasion tension developed between junior ministers who "held the rod" and cross bearers. At Aladura churches junior ministers often assumed special roles denied female cross bearers, such as "controlling the altar." The cross bearer might resent the junior minister's role; in turn, the latter might become suspicious of the cross bearer's envy. A junior minister, who experienced frustration and failure in performing his assignments, might blame others for his difficulties. Almost inevitably this would lead to accusations of witchcraft, as happened in a case involving a junior minister named Edward Saydee and an older, more experienced female cross bearer named Felicia Morgan.

After Tabborrar, Saydee had been assigned to supervise the Faith Home at a local branch. Soon after he began this work, he began to experience a series of "attacks," which he believed were caused by Sister Felicia. The cross bearer was an old member of the branch, and, to my knowledge, had always been in good standing. She first began her work as a cross bearer in the Church of the Lord but left that church when officials accused her of some infraction. They sought to penalize her by taking away her cross, but she refused to hand it over. About that time Olu started St. Peter's and Sister Felicia decided to join the new church. In March 1984, when I first got to know her, she appeared well respected by other members and dwellers. She faithfully attended services and prayers and often assisted ministers with healing rites. I found her to be well versed in Aladura doctrine, always eager to talk about the details of church practice, and generally forthright with interpretations. Church authorities also occasionally entrusted her to instruct new ministers on the meaning and use of religious objects. James Flomo, the Kpelle minister, in particular had found her an invaluable resource about church practices.

A month before Tabborrar a family death required that Sister Felicia travel to Greenville County. She stayed there for several weeks and did not return to church until well after Tabborrar. During her absence Olu assigned Flomo to another branch and replaced him with Saydee. From the start I observed Saydee keep some distance from Sister Felicia. Eventually I learned that there had been a past unpleasant encounter between them. Saydee and I were discussing another minister's use of witchcraft when he commented that the minister was "not the only member with witchcraft in his heart." He then began to talk about Sister Felicia and why he distrusted her. A few years before, when he had just started his work as a minister and was serving at another branch in Paynesville, Sister Felicia had brought him some bread, which, after he ate caused him to become terribly ill. Although he no longer held a grudge, he told me he continued to be careful in his interactions with the cross bearer.

Not long after Sister Felicia had returned to the church, both Saydee and a senior prophet received revelations about the cross bearer's "evil plot in the yard." They confronted her about the suspected activity. According to Saydee, "she had been shamed" but still refused to confess any wrong. She continued to attend church, performing the usual cross bearer duties. Saydee, however, would claim that this was simply a disguise that hid her true "witch nature." For some time he had been having dreams that revealed her opposition to his work in the church. One afternoon he told me about a dream: the cross bearer had changed into a dog with "so-so human" appearance and had bit him in the groin. He managed to kill the dog by piercing it with his rod. The next day the minister narrated the dream to church members but did not publicly name the person who attacked him.

Two other members would also report dreams about Sister Felicia taking animal forms. One told the ministers that she saw her take a snake form; the other, that she became a deer blowing fire. In dreams animals often symbolized witchcraft. For some people the image of a person changing into an animal left little doubt about his or her character. But certainly what became most striking about Saydee's dream was the personal struggle it evoked and the identification between the prophet and the rod. In the dream the effective use of the rod (the weapon of virtue) defeated the dog that had caused him injury and the loss of power. During this time Saydee also had a vision in which he saw the cross bearer seize the senior prophet's rod "to see what power it had." After he told the senior prophet about the dream, they again confronted the cross bearer and again she denied the allegations. She became upset and threatened to sue. Though the ministers never publicly confronted Sister Felicia, the accusations became common knowledge among the dwellers. Over time, though, the senior prophet distanced himself from the matter.

Administrative responsibilities and visits to other branches increasingly demanded the attention of the senior prophet. When he had to be away for a long period he left the church in Saydee's charge. Saydee believed that on such occasions the enemies of the church especially tried to test the inexperience of younger ministers. Once Saydee had a vision in which he saw a black cat drinking from a bucket of water that he was consecrating for a patient. He attested that the cat represented a witch or evil spirit sent by the enemies of the church to "spoil" the water. Saydee included Sister Felicia among the church's enemies, since, as he put it, she had tried to "bring me down." The cross bearer had continued to attend services and prayers. But again Saydee believed "it was all pretending": she came only to spite him and to "quench the Spirit." She would cause a service to become "cold." When she fell in Spirit he claimed that she was simply trying to hide her real "witch nature."

Once during a Divine Worship service in November the cross bearer's falling in Spirit appeared more intense than usual. She moved her head and torso rapidly back and forth and ran from one side of the chapel to the other. This went on for about three minutes, when finally Sister Felicia returned to her bench, knelt, and prayed. A few minutes later she prostrated herself toward the altar and continued to pray. All the while Saydee remained standing before the altar, his stare focused on the praying cross bearer. Later, during Thanksgiving Vows, Sister Felicia approached the altar and knelt. She gave special thanks to God for her husband's recovery from a recent bout of malaria. When it came time for her to receive the minister's blessing, Saydee deferred to another minister.

Two days later I discussed with Saydee what had happened at the Divine Worship. He related that the Spirit had fallen on the Sister Felicia, but that when she was furiously thrashing about the Spirit "was beating her" for her sins. It was also "keeping her from taking her witch form." I was rather disappointed by this interpretation, since Sister Felicia's dancing, praying, and vow had all seemed in earnest. I had always found it difficult to fathom that this woman who had shown me kindness and hospitality could be an enemy of the church.

At services over the next few weeks I did not see the cross bearer fall in Spirit again. In fact, she increasingly appeared less engaged. During shouts she often stood away from the "circle dancing" of other ministers and cross bearers. At one such service Saydee, who had been pacing slowly back and forth in the altar area, with his rod held close against his chest, suddenly urged participants to begin jumping up and down and to shout repeatedly, "Go away with evil spirit." Later in the same service he revealed that someone had tried to take a "witch form" in order to keep the Spirit away. As was custom, he did not name names. I failed to ask Saydee about the vision. My journal includes no reflective entries about it. Perhaps I had assumed that the witch (person) he referred to was Sister Felicia.

Saydee and others in the church continued to make claims about the cross bearer's caprice. Despite rising accusations Sister Felicia would never confess. As the end of the year approached, she came to church less and less often. As for Saydee, he began to appear less concerned about the cross bearer. Increasingly he spoke about his "enemies" in more general terms. He would continue to emphasize the strenuous work—spiritual exercises, dry fasting, beach struggles, and holy baths—he needed to perform in order to build up virtue and defeat his opponents.

Meanwhile the conflict between Saydee and the cross bearer remained unresolved. The minister had the support of other members, but, for me, the episode raised as many questions about Saydee's personality and judgment as it did about the cross bearer. My personal experience with the cross bearer and her family had been a pleasant one. I never directly asked the cross bearer about Saydee's accusation, largely out of respect for her and the embarrassment I feared it would cause. Consequently her voice in this story remains absent. But I had also become friends with Saydee. We often shared personal interests, talked about family and work, and discussed theology. We had many constructive conversations about Aladura doctrine and practice, and he often kept me inside the loop on Faith Home affairs, for which I was deeply appreciative. This story primarily represents Saydee's voice, but it does not unfold without awareness of gaps, ambiguity, and moral uncertainty.

From a psychological perspective it is easy enough to dismiss Saydee's conflict with the cross bearer as paranoid behavior or to see it as simply an expression of predictable structural tension that exists between junior ministers and cross bearers. Both groups indeed professed insecurities and apprehensions about the coordination of roles. Also, we cannot pass over the importance of gender in understanding the conflicts between cross bearers and junior ministers. Most cross bearers were female and most junior ministers male. And the fact that Saydee held the rod may have increased the tension. Such interpretations, however, overlook the harmony that usually exists, at least publicly, between these parties. They also reduce Aladura ritual struggle to an epiphenomenon and neglect how, on the one hand, it implicates "presence," and, on the other, an indeterminate dimension. As Adam Ashforth notes, there are limits in our ability to understand and reduce in meaning an experience such as witchcraft (2000, 253–55).

This account of one man's spiritual conflict and one woman's fall from favor imposes a kind of order indicative of a notion of narrative time. In her discussion about narrative time in the context of therapeutic encounter, Mattingly identifies six features that have relevance for understanding such cases as that of Edward Saydee and Felicia Morgan (1998, 84–97). First, narrative time is always configured: the purpose of a story unfolds through a specific configuration of persons and events with each part contributing to the meaning of the whole. Saydee's account, then, represents one part of a complex of entangled stories, images, dreams, visions, and episodes, many of which remained unexplored. The complexities of any story become more apparent only over time. Second, in narrative time the patterns of action and movement are key structuring devices.

Multiple and interactive, they reveal conflict and dissonance. Thus, in the Aladura "lived space" no one could be totally aware of another person's moods and motives. They often remained hidden. One member's story did not always match another's. But this discordant dimension contributed to the structure, meaning, and dynamic quality of narrative time. Third, the organization of narrative time includes the experience of a gap, the acknowledgment that something is missing, that the account will remain incomplete. In the case of our story a key missing element is Sister Felicia's own version.

Fourth, narrative time tells us something about how people and situations change over time. In this account the change was not necessarily linear but "full of tricks and reversals" (85). Along with the Aladura stories of conversion came also stories of relapse, trials of faith, and self-deception. This relates directly to the fifth element of narrative time, namely, its dramatic character. Aladura stories included experiences of clear conflict, perceived danger, and undeniable risk that often propelled action and created new moods and aspirations. One always needed to be prepared for the unexpected. For instance, in April Flomo had introduced Sister Felicia to me as a model member; but by October his successor Saydee accused her of witchcraft. I certainly would not have predicted that outcome, nor, I dare say, would have Flomo, who may not have accepted Saydee's accusation.

Finally, within narrative time endings are often uncertain: we can recognize an element of suspense in a story and the fear that one's ambitions might not be realized. For a prophet, "temptation" was ever present; he kept guard lest the enemy sabotage his work. If he focused only on the physical or public realm, his work would have empty results. But we should bear in mind that the prophet's work always went beyond the external. A visible failure—the patient was not healed, the problem not solved—did not necessarily disprove a prophet's (or a cross bearer's) virtue, but reminded the faithful of the dramatic, agonistic nature of human experience and the need to remain alert in ritual struggle.

DIVINE MESSAGES

As the biographies of ministers indicate, dreams and visions played a key role in helping one understand and fulfill his role within the church, manage his personal struggles, and define his relations with others. Though usually identified as distinctive experiences, the terms dream and vision were often used interchangeably. A dream, as one prophet put it, was a "kind of vision," while another prophet called the vision a "form of dream." Both experiences were doors to "that side": one during sleep, the other in a waking state. The former experience, of course, was available to everyone; the latter remained more the province of prophets. Similarly Kiernan notes that Zionists of South Africa maintain that dreams are experienced by all but visions are the "prerogative of prophecy." Dreams have meanings that require interpretation, while the meanings of visions are direct (1990:184–207).

The complex nature of dreams and visions (and also of voices) informed structural divisions within the church. Hierarchy enjoined rules about public narration. Reporting dreams and visions always involved deference to the prophet's role. If a member had visions or heard voices—usually signs of spiritual growth—she relied on an experienced prophet's interpretation of their meaning. A dream or vision about a senior church official required caution about discussing it in a public setting. I knew cases of cross bearers or junior prophets who had dreams or visions about senior prophets but did not narrate them in public. For instance, when someone received a vision during shouts about a senior prophet, she or he usually reported it to him in a private conference. I observed only two instances when this decorum was set aside. One case involved a cross bearer who delivered a vision to a minister already accused of witchcraft.

During the shouts at a Divine Worship, cross bearers were given special time to exercise their gifts for prophecy. They frequently received messages while "falling in Spirit." The ability to communicate the message clearly and to interpret it correctly also came through the guidance from the Spirit. Once during a service a cross bearer had difficulty articulating her message. It came across as a series of indistinct mutterings. From the high altar the senior prophet reprimanded her incoherence, telling her to "define your message." Most cross bearers received divine messages or revelations mostly for ordinary members and patients. They often gave messages for certain groups—Armies of Jesus, cross bearers, followers, elders, junior ministers, and Faith Home patients. During special services at St. Peter's, such as the annual conference or the Tabborrar thanksgiving services, senior prophets and senior prophetesses attended in large numbers. On those occasions cross bearers usually deferred to their seniors, who assumed center stage and would deliver the divine messages.

Stories about becoming Aladura were replete with references to the significance of certain dreams and visions. Dreams "carried" patients to the Faith Home where they sought an interpretation from a prophet; members received blessings based on an accurate interpretation of a dream; prophets were called and commissioned through dreams and visions. In the Faith Home praxis, at every ritual function dreams, visions, and interpretations by prophets were crucial to a person's self-understanding and "problem solving." Indeed the Faith Home provided an optimum location for the experience of meaningful dreams and visions. For the Aladura prophet dreams and visions served as vehicles that secured his role and distinguished him from other subjects. Aladura decorum dictated a proper way for reporting dreams and receiving visions that reinforced the authority of the prophet.

Several works have demonstrated the purposive and social value of dreams in AIC. In his work on a Nigerian church Richard Curley shows how dream narration, "the dream-as-told," affects conversion, reaffirms doctrine, and augments authority. A dream often plays an important role in "the process of individuation: it helps to give form to new identity" (1992, 149). Significantly these processes imply tension between the highly personal nature of faith and community expectations, which the dream experience can also help resolve. Therefore it becomes a sign of both sincere faith and the validity of church doctrine. Similarly Simon R. Charsley's study of a Ugandan church (1973, 256) indicates the legitimating work of dreams and their role in the "bidding for status" among members and in supporting authority. Dream narratives, Charsley demonstrates, are used to found churches, confirm prophecies, and mediate healing. In contrast to a functionalist position, Charsley does not see dreams and visions as necessarily stabilizing forces; they can bring on tension as well as harmony, which we observed in Saydee's story and will see in others. In his work on Zionist dreams and visions Kiernan also finds unsatisfactory a functionalist explanation and applies a phenomenological analysis that understands these experiences within the context of purposive activity (1990, 184–207).

These studies make clear the sociological import that dreams have among African churches and the importance of understanding the links between indigenous and contemporary forms. However, in examining the content and meaning of dreams one also needs to be open to their adaptive capacity. Images continue to be applied and understood in both traditional and innovative ways, as examples of both cultural continuity and discontinuity (see Robbins 2007). The cluster of image forms that appear in dreams and visions betrays a mix of new and old elements (Jedrej and Shaw 1992, 18).

In exploring the meaning and purpose of dreams and visions we should not overlook the communicative dimension. Among Aladura churches in Liberia dreams and visions do indeed legitimate authority, confirm identity, create *communitas*, mediate conflict, and order experience; but they were understood by participants primarily as "messages" with intentional meaning. While the study of narrative techniques provides a good starting point for understanding the social value of dreams and visions in these churches, one should not dismiss the persuasive quality of dream and vision narration that testifies to a person's experience with spiritual realities. From the Aladura perspective, dreams and visions (and voices) were usually seen as divine messages: they came from the "other side," "that side;" and they provided an immediate means for supernatural communication. Dreams and visions represented a constitutive dimension of human experience.

In Aladura cosmology the dream and waking life were interwoven. Through dreams and visions, this side and that side met and transformed one another.

With this model of interaction the spatial and temporal dimensions of dreams were fully acknowledged. The psychoanalyst Saloman Resnik (1987) speaks about the interactions of realities in terms of "the theatre of the dream," in which the analyst (like the ancient oneiromancer) plays a key role in helping subjects determine the meaning of dreams. Like Resnik's analyst, the Aladura prophet participated in the reality of the other person's dream through the steps of narration, recording, interpretation, and treatment. Such action on the part of the prophet underlined his role as mediator—between this side and that side, between the patient and the sources of affliction and cure. What Resnik says about the analyst applies as well to the role of the prophet: "The interpreter of the dream is always a reader who has his own way of perceiving and interpreting what the 'dream messenger' is saying. To interpret means to negotiate with the messenger, to dialogue with dreams: interpretation is an inter-prestation" (40). For the involved parties the dream both communicates the message and creates the theater for mediation. It tenders a certain meaning that needs appreciation within a field of relations. Indeed we may see these messages as "speech acts" that obtain value in the context of prophet and member/patient relationships. As such, these acts assisted in providing narrative structure to Aladura experience and contributed to the dramatic, "struggling" character of prophecy and ritual healing.

The prophet's role as negotiator or mediator was reconfirmed through the praxis of dream and vision narration. As one minister commented, the difference between the dreams and visions of the prophet and those of ordinary members, even cross bearers, was that the prophet had messages for others, while the ordinary member had them for himself. Even if the minister overstated the distinction (members' dreams were also relational), he made clear a commonplace expectation of the prophet. A prophet's dreams and visions might be self-revelatory and have personal value but such became meaningful and useful only in relation to ritual praxis and communal values—within the "theater of the church."

On the most pragmatic level the prophet's dreams and visions were diagnostic tools in the healing process. When a person came to the prophet with a problem, he or she underwent a "spiritual interview," which involved questions about the client's present condition and personal background. It included praying over the client, which precipitated a diagnostic vision about his or her problem and what needed to be done to solve it. Sometimes during the spiritual interview the client sought the interpretation of a dream that may have first prompted her to seek the prophet's advice.

Ministers often insisted that true diagnosis of a person's problem did not derive from previous knowledge. Though the prophet might give attention to past experiences and events, the focus would be on the present and the future. As one senior prophet once told me, "African man wants to know his future." The same prophet also required that all visions and dreams narrated in his church be recorded in a notebook in order to determine their accuracy. One member claimed he had joined the church because the prophecies there "became true 90 percent of the time." One should not, however, overemphasize the predictive value of dreams for Aladura members. The major role of the prophet in the prophet-client relation was to effect a transformation in people's lives. Thus, along with its predictive value the interpretation of a dream or vision had instructive and therapeutic value, and this always involved making links with the past.

The "plain meaning" of a dream might nonetheless take years to unfold; it might have to be understood in a series of or in combination with other dreams. During services and prayers prophets often narrated visions in which they claimed the meaning of images or events was unclear; but through faith and struggle the meaning would finally be revealed. Members attended services usually hopeful that ministers would give visions to help them deal with a present situation or problem, but the full understanding of the vision might not become clear until after subsequent trips. Some prophets were very adept at receiving and narrating visions and confident enough to designate church-wide struggles for the express purpose of delivering visions and interpreting dreams. I attended one church service during which the senior prophet delivered visions for everyone present, about ninety people in all. He delivered them row by row, the men's first and then the women's, taking almost two hours. On another occasion he was able to finish only the men's visions and promised the women that they would receive "your visions" at the next service.

The prophet's narration of visions and interpretation of dreams, whether they had auspicious or inauspicious meanings, always referred to a specific course of ritual action for the subject. The positive outcome of a dream or vision usually depended on this. An individual might be urged to fast for a certain number of days, take a holy bath, make a sweet, fruit, or sheep offering, attend a scheduled struggle or special prayers, provide alms for beggars, or recite psalms at midnight. I observed many instances when, based on a vision, a prophet warned a member that unless he did the spiritual exercises or struggles mandated by former messages, her problem would remain unsolved. Ritual performances and social exchanges were used not only to change a person's destiny but also his identity and behavior. Ritual struggle mediated virtue, spiritual power considered vital for that transformation. And, of course, the primary technician and mediator of virtue was the prophet or prophetess. Whether he narrated or interpreted dreams or visions, these performances, these "inter-prestations," enhanced the prophet's role as holy person. They confirmed the prophet's access to the invisible world, the source of virtue, which the church considered essential to church authority. However, the problematic nature of the dream or vision might remain. No one saw the dream but the dreamer; no one experienced the vision but the seer.

THE MEANING OF DREAM IMAGES

As I have stressed, even the most capable prophet was not always certain about the meaning of every dream or vision. The meaning of an image or action often depended on narrative and social context. For instance, in one context an image of a white person might mean something positive; in another context, something negative. One can, however, field an inventory of dream images and actions with possible meanings from which ministers drew for their interpretations. The list below (though hardly exhaustive) includes common images compiled from dreams and visions I heard narrated or interpreted in ritual and social contexts. Although I have ordered them with the binary categories of auspicious images and inauspicious images, the meanings were not static; interpretation depended on context, time, place, and the persons involved. The dreams and visions capitalized on images that were grounded in everyday experience; they were also applied in a way that demonstrated a collapsing of traditional-modern, visible-invisible, and local-remote dichotomies (West and Sanders 2003).

AUSPICIOUS IMAGES	INAUSPICIOUS IMAGES
Holy materials	Bottles, jars, boxes
Sheep, fowl, eggs	Snakes, dogs, deer
Celestial bodies	Dirt, mud, muddy water
Eating fruit, sweets	Eating pepper
A full basket	An empty basket
White gowns	Dirty, torn clothes
Thin person	Fat person
Climbing ladder	Falling down
Store bread	Country bread
Rice fields	Swamps
House	Bush
Stones	Mud
Taking a bath	Being naked
Cutting a rope	Tying a rope
New car	Occupied or wrecked car
New umbrella	Torn umbrella
Ship, train, plane	Wrecked cars
Head	Feet
People praying	People talking and grabbing things
Crying person	Laughing person
Children of Salvation	Soldiers
Paved road	Dusty road, crossroads

Most of the sets above can be clustered into images of church, home or village, body, nature, food, and travel. Many images automatically referred to the ameliorative work of the church. Holy materials signaled the unique values and character of the Aladura. These included candles, white buckets, rods, and crosses and often suggested the need for ritual struggle. For instance, if a member dreamed about a white bucket or candles, or if a prophet saw someone praying over him, a holy bath or some form of treatment was possibly in store for him.

People wearing white gowns or kneeling in prayer confirmed the progress of a subject's struggle. These became signs of persistence in the Aladura way. This mark of identity was also represented by the image of people making gifts and contrasted with the inauspicious image of people grabbing things. To dream of bottles and jars that contained dark liquids or substances, or of boxes with mysterious content, suggested the evil intent of one's enemy. The bottle "planted in the yard" immediately evoked the witch's plan. New or clean white gowns signified the church, while tattered, dirty, or dyed clothing signified worldly temptations. The image of people praying or performing open-air preaching was contrasted with the image of people just talking, perhaps engaged in idle talk or gossip. The Children of Salvation kneeling in prayer found startling contrast in the image of soldiers with guns. In some contexts the soldier evoked protection, but increasingly he represented new dangers.

Images of home or house and domestic materials often denoted security and harmony. Prophets interpreted the image of a house and swept yard as the Faith Home and contrasted this with images of the forest, which evoked uncertainty and confusion. Also, images of domestic light—such as light bulbs, candles, cooking fires, and flashlights—could refer to the church's power to remove the fear caused by darkness. Doors and keys represented the new possibilities and opportunities that came from making the right choices. The cultivated rice field always meant abundance, productivity, and control, whereas the uncultivated landscape, a swamp in particular, represented waste and abandonment. Though water was always seen as a source of power, especially when it appeared in the context of church or home use, muddy or swamp water suggested danger and confusion.

The positive quality of domestic images might also be seen in the value ascribed to certain animals. On the one hand, sheep and fowl always suggested something auspicious. Their appearance in visions or dreams often meant that an animal sacrifice needed to be performed. On the other hand, snakes, crocodiles, lizards, deer, and leopards represented forms of witchcraft.[5] Snakes in particular suggested such artifice: they belonged to the wild but easily entered both church and home undetected. Though connected to the domestic realm, dogs were also scavengers and were therefore considered unclean. Like snakes, they almost always suggested the presence of witchcraft.

When fruit or sweets appeared in dreams and visions, they denoted productivity and sweetness of life. A basket of fruit, biscuits, or candy was interpreted as an indication for fruit or sweet offerings or that blessings were on the way. In contrast, an empty basket could warn hard times. Food products that appeared in bunches, such as bananas, palm nuts, or ears of corn, also represented good signs. There were, however, certain food items that suggested uncertainty, or even misfortune, such as pepper, a mainstay in the Liberian diet. In the case of pepper, Aladura fasting may have informed its meaning. Some fasts allowed rice and fruit, but strictly forbade pepper and spices. Pepper represented temptation, backsliding, and worldly indulgence. Informants also ascribed a punitive value to pepper, perhaps related to the unfortunate practice of punishing children by putting pepper in their eyes. The contrast made between store bread and country bread also suggested the problem of witchcraft. Rules prohibited bringing country bread into the Faith Home, since any food prepared outside the compound could easily become a medium of witchcraft. Wrapped store-bought bread was considered safer, since it was imported or cooked by local Lebanese bakers, who usually were not considered sources of witchcraft. The image of being tied down, or seeing someone tie a rope, also brought about concern for witchcraft. Being tied evoked an obstruction to blessings, to the flow of virtue; an untied rope denoted the removal of obstructions, the possibility of fortune, or the enabling of the flow.

Images related to travel frequently occurred in dreams and visions. The motor road evoked uncertainty and danger but also opportunity and rewards. The single road leading through a forest promised order and hope. The forked road or crossroads, however, usually became an omen of anxiety and uncertainty about wrong choices and unpredictable events. Ships, airplanes, and trains were usually interpreted as harbingers of success and freedom. The interpreter regarded autos and buses, however, as cause for concern, as anyone who traveled the Liberian highways could appreciate. A new car might mean prosperity, while a wrecked car was a foreboding sign. An image of an occupied car might augur an accident. Ritual struggle for the subject, then, was in order. Interestingly, at the Church of Salvation a significant number of members owned cars and trucks. Automobile consecrations were commonly observed, often sanctioned through dreams of vehicular and travel images.

Though one might observe a general tendency to interpret an image one way or the other, the prophet was also capable of ascribing contrary meanings to common images. The dream image of a fat person could signify hunger, poverty, misfortune, or death; the image of a thin person could signify wealth, riches, fortune or health. Someone laughing in your dream or vision portended something bad happening, while someone crying portended something good. Many images, however, had ambivalent meanings. For instance, a letter or envelope could signal fortune or misfortune. A white person could represent a ghost, a jina, or an angel. Indeed the meaning of any image, including those listed above, might shift and be reconfigured depending on context and interpretation.

REVEALING THE SECRETS OF GOD

In traditional Liberian cosmology every person had the capacity to move between visible and invisible worlds. But the zo's power to do so was special. As d'Azevedo (1966) has shown, this skill could be obtained through a jina liaison, which also might contribute to the general well-being of society. Such a liaison might bring about individual genius, artistic accomplishment, and technological innovation. But the zo's pact with the jina could also arouse suspicion and fear: through self-interest and personal animosity the zo could cause harm and havoc.

Similarly the prophet's ability to move between the visible and invisible worlds aroused suspicion about his effect on others. Though members respected the role of the prophet and acknowledged dependency on his virtue for solving problems, perceptions were also marked by suspicion. How do we know his power comes from the Spirit and not from the jina? On the one hand, communication with the other world, as through dreams and visions, enhanced the prophet's image as holy man and as the mediator of spiritual power; on the other hand, it evoked mistrust and uncertainty. The prophet's prowess of the unseen could subvert as well as support the public order. The trust that members had toward an individual prophet was related to how they perceived the consistency between his public and private persona.

Dream and vision narrations made public something that was formerly hidden and secret. These performances also made clear the relational aspect of the prophet's mission. The dream soul was not autonomous; it remained responsible toward the visible, waking world. In the Aladura discourse about witchcraft the spirit of the witch rejected such responsibility: it wandered secretly in order to bring harm on others. Witchcraft became public through the misfortune and ruin it caused others. By contrast, the wandering soul of the prophet sought accord between public and private realms, between waking and dream worlds. Through the narration and interpretation of dreams and visions, the prophet made known a world invisible to most and connected private and public realms.

As we have seen, the notion of a dream soul or dream spirit was central to prophet cosmology, especially in the link it made between the person and the "invisible others." The person or self interacted with those who represented a moral reality—the Holy Spirit, angels, the spirits of prophets—but he also encountered others, such as zoes, jina, and witches, who were perceived as undermining the moral reality. These interactions assumed an interdependent relationship between the visible and invisible worlds that informed the perceptions and strategies of the prophet. The prophet's ability to expose the mutual effects between the waking and dreaming world, especially the harms of witchcraft and the jina's trickery, enhanced the church's appeal.

This ability distanced him from those who used unauthorized secret power or, in Kiernan's words, resorted to "pure allocation." It also distinguished him from the zoes, the ones who "do not speak" the secrets in public domains (Bellman 1975, 68). The prophet, in contrast, seldom minced his words when it came to church knowledge and practice. Ministerial secrets notwithstanding, Aladura authorities stressed the church was not about secrets. One young minister noted concerning spiritual power: "If you cannot speak about it, then it was not from God." Those reticent about discussing doctrine clung to an older way. The prophet's main function was to proclaim church gospel, to make it audible and visible through open-air preaching, delivering visions, interpreting dreams, and performing struggles.

Using dreams and visions enhanced the prophet's image as mediator and negotiator. Dreams and visions became a means by which he discerned the cause of problems and attempted to treat them. In the healing context the prophet's capacities to mediate virtue through communication with the other side—receiving, delivering, and interpreting divine messages—and to hover around the porous boundaries between domains was indispensable for Aladura praxis. In the Aladura way the struggle with temptation offered one of the most poignant images of the prophet's mediating role. The prophet effectively opposed evil because he knew his enemy. He might even entertain the thought of using unauthorized African signs. Thus he must be tireless in proving himself against temptation. Such trials evoked the "radical presence" (Orsi 2005) of subverting powers that might "tie down" the victim, "block" her fortune, and divert the prophets.

We may compare the prophet's strategies with traditional divination practices but need to keep in mind that the prophet's focus on dream and vision mediation pointed in a different direction. In the healing process he or she manipulated words and objects in a fashion that evidenced acceptance of their materiality but assumed a theological model that affirmed the guidance of the Spirit. Ministers and members insisted over and over that true discernment of a person's condition and treatment through the use of dreams and visions depended on "being in Spirit." Dreams can be just dreams, but they can also be doors to the other world, revealing truths and meanings that, if properly understood, can bring new insights and blessings.

This dependency on the dream world demonstrated an acceptance of mystical power. In his study of Kpelle communities William Murphy contends that many of the secular functions of the zo became challenged and replaced by the schoolteacher, who represented a "civilized" form of knowledge as power. The teacher "is essentially a transformation of the traditional identity of the [zo]. Both are knowledge brokers—of civilized and country knowledge respectfully— and both use the same cultural idiom of dangerous knowledge for political and economic purposes" (1981, 679). The Aladura notion of doctrine as power, however, transcended the civilized-country dichotomy about knowledge. As the paragon of mystical power in new communities, the prophet also indicated a transformation of zo identity. Undoubtedly, in the Aladura way, the prophet's gifts and supposed access to virtue implicated a notion of "dangerous knowledge" for which he was respected and feared. The ambivalence and anxiety about his place and work within the world perhaps mirrored something of the zo image. Aladura representations indeed suggested an image of the prophet as a boundary person, which reinforced cautious ambivalence about his character. In the healing process and in the context of ritual struggle, he monitored the conditions of sickness and health and the situations of misfortune and success. It was precisely the capacity to mediate between sides, to manipulate conditions, to negotiate meanings between persons, and to reveal divine secrets that made the prophet the extraordinary person in the Aladura world.

This picture of the prophet as boundary person and negotiator, however, would find its most meaningful interpretation in the context of Christian discourse. To see the prophet's power only in terms of the zo's dangerous knowledge would smack of a functionalist approach that trivializes the impact of historical and theological paradigms. It also privileges indigenous African traits while underappreciating the inspiration Aladura prophets claimed from biblical and missionary sources. As Meyer (2004) indicates, such dichotomies have distorted our understanding of the scope and depth of the new African church. Indeed the model of the prophet or prophetess increasingly gives way to the very visible charismatic pastor or the flamboyant evangelist of global Pentecostalism. It would be shortsighted, however, to write an epitaph for the prophet's role and the regime of ritual struggle. The Pentecostal discourse has simply radicalized various components of the AIC, including the idea of demonic presence, a development that enhances rather than diminishes the prophet's role.

4

The Circularity of Signs

The Aladura prophet engaged an agonistic world of opposing forces and presences. This setting generated a cluster of images that mediated the understanding of the self and of the world. The prophet, the extraordinary person, became the chief player in the ongoing production and acceptance of images, rites, and rules that characterized the Aladura way. The prophet's struggles expressed his mediating role often in spatial terms: movement between this side and that side, between Faith Home and Tabborrar, between church and town. In this regard he became a boundary person who traversed, demarcated, and made links between separate but diffused worlds. This capacity for mediation, for moving from side to side, gave the prophet the skills and authority to divine and heal. It also created ambivalence toward him. The prophet's gifts and skills confirmed his status as the holy man but also evoked uncertainty: he had the capacity to harm as well as heal. Expectations regarding virtue became conflated with ideas about "occult power" (Moran 1990, 36–40), which made for a kind of "circularity of power" as discussed by Geschiere (2006, 226–230).

In the Aladura world the prophet dealt with persons considered unsympathetic to church aims. On this side, the waking reality, there were disobedient patients, hostile neighbors, and members who "prayed against one another." On the other side, the dream reality, there were secret societies, Dragon witches, and bush jina. The two domains intersected to the point that members often did not distinguish between actions or deeds that happened on this side or that side.[1] In the long run, reality transcended this dichotomy. Whether the prophet faced the disgruntled member next door or the jina in a dream, what ultimately mattered was how he responded to such encounters.

The fundamental dichotomy in Aladura cosmology lay between good and evil. In the early history of the Nigerian church, this notion of cosmic conflict was undoubtedly influenced by the Yoruba notion of battle between the orisha and the *ajogun*. The orisha are the benevolent "supernatural powers of the right" who seek to bless humans; the ajogun are the malevolent "supernatural powers of the left" who seek to destroy them. According to Adogame, in the Yoruba world humans are caught in the "cross-fire" between these forces (2004, 503). We need to explore, then, how these polarities were embodied or personified in the Liberian prophet's world. Since the metaphor of struggle always implied an awareness of forces that sought to sabotage the prophet's work, we need to describe these, explore their meaning, and understand their role.

Certainly, when thinking about forms of occult power, the problematic topic of witchcraft immediately comes to mind. Though a Western term, *witchcraft* has gained currency throughout anglophone sub-Saharan Africa. From region to region, from group to group, its specific meaning and use may vary and overlap with indigenous terms and other general categories. When I first began fieldwork, I rarely heard witchcraft discussed, and I found little reason to bring it up. As fieldwork progressed, however, the topic became increasingly difficult to ignore. For one thing, healing ceremonies almost always expressed concern about specific forces or powers preventing successful treatment. The works of other researchers, such as Ray (1993), Olupona (1987), and Adogame (2000), have made clear that much of the popularity of Aladura churches has to do with its insistence on the reality of evil. The general topic of witchcraft or occult power in Africa has received renewed interest in part because it is a phenomenon that simply will not go away. Indeed the contexts of modernity and postmodernity have occasioned its reinvigoration. The belief in witchcraft in particular and in the invisible world in general has simply adapted itself.[2] The adaptive variability of witchcraft has become one of the obvious aspects of this discourse. Concerning ideas of witchcraft in South Africa, Erik Bähre has noted that "the study of witchcraft has revealed that homogeneity should not be assumed. Witchcraft is very much alive today and has found its way in new technologies, media, and forms of inequality in South Africa and as elsewhere in Africa" (2002, 302). Cyprian Fisiy and Peter Geschiere have similarly insisted on the variations of occult knowledge, techniques, and power often subsumed by the term *witchcraft* (1996, 193–95).

Discussions of African witchcraft from the 1940s to the 1960s employed various models for understanding conceptions of negative power. In general, these discussions saw it as "direct attack on the social order" (Geschiere 2006, 223). Witchcraft referred to forms of subversion that produced undesirable consequences for both the victim and perpetrator. Researchers often assumed that as urban cultures grew and Africans became more exposed to modern or Western forms of knowledge, notions of witchcraft would decline. Such prognostications, however, have proven shortsighted and simplistic. Witchcraft and occult beliefs appear to be as vibrant as ever. Former studies fundamentally framed the phenomenon incorrectly. As Henrietta Moore and Todd Sanders note, "far from being a set of irrational beliefs, [witchcraft] beliefs are a form of historical consciousness, a sort of social diagnostics" (2001, 20). Such beliefs participate in a burgeoning discourse about cultural transformations, the meaning of existence, and ethical responsibilities.

Postcolonial studies have advanced an understanding of the ambiguous and fluid dimensions of witchcraft and its overlap with other notions of power. The contributors to Jean Comaroff and John Comaroff's *Modernity and Its Malcontents* (1993) and to Moore and Sanders's *Magical Interpretations, Material Realities* (2001) generally insist on situating the witchcraft discourse in the context of market values, urban creations, new political conflicts, social identities, and globalizing networks. Among them, Rijk van Dijk makes the especially useful point that we should try to see witchcraft in the modern setting more in terms of its "role in the construction of the critical politics of identity" (Moore and Sanders 2001, 113). Van Dijk develops this idea specifically with reference to the rising popularity of Pentecostalism wherein the witchcraft discourse becomes a "creative space where … identities of being 'born-again,' of being 'delivered' from the bonds with a past, are produced" (2001, 112), a soteriological theme reproduced in Aladura churches as well. Among Aladura in Liberia and beyond, the discourse converges with new markets, media forms, technologies, the circularity of goods, and the crisscrossing of medical cosmologies.

Other new works on the witchcraft discourse have combined attention to the postcolonial or global contexts of occult power with philosophical and theological explorations. Adam Ashforth (2005) insists that in order to understand witchcraft one needs to see how the "forms of agency embodied in material substances, objects, and images can be made to seem plausible" (121). This attention to plausibility involves more than translation of "one culture to another"; it includes as well understanding how claims about spirits, witches, and forces apply to everyone, and "not only by Africans" (120–21). Ashforth contends that one needs "to take seriously the notions of 'force' that people use when they worry about invisible forces or evil forces—implicated in matters such as witchcraft, the action of evil spirits, or the wrath of the ancestors—and investigate the dynamics of relations wherein worries about these forces arise" (17). Throughout his body of work Ashforth suggests the unpredictable, indeterminate, and imprecise nature of witchcraft beliefs and that ultimately it evokes something ineffable.

Geschiere criticizes anthropological studies about witchcraft that have posited a radical opposition between reality and fantasy. In its actual context witchcraft assumes an unclear boundary between domains of reality and fantasy (1997, 20; Nyamnjoh 2001, 28–32).[3] Taking a phenomenological position, Geschiere insists that if we seriously explore the concrete depiction of witchcraft we cannot reduce it to other categories or terms. However, Geschiere gives a cautionary note: while the effective researcher must assume a blurring between the real and the imaginary, this does not mean he or she forswears the critical judgment of ideas about witchcraft (1997, 20–22). Cameroonian philosopher Elias Bongmba also criticizes attempts to explain away witchcraft and to reduce it to social and political terms. Bongmba stresses the need for a philosophical and theological critique of witchcraft that places it in the context of cultural ethics. He also explores witchcraft in relation to his own Wimbum background and experience as a pastor in Wimbum Baptist churches. Bongmba acknowledges that he does not understand witchcraft (*tfu*) and even doubts its reality, but he cannot deny the impact of this belief on Wimbum relationships. He develops a hermeneutical approach based on Emanuel Levinas's notion of metaphysical desire and openness to the human other. In his review of African theological approaches he seems to suggest that a truly "emancipatory discourse" must address, if not appropriate, the particular locative dimensions of witchcraft (2001a, 104).

Aladura descriptions about witchcraft, occult power, and unwelcomed spirits had an empirical and intentional quality. Aladura doctrine epitomized practical theology: that is, it became most persuasively articulated through involvement in the daily praxis of ritual and social life. Fortunately for my work, even the formal question-answer interview occasioned such intentionality. The interview offered a chance for one "to testify" to his or her experience with affliction and healing. Such "life histories" indeed provided vivid descriptions about the supernatural world, about the sources of affliction and health. Like Bellman's Kpelle informants, the Aladura demonstrated considerable regard for the context of communication. But, unlike the Kpelle, they discouraged the secret. Indeed the Aladura way and ritual struggle worked for the exposure of power—especially forms that involved witchcraft—of jina liaisons, and of the use of secret texts. Such exposures went hand in hand with the church's interpretations of reality. And yet, the circularity of power, or the circularity of signs, made inevitable the relapse into secrets.

The assemblage of varied stories, performances, miracles, dreams, and visions revealed (and exposed) the intersection of this world and other world realities, which can be understood, in Marc Auge's terms, as a "universe of meaning, a symbolic universe, in which they are inscribed" (1994, 63). Nothing is accidental or happens by chance, because "Everything is a sign." As Auge notes, this does not mean that signs yield proof or suggest totality: they also remain ambivalent, resisting precision. The stories about witchcraft, jina, and powerful persons always suggested uncertainty, the unspoken secret, the moving shadow, and the disruptive happening. Witchcraft discussions took place in the context of constantly shifting and ambiguous relationships. A consensus rarely formed about the character of this or that person with regard to his access to and use of suspect, invisible powers. The more I explored the topic, the more I became aware of the gaps in knowledge and experience.

WITCH FORMS AND SIGNS

Once when I talked with the junior minister Flomo about the problems caused by witchcraft, he listed the following types of witch, or witch forms, and the signs they created:

1) A witch who eats human beings
2) A witch who takes away someone's luck
3) A witch who destroys or kills a man
4) A witch who brings luck
5) A witch who makes someone popular
6) A witch who stops a human being from coming to Earth

Flomo did not intend the list above to represent exclusive types. Indeed, in other contexts he spoke about certain witch figures in terms that applied to two or three of those mentioned above.[4] The list demonstrates that the witch was best known and described in terms of the deeds he or she produced. Thus I encountered situations in which ministers diagnosed different sources causing a patient's problem and saw no contradiction in this. Also, though some informants insisted on a sharp distinction between witchcraft and jina, others did not. Despite invoking horrific images about witchcraft, descriptions, discussions, and social dramas also on occasion included an element of the comic or ludicrous. Van Dijk notes how Pentecostal ideology "created the space to experience witchcraft in terms of mockery, laughter, and amusement" (2001, 99). The ludic element helped soften the edge of confrontation, ease the conflict, or mediate the encounter between opposing sides. The identified witch's secret side, the jina's odd behavior, the effects of placing signs might prompt laughter and derisive judgment as well as tears and words of caution. It was seldom the case that an informant's descriptions did not include an ironic smile or laughing dismissal.

In the ethnography on witchcraft the anthropophagic image appears as one of the most ubiquitous and poignant for suggesting the enervation, disease, and death of an individual (Lewis 1986, 63–77). Aladura informants contended the witch devoured the person physically, spiritually, and materially—body, soul, and fortune. Some applied this representation to any witch; others insisted that it applied to only certain types of witches. Modee once spoke to me about the Society of Earth that increased its membership by eating human beings. When an individual wanted to join the society for physical or material gain, he was expected to offer a sacrificial victim. In a nocturnal ceremony members invoked the name of the victim, whose spirit appeared before them and which they then placed in a fire. The next morning the victim, on this side, would be found dead. The society also caused epidemics and disease by polluting water supplies with "so-so human grease." Modee related to me a story about a female patient with an enlarged stomach who was admitted into the Faith Home and underwent a series of spiritual treatments. During a midnight struggle a senior prophet revealed that he had seen her consuming human flesh in the company of society members. He stressed that unless the woman confessed to this horrific deed, her stomach would remain enlarged and she would die. The patient ignored the prophecy until the victim visited her in a dream. Eventually she confessed and passed, according to Modee, "fresh lumps of meat," which were placed in a jar and shown to other members. It was not uncommon for prophets and healers in Paynesville to keep closed jars or containers of unseemly materials issued and extracted from patient's bodies—excrement, mucus, worms, and vermin—as proofs of magical prowess. The object might appear to the human eye as mucus or vermin, but the spiritually astute could discern the sign of a miscreant's deeds.

Again, it should be stressed, the Society of Earth's anthropophagic deeds took place on the other side, the dream world, but had terrible consequences for their victims in the waking world. Members might look like ordinary people, but the true prophet could expose the invisible witch forms and reveal how an unseen reality could impinge on the visible material realm. Here Gittins's comments concerning Mende references to anthropophagy are appropriate: "What to us might be dismissed as a dream or nightmare, depends first on our determination of what is 'real' experience. For the Mende . . . , the experience of meeting the witches and being given human flesh was 'real'; the details were secondary" (1987, 165).

In *The Mask of Anarchy* (2006), his stunning account of the Liberian Civil War, Stephen Ellis indicates that the "idiom of eating" humans went beyond metaphor. His study, however, deals with events of such extreme violence and unimaginable terror that, by comparison, the cannibal image seems passé. When I lived in Liberia, I heard ministers in mainline churches use the idiom in an obviously metaphorical way. A student (with Mano background) from Liberia Baptist Theological Seminary once delivered a sermon in a Gola village church in which he spoke about Mano "eating" Gola and Gola "eating" Mano. The audience laughed, many nodding their heads in agreement. In the context of the sermon, though, he had used the idiom of eating to talk about hate and envy between tribal groups, insisting that this was not the "Christian way." The idiom of eating obtained power as either metaphor or literal event. The Aladura prophet more often took for granted the porous boundaries between this world and that world. Indeed it was central to how he managed the healing process.

Nege: The Water Witch

Members often used anthropophagic imagery in describing a kind of Bassa witch known as Nege (Neegee), the "Water Leopard." This witch made its home in rivers, streams, and lagoons. Little (1951, 223) and Bellman (1975, 141–42) both report in detail the belief in water spirits among the Mende and Kpelle groups, who called them dream spirits or jina rather than witches. Informants who had migrated to Paynesville from other regions spoke of dangerous water spirits back home, but had come to see the Nege as more threatening. Among coastal Liberians the Nege appeared in the waking world in their ordinary form, but on the other side, the dream side, they had witch forms. They were also believed to take animal forms, especially those associated with water—hippopotamus, crocodile, frog, fish, snake, and turtle. People who loved to fish, swim, or work near the water might be suspected of being Nege.

On the other side, the Nege lived in towns and cities under the water. They tried to live like ordinary people, but they had one big problem: they were unable to procreate. Therefore, in order to increase their fold, they either kidnapped random victims or recruited new members who provided victims. When a person drowned or was killed by a crocodile, it might be thought that his or her spirit had been captured by the Nege.[5] As one prophet noted, the Nege "had the power to call you from a town if they want to have you. You will feel happy just to bathe. When you come they will kill you, by causing you to drown. They will take parts of your body—eyes, ears, toes, fingers, nose, lips, and penis." Those who chose to become Nege were expected to sacrifice a human being, usually a carefully chosen relative or friend. The new member gave the name of the victim to the Nege, who, on that side, feasted on his body for three days. On the first day the victim had a "fever sickness"; on the second day he became medically incurable; on the third day he died.

The Nege's strategy involved deceiving the victim to think that he had only a natural disorder. When he became aware of its true nature, it was too late. The victim's only hope was in the prophet's spiritual treatments. Such patients were not uncommon in the Aladura Faith Home. During Tabborrar at St. Peter's, I became friends with one, a Bassa man in his mid-twenties who was a skilled mechanic. He came from an interior branch and had been brought to the Paynesville headquarters by his minister for special treatments. He had been suffering from fevers and headaches, which were diagnosed as Nege-related. The minister named the man's wife and her lover as the responsible parties. He claimed the wife's lover belonged to the Nege Society and had persuaded her to join. But first they needed to arrange for the sacrifice of the mechanic with the assistance of a "medicine man" who knew the effective technique. The patient told me that without the church's help he surely would have died. He also put his two children in the care of his mother, since he believed his wife wanted to harm them as well.

Whenever a minister diagnosed a Nege case, he almost always requested that the patient remain in the Faith Home, where he might receive greater protection from the witch power. Immediately he began a twenty-one-day "circle bath" with candles and incense treatment. The candles were black, red, and blue. The black candles, which represented a negative power, "broke down" the witch's hold; the red candles revived the patient's life, his blood; the blue candles created a screen of protection around the patient. The treatment also involved using devil's incense, a potion especially effective in fighting witchcraft and jina. The circle formation, the burning candles, the smoke from incense, the declaration of holy names and the recitation of psalms served to wrest the witch's power from the patient.

The Dragon Witch

The witch who used Dragon was among the most feared by the Bassa and people in the Paynesville area. One prophet described Dragon as the witch's "working instrument." This power brought the witch riches, fortune, and popularity but always through someone else's misfortune, sickness, or death. To the natural eye, Dragon appeared like a rope or string. The witch using Dragon kept it in his house, hidden in a pillowcase, bag, or pot, or he wore it underneath his clothes, perhaps around his waist. He might also bury it at the entrance to his home. In the invisible world Dragon had a snake form, with one, three, or seven heads. According to one Bassa prophet, it rarely happened that a person was born with Dragon; more often, he "caught" Dragon either through his own devices or through the assistance of a wayward country doctor. People usually sought knowledge about Dragon during times of desperate financial hardship or social stress, when they hoped for quick solutions. A person who went swiftly from extreme misfortune to startling success might easily be suspected of working with Dragon. Ministers also claimed that village elders and zoes used Dragon in order to punish social miscreants. As such, it became an instrument of law and authority.

Even ministers could become vulnerable to the temptation of using Dragon. Once when I asked an Aladura minister about the church's use of devil's incense, the topic eventually turned to the problem of ministers using inappropriate powers and medicines, including Dragon. He told me about a minister at one AIC church who kept Dragon in a country pot that was invisible to ordinary eyes. The Dragon enabled the minister to receive secret information about people, which he falsely presented as divine messages. But once the church recognized the true source of the minister's power he became insane, and he left the church.

Informants maintained that older women, often barren, used Dragon most effectively. The woman who kept Dragon needed to provide it with an annual sacrifice. If she did not, Dragon would turn against her and cause her misfortune, possibly death. When she chose to use Dragon, she placed the rope on the ground and sprinkled it either with drops of a "blood-black substance" or with a powder made from mushrooms. She then spoke certain words to the rope, which brought it to life, turning it into a snake with "a head that talked." After bringing Dragon to life, the owner might use it in several ways. She might place it in a victim's pathway, which would cause paralysis when he stepped on it. The witch might put Dragon's poisonous saliva in a guest's food and water or send Dragon to his room after he fell asleep. Dragon would study the physical condition of the targeted person, rejecting persons with defects, which might have been caused by jina or an unseen power and made them immune to Dragon's poison.

If Dragon was pleased with the prospects, it usually made two or three trips before completing its work. On the first trip, when it studied the victim, Dragon licked or bit the victim's side. The mild discomfort the victim experienced soon gave way to fever, headaches, vomiting, diarrhea, and a loss of appetite. The symptoms might appear "natural," like a case of pneumonia or malaria. Eventually paralysis would set in through Dragon's constant licking or biting. On subsequent trips Dragon would "suck out the blood" of the victim, evidenced by the victim's growing weakness. If the afflicted one was a child, and she cried out during the night, it meant that Dragon was effectively draining the child of her lifeblood. Ministers described this as "swallowing the soul" of the afflicted one.

One minister told me about an elderly woman in his hometown whom residents believed had kept Dragon. Parents warned their children about crying out loud lest Dragon swallowed the sounds of their cries. A local country doctor was able to defeat Dragon by pounding a mortar and pestle. The Dragon swallowed the sound of each pounding. After a week the woman became sick and the country doctor claimed that she had a stick in her stomach, which had swelled like a pregnant woman's. The country doctor also discovered that the woman had borrowed Dragon from a chief, who kept it underneath a tree in the form of a thread. The country doctor unearthed the thread and burned it. Both the elderly woman and the chief eventually died.

Dragon-related maladies were commonly treated at the Aladura Faith Home. Most involved infants and small children sometimes described as being "fed" to Dragon by the witch. Once during the late rainy season an Aladura cross bearer brought her ten-year-old niece to the Faith Home for treatments. The little girl suffered from fevers, diarrhea, and dehydration. The prophet assigned to her case soon diagnosed her malady as Dragon-related. Later he identified an older female relative as the culprit, whose sudden success had aroused suspicions, though this would never be made public. The older relative stayed in the Faith Home with the child but had disapproved of the treatments being applied. On one occasion she prevented the ministers from giving the child the burning incense treatment, which they believed was necessary in order to keep Dragon away. In the minds of many Faith Home dwellers, the relative's actions confirmed the suspicions about her witchcraft. Eventually the child died.

A young pregnant woman and the fetus she carried were considered especially vulnerable targets of a Dragon witch, who attempted either to kill the pregnant woman or to feed her fetus to Dragon. Informants called miscarriages the work of Dragon. The power represented, in Flomo's words, one form of "a witch who stops a human being from coming on earth." In one Aladura church a pregnant woman was admitted to the Faith Home complaining of nightmares in which a snake attempted to lie with her. The prophets identified the snake as Dragon and accused her husband's first mate, an older barren wife, of sending the snake into her bed. In another church, I knew a woman, actually a senior member, whom prophets had accused of keeping a Dragon, which she had "used to kill many babies." At night she turned into a "zo-witch" and carried out her work. The church tried to get her to confess, but she always denied any wrong. Eventually she suffered from "witch skin," an affliction that caused her skin to spot and to itch without relief. In such cases the only cure was confession.

Aladura informants claimed that only the prophet church could effectively treat Dragon-related sickness, because only the "spiritually trained" prophet saw beyond appearances. Dragon sickness always appeared as natural sickness. Western medicine could treat the symptoms but was unable to deal with the true source. The country doctor was also able to see beyond appearances, but from the Aladura perspective he might also be in cahoots with the Dragon witch, if not be one himself. When Dragon invaded the church grounds, the prophet could see its tracks in the yard, hear its "ca-ca-ca" sound, and protect the victim from its vampirism.

As in the case of Nege-related problems, spiritual treatment always involved using a circle candle bath and burning incense. As the patient knelt within a circle of candles, the ministers prayed over her. The healer also fumigated the area with incense. Both the candle flames and the incense helped create a screen between the patient and Dragon. Such treatments always took place in the Faith Home, which provided the focusing lens, or the grounding, for dealing with spiritual maladies. The treatment usually necessitated a house consecration, which drew from the Faith Home's power and the struggles performed there.

The Personal Witch: "The Witch Who Takes a Man's Luck"

Stories about individuals who incurred financial misfortune because of another's witchcraft were quite common in the church. Some informants called the witch who robbed another person of his success a personal witch. This witch frequently targeted men with steady jobs and businesses, market women, and high-school and college students. He caused a person to lose his money, business, property, farm, or job, and to fail in school and in sports. The personal witch also caused accidents. However, the victim usually did not die but was only made to "suffer badly in the body." A temporary or permanent disability, for instance, would effectively prevent a person from being successful in certain occupations. Any witch might be so described since financial or material misfortune was always a possible outcome of witchcraft. For instance, though he primarily affected the body, the Nege might also cause his victim, say, if he were a merchant, to lose his business. But the Nege ultimately aimed for the victim's death. Therefore it was crucial that the prophet identify the true source of the problem and not mistake a Nege for a personal witch.

In all witchcraft cases I knew about, the witch was a relative, friend, or acquaintance. As one interlocutor put it, "almost all witching is within the family. But if a stranger or non-relation goes against the norm or harms someone, they can be called a witch. It is a dishonor or an evil to witch a stranger who has done no harm." But, as the term suggests, in the case of the personal witch, these associations were even more emphasized. One prophet informed me that witchcraft did not work effectively on strangers. "The witch who took away a man's luck" always used something that had belonged to the victim, either from among his possessions, such as a book, comb, or piece of clothing, or that came from his body, such as hair or nails. He would "take your clothes, cut them up, and put signs inside them. Then he would bury them. This would take away your luck, your job." The personal witch might employ the help of a country doctor, who would place the stolen items in a bottle with other "medicines" and "plant" the bottle in the victim's yard. Landowners and merchants were frequent victims of a personal witch. In Faith Home cases the patient did not return to his home or business until prophets had consecrated the yard or premises. Consecration required locating the bottle and neutralizing its power. But only the country doctor, I was told, could unearth it. The prophets tried to perform the consecration surreptitiously, often after midnight, hoping not to arouse the interest of neighbors.

Prophets frequently warned individuals about the witchcraft of others in workplaces and schools. Members needed to be careful about whom they ate with, whom they shared personal information with, and whom they took home. A personal witch might cause a person to be denied promotion or a raise in wages or salary. He might be a fellow worker who competed for a new position and who believed his success could happen only through the failure of his fellow worker. Interestingly a Nigerian businessman once commented to me that Liberians used witchcraft in order to keep others down. He distinguished it from Nigerian witchcraft, which was used simply for personal gain and not for another's misfortune. Aside from the polemic of difference that this comparison suggests, it underlines the common perception that one's personal gain often involved another's loss. This idea applied to educational settings as well. Patients complained that another classmate's success in school came only at their own failure. The personal witch caused them to do poorly in school, to fail exams, often making them sick with fever, headaches, or stomach pains. Prophets warned students about signs placed in clothes, books, and food.

The personal witch imagery relates to the cultural and social exigencies of the Liberian landscape: urban migrations, new industries, competition among both unskilled and skilled labor forces, and the increased value of technical training. Undoubtedly, in the period since World War II Paynesville City had become a more acquisitive and competitive place. One might argue that the personal witch functioned as an appropriate symbol for the advance of individualism over community. In the Aladura context references to the personal witch betrayed a fundamental distrust about new public arenas. This distrust was also expressed in the traditional city-country dichotomy. The Aladura frequently cautioned members about family and friends back home who might become jealous about their newly obtained success. The village was not an idyllic community but a place where deceit and witchcraft abounded. Some members expressed more concern about the rule of elders and zoes than about the competition of work companions and schoolmates. This trope, however, served to reinforce the more immediate danger of the town environs with their always changing social terrain.

Bottle in the Yard

The consecration of houses, work sites, and private businesses[6] took place when a prophet discerned that a person's affliction was caused by the work of a proximate witch, such as a Nege or personal witch, who had made the area toxic and uninhabitable. The sick person would be asked to remain in the Faith Home for treatments and not return to the affected site until it had been properly purified, consecrated, and made safe. The treatment of Dragon- and Nege-related cases often entailed performing house consecrations. St. Peter's practiced two kinds of house consecration: public and secret. The public consecration occurred during daytime hours on a Monday or Wednesday, which were considered auspicious days for ritual events. The public consecration took place when the patient's condition was well under control; thus it would not matter if neighbors knew about it. The ministers placed candles throughout the property, sprinkled or splashed it with holy water, and fumigated it with incense. The secret consecration, in contrast, took place only at night, with windows and doors closed. Ministers tried to make sure that neighbors were not able to see the struggle.

A place, such as a chapel, house, or business location, became bad for a person when it was believed a witch, say, a personal witch, had "planted something in the yard." Ministers often described this something as a bottle or jar of "medicine" that included a mixture of animal parts and organs; pieces of the victim's clothes, hair, or nails; and bodily issues, such as spittle, feces, and blood. The bottle slowly contaminated the lot, making its owner and those who lived there inexplicably ill. One minister told me the Aladura prophet "did not have the power to dig it up, only to quench it." If he possessed such power, then he was a "juju man also." However, the prophet could "see it in a vision, point to the spot." Through ritual techniques, such as the house consecration, he could prevent the jar from moving about and spreading its cancer, and then he could neutralize its power.

For the house consecration the ministers placed three candles in every room of the house, and in the case of a public consecration, throughout the yard. Candles were set up along the property lines, creating, as it were, a fence of virtue. Then the ministers fumigated the entire property with burning incense. Next they consecrated a bucket of water with prayers and psalms, such as Psalms 23, 27, and 35 that stressed protection from misfortune and defeating one's enemies. The ministers also added salt and Florida water to the water, elements that checked the movement and neutralized the effects of the mystic poison. The water was sprinkled or sprayed throughout the house and yard. Before the doorway the ministers took the remaining salt and formed a cross on the ground. With their rods they signed invisible crosses over each window.

Some house consecrations involved sheep sacrifice, especially when the subject was threatened with death. The life of the sheep replaced the life of the patient. The sacrifice took place at the Faith Home, near the holy bell. With the patient holding the sheep, the ministers surrounded the pair with candles. Psalms and prayers of consecration were read. The immolation occurred at noon. As one minister described it, we "watched for the direction of the sun, since it must directly touch the sheep before you kill it. Mostly this is done in the dry season when the sun's power is greatest, which is the power of God." The ministers cut the sheep's throat, making sure blood flowed into a hole dug beneath the holy bell. The ministers also caught some blood in a pan and carried it to the patient's house for the consecration. They mixed salt with the blood and poured it into a hole dug at the house's entrance, covered the hole, and lit a candle placed over the hole. They waited at the house until the candle had completely burned down. As one minister told me, the blood of the sheep prevented the contents of the evil medicine from spreading into the house. The house consecration completed, the prophets encouraged the patient to return home. The church stressed, however, that reoccurrence of the illness was possible if the patient did not remain strong in the faith, trusting in the church's power. The noxious bottle, after all, had not been removed, only held in check. Its venom could be reactivated if the subject became careless.

Magical Persons: Zoes, Country Doctors, and Twins

Aladura informants considered zoes to be primary practitioners of secret and potentially dangerous power. This included the ability to use African signs, considered a morally neutral power but used by unscrupulous people for immoral purposes. From the Aladura perspective the zo rarely resisted the temptations presented by secret power if it could be used to bring fame and wealth. Though, generally speaking, the Aladura were more charitable toward Western science, this regard was not without ambivalence. The products of Western science (airplanes, weapons, hospitals, cars) also brought new temptations. The emergence of new state orders (or disorders), global economies, Internet commerce, and technologies simply offered new means for the navigation of occult power and witchcraft beliefs.

Liberian ethnography has made clear the role of the male or female zo in indigenous culture. Though they might be guardians of social order, it was commonly believed that the zoes did not obtain power, or live to be old, without engaging in secret transactions. Aladura informants routinely associated the zo with the traditional societies, such as Poro and Sande. Therefore they voiced strong suspicion, and indeed disapproval, about the role of these groups, and the community regarded them with ambivalence. One Aladura prophet described the zo as "the old man of the country, the big witch, who killed children and caused sickness." He claimed that zoes adeptly caused stomach problems with poison. They took the clothing of their victim and "burned it with African signs," causing sickness and even death. In my experience the Aladura church more readily denounced participation in a traditional society than did mission-related churches. For instance, I knew a Baptist minister in a nearby Bassa village who was also a member of a local Poro Society. The Aladura in Liberia, however, insisted that members should leave behind "society business" and trust the Aladura way.

The Aladura often criticized the country doctor (who might also be a zo), whose techniques and medicine might be used for good but also for harmful purposes. Country doctors treated problems caused by witches and spirits; but from the Aladura perspective they also collaborated with forces that brought harm to others. In Paynesville there were AIC Bassa prophets who were also licensed country doctors. They received unremitting criticism from Aladura ministers, who saw the country doctor's medicine as a form of occult power. Depending on context, however, this polemic could turn on itself. The discourse implied the proximity of invisible powers that even the most respected minister might fall prey to and the rhetoric of prophetic mastery used against them.

Informants claimed that twins were also individuals whom others should respect and toward whom they should exercise caution. The Kpelle saw them as anomalies: "they blur categorized boundaries between nature and culture, since only animals have litters" (Erchak 1976, 23). They often became country doctors because they were born with supernatural gifts. Twins were able to see and move through the invisible world routinely. Indigenous Kpelle maintained that twins were "two brained" (Bellman 1975, 156–57) and that they demonstrated two forms of consciousness, one for the waking world, the other for the dreaming. Gittins notes that the Mende believed twins had spirits with "anomalous power" that needed to be domesticated. As he notes, "If not domesticated early on, that child will be volatile, unpredictable, and demanding. The spirits of twins are regarded as particularly strong and a mother may leave the baby exposed in the sun during the day—known as 'cooking the twin'—not to harm or kill it, but to subdue or 'cook' its spirit so that the twin will be obedient and domesticated, rather than too demanding and individualistic" (92).

According to Gittins, the Mende clearly distinguish between those individuals who have *honei*, "witch-power/spirit," and those who are simply called *honamoi*, "witches." The former have power that represents a "disposition," that is involuntary and not necessarily destructive to others. The latter have an inherent power that they willingly activate for malicious purposes. Twins fall under the category of honei, so their power should not be confused with that of witches (158–59).

Twins born into an Aladura family were required to undergo a process of domestication. They must be "churched," or otherwise the children might become zoes, which were always potentially enemies of the church. And any "enemy" of the church, whatever form he or she took, might be considered a witch. By churching twin children, the Aladura transformed the elemental power they received at birth into something beneficial. Such children, provided they continued within the Aladura way, might become prophets and prophetesses. Flomo (who had Kpelle background) believed that twins represented opposite tendencies. One became good, the other bad; one might become a prophet, the other a witch. During a two-month period St. Peter's ministers treated a woman afflicted by a neighbor's witchcraft. Her twins were also closely observed. Flomo, for one, believed the twins had already demonstrated opposite tendencies. His evaluation accords with Gerald Erchak's description of the Kpelle view of twins: they "are said to become medicine-persons (*zonga*) because of their affinity with the world of spirits," and the Kpelle sometimes "allege that only one twin will become a zo; the zo will make himself known through his behavior, e.g., he will be bold, aggressive and demanding" (1976, 23). But, in the case of Aladura twins, Flomo was confident that churching would benefit both twins.

JINA: BUSH SPIRITS AND MIGRATORY SIGNS

Along with witchcraft, the Aladura identified a second major cause of misfortune—the jina. Informants generally distinguished between witch and jina, but these distinctions were not absolute. I heard witches referred to as "evil jina" and jina called witches. One prophet described the jina as "the Great Witch," who, if provoked, could cause more problems than the witch. It should be noted, however, that witches were always humans, which was not the case with jina. Informants claimed that someone who wanted to "bring down" an individual and promote himself might, with the help of an expert in occult power, form a liaison with a jina, who expected absolute devotion in exchange for favors. In such liaisons informants described the jina as being "behind" the client: it affected his thoughts, words, and deeds in both the waking and dreaming worlds. Some prophets called the jina an "evil spirit" that could dwell in a person and cause him or her to think irrationally, do erratic things, and talk insensibly.

Traditionally jina were usually associated with the bush. Some informants called them "bush spirits." The term *jina* is probably related to the Arabic *jinn* used to refer to nonhuman spirits (Crapanzano 1973, 135). Through the influence of Islam in Sierra Leone and Liberia, the term became applicable to mountain, water, and forest spirits. Little mentions that the Mende called nature spirits *dyinyinga*, roughly translated "genii" (1951, 221). According to Vernon Dorjahn, the Temne used *jinn* for "non-ancestral spirits" distinguishable from "ancestral spirits" (1962, 3–8). D'Azevedo indicates that the Gola in Liberia referred to jina as the spirits of nature. They differed from the "ancestral spirits" and from the "spirits of evil persons, rejected by the world of the living and of the ancestors alike, wandering aimlessly about doing terrible deeds" (1966, 17). The Kpelle, as Bellman shows, also used the term for nature spirits and also for human beings called *wulu nuu*, "the stick people," who were "the second or dream brain of living persons who go about in their sleep killing their enemies" (1975, 146). The Bassa referred to bush spirits that lived in bounded spaces and became angry and vengeful toward persons who entered their space. They would demand appeasement with a sacrifice.

Though Liberian ethnography supports the idea of jina as dangerous, they were best understood as amoral, not immoral, beings. In their natural domain, alone and undisturbed, jina were harmless. They became immoral only in their relations with humans but not without an element of ambiguity. As d'Azevedo shows concerning the Gola (1966, 19–21), jina relations were potentially creative or destructive. Gifted individuals, such as artists, blacksmiths, and diviners, were commonly understood to have a jina behind them. Indeed, extraordinary talent and enduring success might be developed through a jina liaison.

Aladura descriptions of jina were similar. Informants recognized the benefits the jina liaison might bring, but more often they described the jina as tricky and dangerous. This view was also consistent with the Aladura image of the zo or country doctor, whose success could depend on access to the jina's power. The jina represented an option for success that thoroughly challenged the Aladura agenda. Furthermore, any success obtained through a jina liaison inevitably led to problems. The jina promised only temporary comfort and security. It was not humanly possible to give the jina the kind of devotion it expected continually.

When a subject's attention deviated, the trouble began. The price of fortune in one area meant loss in another. For instance, a female jina expected absolute devotion from her male partner. If married, he should neglect his wife; he should have no sexual interest whatsoever in her. Cases that involved spouse neglect might be diagnosed as caused by such a jina liaison. Breaking off the liaison meant for the subject depression, insanity, or falling into poverty.

A jina liaison could be chronic or continuous, an example of what Crapanzano (1973) calls a "symbiotic relationship" with a spiritual being.[7] Informants believed that some individuals were born with jina or became subject to one at an early age and found it difficult to break its hold. This could be the case even for church members. The jina helped them to be successful but also brought misfortune to their families. In some cases the jina might always remain with a person. An incorrigible problem, however, was not reason for despair; the person just needed to remain involved with the church, which would help him or her keep in check the powers of the jina.

In speaking about jina, the Aladura often described them in terms of "cold jina" and "hot jina." In the case of a cold jina, the afflicted person appeared normal and controlled; nothing about his or her behavior seemed immediately disturbing. The prophet "in power," however, knew otherwise: the calm might become erratic and the jina cause unexpected harm. He would suggest then that the subject enter the Faith Home for special treatments. At St. Peter's one such case involved a young man named Jonah.

Jonah and his "Cold Jina"

On the advice of friends, Jonah's family brought him to St. Peter's. A senior prophet from an interior branch known for his ability to heal mental disorders had just been appointed to the Faith Home. Jonah's family members hoped he might cure Jonah of his "craziness." When the prophet first prayed over Jonah, he delayed giving an immediate diagnosis. He suspected that Jonah had used drugs; this had made him vulnerable to evil spirits. He recommended that Jonah stay in the Faith Home for closer observation. Because his mental condition was uncertain, the prophet insisted that family members also stay in the Faith Home to help watch over him.

After Jonah had been observed and prayed over for three or four days, the senior prophet revealed that he was afflicted by a "cold jina." The young man often appeared calm and composed, but his mental instability and confusion were profound. Such deception was the special talent of this jina, which only the prophet's superior knowledge might detect. Having discerned that Jonah's "craziness" was caused by the cold jina, the senior prophet prescribed a "blanket treatment" with devil's incense. The treatment took place in the chapel behind the tent. The ministers always administered it during scheduled prayers, which occurred five or six times a day. While one minister or a cross bearer at the altar led the after-noon prayers, the other ministers took care of Jonah's treatment. They instructed him to sit on a cinder block and then covered him with a blanket. The ministers then placed a canister of burning devil's incense beneath the blanket and be-tween his legs. They then began praying over Jonah, reciting psalms and holy names. Throughout the prayers the senior prophet alternated between pressing his hand upon the crown of Jonah's head and tapping him on the head or shoul-ders with the holy rod. The ministers spent much of their time quietly watching Jonah as the incense burned down. It usually took about twenty minutes. They tried to make sure that Jonah stayed as still as possible and did not throw off the blanket or kick over the incense.

The senior prophet informed me that devil's incense "heated up" the patient so that the sickness might come to the surface and bring out the cold jina. Here a homology was assumed between the sickness and the jina. By bringing out the sickness through this ritual heat, the jina would become exposed. Beneath the surface of Jonah's seeming calm the ministers claimed to see the jina's true crafty and dangerous side. From time to time throughout his Faith Home convales-cence, the ministers also administered to Jonah a liquid form of devil's incense, which they concocted simply by adding powdered incense to Florida water. The ministers poured drops of this into Jonah's eye. They believed this prevented him from seeing the jina. They also poured it into his nose, which, according to one minister, sent the incense straight to the brain and "drained out the sickness back through the nose."

Jonah received the blanket treatment for seven days. He began to show signs of improvement. He spoke more coherently. His interactions with others appeared more open and relaxed. He came to require less supervision, though ministers continued to be careful about campus leaves. After the senior prophet suspended the blanket treatment, he prescribed for Jonah a three-day dry fast. It was impor-tant "to keep the heat going" that had been set into motion by the blanket treat-ment. A dry fast continued to help expose the cold jina and draw it out and away from the patient. Once Jonah finished the three-day dry fast, the ministers re-sumed the blanket treatment. This time they also submitted Jonah to a round of holy baths. They began with an ordinary bath, twice a day; but eventually it was revealed to the senior prophet that a circle bath with seven candles was neces-sary. He administered this bath at midnight, when the jina would always try to reassert its hold. Though Jonah's general demeanor improved, the senior prophet cautioned that his recovery had just begun and that other treatments were needed. However, against the prophet's advice Jonah's family decided to take him home. In my conversations with the ministers they worried about Jonah's fate: they believed the temptation of drugs remained. If he returned to using drugs and discontinued his prayers, the jina surely would return and again bring on mental confusion.

The term *hot* was used for jina that acutely and violently attacked their victims with obvious maladies. The cure for these victims would be seen more as a "one-shot affair." We should remember, however, that this distinction between a hot jina and a cold jina and the type of disorder they caused was never as final as one assumed. A jina might become manifest in either way. The prophet's diagnosis often allowed for a chameleon jina. It was more often the case that the prophet/healer determined the kind of jina that afflicted the subject through a gradual process of divination. As in Jonah's case, he did this with great caution. Identification came once the preliminary treatments had started. How a patient responded helped reveal the source of affliction. This was especially the case with jina, which could be more elusive than witches.

Bush Jina: Strangers, Cyclops, and Dwarf

The Aladura retained the traditional view that jina were territorial "bush spirits" that inhabited forests, rivers, swamps, and mountains. They harmed humans only when humans entered their domain. The church often warned members about traveling through the country or into bush, where they stood a greater chance of encountering a jina. The Aladura also referred to more adventuresome jina who became curious about the human world and left their natural abodes. They were warned about bush jina who became fellow travelers. The stranger you meet at a crossroads, in a money bus or bush taxi might be a jina who has assumed normal appearance. The jina might appear like a beautiful woman or handsome man and have "a nice smell that attracts humans." It was hard to resist its entreaties or favors, and if one submitted, one became bound to the jina. The jina might also become offended by the person's resistance and would try to punish her. Informants frequently mentioned mental confusion or insanity as a consequence of such resistance. I knew one woman, eighteen years old, who resisted a stranger "approaching her with love" whom she had met at the crossroads. The stranger caused her to start counting and told her that she would become his slave if she ever stopped. Her family brought her to St. Peter's Faith Home in a state of delirium, in which she was still counting numbers. Apostle Olu identified the stranger as an "evil spirit," performed a preliminary exorcism, and admitted the young woman into the Faith Home for spiritual treatments. The ministers later insisted that the malady was caused by a jina.

The admonitions about the jina as the dangerous stranger resembled those about the witch as family member or friend. The former related to the demographic and geographic disruptions precipitated by new migrations, forms of travel, and the flow of goods; the latter, whether in its traditional or modern context, implied the circumstances of familiarity damaged by competition and self-interest. In either case, for the Aladura one needed to be aware that people were never what they seemed. In her study of Sierra Leonean descriptions of bush spirits, Rosalind Shaw sees possible evocation of the travesties of past warfare and slave trading: "So while bush spirits raided towns and roamed the bush and roads, 'seizing' unlucky and unprotected victims, and light skinned water spirits bestowed money and commodities upon men in Faustian (an ultimately life-depleting) exchanges, the ancestors and town spirits defended the town as invisible warriors" (2002, 55). Other qualities and meanings were layered onto the spirit forms, but, according to Shaw, they also appeared "to crystallize many of the attributes of those who raided and traded for slaves" (55). Undoubtedly the disruptive changes during and since the Doe regime have facilitated the morphing of former domestic or bush spirits into migratory rogue predators.

Informants did not lack vivid descriptions about the bush jina's visible form. Some Aladura spoke about a kind of cyclops jina—it had one eye in the middle of its forehead that shone like the headlight of a car. Human activities especially attracted this jina, and occasionally it left its forest domain and ventured into villages. One minister told me about a boy in Lofa County who received a visit from such a jina while he was preparing a late-night supper in a country kitchen. The jina spoke to the boy, but he was unable to understand him. The jina then hit the boy, who fainted. The family took the boy to a hospital, but the medical staff was unable to treat the malady, since it was a spiritual problem. Finally, they brought him to a Faith Home where he underwent extensive holy treatments. The minister claimed that the jina continued to appear "spiritually" in the boy's dreams,[8] but became incapable of hurting him physically.

Among informants, a frequently mentioned bush jina was called Dwarf. Members spoke about Dwarf (both singular and plural). These small beings had long faces and noses, heavy eyebrows, and long teeth. They had short legs and large torsos, on which appeared a second face. As a group, they blinked, spoke, and moved in tandem; they always walked backwards. If you ever saw a Dwarf in the bush and began to treat it like a little boy, it would become angry, grow into a large man, and beat you. One minister claimed that his conversion to the Aladura church came after he miraculously survived a fight with several Dwarf jina. Early one morning, while he passed through a forest, he came upon a circle of the Dwarf. They were offended by his presence, so they seized him, beat him unconscious, and placed him on the railroad tracks. Fortunately Aladura people who were going for morning prayers found him and carried him to the church. The jina had caused him to become "dumb"; but after about four months of spiritual treatment he recovered his speech.

The Dwarf, however, were not always so malicious. Some were attracted to humans and sought to exchange favors with them. Members often recognized a comical side to the Dwarf; but they were dangerous nonetheless. Informants believed that contact with the jina caused mental derangement and "sexual disorders." At one AIC I visited, the ministers diagnosed a young man's sexual interest in other men as being Dwarf-influenced. They also reported that he had dreams and visions of the Dwarf trying to bite him, causing the erratic behavior of a hot jina. More often, though, informants attributed homosexuality to the work of another jina known as Night-man, who might appear like a cold jina.

Night-man/Night-woman: Dream Liaisons

The jina that caused more sexual and reproductive problems than any other jina was one who appeared as either Night-man or Night-woman. In general, Night-man created problems for women; Night-woman did so for men, though now and then roles reversed. Night-man appeared to women as a handsome man; Night-woman to men as a beautiful woman. In a dream the jina would attempt to make love to the human subject and often succeeded in doing so. The love relation in the dream world had effects for the waking world. The jina provided its partner with material and financial rewards in exchange for the subject's loyalty. But the liaison also caused sexual or reproductive problems—sterility, impotency, and infertility. A man's nocturnal emissions, which in the Faith Home caused pollution, could be attributed to Night-woman's advances. If a man resisted the jina's overtures, or attempted to get out of a present liaison, the jina could cause him misfortune. He might lose his wealth, his family, and his sanity. An individual's life might demonstrate a cycle of fortune and misfortune based on his standing with the jina. In such cases the church's diagnosis and treatment were not considered one-shot affairs.

A self-deluded man or woman might prefer the material success the jina offered. The jina's expectations of devotion, however, always increased, severely testing the subject's commitment. Eventually the jina expected its partner to sacrifice a friend or family member; a man or woman's sexual abstinence was no longer enough to reassure the jina of his or her fidelity. The liaison might indeed lead to the subject's own death, required as a final proof of devotion. Though Night-man usually affected the behavior of women, informants claimed he could affect men as well through a homosexual liaison. Because of a man's relation with Night-man, he lost interest in women and became attracted instead to other men. Night-woman was capable of affecting women in the same way. Such relationships demonstrated the symbiotic characteristics of a "cold jina," which might always remain with a person.

The prophet also had to be careful about Night-woman's sly advances. One minister informed me that the spirit could still enter dreams, engender libidinous thoughts, and cause a nocturnal emission. Such an occurrence resulted in the prophet's loss of virtue and spoiled a struggle he may have been undertaking.

If he happened to be sleeping within the chapel, a church consecration would be in order. Thus the ministers, especially the younger ones, were warned that by "not praying strongly enough you can be overcome by these evil spirits."

One junior minister insisted that the reason that the Aladura church attracted so many women had to do with its ability to treat mental and sexual disorders caused by Night-man. A woman might be affected mentally because she had tried to resist Night-man's entreaties. She might become infertile because she had accepted the liaison. Though Night-man worked mainly through dreams, it was understood that he might enter the waking world, usually as a stranger. The jina's overtures initiated in the waking world could also continue into the dream world. The holy grounds of the Faith Home, if properly consecrated, provided ample protection for the patient: it was too strong for Night-man, who eventually realized his interest best lay elsewhere. Though Night-man might continue to appear in her dreams, his influence decreased through proper treatment.

Mami Wata (Mammy Water)

Mami Wata was usually described as a mermaidlike figure, part woman, part fish, whom men encountered in lagoons, lakes, and rivers. Sometimes she assumed a fully human form, as when she visited diamond, gold, and iron ore mines, which always attracted her. She was often associated with money, banks, and places of wealth. One minister told me that one should never keep money one found in the bush or in a deserted area, since Mami Wata often used it to trap her victim. The minister also claimed that, if in a forest sojourn one came upon a pot of rice boiling without fire, one should not eat the rice, however hungry he might be, since Mami Wata might have cooked it.

Mami Wata beliefs have been well documented throughout West and Central Africa. The recent publications edited by Henry John Drewal and coauthored by Drewal and others (both 2008) attest to the pervasive influence and the cultic ubiquity of Mami Wata (and Mami Wata–like beliefs) throughout sub-Saharan Africa and the African diaspora. These publications also alert us to the perceived ambiguities and contested claims concerning Mami Wata. Among the Igbo of Nigeria, one finds organized Mami Wata cults that mix indigenous, Christian, and Hindu elements (Drewal 1988, 38–40). Mei-Mei Sanford observes the tendency in southern Nigeria to gloss distinctions between female water deities, including Osun, and Mami Wata (2001, 239). One can also observe this tendency in Liberia and Sierra Leone, where ideas about female water spirits were widespread. Mami Wata beliefs have been expressed through public settings in Sierra Leone for several decades. According to John Nunley, the Freetown Jolly Festival has much to do with male access and management of female power, which, for many participants, became recognizable in Mami Wata forms (2008, 73–78). In Liberia I was not aware of any public rites or groups dedicated to Mami Wata; but reports about Mami Wata beliefs have circulated at least since the 1960s. In the late 1960s the psychiatrist Ronald Wintrob, who worked at the Catherine Mills Rehabilitation Center in Paynesville, treated male patients who believed that their mental problems came from Mami Wata's influence (1970, 143–56).

Aladura interlocutors also claimed that Mami Wata had light skin and long golden hair. Her two prized possessions were a comb and a mirror. She loved combing her hair and gazing into the mirror. She could be seen in both the waking and dream worlds. According to one of Wintrob's informants, one usually gained contact with Mami Wata through the aid of an occult expert. The expert provided his client with Mami Wata's comb and instructed him to remain celibate for six months, after which the jina appeared in his dream and asked for her comb. The client needed to withhold the comb since he would then lose everything, become sick, and possibly die if he returned it (1970, 145–46).

Aladura informants stressed that Mami Wata caused greed and deceit in her clients, who put aside their moral qualms for the sake of an amorous liaison and the material benefits it might bring. As in the case of Night-woman, this liaison involved a contract of fidelity: the mermaid bestowed riches in exchange for undivided devotion. She made love with the one who sought her and became jealous at any attention he gave to others.[9] Though other jina prompted greater concern, Mami Wata remained a danger and not infrequently became a topic of discussion among members, who remained aware of the potential harm she could cause. This approach contrasted significantly with that of the Aladura of southern Nigeria, who regarded devotion to Mami Wata in more positive terms. Sanford mentions one case in which an Aladura prophet told a member who had found herself in the jina's hold that she "needed to learn to live with it" (2001, 245). Aladura ministers in Liberia also recommended that in some cases one needed "to learn to live with" a jina, but I never heard a minister say this concerning a Mami Wata liaison. In a world of economic turns and social change, she became a trope for self-interest and greed, which one always guarded against. The mermaid jina revealed, as if holding up a mirror to, the material and sensual obsessions of the pseudoautonomous male.

Several years ago I learned about a Mami Wata case treated at the Faith Home in Hyattsville, Maryland. It involved a married man who had visited Côte d'Ivoire, where on a secluded beach he met a beautiful woman with whom he made love. Before leaving, the man asked for the woman's phone number. She gave it to him and said that as soon as he called she would be there. One day his wife was away and he decided to phone the beautiful woman. When he dialed the number she magically appeared. Again they made love. Afterward she told the man that he belonged to her. On Mondays, Wednesdays, and Fridays, she would come to him. On those days he was never to make love with his wife. The husband, however, was unable to keep the vow. He made love with his wife on a forbidden day, and the beautiful woman became jealous, bringing mental and physical afflictions to both the husband and wife.

When they came to the United States, the female spirit traveled with the man and continued to cause problems. After moving to Hyattsville, the couple learned about St. Peter's and sought out the ministers' help. They told the husband that the spirit was Mami Wata and that she would continue to create difficulties unless the man stayed in the Faith Home and submitted to spiritual treatments. The members fasted for seven days, and the husband slept for seven nights within a circle of candles. On the third night of the struggle, the husband dreamed of a woman with a baby on her back. The baby spoke: "God will take care." When morning came people who had assembled to pray heard a voice from outside shouting: "What is this? What have you done?" According to the senior prophet, the voice came from Mami Wata, who had become distressed by the separation being effected through the struggle. On the seventh day the jina finally left the man.

The *Sixth and Seventh Books of Moses*

Along with admonitions about witchcraft and jina, the Aladura churches warned members about secret writings that made readers insane and suicidal. Probably the most frequently mentioned such text was the *Sixth and Seventh Books of Moses*. When I lived in Liberia, mystical and occult texts (including works of Emmanuel Swedenborg and Hindu gurus, as well as Masonic pamphlets) could be found on book tables of street vendors and in the markets of Monrovia; but I never came across a copy of the *Sixth and Seventh Books of Moses*. Informants, however, insisted that copies could be obtained and told stories about people who, having purchased and read the work, became insane and impoverished. The Aladura ministers advised members neither to obtain nor to read a copy. While some informants spoke about the *Sixth and Seventh Books of Moses* as a physical, visible text that could be purchased like any other book, others described it as a hidden, invisible text obtained through dreams, visions, and supernatural liaisons.

The actual text has an intriguing history. In a 2009 issue of the *Wall Street Journal*, social historian Owen Davies gave a brief review of several early American magical texts, including the *Sixth and Seventh Books of Moses*. According to Davies, the work was anonymously authored in Germany in the late eighteenth century. An English-language publication appeared in the 1880s and was used among the Pennsylvania Dutch. Magical spells from the text also found use in Appalachian and southern African American folk remedies. The *Sixth and Seventh Books of Moses*, however, fell into disfavor in 1916, during a notorious Pennsylvania murder case in which the murderer allegedly used hexes from the text (Davies

2009, 8). Today free excerpts of the text are easily available from online sources, and full copies are for sale at the Amazon website. For the Aladura such availability, however, has hardly demystified the text; it simply demonstrates the adaptability of occult power.

How the *Sixth and Seventh Books of Moses* made its way to anglophone West Africa is unknown. In the 1950s the anthropologist Margaret Field saw a copy of the text in Ghana. She described it as "a collection of translations of ancient and medieval treatises originally in Hebrew, concerning 'Moses's Magical Spirit Art.' It is profusely illustrated with black-and-white representations of 'Seals,' 'Tables,' 'Magic Circles,' 'Schemhemforas,' 'Semiphoras,' and so on" (1970, 41). Harold Turner also notes that a book by the same title published by a Chicago press had circulated among the Yoruba in Nigeria (1967, 2:73–74). More recently Harris mentions that the text was cause for alarm among the C&S in London (2006, 197–98).[10]

In her study of Temne divination Shaw suggests a possible link between *an-yina* Musa divination and the lore about the *Sixth and Seventh Books of Moses*, what she refers to as a collection of "potent secret texts." The term *an-yina* was related to *jina* and the term *Musa* to *Moses* (Shaw 2002, 94–95). I find this link suggestive of the association Aladura prophets made between the jina and the *Sixth and Seventh Books of Moses:* in return for favors the jina might enable one to learn how to use the books. *An-yina* Musa divination also involved an assortment of techniques, including the study of mirrors, the use of black squares and cross designs, and containers of water blackened by ink from words written in Arabic washed from a slate board.

The *Sixth and Seventh Books of Moses* contain formulas for obtaining wealth and fame. Turner suggests that a copy of the text may have had possible influence on Oshitelu's manual *The Book of Prayer with Uses and Power of Psalms and Previous Treasure Hidden Therein* (74). Peter Probst also contends that Oshitelu's idea of a holy script may have been inspired by knowledge of sacred signs and configurations in the *Sixth and Seventh Books of Moses* for the mystical interpretation of Hebrew scripture. Thus, he concludes: "Considering the background, it seems likely that Oshitelu knew of *Moses' Books* and assimilated it accordingly in the elaboration of his Holy Script. Especially appealing to his mind must have been the cabalistic idea that the Hebrew letters in which the sacred texts are written down are not just ordinary signs invented by man to synthesize and render meaningful events but rather are reservoirs of divine power, symbols behind which the Biblical secrets are hidden" (1989, 487).

Probst cites Oshitelu's concern about possible confusion between his text and the *Sixth and Seventh Books of Moses* as indication of his exposure to them. My Aladura informants (including those at St. Peter's), however, would have found this association blasphemous. For some it would amount to a sacrilege to suggest that Oshitelu or any other esteemed Aladura prophet had studied the esoteric text, much less been influenced by it. They insisted on the moral distinction between Oshitelu's work and the *Sixth and Seventh Books of Moses*.

For the Aladura the *Sixth and Seventh Books of Moses* served more mercenary purposes. The work contained secrets about producing food, goods, and money. Its formulas could be used to change sand into rice, rocks into meat, and paper into money. One prophet claimed that an interested client could receive tablets from a jina that would enable him to read the text. These tablets prevented him from becoming insane, but, according to my informant, misfortune was inevitable for those who relied on its magic, since the text came from Satan. According to another prophet, God had actually taught the *Sixth and Seventh Books of Moses* to Satan, who began to use it for evil purposes. The idea that the work really came from God alerts us to the Aladura ambivalence about spiritual power when applied by human beings in the same way that a prophet, the model of virtue, could be tempted by special power that African signs provided. The text represented a secret knowledge that belied the church's open knowledge. Even a prophet was not invulnerable to ignoble desires. At one AIC the head minister became mentally unstable and eventually the church relieved him of his responsibilities. When Aladura prophets were consulted, they revealed that the minister had been reading the *Sixth and Seventh Books of Moses*. They recommended purification of the church grounds and that members undergo midnight struggles.

For the Aladura the *Sixth and Seventh Books of Moses* presented a subversive parallel to Christian scripture; the work represented the flip side of the Aladura liturgical and healing texts. In her discussion of the *Sixth and Seventh Books of Moses,* Elizabeth Isichei makes the important point that the lore about this book relates to the traditional value placed on "secret knowledge" and to a suspicion that European missions may have withheld from Africans a "hidden Bible" (1995, 295–96). In the Aladura imagination, however, the *Sixth and Seventh Books of Moses,* whether a physical text obtained in markets or an invisible text received from a jina, represented a powerful esoteric knowledge, an unspeakable science best left unopened.

THE SIGNS OF DISORDER

The descriptive account above does not present a complete explanation as to why people accept the reality of witches and jina; in any event such a task could not be accomplished. What we have is a description of the patterns, themes, and styles that unfold through narratives, performances, and social dramas. To take witchcraft seriously does not mean that we believe it exists, but, at the very least, that we appreciate why other people do and do not underestimate the power this trope or sign has as an evocation of human malice and collapsed relations. A theography on the Aladura in Liberia must take into account how the church has represented and addressed the matter of unseen occult power and its misuse.

Witchcraft and jina were almost tangible realities, known through the lived experience of individuals—through their dream encounters, personal traumas, narrative testimonies, and the healing praxis. These forces were articulated in the context of persistent problem solving, the church's special mission. Michael Jackson's comments on the relation between beliefs and practices apply to the Aladura context as well: "Beliefs have no objective reality apart from the people who make use of them, and to try to see how beliefs *correspond* to some allegedly 'objective' reality or how they *cohere* as a so-called 'system' seems to me far less edifying than trying to see what people do with beliefs in *coping* with the exigencies of life" (1989, 101).

Ideas about malevolent, invisible forces—jina, for instance—impacted and ordered one's experience of the world. They were, in Bennetta Jules-Rosette's words, "dominant therapeutic symbols" (1981, 144–45) that offered a dual function: they expressed and explained the conditions of misfortune. In his study of South African forms Bähre follows this line of interpretation: "Witch familiars seemed to be a fantastic reflection of the exchanges, desires, and anxieties of sex, blood—as a symbol of life and consanguineal ties—and money featured in the imaginations of the thieving, blood-drinking, rapist witch familiars that the witch created out of jealousy. Talking about witchcraft was therefore a way to make sense of the horrors of everyday life" (2002, 327). However, in theorizing about witchcraft, jina, and spirit familiars as coping mechanisms, as symbols making sense of horrors and disorders, we should never minimize the impact of these beliefs. They do not simply represent beliefs about the spiritual order (and disorder) but suggest actual experiences, encounters, and responses.

The centering in everyday praxis also provides a useful balance to symbolic approaches. As Ashforth notes, the symbolic model sees witchcraft as an idiom, a metaphoric tool for describing and explaining disorder (2005, 114). What symbolic approaches have often underrated was the literal meaning of statements about jina and witches, or the "there-ness" of spirits, as Robin Horton would put it (1993, 337). For the Aladura, jina and witches were not just symbols representing disorder but signs (with power) that actively and effectively brought it about. Speaking about the South African context, Ashforth strongly criticizes the "discourses of statecraft" that see witchcraft as a "matter of belief, as a property of mind"; rather, he sees witchcraft as "a matter of action leading to real, material consequences for living human beings—action, moreover, that creates injustice" (2005, 11).

The study of witchcraft always returns to ethics, which in the Aladura setting becomes a theological and ecclesial issue. Anthropological, historical, and comparative approaches continue to assist in the analysis of the cultural constructions of witchcraft and occult power. However, I find explanations that evoke the theme of human vulnerability, disorder, and weakness the most useful. Moore and Sanders describe discussion about witchcraft or occult power as "a set of discourses on morality, sociality, and humanity: on human frailty" (2001, 20). The phenomenon of witchcraft thus has implications for the theological understanding of the human person, a discourse that even African theology has largely neglected. Vanden Berg notes that many African theologians have taken on the topics of doctrine and practice from an elitist advantage. He faults African theologians for not using a grassroots approach in addressing the topics of witchcraft and occult power (2005, 58–59). They have largely written for African and Western academics and have relied too heavily on theology of liberation models to explicate the character of African Christianities. The theology of liberation has provided useful strategies for redressing political oppression and injustice; however, in brushing off the matter of occult cosmologies (including witchcraft) it has offered a limited picture of the human subject and the ambiguities of everyday practice.

In the end, while we try to understand the meaning of witchcraft in terms of social relations and values, epistemic systems, performative expressions, and psychological states, it remains a theological and an ethical issue. As Ashforth insightfully states: "Questions of witchcraft also intrude upon considerations of what might be termed a theological problem of 'unknowing' in relation to unseen powers. I would argue that it is necessary to countenance something akin to the phenomenon known in religious experience as the Mystery in relation to these matters pertaining to unseen powers, that is, an engagement with something transcendent beyond human apprehension. . . . The putative action[s] of witchcraft, along with the very real fears relating to them [the unseen powers], spring from, relate to, and are located in realms of being which are both ineffable and open to transcendence—that are not subject to forms of knowledge adequately represented by clear and distinct ideas" (2001, 219). Ashforth contends that when witchcraft is identified as a "religious phenomenon," it evokes a "sense of metaphysical openness [that] can also co-exist with a sense of vulnerability" (219). His coupling of the ineffable with the theme of vulnerability helps us to appreciate the indeterminate nature of occult power, the perceived incongruity of ritual actions, and the distrust among human performers. At the same time, as one explores the murky clouds of "occult cosmologies," the "metaphysical openness" should remain grounded in ethical responsibility.

The tenacity of the witchcraft discourse and of occult cosmologies contradicts a linchpin of modernity: the assumption of trust (Sanders and West 2003, 10–12). The Aladura, while thoroughly "Christian Moderns" (Keane 2007), recognize the ubiquity and impact of hidden operatives and insist that we neglect this circumstance at our own peril. The emphasis on human frailty and temptations involved openness to conversion and renewal. The Aladura community consistently advocated for the transformation of fallen brothers and sisters. Ritual struggle paradoxically coupled exposure of malice with hospitality for the neighbor and the stranger. It assumed the influence of a plethora of signs and demonic powers but rejected a notion of absolute evil. The Aladura saw evil more as potentiality than as substance or entity. Therefore they sought redemption for the agent placing signs as well as for his victim. In this process the connection to place played a critical role. In the Aladura world the Faith Home was the central location for the prophet's demonstration of power and for remaking persons in a ritualized world.

5

The Faith Home

FOCUSED SPACE

More than thirty years ago, James Fernandez stressed the creative response of African religious movements to the decentering impact of colonialism and modernity: "We miss the heart of such religious thought if we neglect the fact that this decentering and the acute sense of peripherality it produces is imaginatively negotiated in primary images of body and household, field and forest life" (1978, 229). This insight is no less relevant today for understanding the church's role amid the postcolonial traumas. As what Fernandez terms "a grounded image," the Faith Home provided dwellers with a sense of place and belonging. At the same time, *dwelling* implied the idea of being on a journey and the readiness to move on, and so the Faith Home provided strategies for coping with experiences of conflict and misfortune that went beyond its fundamental mission of offering refuge.

In understanding the Aladura Faith Home as a grounded image, I have also found useful Web Keane's notion of semiotic ideology, which refers to a "people's background assumptions about what signs are and how they function in the world" (2005, 191). Adapting a Piercean model, Keane understands signs, first, as processual and generative, while laden with contingency and sociability. Second, he insists on the "complex range of possible relationships among signs, interpretations and objects" (186). Signs involve more than meaning or representation. They are also layered into a web of material objects with distinct and malleable qualities: "a given quality is contingently ... bound up with other qualities" (194). The image of the Faith Home becomes bundled with verbal strategies, physical structures, habits of dress, material forms, and performative acts. Particular forms, acts, and meanings may refer to other forms, and the complex of associations can generate new forms, acts, and meanings. In the Faith Home one recognized a "space of ritual encounter [that] must be mapped out" (198) if meaningful and effective contact between the Aladura subject and the divine realities was to occur.

St. Peter's Faith Home provided a kind of spatial threshold that dynamically mediated a person's entry into the ritual life of the church: the daily regimen of prayers, the weekly services, the holy treatments, the acceptance of rules and regulations. The expected behavior of prophets and patients demonstrated persuasively the role that bodily praxis played in the Aladura world. During the week the number of scheduled events, let alone improvised "Spirit-led" events, challenged even the most ritually avid devotee. Along with the five daily prayers, the church scheduled Divine Worship for Wednesday evening, Friday evening, and Sunday morning. A prescribed healing ceremony occurred on Friday morning. Though worship leaders endeavored to conclude services within a certain period of time, one could never predict the Spirit. Most Divine Worship services lasted about three hours, but occasionally one might last twice that long. Also contributing to the rigor of the Faith Home schedule were the endless series of beach struggles and midnight struggles, healing treatments, and consecrations. The complex of somatic actions, which gave form to ideas and concepts, nurtured the "aura of factuality" (Geertz, 1973, 109) in the Aladura Way. Through the prophet's manipulation, through his insistence on a particular praxis, the Faith Home offered an effective strategy for the constitution, or rather for the reconstitution, of the self. The perceived ambiguity about the prophet's role, however, remained embodied through ritual and moral action. Such embodiment simply enhanced the paradoxical dimension of Aladura Christian experience.

A location of spiritual power, the Faith Home provided an exacting setting for a person's recovery and spiritual growth. Of course, this role was directly related to its being the home of the prophet and to his ability to affect in a positive way the persons who dwelled within his domain. In a strict sense the Faith Home referred to the minister's residence. Concerning the relationship between the Aladura minister and his members, Harold Turner notes that he "lives among them, sharing their life and their level of education, and his residence is known as a 'faith-home' and serves as a spiritual clinic as well" (1967, 1:51). In keeping with the consanguineous quality of church life, members frequently referred to the head minister as Father and to his wife as Mother. At St. Peter's members often referred to Apostle Olu in familial terms as "Pa Olu." They regarded him as the head elder of the household, the one who represented the church's unique spiritual lineage. Ray relates this communal aspect to the Yoruba notion of group unity. As he states, for the Aladura the church "is a new spiritual family, whose members become one's brothers and sisters and elders, which constitutes the believer's new 'home.' Aladuras therefore see themselves as a community distinct from the rest of society. Each congregation usually refers to itself as an *egbe*, a group or fellowship, joined together in the pursuit of a better life" (1993, 272). In an essay on the Celestial Church of Christ, Adogame also underlines the consanguinity of church life. The church operates as a "substitute kinship coterie" that supersedes biological ties (2000, 19–20).

The Faith Home introduced an order of activity centered on recovery through ritual, moral, and social means, a healing process that supported participants in their efforts to become Aladura persons. Through his ritual struggles the prophet mediated virtue that consecrated and maintained the purity of the Faith Home. The term *Faith Home,* then, designated not simply the home of the prophet and his family but also the place for the ritual mediation of virtue. This association helped reinforce its image as a holy place separated from ordinary space. Again Ray indicates the Yoruba basis for the Aladura idea of home as a place for auspicious interaction between living humans and the spirits of ancestors. The Yoruba word *ile* refers to a family compound protected by lineage ancestors. The Aladura saw their church and its compound as a special location that promoted the interaction between the family of God and "spiritual allies." The compound represented a "heavenly space," the descent of the "sacred archetype of God's heavenly church" (1993, 274–75).

In the Aladura compound the Faith Home was usually distinguished from the chapel. Many Liberian churches, however, lacked sufficient means to build separate facilities, and the ministers then operated the Faith Home within the chapel. Some churches simply identified their Faith Home with the compound itself. Informants stressed that, in any case, a church did not become an official branch until it had started a Faith Home. The Faith Home made the church a station, "a place to sit down." Members likened a true church to a shelter for the traveler, who might find safety from danger. Not infrequently traveling represented a temptation that one inevitably must face. Whether one traveled near or far, "dwelling" ideally prepared one for the journey.

The word *faith* denoted the quality of the dweller's commitment: not just an affective act but a position expressed through strict adherence to rules and regulations; steady participation in services, prayers, and prescribed healing rituals; and unwavering reliance on the prophet's authority. These were acts of faith, testaments to the dweller's resolve to participate in "problem solving" and to doing what was necessary to become a Child of Salvation. Though ministers often insisted on an inward quality of faith, they also stressed that faith became shallow and wavering without outward demonstrations, such as fasting, struggles, and sacrifice. Finally, the use of the term *faith* distinguished the Faith Home from other homes. At times Aladura branches evidenced strong regional, national, and ethnic relations among its members, but the idea of dwelling evoked a household of God (a kind of parallel household) that ideally transcended the conventional claims of kin.

Though she writes about a different time and place, Elizabeth Fox-Genovese's description of a household has relevance here. She defines a household as "a basic social unit in which people, whether voluntarily or under compulsion, pool their income and resources. As such, it has no necessary relation to family, although members of households may be related and many households may be coterminous with family memberships. Above all, it has no necessary relation to home, which is a modern and ideologically charged term" (1988, 31).

Without the daily, weekly, and monthly involvement of all dwellers, a specific "household of God" was hardly sustainable. Many dwellers had permanent residences elsewhere. For instance, a junior minister assigned to a branch might visit from time to time a wife and family living nearby. Each dweller was expected eventually to leave the Faith Home. Still, everyone who participated in the life of the Faith Home became part of what Fox-Genovese describes as a "web of interdependency" (87). This web was obviously reinforced by the hierarchical but reciprocating formalities worked out between ministers, members, and patients. The perceived success of the Faith Home depended on the character of relations, which were always shifting and changing. What remained constant was the structure of ritual space, the expectations for ritual engagement, and the rules and regulations that provided the template for the moral and spiritual order.

THE STRUCTURE OF RITUAL SPACE

The physical layout of the St. Peter's compound represented an intended ordering of ritual space that imitated the traditional CLA Faith Home compound.[1] The various elements and dimensions of that space function to support and express the ongoing life of the Faith Home.

The St. Peter's branch was only a few hundred yards from the Tubman Boulevard and Scheiffelin (Airport) Road intersection or "red light juncture," as dwellers frequently called it. There were several small businesses in the vicinity: a pharmacy, an African herbal medicine center, a boutique, a Lebanese-operated grocery store, a rice distributor, a snack bar, and a gas station. Outside the grocery "market ladies" also sold goods and daily produce. On the intersection's street corners there were vendors selling cigarettes, fruit, fried plantains, country bread, biscuits (cookies), and candies. Two country markets were within a quarter mile of the juncture. Several church members worked at the markets, where dwellers frequently shopped. The cement and rock companies in the area and the construction of the "Chinese Football Field," located across from St. Peter's on Scheiffelin Road, made for a constant flow of temporary workers. Not infrequently, unskilled workers seeking employment in the area came to St. Peter's for treatments. Buses and taxis stopped nearby, heading into Monrovia or out to the countryside. St. Peter's often received travelers who delayed their trips or missed their rides. Dwellers regarded the juncture area with a mixture of wonder and caution. The site offered occasions for delightful exchanges among friends, for

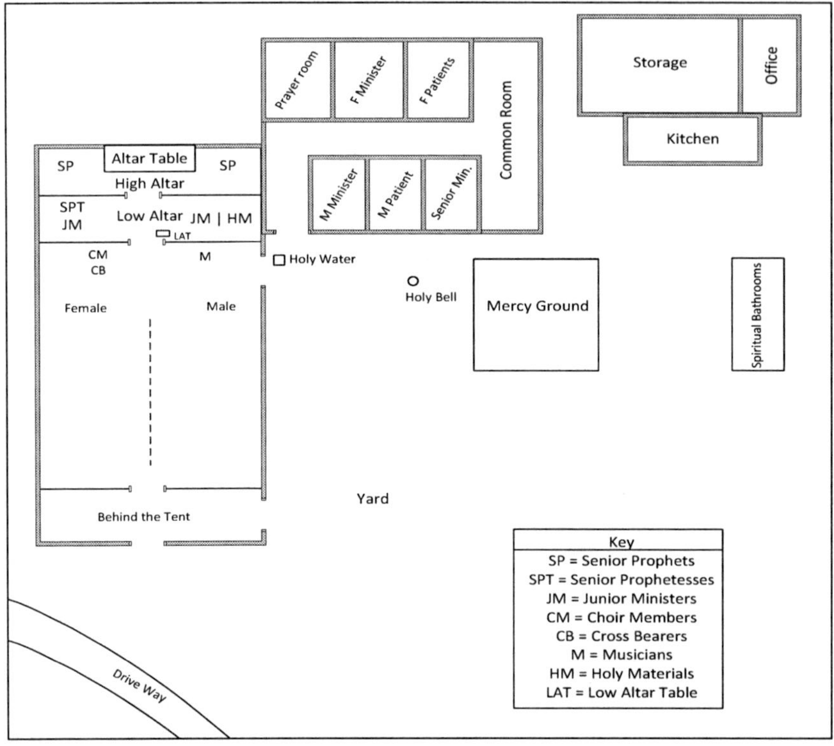

Outline of St. Peter's Faith Home compound.
Prepared by Peter Valdina, not to scale.

welcomes to family members just arriving from interior homelands, for buying and selling goods, for open-air preaching and extemporaneous praying. But one also risked encounter with harassing policeman, soldiers with guns, the transient pickpocket, the peddler of suspect things, and the leering eye of the stranger.

From Scheiffelin Road a narrow dirt road led down into the Aladura compound, a zinc-sided chapel with a green roof crested by a cross. In the yard a tire rim suspended from a wood frame served as a church bell. From the road the compound structures—the chapel and Faith Home, the cinder-block kitchen area and Mercy Ground—were clearly distinguishable, but not ostentatiously so. During my first few months in Liberia, I had passed the compound countless times before realizing that it was a church. At the Aladura compound the dirt road veered left toward a cluster of corrugated iron, cinder-block and mud-stick homes, eventually becoming a pathway impassible by car, though not by motor bike. The road by default became a boundary between the compound and the other dwellings. Unlike other compounds, such as the CLA Center Street branch, the compound at St. Peter's was not separated by a wall from its surroundings. Thus the church members frequently warned passersby about trespassing and misusing the yard. Neighbors and strangers using the road were told not to loiter on the compound nor to cross it without good reason. For members, the grounds were holy, and those who trespassed or misused the grounds (by urinating in the yard, for instance) could potentially spoil them. Despite this posture of seriousness, life at the compound often appeared mirthful and easygoing. The presence of children had something do to with this. Even children's playmates from outside the compound were tolerated. Olu and his wife, the spiritual mother, had seven children, ages two to twelve, who all stayed at the Faith Home. Prepubescent children, unlike adults, usually were not considered potential sources of danger or pollution.

The neighbors were mostly Bassa and Kpelle, some of whom belonged to the church. Directly behind the St. Peter's compound was the Pentecostal Bassa church named African Glory. St. Peter's members simply called it the Bassa church. The two churches kept a polite relationship, often sharing items, such as chairs, benches, and musical instruments. Both held Sunday services at about the same time, but this did not seem to create competition or tension between them, as was sometimes the case among prophet churches on adjacent lots. African Glory attracted primarily the Bassa people in the immediate area, while St. Peter's attracted a more ethnically and geographically diverse group. Also, the Pentecostal church did not sponsor healing rituals, which were potentially a source of competition and resentment among prophet churches.

A Lived Space

The Faith Home clearly represented, in W. Penn Handwerker's terms, a "household configuration." Handwerker's study of the urban Bassa calls attention to the variety of households that develop in urban settings in relation to shifting kinship systems, residential structures, educational interests, technological skills, and job opportunities. He lists at least eight household configurations among Monrovia-area Bassa that "take shape as a series of individuals and groups of people dependent on themselves or on one another for subsistence—single adults, single children, parent-child, and other consanguineal structures, and nuclear families—coalesce in the process of obtaining and maintaining a livelihood" (1973b, 187–88). The Faith Home as a specific household configuration was to be distinguished from both indigenous households and from mission-based and mainline churches. The Faith Home brought together individuals with multiple social, economic, and religious backgrounds. It created a "household of faith" comprising people who gained a palpable haven from the unpredictable exigencies of urban life.

The household, however, was never a fixed body. A dweller was always a temporary dweller, since ministers were reassigned, new patients admitted, and others discharged. The emergence of a core group might have to do with the influence of the ministers: Bassa prophets tended to attract Bassa clients, Kpelle prophets, Kpelle clients, and so. It would also happen that a Faith Home supervisor's relatives might stay for long periods. At one Faith Home the avuncular relations of the spiritual mother often stayed there on their trips from the country. The ministers complained about the undue favors they received. One "brother" especially provoked the junior ministers: he showed little respect for their authority and was cavalier in his observances of Faith Home rules: he treated it "like a hotel."

As a household the Faith Home represented a livelihood supported through a network of minister-patient relations. Ministers received a stipend from the church, but much of their material support came through ties to clients. At some churches, I knew ministers who went months without a stipend, because members had not paid tithes and dues. Water and electric bills took priority, since, as one minister noted in a sermon, a prophet church could not effectively function without light and water. During such times private donations from clients in the form of cash, candles, clothes, rice, or fruit would greatly help. The Faith Home praxis necessitated an exchange of goods and services that maintained the livelihood of the minister and supported the general household.

People became patients through various routes: on the basis of a prophet's vision or his interpretation of a dream; through friends and family already involved with the church; or through another minister's referral. Each patient was assigned to a particular minister who became primarily responsible for the treatment. The number of patients varied from week to week, depending on available space, on the seriousness of the cases, and on how many experienced and reliable healers were on hand. Sometimes the number of patients admitted as dwellers would be as high as fifteen or twenty; at other times as few as two or three.

Though from time to time St. Peter's accommodated several male patients, throughout the year the majority of patients were women. Most of them were from eighteen to thirty-five years old and were married. If a woman had small children, the supervisors usually allowed them to stay with her in the Faith Home. The majority of the patients had strong "tribal" backgrounds—Kpelle, Bassa, Kru, Mano, Kissi, and Grebo being the best represented. I seldom met a female patient who was America-Liberian or Congo. If she came from the central and western regions of Liberia, more than likely she had been initiated into Sande Society. Many patients had exposure to Christian missions and schools and already belonged to another church. Although most had attended school, I met only one female patient who had finished high school.

Most patients sought treatment for physical ailments, but others came burdened with concern about a child's health, an unsuccessful market business, or domestic strife. Many dwellers first came as visitors traveling from the interior in pursuit of a new job or to look for relatives. Others sought the church's help in holding a job or with finishing their education. Having heard about Olu's work, many came from other parts of Monrovia seeking spiritual protection: a landlord having difficulty with boarders, a store owner concerned about a neighbor's jealousy, a government employee insecure about support from his work companions. Diagnosis and treatment for all patients almost always implicated the negative influence of occult powers.

The Chapel

Located on the left section of the compound, the chapel was a yellow zinc-sided rectangular building with green doors and shutters. Every evening after services or prayers the ministers closed the doors and shutters as an added measure for protection from evil spirits. The chapel had three entrances, a seldom-used front door and two smaller side doors that were routinely used. The only times I saw the front entrance ritually used was for the Tabborrar thanksgiving service procession and during midnight struggles when dwellers knelt at the door to make confession. One side door led into the chapel area referred to as "behind the tent," the section reserved for menstruating women, special patients, and penalized dwellers. A wood rail separated it from the rest of the chapel nave. The second side door led into the front section of the nave, with the altar on the right side and the first row of benches for worshippers on the left. At Sunday services the ministers, elders, cross bearers, and choir members processed and recessed through this door as well. During the week the door served as the main entrance for prayers and special treatments. At this entrance a white bucket of consecrated water was placed on cinder blocks for washing hands before entering. Some individuals would wash their faces as well. As was custom in Aladura churches, no one wore shoes into the chapel. These were always left at the doorstep, which was in keeping with God's warning to Moses to remove his shoes before the burning bush (Exodus 3:15).

The chapel had at least twelve rows of benches divided by an aisle. Again, following the Aladura pattern, at worship services men sat on the right side and women on the left. In Aladura branches with much smaller chapels this kind of separation was more difficult to maintain. For instance, Prophetess Miatta Tagoe's CLA branch had a very small chapel. Participants were overwhelmingly women and children, so they hardly observed the left-right separation. The few men in attendance usually sat on one bench placed along the right wall of the chapel, but women moved freely about. At St. Peter's services choir members (many of whom were cross bearers) always occupied front benches on the left side of the nave, and musicians used the area immediately in front of the right altar wall, where they kept their drums, rattle gourds, and other instruments. A lectern was usually placed before the right altar wall. During services, when ministers gave sermons, read scripture, or made announcements, the ushers moved the lectern before the first altar step so that the ministers could remain within the altar space.

The altar area was divided into the low altar and the high altar, with the low altar elevated a step above the nave, the high altar a step above that. A three-foot-high curtain separated the low altar from the nave. On the right side of the low altar sat male junior ministers, elders, deacons, and noted guests, such as visiting ministers from other denominations; on the left side sat male and female junior ministers. The spiritual mother and visiting senior prophetesses would also sit on the left side. In the low altar space was a small table covered by a white cloth on which were placed a three-branched candelabrum, a bell, the Psalter, and an Aladura hymnal. For some prayers and healing treatments, ministers often moved this table from the altar into the nave for ready use of its objects. On the right side of the altar area, behind the elders and deacons, was the consecration area for holy materials, for containers of water, oil, and honey. Another short curtain separated the low altar and high altar areas. It included the high altar table and four seats for senior prophets. Ordinarily the only individuals allowed into the high altar were the senior prophets. A white cloth covered the table, on which were placed another seven-branched candelabrum, a small cross stand, a box of candles, and vases of artificial flowers. On the wall above the altar table hung gold plaster images depicting two orders of angels, the cherubim and seraphim, with a light bulb glowing between them. Also tacked on the altar wall were two large posters: one, a portrait of a white-robed Jesus with nail-scarred hands; the other, a colorful, ornate Christian calendar with an inscription that read: "Jesus died for our sins."

Members claimed that the high altar was the "most powerful" area within the chapel. Within this space the senior prophets led liturgies, said special prayers, and delivered prophecies. Junior prophets entered the high altar only with permission from their seniors. Before services they might arrange the altar table or help purify the area with incense. They never routinely entered the space. During Divine Worship services, kneeling within the high altar, the senior prophets delivered the Victory Prayer, invoking the presence and power of the Holy Spirit. It was necessary that the high altar always be pure and consecrated and the senior prophets ritually prepared. If these conditions were not meet, the service or prayers would be unsuccessful. The Holy Spirit became known in many ways and places, but the church considered the senior prophet's work within the high altar area as central to the mediation of virtue within the Faith Home.

In the rear of the chapel, marked off by a rail, was the space called "behind the tent." This was the only section of the chapel where menstruating women were allowed to enter and worship. During a service they received holy water and palm leaves ("Victory leaves") from ministers who took special care not to touch them.

Dwellers might also be penalized for an infraction of Faith Home rules by being sent behind the tent. Senior prophetesses at local branches used the area to punish male junior ministers for disrespecting their authority. Even the spiritual mother or a senior prophetess during her monthly cycle went behind the tent. Though the high altar and behind-the-tent spaces might appear to contrast with one another in terms of a purity-impurity grade, it is important to see both as related and integral to the Aladura notion of the church and Faith Home as a holy place. Healing rituals and prayers also took place in the behind-the-tent area, which was configured into the structure of sacred space.

The Faith Home and Compound

In the Faith Home yard were two sites critical to everyday praxis—the Mercy Ground and the holy bell. Every Aladura church had an enclosure called a Mercy Ground. According to Turner, Josiah Oshitelu based its invention on a revelation he received in 1930. Concerning its physical structure and purpose, Turner comments that "it has become a specially sacred open space attached to many churches, for private prayers and struggles, or where the congregation may repair after service for final prayers of dismissal, or a group of women may receive special prayers from the minister. It may be enclosed with a fence or hedge, or merely marked out by stones; the surface may be sanded for rolling, or swept hard earth; at one side there is usually a wooden cross several feet high" (H. Turner 1967, 2:103).

In Liberia, Mercy Grounds might have different shapes and be constructed from different materials. Some had walls of corrugated iron, others of grass mats or mud-sticks. Some Mercy Grounds had roofs, others did not. St. Peter's Mercy Ground was roofless space with a cinder-block wall about seven feet high. The ground inside was beach sand, making the surface more appropriate for rolling. A wooden cross four feet high was placed before the rear wall. When performing prayers or healing rites, the minister normally stood next to the cross as the patient knelt before him. Special treatments that prescribed that a patient sleep within the Mercy Ground frequently took place. Members and dwellers routinely used it for personal prayers and confessions. In his study of the Celestial Church of Christ, Adogame (2000, 21–22) emphasizes the "wilderness" imagery of the Mercy Ground among Aladura churches, which underlines its separateness.[2] In Liberia as well, the Mercy Ground evoked an element of the "bush," a place for struggle.

Located outside the Mercy Ground was the holy bell, a tire rim suspended from a wooden frame, typical at most AIC branches. A minister clanged the bell with a metal object to announce the beginning of prayers and services. The ground around the holy bell was regarded as a special place for the consecration of holy materials and for special prayers over patients. On occasion an animal sacrifice (usually a sheep or chicken) took place there and the animal's blood allowed to flow onto the ground.

Like the chapel, the Faith Home proper was made of zinc siding and painted yellow with green doors and shutters. A rectangular building about fifty feet long, it had eight rooms: a prayer room, a large common room, and bedrooms for Olu and his family, for the minister-in-charge, for male ministers, for female ministers, for male patients, and for female patients. Ministers considered the prayer room, which one faced immediately upon entering the Faith Home corridor, to be the most important room in the building. In the prayer room holy materials were consecrated for later use in services and treatments. The ministers consecrated materials for common use, but quite often they had their personal items "recharged" in the space. For instance, a minister might leave his special gown in the prayer room to obtain more protective power. Along with the consecration and preparation of holy materials, special prayers and treatments took place there. Within the compound the prayer room's power was considered second only to that of the chapel's high altar. Therefore, ministers closely guarded its use. They prohibited other dwellers from entering, except for supervised prayers and treatments. During menses, female ministers could not enter the space; nor could they sleep there for special struggles, as male ministers were allowed to do on occasion. The major exception was the church's spiritual mother, who on one occasion stayed in the room while recovering from an illness believed caused by a member's witchcraft.

The bedrooms for ministers and dwellers were on both sides of the hallway. On the right, there were quarters for male ministers and patients; on the left, quarters for female ministers and patients. Each room could accommodate as many as four dwellers. The male ministers' room was the most restricted in use. The male ministers often used their bedroom for administering routine prayers and treatments, as when other preferred spaces became crowded or unavailable. Consequently they monitored closely the daily use of their room. For instance, the room should not be used for saying prayers over a woman in menstruation; in such cases, the female ministers' room became more appropriate.

At the end of the hallway was a large common room used for a variety of activities. Before Divine Worship services, it became a vestry for members of the procession where they assembled for prayers and returned for the last benediction. The room was also frequently reserved for prayers and healing ceremonies, especially when the workload became heavy. Simultaneously, during busy seasons treatments might be taking place in the chapel, prayer room, ministers' bedroom, Mercy Ground, and common room. The church also used the common room as sleeping quarters, especially during special events, such as Tabborrar, when the bedrooms and the chapel were full. It also provided a convenient space for seriously ill patients who needed family members to stay with them. At times the room became a kind of recreational center. During heavy rains children often played there. Also, a television in a corner might draw occasional interest, though ministers occasionally chided dwellers for watching secular programs.

A two-story cinder-block building with a porch was located just a few feet from the side exit of the common room. The porch area was used as a kitchen and the first floor for a storage area. The second floor provided a waiting room and office for Olu, where he attended to many administrative tasks and conducted spiritual interviews. The porch area and facing yard often became a center of routine Faith Home activities: cross bearers cooking meals, followers washing clothes, children kicking a ball, visitors, dwellers, and members sitting around conversing while they waited to see the prophet. But even ordinary work and play could be charged with religious significance. Members stressed that any activity that occurred within the compound had spiritual value, however convivial or mundane it appeared. This included taking care of toilet. On the right border of the compound was a rectangular structure divided into three separate compartments called the "spiritual bathroom." One compartment was set aside for the apostle's use. The spiritual mother also used this facility, except during her menses. Then she used a second compartment available to all dwellers for ordinary use. Here also ministers administered enemas and inspected patients' feces for signs of witchcraft. The third compartment was used only for holy baths.

The Protection of Angels

Samuel Olu once told me that when he founded St. Peter's he asked UCL founder David Fyneah to consecrate the Paynesville compound. The elder Fyneah, however, said it was unnecessary. He claimed that God had already made it holy and now protected it with angels. The association of angels and sacred space was a commonplace notion among Aladura churches. St. Peter's contended that four angels—Michael, Gabriel, Uriel, and Raphael—mediated the presence of the Holy Spirit. They also protected the four sides of the compound, which represented the cardinal points of the universe. On the role of these angels in Aladura cosmology, Adogame comments: "*Michael* is the 'chief archangel' under the "power of chief" who wields the *ida* (spiritual sword) that demolishes *ajogun, aje, oso,* the malevolent supramundane forces which populate the world. He is the angel of victory and the protector of the church. . . . He occupies the east axis of the church. . . . *Gabriel* is the angel of protection and benediction. He is also the angel of healing and humility. He is believed to cure barrenness. His jurisdiction is located in the west. *Raphael* is the angel of force that resides on the side of the ocean in the south. He prevents all sorts of ailments and health hazards. *Uriel* is the least invoked of the four archangels. He represents the angel of gifts, and dwells in the north axis. He is called upon to activate and render potent private devotional prayers" (2000, 15).[3]

Accordingly, at St. Peter's compound members frequently reported visions of angels. The four noted above were frequently mentioned, but visions and dreams also referred to large groups of angels. I was told that angels in visions or dreams assembled in numbers of one, three, seven, thirteen, or twenty-one. They walked among the dwellers in the compound. During services they entered the chapel and facilitated interaction between the prophets and the Holy Spirit. Aladura informants in Nigeria told Ray that angels "hovered" over the altar (1993, 275). During shouts, Liberian prophets claimed to see them "spiritually" multiplying among worshippers. Angels assisted the church in its battles with witches and evil spirits. At night, it was believed that they "walked over" dwellers while they slept in the chapel, providing them with more protection.

Though members always saw the Faith Home complex as holy, an element of ambiguity about its power also existed. Informants claimed that immorality and social discord could always sully the Faith Home's sanctity. The imperfections of human nature applied to dwellers as well as to those who lived outside the Faith Home. With this awareness, the ritual observances took on even more urgency. Jonathan Z. Smith's notion about the emplacement of ritual being in tension with the way things are is certainly applicable to Aladura ritual (1987, 109–11). In general, the Faith Home praxis involved redressing problems and notable tensions between persons: as between victim and jina, prophet and witch, church and neighbors. When the Faith Home received patients afflicted by evil spirits, this automatically risked bringing impurities into the premises. The variety of ritual events and the commitment to ritual struggle, then, constituted a place of "ritual closure" (Masquelier 2001, 62–76) amid the realities of frailty, loss, and death. Practice also required the close observance of rules and regulations.

RULES AND REGULATIONS OF SACRED SPACE

Like all Aladura churches, St. Peter's posted a typed list of rules and regulations that Faith Home dwellers were expected to follow. The list may be seen, in Searle's terms, as an example of regulative rules that "constrain action in an already existing context" and constitutive rules that "create a context, and hence a field of action" (Humphrey and Laidlaw 1994, 117). Ministers urged dwellers to study the list and commit it to memory. St. Peter's model for the moral order of the Faith Home followed closely that of E. O. A. Adejobi, a former primate of the CLA, who, in a pamphlet entitled *An Exposition of the Faith Home: Its Rules, Regulations and Special Faith Home Prayers of the Church of the Lord Aladura*, described the Faith Home's purpose, admission procedures, schedules, and special treatments, as well as various rules and regulations. Adejobi notes that membership was not required for admission into the Faith Home, but the church hoped a successful stay would lead to it. He writes, "We do not entreat one to come to the

Faith Home except that the spirit of the Lord reveals that a person should be admitted" (6). This guideline was true for St. Peter's as well. The ministers always claimed that one became a dweller only through the direction of the Spirit, through revelation. Whether you were a member or a stranger did not matter.

A patient was admitted only after a spiritual interview between a Faith Home minister and the patient or the patient's family or friends. At St. Peter's the interview often took place in Olu's office above the kitchen, but other locations, such as the prayer room, the Mercy Ground, or before the chapel altar, were also used for this purpose. The interview involved routine inquiry about the patient's present problem and background. The most important act in this process, however, was the minister's prayer over a kneeling patient. During the prayer the Spirit revealed the nature of the problem, its real source, and the preliminary treatment for its removal. Ministers often administered treatments on an outpatient basis, but cases often led to a stay in the Faith Home. If there were no vacancies, the patient could be seen as an outpatient until space became available. It seldom happened that a person waited more than a few days for a place.

When a patient was admitted, the ministers registered her in the Faith Home notebook. They called this process holy registration. From then on the dweller was expected to obey Faith Home rules and regulations faithfully. Among Aladura churches, the matter of payment created some concern, since reports did circulate about prophets who treated only for money. In his manual Adejobi makes clear what the church's proper conduct should be regarding expenses. He insists that "we do not receive money from any person who comes to the Lord for protection, care and hiding." This became the norm for most Aladura and prophet churches I encountered, though they welcomed gifts and donations. Frequently, after a successful treatment, a patient made a thanksgiving offering, which included gifts of fruit, candies, biscuits, or animal sacrifice. Also, for any treatment the patient was expected to provide holy materials, such as candles, incense, new towels, or special foods. When the patient did not have the means to provide these, the church could lend materials in stock, which the patient could replace later. In any case St. Peter's emphasized that ministers must never independently ask for money or donations, either for themselves or for the church.

Once registered, the dweller took an "admission oath" that underlined obedience to the ministers. A successful treatment depended on such obedience. Without trust in the minister's inspiration, the patient harmed himself and undermined Faith Home morale. The dweller was immediately made aware of the rules and regulations. St. Peter's posted list included eleven rules:

1) No woman is allowed to open her chest in the compound.
2) All dresses and shirts should have sleeves so that the body cannot be exposed.

3) No minister or ministers are allowed to enter the bishop's room without permission.

4) No male minister is allowed to enter the lady minister's room without permission while they are dressing.

5) Patients should submit themselves to the ministers and not criticize them.

6) Patients should wear their sleeping suits only in their rooms and not outside.

7) Ministers under training are not allowed to leave the Faith Home without permission.

8) Patients are not allowed to leave the church compound without permission.

9) No woman should wear trousers in the Faith Home.

10) Patients, ministers, and residents of the Faith Home are asked to attend all services.

11) Ministers, patients, and residents of the Faith Home are asked to bathe before entering the church.

The list was by no means exhaustive or uniform with other churches. Ministers also implemented unwritten rules that were standard fare in Faith Homes. For instance, the list does not refer to food or menstrual customs, which were important aspects of Faith Home life. The church claimed that all established rules came through the direction of the Spirit. St. Peter's list, though hardly complete, covered what the church considered to be major areas of behavior and practice for the Faith Home. The list focused on the matters of dress, use of rooms, campus leaves and reentries, and propriety between dwellers. The rules addressed conditions of purity and pollution, relations between male and female, and relations between juniors and seniors.

Rules 1, 2, and 9 concerned the exposure of the body. Undoubtedly the church's conservative stance distanced it from aspects of indigenous culture. Informants stressed that the Aladura way was not the way of the village, of the country. Even when nursing her infant, a woman needed to be discreet. In the chapel she kept her chest completely covered when doing so. During services ministers reprimanded women who exposed their breasts and threatened them with penalties if they did so again. As rule 2 indicates, the concern about the body's exposure applied to men as well. Both men and women were warned about exposing armpit hair, which the church considered indecent. Senior officials also discouraged wearing shorts. The exposure of knees was seen as inappropriate for either sex, but more so for women.

For special treatments, during services and prayers both ministers and patients were expected to wear white gowns. If a patient did not own a personal gown, the church might lend her one. For many functions the church approved the wearing of a white T-shirt and a lappa (a colorful wraparound garment).[4] However, it usually found unacceptable the full two-piece lappa outfit. Ministers stressed that dwellers and members should not wear multicolored suits or outfits to services and prayers. As one minister noted, "it caused confusion, temptation." Eventually a dweller, whether male or female, purchased a white robe or suit, especially when he or she became a member. For the church the white clothing denoted both purity and equality; indeed it could be listed among "holy materials." The clothing also represented the subject's new standing before God, which was not determined by status or wealth. For some, its cultural implication was clear: it undercut the civilized-country dichotomy that continued to inform Liberian society. During open-air preaching, members and cross bearers were required to wear white gowns. They were also encouraged to wear shoes, not sandals or flip-flops. In the compound, however, they regularly wore sandals or flip-flops, which were easily removed when entering the chapel, the prayer room, or Mercy Ground.

Rule 6, that "patients should wear their sleeping suit only in their rooms," expressed a concern for proper dress. It also reminded the dweller that the Faith Home was a place of spiritual work, of struggle, not relaxation. The sleeping suit suggested slumber and idleness. Openly wearing pajamas undermined the morale of the compound. Dwellers were told that they should not wear pajamas when they slept in the chapel for treatments. Proper attire prepared one for dream contact with the other world. In this sense, clothing not only represented reality but also affected it.

Rules 7 and 8 indicate the importance of recognizing the Faith Home supervisor's authority and the concern about leaves. Successful training of followers and successful treatment of patients depended on strict adherence to the rules of obedience. Thus, applications for campus leaves were closely evaluated and curfews carefully enforced. Among Aladura Faith Homes, including St. Peter's, nine o'clock was the usual curfew time, though a supervisor could extend it depending on circumstances. Monitoring absences and reentries not only related to the dweller's spiritual condition but also to the purity of the Faith Home compound. Thus, a dweller's reentry received major attention. Dwellers were strictly forbidden to have sexual intercourse when they left the compound. An allowance might be given to a minister-in-training to visit his spouse if he was not presently engaged in a struggle, fasting, or a special healing treatment that required him to be in a "holy state." Returning from such visits, he should not reenter the compound unless he had bathed. During services or prayers a minister might receive a vision that revealed a dweller's transgression. The dweller was then disciplined and a special cleansing of the compound might be announced.

The prohibition against sexual intercourse on the premises applied especially to ministers. As we have seen, the church approved off-campus visits on a case-by-case basis. When I first attended St. Peter's, one minister's wife lived in Kpelle Town, and he visited her as his schedule allowed. After conjugal visits he bathed before returning to the compound. Once back at the compound, he bathed yet again—this time with holy water—before he reentered the altar or prayer room. Ministers also bathed with consecrated water after any physical contact with menstruating women. After her period, a female dweller bathed before reentering the chapel nave or the prayer room. Similar stipulations applied to individuals who had open or bleeding wounds. Buckley and Gottlieb (1988) contend that menstrual blood needs to be seen in terms of blood "out of place" (outside the body). I think this is a helpful way to understand the Aladura concern.[5] If a minister "spilt his seed" on holy ground, he also created impurity and needed to undergo a rite of purification. The two cases differed, however, in terms of necessity and choice. Even a minister's nocturnal emissions could be interpreted as a matter of choice: these could happen through choosing to make love with a jina. Interestingly enough, despite the attention the church gave to such bodily issuances, there were no posted rules regarding them. Nor did Adejobi's manual on Faith Home decorum include any such reference. Perhaps this absence could be attributed to some sense of propriety. However, in both formal and relaxed settings the topic (especially menstruation) was hardly taboo. The nature of Faith Home behavior and social exchanges and the concern about the integrity of sacred space required frank discussion and steady attention to such matters.

Purity rules also governed how St. Peter's handled the dead. Like other Aladura churches, it did not "church" a corpse, since members believed it polluted the compound.[6] Funeral ceremonies took place at the home of the deceased and at the graveside. Since the church frequently admitted individuals with serious illnesses, there was always the risk of a death occurring on the premises. However, a prophet who was "in power" would be able to predict death and take the necessary precautions, which involved moving the dying person to a sheltered area behind the Faith Home. A senior prophet told me that when he did a spiritual interview he knew then whether a person would live or die. If prayers revealed death, the patient was not admitted, though treatments might be administered at home. Once at St. Peter's a junior prophet admitted a patient, a small boy near death. At the time the senior prophet was away. For several days ministers treated the patient in the Faith Home, where he and family members stayed in the large common room. But his condition only worsened. When the senior prophet returned, he prayed over the patient and then ordered the other ministers to carry the boy behind the compound, where he expired an hour later. One minister later told me that had the boy died within the Faith Home the grounds would have become spoiled.

Though regulations about food do not appear on the list above, the topic received major attention in the everyday praxis of the Faith Home. Effective healing necessitated control over the preparation, cooking, and consumption of food. Such control made dwellers less vulnerable to witchcraft, which often used food to harm its victims. Food prepared and eaten within the church grounds was frequently contrasted with food prepared and eaten in a country kitchen, at home, at school, or in the workplace. Food prepared and eaten outside the compound was more easily poisoned by one's enemies. Witchcraft incidents that involved food did occur from time to time within the Faith Home compound, but these usually happened because someone had brought in something from outside. As we have seen, Minister Saydee believed he became ill from bread prepared at home by Sister Felicia, whom he later accused of witchcraft. At St. Peter's a female cross bearer was usually assigned the cooking chores. Ministers who undertook special struggles or who fasted often appointed a trusted cross bearer to prepare their food.

As St. Peter's list of regulations indicates, Faith Home praxis depended on a system of propriety among dwellers. Rule 3 implied the general respect junior ministers exercised toward senior ministers. The rule regarding the bishop's room also applied to how dwellers should respect the quarters of any ranking minister. Dwellers recognized a correlation between rank and personal space. Senior prophets were granted the most privacy, while patients had the least. Junior ministers usually shared facilities with one another. Rule 4 stressed the need for male and female ministers to respect gendered space, a rule that applied to male and female patients as well. In general, however, male ministers took more liberties with female space than vice versa. At St. Peter's this had as much to do with seniority as with gender, since during my time at the branch headquarters the only female minister who outranked the male junior ministers was Olu's wife, the spiritual mother.

At the heart of the Faith Home praxis was the relationship between the prophet and the patient. Rule 5 emphasized the importance of the patient's respect for the minister's role and trust in his guidance. Similarly Adejobi's manual states that the dweller should always "observe and follow the instruction, advice and helpful suggestions emanating from the Faith Home Supervisor . . . [and] avoid idle talks, wandering, irregular actions, untoward conduct and all those things which are capable of causing blemish and scandal" (9). At St. Peter's Faith Home acceptance of the prophet's instructions signified a quality of faith considered crucial for an effective cure or solution. This involved not only the patient's submission to the prescribed treatments, but also completing the Faith Home tasks assigned to him or her (such as collecting firewood, sweeping the yard, washing clothes). Again, concerning this role, Adejobi insists that the dweller (the patient) should "perform willingly and humbly all such duties which may be allotted to him or her, or worthy to be performed in the Faith Home, such as sweeping, fetching water and cleaning the house of worship, and all such works which give health and are beneficial to the body and impart blessing and grace to the spirit" (9). At St. Peter's the most menial tasks performed by the patient were considered spiritual activities and part of the healing process.

One sign of the dweller's submission to Faith Home praxis was regular attendance of hourly prayers and worship services, as expressed by rule 10. Prayers took place in the chapel at least five times a day, every three hours, beginning at five thirty in the morning and concluding at six o'clock in the evening. As the Spirit led, prayers also took place at nine o'clock, after the usual conclusion. Indeed six, instead of five, daily prayers became the rule in many Aladura churches. Also, when a midnight struggle was called for prayers could take place through the night. Each regular prayer had a definite focus and drew from a list of designated psalms. Aladura churches by and large used a schedule like the one below taken from St. Peter's church bulletin:

HOURS	PRAYER
5:30 A.M.	Adoration Prayer and Victory Prayer
9:00 A.M.	Prayers for the Holy Spirit
12:00 P.M.	Prayers for all churches
3:00 P.M.	Prayers for all ministers
6:00 P.M.	Adoration Prayer, Thanksgiving Prayer, Confession Prayer
9:00 P.M.	Bedtime Prayer

Weekly services occurred three times: the Sunday morning Divine Worship and Wednesday and Friday evening services. Also, depending on circumstances and ministers' divine messages, other congregational services might be planned: healing clinics for Wednesday and Friday mornings or beach or midnight struggles for the Faith Home dwellers. Dwellers, their health permitting, attended all scheduled and announced events. During special struggles ministers expected them to be on their best behavior. One minister informed me: While a midnight struggle is going on, the Faith Home dwellers must keep themselves from intercourse. The same applies to beach struggles in the morning. If you are caught, if it is brought to light that you have done so, you will be punished, since you have spoiled the prayer." The combinations of rites created a kind of rhythm of activities with which dwellers engaged in varied ways.

For Faith Home violations the most common punishments were fasting and spiritual exercises. Sexual intercourse within the compound or while on leave, breaking the curfew, and rebuking a minister could result in dismissal. More often a patient was allowed to stay at the Faith Home but was penalized with a strenuous fast or assigned extra chores. Violators might also be required to run laps around the compound. An effective punishment for ministers, followers, and cross bearers was confinement behind the tent during prayers and services for one, three, or seven days. In large measure, the type and severity of a punishment depended on the supervisor's revelation and what the violator was capable of performing. Ministers might alter any punishment depending on new revelations. A punishment was intended to promote the welfare of a dweller, not to alienate him or her from others. The church interpreted these as trials that tested a person's commitment to the church's work, as well as her seriousness about solving a problem.

The system of rules and regulations at St. Peter's was understood as an intrinsic part of the dweller's healing and growth. Any violation became a serious matter. But violations were also expected. A Faith Home goal—whether a patient's cure or a follower's ordination—was rarely accomplished without awareness of some violation, mishap, or demonstration of doubt. The cycle of keeping and breaking rules implicated, in Bourdieu's terms, a habitus, [7] in which the struggle with temptations helped shape personal identity. Of course, the ritual dimension complemented the regulative, moral dimension of the Faith Home. Together these helped reinforce the structure and ordering of sacred space and time.

Among ritual struggles, the practice of fasting helped inform and structure the daily praxis of the Faith Home dweller. Earlier we examined the prophet's investment in fasting, which some considered the most important type of struggle—indispensable for the minister in his or her obtainment of virtue. The practice of fasting also informed and structured the relation between the minister and other dwellers. It helped create a bond of shared identification. In Handwerker's words, the Faith Home was "a consuming unit, that is, a group of people who customarily ate together or an individual who customarily ate alone" (1979, 189). Unlike the diet of Liberian households included in Handwerker's study, the diet of the Faith Home household involved intentional abstinence from food and water. Even an ordinary meal without intended religious purposes, in the context of the Faith Home and in relation to a fasting routine (whether the minister's, patient's, or both), gained a kind of sacramental value. Each day, food for ending a fast was prepared, consecrated, and blessed in a way that changed it into superordinary nourishment. Whether standing alone or accompanying other rites, whether performed by the minister or the dweller, the struggle of fasting ideally enhanced the efficacy of ritual, the bonds among dwellers, and the sanctity of the grounds.

The Holy Bath

Holy baths were frequently prescribed spiritual treatments. A holy bath was a fundamental healing technique in which a patient received prayers from a prophet and bathed with consecrated water. For the Aladura the term *consecration* applied only to things and places. The term was used to denote a process of purification: through a ritual procedure, a thing or place was changed from an impure, or spoiled, state to a purified one. Many Aladura informants however insisted that it was a mistake to see the holy bath as representing a kind of purification.[8] In order to perform a holy bath it was necessary to use consecrated elements, which had been purified. But the holy bath itself did not purify; it offered protection and empowered the subject.

The Aladura generally identified three types of holy baths: ordinary, candle, and circle. These were administered in the Faith Home as part of a dweller's treatment or on an outpatient basis. The details of any holy bath—regarding number and color of candles and day and location of the ceremony—varied depending on the circumstances of each case and the prophet's revelation.

As the word *ordinary* suggests, the ordinary holy bath was the most commonly performed at St. Peter's Faith Home. It usually took place over one or three days. Candles might be used, but the patient was not always expected to supply them. The ordinary holy bath was performed mainly to ensure blessings and to avert misfortune. In the course of a year some members took several ordinary baths, often with one-day treatments. It was easier to schedule the one-day bath around a work or school schedule. Sunday mornings and evenings and Wednesday nights after church were typical times for administering baths. For established members the ordinary bath provided a booster, as it were, that maintained the effectiveness of previous treatments. Also, both members and patients took ordinary baths as a stopgap for more complicated treatments presently not feasible or affordable. Migrants newly arrived from the country often came to St. Peter's for a one-day bath to empower them in their search for work or to reunite with a relative. For the ordinary bath the patient provided necessary materials: towel, soap, olive oil, and Florida water. If he could not afford them, the church drew from its stock of materials donated or left by previous patients, provided that these had not been consecrated in another person's name. The Faith Home supplied a white gown and white bucket needed for the water consecration.

The first stages of the ordinary bath involved consecration of the patient and the elements. The chapel sanctuary, prayer room, or Mercy Ground were the ideal locations in the Faith Home at St. Peter's, but ministers also presided over ordinary bath rites in their quarters or in the common room when the former spaces were unavailable. The rite included a prayer for protection and deliverance and reading the psalms prescribed in Oshitelu's manual. In most cases, however, Psalm 23 was recited. The minister also voiced several holy names during the blessing. He used the holy rod, a cross, or simply his right hand in praying over the patient and elements. A canister of burning incense was usually placed nearby. The patient faced the minister, knelt before him, bowed her head, and raised her hands with open palms. The patient was usually instructed to hold her soap and towel. A bucket of water was set before her. During prayers the patient remained still as the minister performed a variety of gestures. He stirred the water with the holy rod and signed the cross. Palm leafs were usually placed in the water. If he was a rod holder, the minister often inserted the rod into a bottle of olive oil, moving it back and forth several times. Often he waved a candle or incense around the patient's head. After the prayer of consecration, the patient took the water, soap, and towel and entered the spiritual bathroom for her bath. When she had finished bathing, she returned for concluding prayers. The minister poured olive oil into her palms, which she rubbed together and over the exposed areas of her body. The olive oil provided a layer of protection from evil spirits. Then the prophet delivered a divine message about the patient's condition that he may have received during the prayers. A benediction concluded the holy bath. Afterward the prophet and patient would discuss the further steps needed to ensure a successful treatment.

Like the one-day bath, the three-day ordinary bath was performed primarily for the obtainment of certain blessings that the minister had announced "will surely come your way" by doing the struggle. As one might expect, the three-day bath was considered stronger. It generated more virtue and created a stronger layer of protection. While I attended St. Peter's, I underwent a three-day ordinary bath, which three different ministers had told me I needed in order to receive certain blessings upon my return to the United States. The first phase of my bath took place at 3:00 P.M. in the prayer room. The church provided the bucket, the water, the gown, and the palm leaves. I had been asked to purchase the soap, the towel, and the bottle of olive oil. These had all been placed in the prayer room for consecration. A senior prophet supervised the ritual, giving the opening and closing prayers. He was assisted by a male junior minister and a female cross bearer. Otherwise the procedure followed what has been outlined above.

The next day at three I returned for my second day of prayers and bath. This time the cross bearer led the opening prayers. She provided me with the same soap and towel I had used the previous day, which I left in the spiritual bathroom after each bathing. On the first day the senior prophet had consecrated the water using the holy rod; on the second day the cross bearer simply stirred it with her right index finger. After completing the bath, I returned for the oil and prayers to the prayer room, where I received the day's final benediction from the cross bearer. On the third day the senior prophet returned to lead both the opening and final prayers. More palm leaves had been added to the water: on the first day ministers used three; now there were seven. For final prayers the senior prophet was joined by the junior minister and the cross bearer. And as was customary, they simultaneously voiced individual prayers, each emphasizing the blessings I would receive. The concluding prayers of any holy bath that occurred over a period of three or more days often involved several ministers and cross bearers. Strength in numbers boosted the power of the holy bath.

The candle bath could take place over one, three, or seven days. Candles were used directly in consecrating the elements and the patient. White candles were used most often. Ministers considered the candle bath more powerful than the ordinary bath. At the ones I observed, a minister used candles previously consecrated within the altar. When he prayed over the patient and elements, the minister instructed the patient to hold one candle or a cluster of three over a bucket of water. As he prayed over the patient, he would take the candle and wave it around her head, first three times clockwise and then three times counterclockwise. He would make the sign of the cross over the water with the candle and finally dip it into the water. The circular motion of the candles around the head almost always indicated protection against the threat of evil spirits. The Aladura considered the head of a person to be his or her most vulnerable part, where an evil spirit might easily enter. During services and prayers, whenever a prophet gave a vision about the threat of witchcraft or evil spirits, members and patients frequently waved their right hands with a circular motion over their heads: they were shooing away the evil spirit. I was told the candle represented the descent of the Holy Spirit. The waved candle created a screen of smoke and fire that protected the subject from the advances of malevolent power. The melted wax that dripped into the water and the flame that was extinguished in it transmitted the protective power of virtue.

The importance of circle symbolism becomes fully apparent with the circle bath, which prophets prescribed for life-threatening problems. The patient and the bathing materials were blessed within a circle of candles. Circle baths took place over three, seven, thirteen, or twenty-one days. If the Spirit so directed, a candle or circle bath could be scheduled with one- or three-day intervals between each bathing. The intervals allowed time for the holy materials to obtain greater strength. In most cases the ministers used seven or twenty-one candles. White candles were used most often; but in cases in which the power of jina or witches had become stronger, black and red candles were called for. The white candles helped protect and build up the patient's power, whereas black and red candles more effectively destroyed the witch's power and helped free the subject from its hold. The circle of candles created an invisible screen between the patient and holy materials and the evil spirit, who attempted to spoil the materials, to make them ineffective. For circle baths with twenty-one candles, the patient sat within a circle of fourteen candles and held a cluster of seven candles over the bucket of water. After a prophet concluded his prayers over the patient, he took the seven candles and, as in the candle bath, waved them around the patient's head. He took each candle, first the seven hand-held candles and then the fourteen from the circle, and extinguished them in the bucket of water. Again, the wax and flame of each candle was not wasted, its potency transmitted materially into the water that the patient used for bathing.

It is important again to emphasize that any holy bath was accompanied by an assortment of other procedures that were understood to increase the effectiveness of the bath. Dwellers especially were expected to follow stringently the rules and regulations of the Faith Home. Fasting always accompanied the bath, whether it was performed by the minister, the patient, or a substitute. If any broke the fast before the bathing sequence was completed, then the healer considered the bath ineffective. An effective holy bath always depended on the guidance of the prophet, on how much he inspired the trust and obedience of the patient, and on his diligence in obtaining personal virtue.

Beach Struggles

Services, prayers, or treatments that took place at the beach were called beach struggles. Ministers underwent private beach struggles but more often they led group performances that involved the entire church, or a smaller group, such as cross bearers, Army of Jesus ushers, or dwellers. Aladura churches generally discouraged members and patients from taking beach struggles on their own without a prophet's supervision. Ministers required their patients to take beach struggles for a variety of reasons—for confession, protection, penance, or thanksgiving. Individual and group beach struggles were one-, three-, seven-, and thirteen-day events. For the beach struggle the minister usually prayed over the patient and then told him to bathe in the ocean. He might also instruct the patient to perform several sets of spiritual exercises: jumping, running, and rolling. If the Spirit so directed, the prophet did these along with the patient. The struggle also involved the minister and patients sharing visions and dreams.

At St. Peter's the ministers usually chose a beach near the property that served as the church's Tabborrar site. The association was important, but any fairly secluded beach location could work. The Aladura believed ocean water was invested with special potency—its appearance demonstrated the power of God; it also contained salt, which was used as an additive in other healing procedures, such as house consecrations, animal sacrifices, and incense treatments. Ministers believed salt was an effective medicine for treating advanced cases involving witchcraft.

I knew ministers who took private beach struggles on a regular basis. In the Aladura world the minister's time mostly belonged to others—to seniors, members, patients, and dwellers. But even junior ministers who, among Faith Home dwellers, had little time available for private pursuits, were encouraged by their seniors to do private prayers away from the compound. Still, the authorities cautioned the junior minister about private struggles that turned into personal quests for power over others, and the minister who often prayed alone in an isolated place could also arouse suspicion. Such ambivalence, however, contributed to the power of the beach struggle: the struggle was a necessary venture, but it also brought risks and temptations.

The beach struggles that I attended involved those performed by dwellers—the ministers and patients presently living in the Faith Home. At St. Peter's, beach struggles for dwellers usually happened in the morning, beginning with nine o'clock prayers. Group struggles usually numbered between ten and twenty people. The ministers would clear out area that would represent the altar for the prayers, mark it with a circle drawn in the sand, and then dig a hole into which they placed a candle. A wood cross or staff was placed near the hole. Bottles and containers that had been filled with ocean water were placed within the space. Then a prophet faced the ocean with arms stretch wide, held the holy rod high, and began prayers. Dwellers would kneel behind him. A cross bearer would be busy fumigating the area with incense.

The prophet (or prophetess) rang the altar bell and began the liturgical prayers. He would deliver a series of invocations and, after completing them, prostrate himself on the ground. The other ministers and dwellers followed suit. Once he had finished, he entered and knelt within the circle altar and began another set of prayers. From here, the struggle began to resemble usual services: with the Adoration Prayer, psalms, hymns, the Lord's Prayer, the Victory Prayer. The beach struggle also included shouts—introduced by three songs with each picking up in tempo and intensity. During the fourth song the prophet left the circle altar and moved freely among the participants. The dancing became more charged, as participants began moving over a wider space. Over the next thirty minutes or so some of the participants would fall in Spirit. Some would run to and from the sea, others would collapse on the beach and begin to roll. Moving among the dwellers, the prophet would instruct each to kneel; he then placed his hand on her and prayed. Sometimes he commanded a patient to stretch out on the sand and roll. At some point in the struggle, as dwellers looked on, the ministers would perform a series of spiritual exercises and dances.

After shouts, the prophet in charge told the other ministers and cross bearers to form a circle and then instructed successive groups of patients to enter the circle to receive prayers: first children, then pregnant women, other women, and finally men. After each person had been blessed within the circle, he or she would sit on the sand, facing the ministers. For the next several minutes the ministers and patients shared dreams and visions. Eventually the prophet reentered the circle altar, knelt, and gave concluding prayers. For the benediction he stood, faced others, and stretched his arms toward the sea. Even with the struggle concluded, the ministers continued to pray over the dwellers and to consecrate containers of water. They reminded some dwellers that they needed to bathe in the ocean before they returned to the Faith Home.

Faith Home ministers dance and perform spiritual exercises during a beach struggle. Photograph by author.

Faith Home ministers leading dwellers during a beach struggle. The participants march counterclockwise around altar indicated by staff next to hole wherein a burning candle has been placed. Photograph by author.

Beach struggles for a group of dwellers or members followed the basic structure described above, but the ritual movements that occurred during shouts could vary considerably, depending on the direction of the Holy Spirit. I attended one St. Peter's beach struggle in which the ministers instructed dwellers to march counterclockwise around the altar. They marched while singing hymns for well over an hour. The marching eventually segued into a period of rolling. When I asked about the reason for the circle marching, the prophet simply explained it as the will of the Spirit. Whatever the reason, the circle movement immediately evoked for me other forms of bodily praxis that involved circle images or motions: the circle bath, the circle of smoke for incense treatment, the dancing circle of cross bearers consecrating a patient, and the fence of Tabborrar that enclosed ministers.

In her work on Kpelle dance Ruth M. Stone notes how performers mark out a dance space "in a counterclockwise direction, moving in slow, nondance steps to the music sound" (1994, 391). The movements suggest clearing out village space within a forest and creating a protective fence. The performance always assumes interaction between visible and invisible forces. The human specialists are indeed mediums of the supernatural, their instruments the voices of spirits. Within the imagined fence, the Kpelle performers invite the presence of supportive powers while they attempt to exclude the harmful.[9] Similarly, for the Aladura the circle motion in the beach struggle evoked a clearing-out process whereby the Children of Salvation separated the wheat from the chaff through arduous, but enlivened, work. Through movement and music they enclosed themselves within a protective zone. Participants obviously obtained new insights about the meaning and use of various ritual insignia, but what appeared most striking was the rite's sense of motion, directionality, and position. For the Aladura these forms of embodiment expressed and created connections between the self (or body), a specific space, and the efficacy of ritual struggle.

A FOCUSED SPACE

The Faith Home served as the hub of ritual, moral, and social life and provided a primary image, in Fernandez's terms, a "grounded image" (1978, 229), that helped subjects obtain meaning and purpose in their lives. For many individuals in the urban setting, the Faith Home represented an alternative location that offered strategies for self-renewal. Through ritual, moral, and social means, it offered a refuge from the malevolent forces that caused misfortune, pain, and uncertainty. According to Aladura theology, the Faith Home made this possible through its mediation of spiritual power. As a "lived space," it projected the idea of a household where ministers, members, and patients interacted and consequently shaped the Aladura way. The Faith Home constantly evolved a "web of interdependency" (Fox-Genovese 1988, 31) that expressed the importance of both hierarchical and reciprocating functions.

The idea of the Faith Home as refuge was embedded in Aladura doctrine. In his manual Adejobi offers biblical support for this image, citing Numbers 35:6, 29, which mentions certain cities of refuge as havens for Israelites and strangers. He also cites Galatians 6:10, in which the apostle Paul states, "As we have therefore opportunity, let us do good unto all men, especially unto them who are of the household of faith." The representation of the Faith Home as shelter from evil and misfortune became especially meaningful in the African context. The ministers saw ritual struggle in the Faith Home as an effective way to deal with problems caused by witchcraft and evil spirits. The image of refuge undoubtedly implied a surrounding world of danger and uncertainty. At St. Peter's the sermons, dream and vision narrations, and prayers made constant reference to the "protection" that the church dispensed through the Faith Home.

In Liberia the Faith Home image also implied the transformation of a traditional social model, the contrast between village and bush. Both Liberian and Sierra Leonean ethnographies support a village-bush dichotomy according to which the village represented the safe cultural domain and the bush the foreboding natural realm. The village was a bounded, domesticated space supported by ancestral traditions and laws, while the bush was free, undomesticated space controlled by supernatural forces, such as jina. But the creativity and continuity of society actually depended on the interactions between these domains. As d'Azevedo (1966) notes about Gola culture and Bellman (1975) about Kpelle, the architects and artisans of society obtained their extraordinary genius and power through liaisons with bush spirits. Ethnographies on Poro and Sande initiations demonstrated the importance that social mediations between village and bush had for making new persons. The traditional cosmology thus indicated an ambiguous, but necessary, relationship between the two domains.

The traditional imagery appeared in the prophet's emphasis on the bush struggle. Ministers frequently alluded to the bush struggle as a necessary event in their spiritual growth, an endeavor that imitated Moses on Sinai and Jesus in the wilderness. As in traditional Liberian cosmology, the bush represented a place inhabited by supernatural forces; but in the Aladura cosmology these forces obtained an image of negative power that challenged the prophet's virtue. The struggle with such forces was considered necessary for spiritual progress. In prophet cosmology the term *bush* continued to evoke a meaningful concept. For the church, the Faith Home–town opposition became more dominating, with the term *town* assimilating the attributes of the bush. Prophets warned patients and members about catching jina "behind" them when they traveled through both bush and urban areas.

The cultural values ascribed to the village-bush dichotomy, then, became absorbed into the Faith Home–town dichotomy. Though the new urban setting evoked the bush or forest as unknown, uncertain, and dangerous, it yet held promise for new knowledge and experience. In Richard Werbner's terms, the Faith Home represented an "ambiguously focused space" that contrasted with town-bush "ambiguously unfocused space" (1989, 303–10). Consequently the exchanges and movements between Faith Home and town—the new bush, as it were—became serious undertakings. Though the Aladura understood that the Faith Home offered protection from negative forces, the boundaries were vulnerable. Violations, transgressions, and impurities occurred from without and within, creating unavoidable ambiguities and always prompting ritual struggle.

For St. Peter's, witchcraft often represented a greater challenge than jina. Competition among prophets and members and the laxity of patients made witchcraft, even within the compound, an ever-present reality. Faith Home consecrations were often authorized because witchcraft was perceived within the church or at the compound. Ironically its occurrence became a catalyst for creative response. Aladura healing always assumed the reality of unseen forces, positive and negative, and the Faith Home, the healing clinic, became the vortex, as it were, of interaction between these forces. In this "ambiguously focused space" the sacred was always relational and never "mutually exclusive" with the profane. Even if the church presented an ideal of inviolate holiness, it constructed a place that commingled sacred and profane realities. And awareness of this ambiguity mandated ritual struggle.

In his discussion of ancient Hebrew temple rites, Jonathan Z. Smith notes:

> Ritual is a means of performing the way things ought to be in conscious tension to the way things are. Ritual relies for its power on the fact that it is concerned with quite ordinary activities placed within an extraordinary setting, that what it describes and displays is, in principle, possible for every occurrence of these acts. But it also relies for its power on the perceived fact that, in actuality, such possibilities cannot be realized. There is a "gnostic" dimension to ritual. It provides the means for demonstrating that we know what ought to have been done, what ought to have taken place. . . . Ritual thus provides an occasion for reflection on and rationalization of the fact that what ought to have been done was not, what ought to have taken place did not. From such a perspective, ritual is not best understood as congruent with something else—a magical imitation of desired ends, a translation of emotions, a symbolic acting out of ideas, a dramatization of a text, or the like. Ritual gains force where incongruency is perceived or thought about (1987, 109–10).

Aladura ritual also demonstrated the tension between what is and what ought to be. The architectural, moral, and social images of the Faith Home all reflected how ritual worked within the Aladura way. In Smith's terms, the Faith Home also became a place for "marking attention" (see 103–4) and effectively connecting ritual and spatial interest. Through Divine Worship, the five daily prayers, special healing events, beach struggles, and church consecrations, participants demonstrated their faith and commitment. These struggles helped redress the moral violations that occurred within the lived space. Here ritual simply simulated cosmology, the latter being distinguished by moral division.

In his work on the role that tropes about home have in religious life, Thomas Tweed notes that "bodies cross and dwell" (2006, 98). In the Aladura way this became expressed through a variety of temporal and spatial orientations: between this side and that side, village and forest, Faith Home and town, ritual time and ordinary time. The Faith Home in particular provided a centering space for the self's meaningful and effective crossing and dwelling. The prophet was seen as both the daring traveler and the one most at home. Dwelling implied stability, but also movement and adaptability within and beyond the Faith Home's ritual and moral space. As a focusing lens, a centering space, a place for marking attention, the Faith Home helped emplace the self (the body) through the praxis of ritual struggle.

Such emplacement enabled a synthesis of the Liberian and Christian selves. This assertion does not suggest a finished coherency between the two, which can hardly be claimed for any Christian culture. It simply underlines the specificity of Faith Home praxis in the meaningful and effective connections accomplished between bodies, ritual, and place. The Faith Home praxis also prepared the Aladura self for a more episodic form of "crossing and dwelling": the Mount Tabborrar rite.

6 ——

Mount Tabborrar

THE SACRED PASSAGE

In August came the most important ritual in the Aladura calendar: the celebration of Tabborrar. Ministers would "ascend" a sacred enclosure called Mount Tabborrar for thirteen days of "strong praying and fasting." The Mount Tabborrar observance was a rite of renewal and revival. St. Peter's members referred to it as the "battery" of spiritual power that sustained the church for the coming calendar year. The ritual occasioned prayers for redressing specific concerns, such as tensions and hostilities between branches, and the various physical, economic, and spiritual hardships that individuals faced. More than any event during the year, the Tabborrar season emphasized the dialectical relation between church habitus and the restructuring and renewing dimension of prophecy. Tabborrar was the event deemed most necessary for the church's well-being.

All Aladura churches in Liberia observed some form of the Tabborrar rite. The construction and observance of multiple Tabborrars, however, created controversy. The CLA authorities insisted that there could be "only one Tabborrar" and spoke of those founded by "breakaway churches" as inauthentic, examples of "stealing our doctrine." In the early 1970s David Fyneah's UCL had established the first independent, or breakaway, Tabborrar. Thereafter other breakaway churches followed suit, including St. Peter's. In the mid-1980s an extended August ritual of fasting and praying that resembled Tabborrar was commonly practiced among other AIC, many lacking any formal Aladura history but influenced by the CLA model. In 1984 Olu authorized that St. Peter's change the name of Tabborrar to Mount Olive. The name change would further distinguish the church from CLA. Two decades later, however, Tabborrar remained the preferred colloquial name.

During the thirteen days of Tabborrar, the ministers selected for Tabborrar remained secluded from the outside world. On the mount they were under the authority of the "head of the mount," a position assumed by the church's highest official. The ministers maintained a strict regimen of fasting and prayer. They did not shave or bathe until the final evening, when they donned new robes and welcomed members onto the mount. During Tabborrar, members and patients submitted "special requests" written in blue notebooks, which the ministers took with them onto the mount. The ministers prayed over each request and sought Spirit-revealed answers. A minister then wrote the answer—the "revelation"—into the notebook, tore out the pages, and enclosed them in an envelope to be returned after Tabborrar. While ministers were on the mount, other ministers, members, and patients assembled at the Faith Homes for the "holy struggle." On the evening of the thirteenth day, they marched to the mount, where they joined the ministers for a final service. The following Sunday, a thanksgiving service took place that celebrated the ministers' accomplishments. Weeks later, the church would publish a pamphlet of "Divine Revelations," in which the head of the mount reported the visions he received during the struggle. These included general prophecies for the next year concerning nations, churches, and associations.[1]

The 1984 observance of Tabborrar at St. Peter's is explored herein. That year witnessed the merger between St. Peter's and David Fyneah's UCL. The Tabborrar ritual therefore set into motion shifts, alignments, relocations, and promotions with repercussions for both parties. The event also happened against the backdrop of civil violence at the University of Liberia, which almost prevented the concluding ceremonies of Tabborrar from taking place. But what became the most distinguishing feature of the 1984 Tabborrar, which members discuss even today, was the conflict that developed on the mount between the head of the mount (Apostle Olu) and another minister, here pseudonymously named Daniel Solomon. According to informants, Solomon attempted "to witch" Olu and undermine the struggle; Olu, however, prevailed against him and exposed his plot. The 1984 event demonstrates forcefully the Aladura concept of prophecy, especially the importance of the founder paradigm articulated in Aladura practice: through a performative act, that is, by declaring in ritual settings that followed Tabborrar his conquest over adversity, Olu confirmed his authority and his power to renew the church. At the same time, the episode involving Solomon expressed the ambiguity and the indeterminate nature of occult power—whether articulated through unauthorized means or through a prophet's own ritual struggle. The narrative also testified to the church's capacity for absorbing a perceived misdeed. Though the Aladura spoke about the agonistic context of ritual action, they did not see evil as an absolute will but as a propensity shared by all.

"It will always be there"

The first Tabborrar was observed by CLA in Nigeria in 1937, based on a revelation to its founder, Josiah Oshitelu. Harold Turner notes that the name Tabborrar resembles the name Mount Tabor mentioned in Judges 4 (1967, 2:222). In that passage the prophetess Deborah commands Barak: "Hath not the Lord God of Israel commanded, saying, 'Go and draw toward mount Tabor, and take with thee ten thousand men.'" Barak requests that Deborah accompany them. Thus, she "went up with him," and later Barak "went down from mount Tabor, and ten thousand men after him" and defeated the Canaanites (4:10–14). The motifs of followers ascending and descending Mount Tabor with their leader and fighting the enemy suggest parallels with an Aladura Tabborrar. A notable contradiction, however, between the Tabor in Judges and the Aladuran Tabborrar concerned the role of women. In the former the ascent includes the prophetess Deborah; in the latter even senior prophetesses were excluded from "ascending" the mount until the final evening. There are other possible references for the name, but Turner contends that these still do not account for the church's choice (221–22). The biblical imagery of praying in a private place, often a mountain site, certainly informed the meaning of the Aladura Tabborrar. Moses' encounter with God on Mount Sinai and Jesus's praying on the Mount of Olives provided paradigms of struggle, not only for the Tabborrar ritual but also for periodic bush struggles.[2]

By 1944 the Tabborrar ritual had become a regular event in the calendar of the Nigerian CLA. By the late 1950s the ritual centered on the "mount" consecrated at Ogere, near the home of Oshitelu and the headquarters of the church. In Aladura sacred geography this became the church's holiest location (Turner 1967, 2:222). Its celebration also became an important aspect of the adaptation of the church in Liberia, Sierra Leone, and Ghana, but since it was difficult for members in those lands to journey to Ogere for the August event, it became necessary for them to sponsor the construction of their own Tabborrar sites. Under Samuel Oduwole's guidance, the Liberian mission established its own holy mount, but |it would always acknowledge the primacy of the Ogere Tabborrar. Every August representatives were sent to Ogere, carrying with them the special requests from Liberian members. I knew Liberian ministers, who, though firmly involved in their dioceses' celebration of Tabborrar, annually arranged for messengers to travel to Nigeria and to bring home containers of water and oil consecrated in Ogere. Although the CLA in Liberia claimed their mount was the holiest site in Liberia, and that the celebration of the Tabborrar ritual strengthened the church, for them, as for many others worldwide, the Ogere mount and the ritual that took place there remained unsurpassed.

Tabborrar expressed both the notions of sacred time and sacred space. Originally it seems that the idea of sacred time dominated. Tabborrar represented a special time for individual and collective praying and fasting. The actual location of the holy mount—the consecrated area where the selected prophets observed the ritual—was often a matter of expediency. In writing about former Tabborrar sites in Nigeria, Turner claims that the chosen site "cannot possess any intrinsic sanctity, and it becomes no more than a suitable place set apart for a sacred purpose" (222). Early observances of Tabborrar certainly implied an idea of the site's functional and impermanent nature. However, many of my Aladura informants insisted on the sanctity of Tabborrar mounts, including former sites. They considered the mount to be a "sacred place," and they would question Turner's claim that the site was "no more than a suitable place set apart for a sacred purpose." Some sacred sites, whether Tabborrar mounts or church compounds, became sacred, or holy, through revelations that a particular location was special. Former sites always remained revered, even if they became deserted, disused, or spoiled. Through ritual action, the sacred power of the place could always be reactivated. As one St. Peter's minister put it, a former site "will always be there, even if not used like a new one, since God had made it holy and it could not change." The CLA indeed had converted former Liberian mounts into branches, since they had a unique holiness, if not an "intrinsic sanctity."

When I lived in Liberia, St. Peter's had not established a "permanent" mount of its own. In 1984 the church observed the ritual at a beach lot that it had leased the year before. Members considered the location still "powerful," but the prophets would have to reconsecrate it for Tabborrar use. As I was told, former holy sites that lay in disuse attracted evil spirits curious about their power. Without a prophet's watchful eye, the site became polluted or spoiled. In the late 1980s and during the civil war, St. Peter's continued to use the beach lot. When battles raged in Paynesville, the church suspended open celebration; the Tabborrar struggle was quietly observed in homes and local branches. The beach site, however, continued to be revered. When he began a new church in Washington, D.C., Reverend Sandy would continue to speak about beauty and power of the site, which was special also because it was there that Sandy had experienced his first Tabborrar.

PREPARING FOR THE STRUGGLE

In 1984 St. Peter's began preparing for Tabborrar about two months before the event took place. The CLA always started its Tabborrar on August 10, so St. Peter's decided to begin its observance on the thirteenth in order to avoid possible conflict. The church also believed the rescheduled date would enable members from the mother church to attend its concluding ceremonies. A series of letters was sent to the different branches announcing the event and explaining its purpose. Members were reminded of the importance of submitting prayer requests along with paying the four-dollar fee. The monies raised would help pay for leasing the land, constructing the mount, and securing food stuffs, advertisements, and the brass band that would lead the closing-day procession. Instead of relying on the postal system, the church appointed messengers to deliver letters by hand to the branches. The special prayer requests needed to be submitted a week before Tabborrar. Authorities strongly discouraged late submissions but, as it turned out, they would not refuse requests that arrived late, even after the ministers had ascended the mount. The church also honored pledges from individuals.

In the weeks before Tabborrar the matter of who should ascend the mount became an issue. In the past both St. Peter's and the UCL had invited ministers from unaffiliated churches to take the struggle with them. But some, after ascending the mount and receiving its blessing, including ordination and the holy rod, "were never seen again." The recent merger and growth had prompted greater interest in self-definition and how the church dispensed its power. To invite outsiders to attend Faith Home struggles and church harvests was one thing, but to bring them onto the mount was another. All Aladura churches, like CLA, voiced concern about other churches "stealing" their doctrines, their blessings, and their power. Among Aladura prophets I knew, Olu was among the most generous with sharing sacred facilities and spaces. Regarding the 1984 Tabborrar, he insisted that invitations and appointments were a matter of spiritual direction and should not be based on past history. All the same, in 1984 the selected ministers came from the two divisions that had formed the merger.

A major part of the preparation for Tabborrar centered on life at the local churches and Faith Homes. Ministers had the responsibility of instructing members and patients in the mechanics and meaning of Tabborrar, in both formal and informal settings. As the ritual drew nigh, the Divine Worships, the prayer services, the healing clinics included more allusions to Tabborrar and the power it would bring for solving problems. The special requests that were being collected often referred to the affliction or problem that a person presently faced. For many patients participation in Tabborrar addressed in a more focused way certain healing treatments that had already been started. The site chosen for Tabborrar was about two miles away from the headquarters, just off Old ELWA Road. The site faced the ocean through a ridge of palm trees. There were several mud-stick and thatched-roof homes in the area. The inhabitants were mostly Bassa, and some attended St. Peter's. At the time the church had plans for constructing the mount on a hill at another location, but the ocean site was also suitable, even preferred by some members. In general, Aladura churches considered the ocean to be a place of power and used ocean water for special treatments. On the chosen lot sat an unfinished cinder-block house with two rooms, which the ministers would use for shelter and sleep. An elderly Bassa woman currently owned the land. She belonged to the Assemblies of God but planned to participate in Tabborrar, as she put it, "to see God's power."

The lot had been used for Tabborrar the previous year. But since then the landlady had rented the house to boarders who had not taken proper care of the place. Most alarmingly, the ministers claimed, evil spirits had come to dwell on the property. Disturbed by the haunting spirits, the residents vacated the house and the landlady had been unable to find other renters. So she came to the church asking for help and offered the property again for their use during Tabborrar. The ministers insisted that the site needed purification, which they would do at the beginning of the August rite. Rather than representing an obstacle, the presence of malicious spirits would immediately remind the ministers of the seriousness of the task before them.

The actual renovation and construction of the Tabborrar site took about two weeks. A senior prophet in the church was given responsibility for supervising its construction. The Faith Home ministers had taken one week to pull up the grass and roots and rake the ground smooth for rolling. They created an oval-shaped yard that extended from the building's entrance to the row of palm trees before the ocean. During the second week before Tabborrar, the ministers surrounded the yard with a bamboo-stick fence covered with palm branches. The fence was about seven or eight feet high. On the right side of the wall was the enclosure's only entrance. The junior minister Flomo used the entrance as the mount's "mid-runner": one who delivered messages between the Faith Home and the mount. At the rear of the fence, facing the sea, was a small opening by which ministers left for toilet. Other major features of the mount, such as "behind the tent," which was to be used to penalize ministers, and the altar, would be marked off and constructed once the ministers began the struggle. An elder in the church who lived nearby built a bathing hut for members and patients who came to the mount for holy baths.

Just before Tabborrar, the Faith Home at the headquarters buzzed with activity. The workload of the Faith Home ministers became especially heavy. The junior minister Flomo found himself overwhelmed with treatments, prayers, and house calls. In early July the other junior ministers had been temporarily assigned to other branches, and Flomo had also assumed many of their chores. The junior minister, though, rarely complained. He saw this period as a trial in his progress as a prophet. Virtue did not come without work. He remained mindful toward his seniors and attentive to his patients. During this time he dreamed that he saw himself before an altar. "Someone gave me directions about how to control the altar and they put oil in my hands." Olu later told Flomo that the dream represented "power, blessing, promotion." His present work would bring reward. Fortunately Flomo received assistance from other ministers, who began arriving at the Faith Home in the days and weeks before Tabborrar.

The assurance of victory through faith, the need for obedience, and the importance of confession and forgiveness were themes that repeatedly appeared in homilies, announcements, and prophecies in pre-Tabborrar services. Such

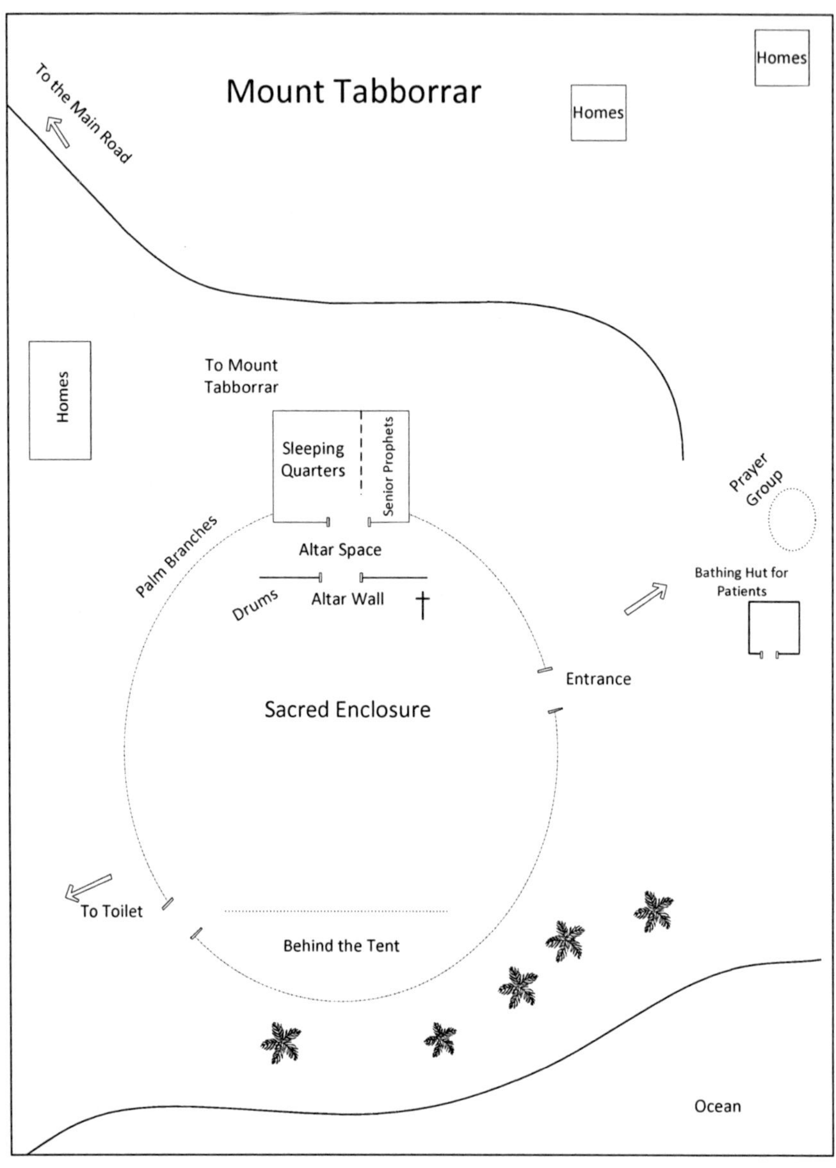

Diagram of the sacred enclosure of Mount Tabborrar.

Prepared by Peter Valdina, not to scale.

references gave a clear picture of Tabborrar as a process, not just a place; as an event in which all of the faithful must take part. The holy struggle represented a sacred passage that would strengthen the church for the coming year. It is important to stress, however, that the temporal understanding of struggle became stronger only as the spatial sense became more defined. For St. Peter's, what gave the struggle its redemptive power was the prophets' specific engagement on the mount.

Both attendance and enthusiasm increased at the weekly services and daily prayers as Tabborrar drew closer. At services, shouts become progressively "hotter," with more individuals than usual "caught up" in the Spirit. The two successive Sunday morning services before Tabborrar occasioned more visions than any services I had previously attended. The first happened to be the monthly "cleansing service," when ministers sprayed the congregants with holy water and gave them palm leaves. These acts heralded blessings of the coming month. Every cleansing service was festive, but the August cleansing service was especially enlivened by the anticipation of Tabborrar. The second Sunday service on August 12, the morning before the ministers' evening ascent, was even more dynamic. On Saturday evening in a private meeting with St. Peter's male clergy, Olu disclosed the names of the thirteen mount ministers and assigned their roles. Among the thirteen, three made quick visits to their home branches before returning for the ascent; but the other ministers remained at the headquarters through Sunday. During Sunday's Divine Worship, the ministers delivered homilies, narrated visions, and interpreted dreams that repeatedly heralded Tabborrar's coming victory over evil and misfortune. One minister called Mount Tabborrar the "friend" that would see the faithful through their hardships.

The Divine Worship that Sunday extended well into the afternoon. In the evening, activities on the church grounds became more relaxed. One sensed a welcome interlude of rest before work resumed. Members and patients made last-minute preparations for their stays in the Faith Home. Ministers completed final errands, family visits, and house calls. Some partook of favorite meals before starting their fasts. The Sunday evening service, which preceded the ascent by only a few hours, appeared considerably lackluster in comparison with the morning Divine Worship. Only one senior prophet attended. Shouts were unusually short. The senior prophet's sermon, however, drew special attention. He emphasized that dwellers needed to obey the junior ministers who were appointed to serve the Faith Home. One was Flomo, whom Olu had also appointed messenger between the mount and the Faith Home. The other appointee was a young Krahn man named Charles Isaiah, who had arrived at the compound from an interior branch only a few days before. Neither Flomo nor Isaiah was a rod holder, a significant detail. But the senior prophet reminded dwellers that the junior ministers represented the authority of the mount.

FIRST WEEK

Late Sunday evening, August 12, the ministers collected the necessary materials: special requests, writing materials, Bibles and booklets of psalms, buckets of small crosses and iron rods requiring consecration, and boxes of other holy materials, such as candles, incense, and bottles of Florida water and olive oil. Around nine o'clock, some junior ministers loaded my car with bags and boxes of materials, and we drove on to the mount. After helping unload materials, I waited at the mount while the ministers began consecration rites—fumigating it with incense, sprinkling it with holy water, and placing candles throughout. Once the first set of candles had burned down, the remaining holy materials were taken in. About two hours later, I drove Olu and two other senior prophets to the camp. After they entered the mount, Flomo and I returned to the Faith Home. At midnight Olu started the prayers that marked the official start of the thirteen-day struggle. At the various faith homes dwellers also began midnight struggles.

For the struggle Olu assigned ministers with special roles. There were ten official positions that needed to be filled: head of the mount, assistant mount leader, food inspector, foreman, disciplinary minister, secretary, cook, timekeeper, gatekeeper, and mid-runner. Olu, of course, assumed the office of head of the mount. The success of the Tabborrar, and therefore the empowerment of the church, depended on his direction. As its leader, Olu epitomized the church. As head of the mount, he supervised all services, prayers, interviews, treatments, and meetings. When he was unable to conduct a ceremony, he delegated that function to other senior prophets. On the mount he would receive special divine messages about healing cases, church policies and issues, and future promotions and assignments. Some required urgent response and needed attention during Tabborrar, while others could wait until after struggle.

For the position of assistant mount leader, Olu appointed a senior archdeacon from St. Peter's Grand Gedeh branch. A Krahn man in his forties, he had once belonged to the CLA but joined St. Peter's soon after it was founded. Olu considered him to be one of the most capable leaders in the church, though he was not well known among many Monrovia-area members. As assistant mount leader, he helped Olu with prayers and treatments, and on occasion took over for him. His chief responsibility was supervising visits by other ministers and members, and he paid special attention to the performance of the younger and less experienced ministers, who might be tempted to break their fasts or leave the camp surreptitiously. Such conduct could harm the entire struggle. For instance, if a minister stole his way out of the camp, it was best that he not return. Leaving the camp showed a lack of commitment and disrespect for seniority. Furthermore, reentering risked bringing in impurities from outside.

The food inspector examined the food that was brought into the camp each day by the mid-runner. For this role Olu appointed an archdeacon from the Bong Mine branch. The prophets broke their fast every evening after six o'clock prayers. The food inspector made sure that each minister ate the food prescribed for breaking the fast. In the first week the prophets underwent a white fast that prescribed eating only raw foodstuffs—vegetables, fruit, nuts—and cooked cassava or rice. The preparation and cooking of food only occurred within the camp, since cooked food brought in from outside could more easily be witched. The food inspector, then, worked closely with the mount cook, a position assigned to a junior minister. As one minister put it, both needed "to have the knowledge and strength to prevent witch food." The cook also had the special task of preparing food for the head of the mount, who ate alone after the others had finished eating.

For the position of foreman, Olu appointed the senior prophet who had supervised the clearing and renovation of the mount. The senior prophet had also been mentored by Bishop David Fyneah and, like Olu, had regarded him as his "spiritual father." The foreman supervised the construction of the altar area and the maintenance of the camp fence. During the first week of Tabborrar the altar was built as the prophets gradually obtained the necessary spiritual power. Its completion was paced over a period of seven days. On the seventh day the prophets were considered empowered enough to sustain its sanctity. The altar fronted the building's entrance, marked off by a cinder-block wall made four layers high. Within the altar were placed benches and an altar table, before which there was a white cross. The foreman also gave special attention to the condition of the fence. The fence served a very practical purpose—to keep ministers from looking out and outsiders from looking in. A prophetess once told me that it was especially useful for preventing ministers from seeing women, which might distract them from their struggle.

A minister from a former UCL branch in Bomi Hills held the position of disciplinary minister. This officer reminded ministers of the rules and regulations that governed conduct on the mount and determined the punishments for those who violated them. The usual violations were sleeping at inappropriate times, missing prayers, partaking of proscribed food, challenging superiors, and speaking in anger. Violations caused enough harm to the struggle, but an unpunished violation made matters even worse. Punishments varied, but they often involved confining the offender to behind the tent, marked off by a line furrowed in the sand near the camp's back wall. The offender might also be required to undergo a more severe fast, such as a dry fast.

The mount secretary played a special role in transcribing the divine messages revealed to senior prophets. He recorded dreams and visions and their interpretations. For this task Olu appointed Kennedy Sandy, then a junior minister who had only recently been ordained. He had been a follower at the headquarters for only about four months. His appointment to ascend the mount came as a surprise for many, but Olu undoubtedly had confidence in the junior minister's ability as a recorder and promise as a prophet. Tabborrar on the mount focused on the work of senior prophets, but the inclusion of junior prophets promoted the continuity of power and authority. A minister's first mount experience marked an initiation into deeper levels of prophetic knowledge. Olu had already recognized in Sandy prophetic skills, since recording also involved the talent to receive a revelation. The transcription of revelations necessitated gifted concentration and accuracy in writing down messages without distortion.

Olu appointed as time keeper David Modee, a junior minister who had apprenticed under a senior prophetess at a UCL branch in Paynesville. The timekeeper's major responsibility was to announce prayers, which occurred every three hours. The regular Faith Home schedule designated prayers five or six times daily, beginning at six in the morning and concluding at six in the evening. For Tabborrar, both in the Faith Home and on the mount, prayers continued every three hours through the night and into the wee hours of the morning—at nine, twelve, and three o'clock. The mount timekeeper, then, took care to signal time for prayers. He needed to make sure he did not oversleep or let others do so. During the first week Modee once slept past the starting time for 3:00 A.M. morning prayers, which, as he told me, "weakened" the mount. For this slip he was put on a dry fast. It had also been revealed to a senior prophet that Modee fell asleep because an "evil spirit" had entered the camp. This occurrence implicated the gatekeeper, a position that rotated among junior ministers. The ineffective gatekeeper was also placed on a dry fast. The gatekeeper's job was to make sure uninvited people or animals did not enter the compound. He also inspected the yard, the altar, and sleeping quarters for snakes. Snakes in the area always indicated that "evil forces might try to enter." During prayers the gatekeeper was the only minister who remained standing.

The last mount position was the mid-runner, which Olu gave to Flomo. For multiple reasons the mid-runner traveled back and forth between the mount and the headquarters: conveying messages, reporting on a patient's treatment or on a member's acrimony, bringing patients to the mount for special treatments, obtaining food appropriate to fast, and sometimes just to pray for his own spiritual wisdom. On some days Flomo made as many as seven or eight trips back and forth. Occasionally he was offered a ride from a member visiting the compound. I was able to drive him back and forth several times during the struggle, which proved especially useful for Flomo when he needed to communicate urgent messages. The frequent walks back and forth, however, were unavoidable; indeed these testified to his sacrifice.

During the first week the prophets prayed mainly for the strength to carry out their struggle. In their prayers they professed the sacrifice they were making "in order to be holy in God's sight." Early prayers focused on the meaning of the struggle: what it would accomplish for the church. For the first week they undertook a white fast, which was designed to build up their physical strength and virtue for the second, more serious week. Fasting was in many ways the exemplary sign of a prophet's commitment; during Tabborrar its performance took on even more significance. When the prophets broke their daily fast, they always encircled and prayed over a bucket of holy water and the food for breaking the fast. The senior prophets placed holy rods in the water, while the head of the mount read psalms. Then he prayed the "prayer of consecration" that blessed and purified the water and food. The ministers then knelt toward the altar area, which was being constructed, in rows according to rank. In the second week after the altar was completed, they would kneel before the head of the mount who, from behind the altar, administered to each a cup of holy water to end the day's fasting. After the ministers had received their portion of food, the head of the mount took his food and entered a back room. There he recited a short prayer and ate his meal alone in silence.

The first week was also taken up with meetings and discussions about church bylaws, regulations, changes, and doctrines. The ministers spent much time exploring the meaning of Aladura doctrine. For the first time senior prophets introduced junior ministers to certain special curative techniques and told them about the meaning of the most effective holy names. They were guided in the study of the Bible and especially on how to use certain passages, such as the psalms, when treating patients. They were told more about how to interpret signs and symbols in dreams and visions and how to detect and expose witchcraft. The church made the customary distinction between "trained" and "revealed" knowledge, but during Tabborrar this became somewhat superficial, since all knowledge communicated by senior prophets to junior ministers was considered revealed. Of course, the exploration of the meaning of Aladura doctrine went hand in hand with its constant performance. Besides persistent praying, fasting, prophesying, and rolling, the ministers implemented a regiment of consecrations and treatments. They received messages that sometimes required immediate treatment of patients. Often the Faith Home ministers administered these, once they had received the message through the mid-runner; but sometimes the patient's journeying to the mount was required, and if the patient was a male, even admission into the mount for consultation and for treatment.

With the ministers' focused praying and fasting, the construction of an altar, the consecration rituals, the younger ministers' initiation into new forms of Aladura doctrine, and the performance of spiritual treatments, the camp members became more prepared for the demanding tasks of the second week. Seen from the angle of life in the Faith Home, life within the Tabborrar camp at first appeared to move along in a predictable fashion. Later, though, it was learned that the head of the mount had faced a challenge in the first week that almost sabotaged the event. Indeed this particular struggle helped define the character of St. Peter's 1984 Tabborrar. Members came to interpret it as a confirmation of Olu's authority and as a sign of future blessings. For now though, I return to life in the Faith Home, the arena that engaged most participants, including myself, more immediately.

The Faith Home Struggle

The junior prophets James Flomo and Charles Isaiah shared the responsibility of running the Faith Home. Female cross bearers, such as a long-serving one named Amelia, assisted them, but for the most part the burden of the healing chores rested on the ministers. Flomo had worked at the Faith Home for more than a year and was trusted by members and patients. Isaiah, though, was new to the compound. In his mid-twenties, he had belonged to several different groups— CLA, the Assemblies of God, the Never Die Church,[3] and the Roman Catholic Church. He had also experimented with "country medicine," which he called the "devil's business." In the year preceding his participation at Tabborrar, Isaiah had become a protégé of the senior prophet from Grand Gedeh, who had helped to set up his present assignment. Relatively inexperienced, Isaiah nonetheless showed self-confidence; but to some he appeared boastful, especially when leading prayers and services. His style contrasted notably with that of Flomo, who appeared more modest and calm. Since much of Flomo's time was taken up with mid-runner chores, Isaiah often led the Faith Home services and prayers.

In the first week the Faith Home quickly became crowded. Members wanted to take advantage of the spiritual invigoration the ministers were presently securing. They came as their jobs, daily tasks, and family and school situations allowed—usually for morning prayers or an evening service. On a day-by-day basis, they might come for the midnight struggle and sleep in the chapel. Others remained at the Faith Home for the entire struggle. The pattern of attendance and participation varied. Several patients were brought to the Faith Home by mount ministers, who continued to monitor the patients' treatment through the work of the mid-runner Flomo. Other patients were admitted well after Tabborrar was under way. The church relaxed its rules about admitting new dwellers and created new sleeping spaces in the chapel. And, even after the start of Tabborrar, the ministers continued to receive special requests.

The Faith Home's healing praxis became central during Tabborrar as each dweller focused on solving his or her problem. At the Faith Home of the headquarters, there emerged a nucleus of dwellers receiving persistent attention from the ministers. Among these were Rachel, a Mano woman with twins; her landlady Ma Martha, who came to the Faith Home because ministers believed her home was besieged by evil spirits and unsafe for habitation; a twenty-year-old

Bassa woman, with a small son, admitted for stomach problems that ministers attributed to witchcraft; a young Kissi woman, Mary, effected by a jina stranger she encountered at the nearby juncture; an old Gola man called Old Pa, who prayed that God would restore his vision; a young Bassa man who believed his estranged wife and her lover had plotted to sacrifice him to Nege; and a successful electrician and landlord who suffered from high blood pressure caused by "bad spirits" at his residence. In running the Faith Home, Flomo and Isaiah were assisted by two cross bearers—Sister Amelia, who was nanny to a senior prophet's children (she had submitted a special request for a husband), and Sister Annie Jackson, a young Bassa woman who had only recently arrived from an interior branch.

In the Faith Home the ministers performed treatments with even more regularity. They believed the rituals and holy materials they used were now considered more efficacious. On occasion the ministers led simultaneous treatments for individual patients in the chapel, the Mercy Ground, and the minister's quarters. The prayers always made reference to the work of Tabborrar and the "God of thirteen-day power." The altar area became cluttered with containers of water and oil, which became newly endowed with Tabborrar virtue. The materials being consecrated on the mount were especially effective for treatments. The ministers urged all dwellers and members to keep their fast. They were especially encouraged to perform the white fast being observed by the mount prophets. The daily prayers, which punctuated the daily Faith Home routines, seemed to occasion more extended dream interpretations and evocative visions. On one occasion Flomo reported a portentous dream about the mount struggle, alluding to some difficulties the mount ministers were facing. Faith Home dwellers needed to pray for the work of the brave ministers. Our conversations during the struggle frequently turned toward the meaning and purpose of Tabborrar. Flomo emphasized the ministers' sacrifice on the mount and the rewards these would bring to the church. He frequently used the filial metaphor to refer to the relation between the ministers and dwellers. Olu was father, and dwellers were "children of the mount."

Often when I drove Flomo to the mount, I would wait for him to complete his work there. This was a good way to learn about new developments and also gave me an opportunity to provide a needed service. On one such trip Flomo, Isaiah, and I arrived as the ministers were in the middle of prayers. Flomo entered the compound to share and to receive new messages. Isaiah and I waited outside the fence. When we returned to the car Flomo reported that while he waited for the prayers to end he fell asleep on the sand. While he slept he received a vision in which he saw a lady facing the ocean. She delivered a warning that those who approached the mount with witchcraft in their hearts would be "drowned in the ocean."

After Flomo shared his vision, Isaiah immediately proffered an explanation: the old woman represented the CLA, which was jealous of St. Peter's Tabborrar. The CLA was trying "to spoil" their struggle. Flomo, though, did not accept this interpretation and actually seemed miffed by it. Later he told me that Isaiah "just guessed." Flomo had always stressed harmony between St. Peter's and the mother church. He refused to see the old woman as a negative force. As he saw it, the old women represented the church's virtue that would enable victory over its enemies. While Isaiah believed the dream suggested the church's difference with the CLA, Flomo saw the dream image as simply heralding, like a kind of performative utterance, St. Peter's eventual triumph. Interestingly, Flomo's interpretation had also inverted the stereotypical image of an old woman from one of witchcraft to one of hope.

As the first week wore on, Flomo became noticeably fatigued by the load of work. The Wednesday night service was especially uninspiring, which he blamed on his lack of energy. "The Spirit had not come down," and the service was "cold." Isaiah had actually been stunningly demonstrative in his attempts to "bring down" the Spirit. He would approach a patient or member, press his hands down hard on her forehead, calling on the Spirit to come down, but it seemed to no avail. That evening he aroused more laughter than respect. But, as he later admitted, one can never force the Spirit. As the week wore on, Flomo suffered from mild laryngitis. He could hardly speak, which hindered his ability with prayers, reciting psalms, delivering homilies, and performing treatments. By Sunday, however, his voice had returned, as he insisted, "through the power of the Holy Spirit." That morning Flomo delivered a sermon that stressed the need for confession and forgiveness. Such was necessary if people wanted their problems solved. Without confession and forgiveness, the triumph of Tabborrar would never take place. The struggle pointed to a new day, to the Kingdom of God. He concluded his sermon with these poignant words: "The earth will pass away, the body melt, the soul go to heaven. We must speak to one another face to face, and keep nothing secret in our hearts."

The Midnight Struggles

During Tabborrar, every night occasioned a midnight struggle. Often the midnight struggle was coupled with a church consecration, when ministers fumigated the compound with incense and sprinkled it with holy water. The midnight struggle became a special time for confession and forgiveness. All dwellers were required to attend, and members came as they were able. A struggle always began at twelve o'clock in the chapel with prescribed prayers. The singing might segue into shouts, a series of healing procedures, and spiritual exercises, such as jumps and rolls, the narration of dreams and visions, and a short homily. The midnight prayers might last only fifteen minutes or as long as two hours. If the twelve o'clock prayers were "weak," the ministers would call for more at three o'clock. If they were "strong," the participants might be allowed to sleep until time for morning prayers at five-thirty.

Often ministers allowed time for the performance of spiritual exercises. Among these, rolling appeared to hold the greatest interest. The first sets were performed by Flomo and Isaiah. Some evenings they were joined by ministers who had earlier gone to the mount for special prayers. The ministers prostrated themselves toward the altar, about three feet apart. Then they slowly began rolling—first toward the right wall of the nave until they bumped against one another, and then toward the left wall. They did this seven times. With each round they increased speed and shouted out words and phrases. They repeatedly shouted "loose!," which was an evocation of release from the devil's rope. Some evenings only the ministers rolled. But other evenings they instructed other participants, three at a time, to do the same. They claimed that rolling built up the ministers' virtue and prompted confession from patients and members.

Dreams and visions were a valuable part of midnight struggles. Tabborrar became a particularly auspicious time for sleeping in the chapel and receiving revelatory dreams. During the night a dweller might ask a minister to interpret a dream or a minister might wake everyone to report a vision. Most dreams and visions pertained to individual problems and treatments, but they also included numerous allusions to the struggle on the mount and its triumph—images of the Children of Salvation praying on beaches or climbing up hilltops, their eyes and hands lifted up to God.

An important aspect of midnight struggle was the early morning confessions that began with the five-thirty prayers. With the ministers standing before the low altar, each dweller knelt at the chapel's entrance and confessed—to lying, cheating, stealing, coveting, causing injury to others, going to the juju man, and so on. After each confession the ministers asked the subject three times "Will you do so again?" After the third "no," the congregation responded, "Lord have mercy and forgive her." The confessant then stood, went outside, and ran around the chapel before reentering by a side door. Once each dweller had performed confession, everyone knelt before the altar for general confession. The ministers then began the morning prayers, which included narration and interpretation of dreams that dwellers had experienced during the night.

After prayers, cross bearers would leave the compound and head to the Paynesville juncture for open-air preaching. Donning white gowns, carrying Bibles and crosses, they went along the roadside throughout the morning, pausing before nearby dwellings, businesses, booths, and marketplaces, proclaiming the news about Tabborrar and urging others to join the struggle.

The Second Week: "Praying for Others"

For the mount ministers the first week of struggle focused on building up virtue. The ministers prayed for themselves, that they might be spiritually strong enough to perform the difficult tasks that lay ahead. They also prayed for protection against those who plotted against their work. Members generally thought of such opponents as "outsiders"—neighbors bothered by the noise, disgruntled former patients or members, competitors from other churches, or missionaries critical and envious of the church's accomplishments. Eventually news arrived about a conflict that had emerged within the camp. After Tabborrar it would become known to all that the head of the mount had been engaged in a personal battle with another mount minister. He believed this minister wished to usurp his authority and take over the mount. As Tabborrar progressed, Flomo would make allusions to the conflict, but he would never refer to anything specific. Isaiah gave no indication that he knew anything about it.

The mount ministers continued with the white fast into the second week. During the last three days they would take the dry fast, a fast that more aggressively produced virtue and undermined the work of evil spirits. The Faith Home ministers and cross bearers would follow suit, while most patients and members continued with the white fast. The intensified fasting also empowered other healing treatments, such as holy baths, and holy materials, such as water and oil, which had been intentionally prepared for those treatments. Several male patients were received onto the mount for three-day holy baths that were staggered over three-day intervals. This allowed more time for the holy materials used to obtain greater potency.

In the second week the ministers began praying over the special requests. By then they had obtained greater virtue and their prophetic skills were considered sharper. They prayed collectively and individually over the requests. Each prophet was responsible for a collection of requests, usually comprising those from his branch. I knew some ministers on the mount who were responsible for more than two hundred individual requests. The prophets prayed over these day and night. In most cases they wrote down their answers. A senior prophet might sometimes order a junior minister to record the revelation for him. Often, as Modee later explained to me, the revelations were not immediate but came much later: "When we would pray over a person's problem, sometimes the vision came then, but it also came later, even after the other person's problems had been prayed over and answered. Messages have no specific time. They may come during the next prayers, the next day, or the next week."

A written revelation usually began with a declaration of its divine source: "Doth saith the Lord of Host" or "I heard a voice speaking." It then immediately referred to the subject's request, such as finding a job, passing an exam, becoming pregnant, keeping a spouse, or improving health. The revelation usually stated the reasons why petitioners might have been unable to accomplish their own requests—they lacked faith, had friends or family who worked against them, impudently disregarded God's laws, or were afflicted by witchcraft or jina. A revelation always included a prescription for holy treatments: a three- or seven-day holy bath, sweet offerings, a twenty-one-day white fast, a sheep sacrifice, a beach struggle, or the giving of alms to beggars. Finally, the revelation emphasized that if the subject had faith and did the recommended rites, his or her request would "surely come to pass."

During the last three days of the struggle the ministers' daily prayers gave special attention to national and world events. This became a highly appropriate focus in 1984, since four days before the struggle was to end, government troops under President Samuel Doe's orders entered the University of Liberia campus grounds and attacked students who were protesting the recent arraignment of Amos Sawyer, a law professor and political opponent of Doe. Reports varied about the number of casualties and the amount of destruction caused by the attack. That day I had arranged for the videotaping of the CLA procession from their Center Street Headquarters to their holy mount in Paynesville, but by the time we set out to film, the government had set up roadblocks and imposed a curfew. The curfew lasted two days, which prevented me from going to the seminary for classes or making trips to the Faith Home.

Earlier that week I had been allowed to enter the mount and speak with Olu and observe some procedures. Among other topics, Olu and I discussed videotaping the procession of St. Peter's members from the headquarters to the mount, scheduled for Saturday evening, August 26. He thought this was an excellent idea. Because of the curfew, though, there was uncertainty about whether the procession would take place. Over the next two days, mid-runner Flomo would furtively make his way to and from the mount. Fortunately by Saturday, the day of the "descent," the government lifted the curfew and churches began to prepare for the closing ceremonies.

On Saturday morning I returned to the Faith Home. Dwellers appeared in good spirits as many anticipated the day's coming event. Pilgrims began arriving from other branches. Some CLA members also showed up. Because of the roadblocks they had been unable to go to the CLA Tabborrar service that had occurred three days before. Ministers from various branches brought their patients for treatments, hoping to take advantage of the mount's special power. Members carried with them containers of water and oil and buckets of food, which they planned to have consecrated by the mount ministers. I spent much of the morning talking with dwellers and pilgrims. In the afternoon I returned home to rest and make preparations for the evening, which included picking up my friend with the video camera.

The Captain and His Ship

At about 5:30 P.M. we drove to the Faith Home. The chapel and grounds were crowded with people. Organizers were concerned that representatives from the Logan Town branch had not yet arrived. They had hoped to begin the march at six o'clock but knew they could not start without the Logan Town party. When those from Logan Town finally arrived, they took their place in a procession line that extended to the main road. The police closed one lane of traffic on the main road and the procession, eventually about three hundred strong, began the march to Tabborrar. St. Peter's members led the way, immediately followed the by Logan Town group. Members were positioned within each group according to rank: male ministers, dressed in white and khaki, were in front, followed in succession by female ministers, elders, cross bearers, members, and patients. As they marched, they sang songs about Tabborrar. We filmed the procession as it moved down the main road. Once it turned onto Old ELWA Road, we decided to drive on to the mount, about a mile away. The ministers had asked us to give rides to two patients and Olu's son Oshitelu. When we arrived, Oshitelu dashed into the compound, a liberty he had exercised throughout the struggle. We began filming the surroundings—the mud-stick dwellings, the palm trees lining the beach, a young Sande girl covered in white chalk nearby watching with her family, and the exterior of the mount enclosure.

The prophets had been waiting for the arrival of the pilgrims for more than an hour. Just outside the closed gate were piled cinder blocks, which I climbed so to look over the fence. I saw the prophets seated behind the altar wall, hardly moving and silent. Each one wore a headband made of palm leaves, a symbol of their power and victory. The only minister not behind the altar was Modee, who was serving his rotation as gatekeeper. The ministers had already broken their fast, but they would not speak until the procession arrived.

We walked to the dirt road to meet the approaching procession. In the short time since we had driven ahead, the number of participants seemed to have doubled. The ordering by branches and rank also seemed to have collapsed. Once the ministers leading the procession reached the gate, they halted and waited for the gatekeeper's signal. The gatekeeper Modee welcomed them with a blessing from the "God of Tabborrar" and uttered the holy name Sawwullakkaa, which meant "Peace be unto you." He then turned and ran to the altar. Procession participants removed their shoes and filed into the camp, continuing to sing and dance. My friend and I were directed to the front, where we continued filming. Once the grounds were full, the foreman, using a megaphone, announced that everyone should kneel for the beginning of the Tabborrar service, which proceeded with the Adoration Prayer, Victory Prayer, General Confession, and shouts. The service

Church members prepare for the procession to Mount Tabborrar where they will join the ministers for a concluding service at the mount. Photograph by author.

Ministers on Mount Tabborrar seated in silence behind the altar wall. They await the procession of members from the Faith Homes. Photograph by author.

would also include the litany of Thirteen Questions, through which members renewed their vows to the church.[4]

During shouts, the mount ministers left the altar area and moved through the crowd of worshippers. Some danced, spinning in trance. They were cheered on by participants who tried to touch them before they reentered the altar. They were passing on the virtue of the mount. As the ministers moved freely about the crowd, they touched containers of water and oil and baskets of fruit, vegetables, and sweets that participants had brought into the camp; and they performed prayers, gave libations, and delivered visions to kneeling subjects. Throughout the service, ministers and cross bearers fumigated the mount with burning incense. As dusk arrived, filming became impossible. I prepared to drive my friend home. When we left around nine o'clock the mood on the mount seemed jubilant and expansive. I returned about an hour later and was surprised to learn that the service had ended and to see people leaving. I saw Flomo and asked what had happened. He told me that during shouts Olu stopped the singing and dancing. He then delivered a vision declaring that many had come to the mount with "witchcraft in their hearts." They had spoiled the mount. The Spirit, therefore, had "cut short" the service. The service had ended climactically but not in the manner hoped for. Flomo asked that I take him, the spiritual mother, Oshitelu, and another dweller back to the Faith Home. He told me that the Tabborrar prophets would soon be returning as well to eat a full meal prepared by the Faith Home cross bearers.

As it turned out, the real victory celebration of Tabborrar would be the Thanksgiving Divine Worship that took place the next morning at church headquarters. The chapel was full and the yard bustling with activity—ministers praying, members singing, and children playing. The service began with a procession of the mount ministers down the middle aisle, the "path of angels." Ministers wore flamboyant blue, green, brown, and maroon uniforms. Behind them came Olu, the head of the mount, wearing a leopard-skin robe and an ornate headdress. In many West African cultures the leopard symbolizes regal authority and power. For some, the attire undoubtedly enhanced the founder's aura. During the service Olu announced promotions and assignments, ordained ministers and cross bearers, and bestowed holy rods and crosses. The church elders voiced special thanks to the prophets who had struggled for them on the mount. During shouts, the senior prophets again took center stage with improvised cleansings and revelations for the worshippers. Olu's sermon, though, produced the strongest effect. He told congregants that Tabborrar had become a test of obedience, a "temptation," that he alone faced. But he knew that the church's survival depended on his being able to overcome the surge and stay the course.

Olu presented himself as the "captain of the ship" who had almost lost control of the vessel. Adogame notes that the ship/boat metaphor has been amply used in Aladura churches with reference to the church's soteriological role (2000, 8–9). In Liberia the metaphor has appeared in dream narratives, the ship usually representing an image of security and protection through danger and hostility. In Olu's usage the ship was Tabborrar whose safe and steady crossing procured the desired blessings. But, as Olu proclaimed, there were forces that tried to prevent the ship from reaching the distant shore. In his sermon the prophet spoke of a series of attacks that had diverted his attention. The attacks came in the form of snakes that entered the compound, always a sign of witchcraft. He also mentioned that throughout the struggle he had been tempted to break the fast, even on the last day. The prophet suggested that other churches that were jealous of St. Peter's success had perhaps tried to bring him down. He also referred to the recent civil disturbances that had threatened to capsize the vessel. These circumstances all added to the urgency of his task. But, as we learned later, the main threat had come from within the camp.

THE SECRET STRUGGLE

After Tabborrar, Olu repeatedly referred in sermons and prayers to his struggle on the mount with "enemies" who sought to usurp his power. At first he spoke in general terms about the temptation. He referred to the invasion of the compound by evil spirits that sometimes took the forms of snakes or dogs. Gradually a more detailed story unfolded and was shared among the dwellers. Before only the mount ministers, including Flomo, had known any particulars about Olu's personal struggle. But eventually most dwellers learned that a contest of power had taken place between Olu and Daniel Solomon.

Solomon, a forty-year-old Grebo man, had arrived at the headquarters in early July. He came from a UCL branch in Buchanan where he had served for five years. Before becoming a minister, Solomon had spent several years in the military and became a trained medic and embalmer. After military service he worked with a mining company near Mano River. There he had a dream that he interpreted as a divine call to heal people. He began attending a branch of the CLA and moved to Monrovia to begin training as a minister. He did not stay long with CLA, however. He eventually learned about the work of David Fyneah's church, which he joined, and soon after received ordination and was assigned to the Buchanan branch.

When Solomon arrived at St. Peter's in July, few people at the church knew anything about him. Some Paynesville members remembered that several years before he had helped with a revival at a local Aladura branch. At St. Peter's Faith Home Solomon proved a resourceful and assiduous worker. He helped Flomo and the other junior ministers with treatments, led daily prayers, and appeared to command respect during services. In those weeks before Tabborrar I never heard anyone express any doubts about Solomon's character or motivations. At the time Olu had enough confidence in Solomon that he included him among the mount ministers.

During the week before Tabborrar I had two exchanges with Daniel Solomon that I would later look back on as possible earlier signs of how things would play out. The first time, we were talking about the importance of special requests, and I asked Solomon if he had one. He told me that he hoped to find a new girlfriend to marry. His answer confused me because Solomon was already married, and I knew that the church disapproved of polygamy among clergy. I learned later that Solomon's wife had left him. The second exchange with Solomon concerned his behavior at one Sunday morning service. During shouts, Solomon entered a trance state, his body tense and shaking, his eyes staring fixedly. He remained like this for several minutes until finally he collapsed onto a bench nearby. A female cross bearer then approached and spoke to him. Soon she moved on, re-joining the others dancing. For the rest of the service Solomon remained hushed and hardly moved from the bench. The next day I talked to him about what happened during shouts. He told me that he had had a vision in which he saw the corpse of a man he knew in a coffin. The cross bearer had asked him why he did not reveal his vision to the church, as was custom during a service. He answered that he could not because the vision "was not a good one," nor could he publicly reveal the man's identity.

In the Aladura church prophets often have visions about death, some including the coffin image. But certain rules of propriety govern when and how one should deliver such visions. One rule is that a lower-ranking minister did not reveal in public a vision concerning a senior prophet. I have since wondered: Was Solomon's vision about a senior prophet? Was it about Olu? If the vision was about Olu, then this would have presented a problem for Solomon: there were risks in communicating a foreboding message, especially one with an image of death, to a superior. The Aladura saw visions and dreams as doors to the other, unseen world, but visions could also unveil hidden ambitions. Was the subject here a medium of the Spirit, or did the vision manifest self-interest or secret ambitions? Thus a prophet might interpret another minister's vision about his death, especially one coming from his junior, as an unconscious desire for power and mastery. I have also since wondered whether or not Solomon ever told Olu about his vision.

In the few weeks after Tabborrar, Olu talked often about the menace of enemies he had faced on the mount. Snakes had repeatedly been found in the camp. But he gave no indication that an enemy might have come from within. He did not identify an antagonist. His only specific reference was to the possible affront "from Nigeria." But, most significant, he stressed his eventual victory over the temptation. During this time other mount ministers also said nothing regarding a particular opponent. I had had no reason to suspect Solomon of any untoward activities. At the concluding Tabborrar service and Thanksgiving Divine Worship, like the other ministers he sat within the altar, appearing poised and resolute. When shouts took place he seemed as engaged as other ministers, dancing energetically and joyously among the pious throng, many of whom reached out to touch his robe, his head, and his feet.

For the next three weeks I had sporadic contact with the Faith Home. I had all but forgotten about Olu's struggle on Tabborrar with "an enemy." Then one day I attended a beach struggle that ministers had arranged for Faith Home dwellers. For more than an hour we marched counterclockwise around a hole dug in the sand with a candle placed in it. Once we finished marching, everyone sat for several minutes watching the ministers dance and roll on the beach. Once they completed their spiritual exercises, they joined the others and began delivering visions for each dweller. One minister reported a vision in which he had seen Solomon sleeping with a snake. I may have been the only person surprised by the vision. I had noticed that Solomon was absent from the struggle. His absence puzzled me, but I assumed he had other responsibilities at the Faith Home.

Later, at the Faith Home I asked Modee about the vision concerning Solomon. He told me that on the mount Solomon had attempted to steal Olu's power. Several times he took the form of a snake that entered the camp. Once, in his snake form he entered the altar and wrapped himself around Olu's holy rod. Olu discovered the snake and hit it with a knife, severing its head. At precisely that moment, according to Modee (at the time, the gatekeeper), Solomon cried out with terrible pain in his leg. Eventually this pain spread to his arm. At first Olu kept the matter a secret, hoping Solomon would confess his sin. But he would not "come around." According to Modee, other mount ministers had also received revelations about Solomon. As one junior minister put it, "the pain had brought out his real form." Any time the ministers asked Solomon about this, he would deny any wrongdoing. He showed no desire to leave the mount. Olu, for that matter, hoped to bring about a change in Solomon, who was allowed to remain. Besides, his presence no longer posed a problem. Once Olu had discovered Solomon's plot, his placing signs, and had struck the blow, Solomon lost his power. Modee noted that, despite appearances, the ministers knew Solomon "was being used by Satan, who knew that after Tabborrar many prayers would be answered and many healings take place. Though he was used, he still made an agreement; a choice was made."

For two months after Tabborrar Solomon remained in the Faith Home. He regularly attended prayers and services, but he seldom had an active role, as he had before Tabborrar. Occasionally he was asked to give the Victory Prayer or benediction, and sometimes during shouts he could be observed entering a trembling trancelike state. The other ministers, however, would insist that at those moments Solomon was receiving "punishments" from the Spirit. Before the accusations of witchcraft became common knowledge, other Faith Home dwellers had been complaining about Solomon's behavior in the compound, especially toward women. He worked "like a jina" in the way he "got behind" the women. One minister revealed that in a dream he had seen Solomon sleeping with a snake and that he had sent it into the bed of another dweller. The patient Rachel claimed that Solomon made inappropriate sexual advances toward her. When she resisted, he tried to witch her. She later blamed the minister for her "heart problems." The ministers also reported that he had once spoiled the water for her holy bath. Olu would eventually reprimand Solomon about his harassment of female dwellers, and this, according to the ministers, appeared to have some effect; at least the complaints stopped. Solomon, however, continued to deny the witchcraft accusations.

Solomon's arm continued to hurt, which, from the ministers' perspective, indicated his persistent embrace of witchcraft. Once, during daily prayers, a minister narrated a vision in which he saw an angel shoot an arrow into Solomon's arm. The same minister, however, stressed that everyone should pray for his recovery, since "he was not aware of what he was doing." Solomon often smeared his arm with white chalk, a "country medicine," which, according to one minister, indicated he had little trust in God's virtue. At services, during shouts, other dwellers usually stood and danced apart from Solomon. But they continued to show sympathy toward him and to pray for his recovery. At one service a cross bearer told of a vision in which she saw Solomon crying alone. She said the vision meant that he needed to pray hard in order to overcome temptation. The cross bearer then instructed Solomon to give a shout. Standing alone, he began singing a heartfelt Grebo song. Others watched and listened. When he had finished the song, he moved before the altar and began dancing, which kept everyone's attention. A minister would later tell me, however, that Solomon "in his spirit form" was actually dancing on his hands. Still, the scene at that time evoked for me the church's patience toward and sympathy for Solomon, rather than its refusal and judgment of him. General discomfort about Solomon, however, continued among the dwellers.

One afternoon about siesta time, several of us were seated on the kitchen porch. Dwellers were taking care of various chores: washing clothes, cleaning vegetables, sweeping the yard, and watching the children. The ministers had left the campus to make house calls. I decided to photograph dwellers doing some daily tasks. I took the Nikon from my leather shoulder bag. After taking a few shots of Ma Martha, Sister Amelia, and some of the children, I turned toward Rachel, a patient who had been staying in the Faith Home with her twins for several weeks. She began to make herself ready for a pose. As I focused the lens, Daniel Solomon moved next to Rachel, also wanting to get in the picture. I tried to pull the lever to move the roll of film, but it jammed. Rachel was miffed and chided Solomon rather harshly: he had "witched" the camera. Solomon immediately retorted "You woman!" and walked away. Sister Amelia and Ma Martha laughed. I told them that the roll of film was finished, and I had failed to bring an extra one. Rachel mumbled to herself, looking askance at Solomon. I remember feeling sorry for Solomon, and regretted I had not come better prepared.

In late October, Olu assigned Solomon to a branch in Grand Gedeh. The ministers expressed relief about his departure. They believed Grand Gedeh would be good for him, since the senior prophet there "knew how to handle his problem." If he continued to create difficulties, at least it would be somewhere else. They had done all that they could do. Rachel seemed especially glad to see the lonely prophet go. Up until the very end, though, she wanted reassurance from Solomon himself that he would no longer "witch" her. Later she told me that she followed the minister as he walked to the juncture to meet his taxi, begging him to remove his spell. He continued to deny that he had placed signs on her, but Rachel would remain unconvinced.

There were many unanswered questions about Daniel Solomon. Hope for his confession, repentance, and recovery remained in doubt. Undoubtedly he provided a convenient foil for the demonstration of prophetic authority and virtue during Tabborrar. The narratives about him represented the power of temptation that the minister always faces. Interestingly his convalescence in the Faith Home received little direct attention from Olu, as though Solomon no longer presented the same hazards to others as he had before. And other ministers were now able to handle the fallen prophet. In the end Solomon's recovery depended on his genuine "change of heart." Without such conversion, all Faith Home efforts would continue to fail.

THE SACRED PASSAGE

In this description of St. Peter's Tabborrar, major themes and aspects of the Aladura way unfold: the synthesis of biblical and Liberian spatial paradigms; the legitimation of prophetic authority; the relation between Faith Home and mount; the secrecy of the struggle; the morally dualistic context of healing; and the pragmatic soteriology. On an institutional level one can identify a unity of purpose in the performance of Tabborrar in the strengthening of the church's virtue through focused praying and fasting. Secondary purposes and meanings developed, shaped by circumstances, such as, the merger of St. Peter's and the UCL. Still, the basic rationale for the ritual remained: without its annual performance, a church could not be "Aladura." Tabborrar secured the vitality of the church's "problem-solving" potential through its expressive and instrumental dimensions. It represented the community's, and especially the prophet's, struggle with contesting forces. If old problems remained unsolved and new ones emerged, this did not diminish appreciation of the rite's efficacy.

The sacred ceremony both integrated and disrupted Aladura experience. Bourdieu stresses that ritual "always aims to facilitate passages and/or to authorize encounters between opposed opposites" (1977, 120), which fittingly describes Tabborrar. Promotions, initiations, mergers, separations, treatments, witchcraft exposures, and relocations that occurred through Tabborrar underscored its capacity to precipitate changes, create uncertainties, and disrupt routines. David Parkin speaks about the unpredictable turns that ritual can make in terms of "tangled states," an insight that can aid our understanding of Tabborrar. Parkin comments, "Perhaps it is only through ritual that humans will collude collectively in their movement, transformation, dispersion, and partition. I would even go so far to suggest that, through ritual, people set up what I have called 'tangled states'—spatial and bodily states of confusion, admixture, and complexity— which they then seek to disentangle. Through such disentanglement, people reimpose order on themselves and on the parts and places that make them up. These tangled states are not, I imagine, calculated in advance. Rather, they arise when participants interfere in each other's interpretations of the ritual 'ruling.' Human agency here, then, develops through its denial to others: it is the denial of the other that, by default, promotes the self" (1992, 23–24).

Aladura ritual creates the simultaneity of entangled and disentangled roles, desires, and expectations. St. Peter's performance brought together (entangled) what previously may have been disparate narratives, characterizations, interests, and goals. The Aladura described Tabborrar as the great problem solver, but the rite also created new doubts and challenges and other entanglements, as the conflict between Olu and Solomon attested.

The fundamental opposites of Aladura life in Liberia—between male and female, senior and junior, prophet and patient, pure and impure, ritual time and ordinary time—were effectively accentuated during Tabborrar. More than any other event, it evoked the agonistic dimension of ritual and earned the description of holy struggle. And this evocation was most powerfully expressed through the personal temptation of the head of the mount. His ordeal, sacrifice, and triumph epitomized the value of struggle for others and ensured the church's pragmatic success for the coming year. The major spatial relations between the mount and the Faith Home, between headquarters and other branches, and between ritual sites and city environs grounded the experience of participants. During Tabborrar, each Faith Home became the location for a series of discrete but related performances that were centered on the struggle occurring on the mount. The movement between the Faith Home at headquarters and the mount became the axis of ritual activity among church branches.

Undoubtedly the merger between St. Peter's and UCL had raised questions concerning authority, which Tabborrar helped to negotiate. The ritual, at least for the time being, affirmed Olu's authority over the Logan Town group. The UCL's observance of Tabborrar was now subsumed into St. Peter's; the former Logan Town headquarters now simply another branch with its eyes toward Paynesville. Significantly Olu had distributed mount positions evenly among St. Peter's and UCL ministers. But some UCL ministers had already ingratiated themselves with the St. Peter's community. The former head of UCL was on assignment in Washington, D.C., and no Logan Town ministers were selected as mount ministers. Those who were selected came from less influential branches. And the fact that Solomon came from a former UCL branch was not lost on mindful members.

Tabborrar also reminded participants of the porous boundaries between sacred space and profane space. In Aladura cosmology the mount represented a reservoir of virtue, but its activation depended on the prophets' rituals, which built up, maintained, and recycled holy power. This temporal dimension did not undermine the mount's spatial image. For participants the enclosed camp became a "high place," removed from the common plain. But its separateness was established by what prophets did there. A place might be intrinsically holy, but only the prophet made it useful or productive. Without his intervention, a holy place became spoiled. Inactive Tabborrar sites and church compounds that were abandoned and overrun by bush or trashed with debris more easily became inhabited by coveting jina and conniving witch spirits. Aladura members spoke about the camp fence in terms of ritual enclosure. The fact that one among them submitted to self-interest and embraced the "witch's way" did not undermine the real effectiveness of enclosure. It simply alerted members to the unavoidable tension between the ideal and real.

As an initiatory symbol, the indigenous bush camp provided a strong analogy to the sacred mount. The bush struggle, as we have seen, was significant for the prophet's obtainment of knowledge and virtue. Undoubtedly this practice assimilated the Liberian associations of the bush with the supernatural. For their initiation Poro initiates were taken from the village and confined to the bush camp, the place of transformation. The bush camp represented a place of order within an inchoate and foreboding forest, but proximity enabled the campers to have more immediate access to its supernatural secrets. The relations with bush spirits were marked with ambiguity: they could harm or help. Whether these encounters proved beneficial for the individual and for society depended on appropriate mediation. The bush camp became a locus of mediation between the village and the forest. Ethnographies (see Leopold 1983) describe the camp as the forest spirit's stomach digesting the initiates or as a womb wherein they gestate. Scarifications they received represented the teeth marks of the spirit. The white clay that initiates covered themselves with day after day denoted the spirit, but also a medium of culture. In Bourdieu's terms, a "mimetic representation" takes place: just as clay baked in the kiln becomes vessels or pots for everyday use, so also the initiates were being made into cultural agents (1977, 116).

Tabborrar transformed and legitimized social roles. In this capacity the ritual became an initiation rite, as participants assumed roles consistent with a new order of experience and knowledge. Aladura ministers frequently mentioned the importance of taking the Tabborrar struggle "on the mount" and the special honor received when one was selected to do so. Within an Aladura church the experience established differences among ministers, between those who had ascended the mount and those who had not. Junior ministers who took the struggle together formed a special bond not shared with ministers who stayed in the Faith Home. The new lessons they received about church doctrine and practice, about how to interpret dreams and visions, about the use and meaning of holy names, and about special healing treatments undoubtedly strengthened the young ministers' confidence. But it was the experience itself, the actual fasting and praying, the struggling night and day within a camp demarcated from the common world that distinguished the minister from others. Bellman's interpretation that the Poro dictum *ifa mo,* "you cannot speak it," referred more to a structured social experience than to a body of secret knowledge has relevance here (Bellmann 1975, 1984; De Jong 2004). Knowledge that ministers received on the mount could easily be taught in the Faith Home, but the mount struggle provided an indispensable context for affirming the prestige of prophetic knowledge. The initiatory, gnostic aspect of Tabborrar was fundamental: the ritual maintained a boundary between those who had taken it together and those who had not. In this process the rhetoric of secrecy helped structure space, time, and relationships.

In St. Peter's case ritual healing, hourly revelations, the struggles with witches, snakes, and jina were linked to the founder's original acts. This does not mean that we should see Tabborrar as the ritual re-creation of the church's origins, as something that happened in *illo tempore,* but that we recognize the ritual affinity between the image of the founder and his establishment of the church. Tabborrar effectively synthesized, in Harvey Whitehouse's terms (2000), the imagist (or episodic) and doctrinal (or semantic) modes of religiosity.[5] As J. D. Y. Peel (2004) has shown (using Whitehouse's model), the Aladura fused the two modes: Its semantic conventions—such as sermons, hymn singing, Bible readings, and giving testimonies—revealed the imagist, while healing rites, fasting exercises, divinatory techniques, and Faith Home routines embedded the doctrinal. The Aladura performances also inscribed knowledge, an "Aladura science," as it were, onto ritualized bodies, expressing and generating a plethora of "Aladura signs."

Tabborrar also reinforced the Aladura relation between virtue and male authority. Only male prophets were allowed to take the struggle on the mount. Ministers and members, male and female, insisted that the presence of women created problems that jeopardized the success of the ritual. To begin with, they stressed the problem of sex. The struggle required total abstinence and control of impure thoughts. A mixed camp made such discipline and concentration more difficult. Both male and female ministers insisted on this point. The palm-branch fence prevented ministers from seeing women, a source of temptation. A second reason why women were prohibited from taking the struggle or entering the camp had to do with menstruation, which was understood to compromise sacred areas. According to this logic, it would seem then that a postmenopausal prophetess might be allowed on the mount, but this did not happen until the closing ceremonies on the last day. When a senior prophetess came to the mount for a holy bath, she always remained outside the fence where she received the water and oil to bathe in a nearby hut. In any case, when women talked about parity during Tabborrar, they still saw this in terms of segregated camps: creating a female Tabborrar that paralleled the male, an idea that suggested the pattern of the gendered bush camps of Liberia.

Though virtue was ultimately genderless, the patterns of ritual segregation supported the authority of the male senior prophets. Only the male prophets could ascend Tabborrar for the ritual's duration and thus obtain optimal power. And as a rule they were able to fast for longer periods of time. Younger female ministers were limited by menstrual cycles, which ruled out fasting. From the Aladura perspective, however, this rule did not so much limit the institutional role of women as provide a means for framing their power. The postmenopausal senior prophetess remained among the most powerful leaders in the Aladura churches, especially in matters of prophecy and healing. It can be argued that in certain contexts the rules regarding menstruation reinforced the notion of female power (Crumbley 2008, 73).

Most participants believed that Tabborrar removed obstacles. We cannot understand the value of Tabborrar unless we take seriously the frustrations, disappointments, desires, and hopes of those involved in the ceremony and the faith they expressed in its efficacy. Whatever functional, symbolic, and communicative patterns we might identify in the struggle, we need always to keep in mind its decisively "instrumental" value. The church annually performed the ritual because it worked. The perceived reality of invisible forces that caused harm and misfortune made Tabborrar a necessity. Tabborrar did not always lead to complete resolution; but resolution was not the measure of success anyway. I knew many cases of members listing prayer requests from previous years that had not been resolved: the fault, however, did not lie with Tabborrar, but with a prescribed rite never preformed, a fast suspended, or a neighbor's unexpected churlish scheme. The members remained dedicated to this episodic struggle, a sacred passage that continued to express and reproduce the Aladura way and shape Aladura selves.

TABBORRAR IN DIASPORA

As we have seen, the Reverend Kennedy Sandy's work among expatriate West Africans in Washington, D.C., began with the operation of a Faith Home in his apartment and his ministering to a regular clientele. As his ministry progressed, the prophet ordained capable cross bearers, who assisted him with worship services, prayers, and treatments. This pattern of supervision for the prayer group continued until the opening of a chartered branch in 1993. Since Kennedy had arrived in D.C. he had observed Tabborrar in some fashion, either independently or by teaming up with other Aladura-like healers. But 1993 marked the first observation as a new chartered branch, and, interestingly enough, this initial rite was shared with a Pentecostal church named St. James.

The minister at St. James, in fact, offered his apartment as a location for the ministers to take the Tabborrar struggle. The Pentecostal minister, a Liberian, had been in D.C. since 1984. He had once belonged to CLA and had continued to observe Tabborrar rites even after leaving the church. He was blind and depended on a seeing-eye dog, which required a new "ritual ruling" (see Parkin 1992, 14–15). During Tabborrar, the dog remained in the apartment, always in a small entrance space where male visitors also left their shoes. The dog's presence would have been unimaginable for an Aladura observance in Liberia. In fact, his presence did eventually become an issue that prevented the Pentecostal minister's participation in future mount struggles.

The apartment's living room served as the major praying space. The window shades were always drawn, which signaled the minister's separation of their "sacred enclosure" from the outside world just as the palm-branch fence had signed the Tabborrar mount in Paynesville. The furniture had been moved against the walls or to another room. On a small altar table were placed the necessary ritual objects and alongside the table buckets and containers of water, oil, and honey for consecration. One box contained small wood crosses that would be given to newly ordained cross bearers. The ministers prayed every three hours, which also included spiritual exercises such as rolling and jumps. They began the thirteen-day struggle with a three-day dry fast, followed by a seven-day fruit fast, and concluded with a three-day dry fast. For the fruit fast, the ministers faced a complication—a male cross bearer or member was unavailable for the regular task of bringing foodstuff to the apartment for breaking the fast. Consequently Sandy usually left the sanctified space of the apartment for a nearby grocery. Such leaves might have compromised spatial purity, but the strength of the fruit fast would effectively make up for this lack. Because the food for the fruit fast came "directly from God," it required no cooking. On this matter the dry fast did not present a problem since it proscribed food. Therefore trips to obtain food items would be unnecessary.

In the days before Tabborrar, the church started leasing a basement apartment in Silver Spring, Maryland, which would be used as a new Faith Home. The lease on Sandy's apartment would run out by the end of the month, but the church would continue to use it for prayer and treatments during Tabborrar. Despite work schedules, the cross bearers implemented holy treatments authorized by the two Tabborrar ministers. In conveying messages from the mount, the telephone conveniently replaced the need for a mid-runner. For members, there were two major ritual expectations—they must perform the white fast and observe midnight struggles. The midnight struggles led by cross bearers usually lasted for about an hour. A condensed version of the Liberian rite, the midnight struggle included a series of prayers, vision and dream narrations and interpretations, and the performance of spiritual exercises, such as rolling and jumps. People met at Sandy's apartment or in a cross bearer's home, although in some cases they prayed, interpreted dreams, and gave blessings by phone. During the last week the church also began preparing the Faith Home space at the new apartment in Silver Spring.

After the final prayers of Tabborrar, the ministers and members met at the new Faith Home location for a Saturday-night midnight struggle. During that last meeting the ministers consecrated and officially opened the space. The new location would prove more appropriate for communal celebrations, since it was located between a storage room and an elevator shaft. In that setting, the steady traffic of members and patients and the shouts, drums, and incense so integral to ceremonies would be more easily managed without causing the attention and disapproval of neighbors.

At the Tabborrar Thanksgiving service that took place on Sunday morning, the empowered ministers returned the members' prayer requests. Sandy had written into each prayer-request booklet a revelation that specified the treatments a person needed to undergo in order to remove an obstacle and obtain a blessing. Also at the service, Sandy had other exciting news. He announced his intention to marry a Sierra Leonean woman who was the church's most active cross bearer. They would reside in an apartment on another floor in the same building. This arrangement offered more privacy for the couple while still allowing Reverend Sandy and the new spiritual mother to remain close enough to manage the Faith Home and monitor the progress of their patients. The service was also distinguished by the increased number of participants who now wore white robes or clothing—an act that inscribed on their bodies a new Aladura identity.

Throughout the 1990s the church similarly observed Tabborrar. Reverend Sandy would undergo the struggle in another location, usually at an apartment or home provided by a member, a client, or supporter. He performed the struggle alone or with other ministers free to commit themselves for the thirteen-day duration. Unfortunately work schedules prevented participation of worthy male candidates who might otherwise have been granted the holy rod. The spiritual mother and cross bearers directed the Faith Home observances, administering spiritual treatments and leading the midnight struggles. Though some patients stayed throughout the day, most treatments were not administered until the spiritual mother returned home from work. Again, work schedules limited full participation, even from cross bearers. Most members tried to attend the evening prayers, the condensed midnight struggle, or the morning prayers before going to work.

One year Reverend Sandy performed the rite in a vacant home in a rural part of northern Virginia. It was about thirty miles from the Faith Home in Silver Spring, and it took almost two hours to drive there during rush hours. Nonetheless, male members and clients regularly made trips to see their leader. Because of the more secluded location, with no store in walking distance, the prophet became even more dependent on members arriving with necessary foodstuffs for breaking the daily fast and transporting holy materials to the Faith Home. Along the way, a few male members and patients stayed from one to three days for special treatments. This became an effective strategy for initiating male patients into the Aladura way.

In 1998 the church bought a former post office building in Hyattsville, Maryland, a suburb of D.C. The building was renovated for a chapel space, Faith Home, the ministers' residence, and office. Formerly the church had usually held Sunday Divine Worships at rented spaces in nearby church or school buildings, even during Tabborrar. The new location provided sufficient room so that this would no longer be necessary. Major changes were also taking place in Liberia. The civil war had ended, and though under Charles Taylor's rule the social and economic life remained unstable, it had become easier and safer to travel to the Monrovia area. In 1999 Sandy journeyed to Liberia for the church's Mount Tabborrar rite and participated in the church's first public performance of the rite in almost a decade. It is significant that a former head of CLA in Liberia, Apostle Lewis Thomas, also participated in St. Peter's Tabborrar. After the ritual the apostle ordained Sandy as bishop and appointed him General Overseer for International Operations. In ensuing years Bishop Sandy would make more Tabborrar trips to Liberia. These pilgrimages also demanded the watchful prayers of members back home and served to reestablish community connections to the traditional site.

The disruptions caused by war and diaspora have required adaptive strategies in celebrations of Tabborrar. The ritual itself reflects, in Parkin's terms, a process of "dispersal or fragmentation" (1992, 14) that modified and condensed the traditional West African form. The rite, nonetheless, continues to be the "friend" or "power" necessary for the church's everyday praxis in the new world setting. Witchcraft, jina, and placing signs remain constant concerns, and members show no hesitancy in talking about these. But drugs, worldly lifestyles, keeping jobs, safety of relatives back home, and finding ways to bring those relatives to the United States have become immediate concerns. In the new culture the Tabborrar ritual provides a temporal and spatial focus for addressing these issues. Its American adaptation has demonstrated a style and a directionality that has promoted a transatlantic Aladura discourse. In its adaptive form the struggle continues to express the relation between prophet, members, patients, and supporters. But while the diaspora strategies demonstrate a creative approach; in Bell's terms "no ritual style is autonomous" (1992, 101). A ritual model is always relational and reflects the context that it presently produces.

Ritual struggle also evidences the regenerative effects of ritual activity and the importance of models of orientation, passage, and purpose. The American Tabborrar rite grounded experience in a new place and made connections with the old. It created a virtual simultaneity of experience between places: the Faith Home and the mount, Washington, D.C., and Paynesville. These connections generated new relationships, aspirations, and a sense of agency. While new complications, ambiguities, and uncertain expectations emerged, the adaptive process demonstrated a kind of "ritual mastery" that re-created a ritualized environment (or space) and ritualized persons (Bell 1992, 107–8). The Faith Home continued to be seen primarily in terms of a location, but its meaning and purpose were inseparable from the everyday praxis of ritual struggle. Analogously the Tabborrar rite continued to register initially in the minds of many as an episodic ritual event, but its meaning and purpose always involved emplacement—whether occurring in an enclosure on a Liberian beach or in an apartment in a Washington, D.C., suburb.

Conclusion

The theography of the Aladura way stresses the value of seeing the body as an irreducible presence (Csordas 2002, 72): for instance, as when looking at varied sets of rituals, the relation between practice and place, the performance of fasting, the role of dream and spirit narrations and revelations, and the reported experiential encounters with spiritual realities. During fieldwork in Paynesville, I began with what I could see, which dovetailed multisensory responses to Aladura practice. These descriptions converged with testimony, becoming discourses about an extraordinary reality inscribed into everyday experience through the interpretive tropes of body, ritual, and place.

The focus on the body, on ritual, and on place also relates to the process of materiality, a theme discussed by Keane. The context of globalization has reminded us of the power of this process. It has brought on the "promiscuous articulation of people, texts, and identifications" (2007, 289), which helps translate culture beyond the local. Christianity's "universalizing" mission has always had the capacity to generate new strategies and ideologies. In the case of Protestant Christianity, the mission of purification—the abolishing of material forms such as the fetish—led to inevitable contradictions. Aladura churches found in the Bible itself support for the reality of arcane powers (jina, witchcraft, African signs) often dismissed in modern and missionary Protestantism, as well as trust in the power of names, words, holy materials, and rituals to affect the physical world.

Though the Aladura have collaborated or converged with Pentecostal-Charismatic Churches (who have recapitulated the "anxious transcendence" of the Protestant mission), they nonetheless remain situated in a cosmology where the lines between trust and deceit, virtue and misused power are experienced "through a glass darkly" and wherein the strategies of ritual struggle evoke the forms and energies of concrete malice, the "placing" of material agents, and the urgency for ritual praxis.

In Liberia the Aladura idea of struggle related to very palpable cultural and social changes in the forty-year period following War World II—increased urbanization, burgeoning bureaucracy, introduction of new industries, new migrations, the fall of the First Republic, and the economic and political turmoil of the Doe regime. These created new uncertainties that appeared to support rather than erode witchcraft and spirit beliefs. As Ellis indicates, the civil war (1989–97) reinforced notions of occult power, which often took on disturbingly bizarre transformations (2006). In the new world economies and migrations, the signs of malice also have traversed geographic distance. Among the Liberian expatriates I have worked with for more than two decades now, the notions of secret power, witchcraft, and jina have shown stark persistence, even if they have taken on new forms and created new associations. These images need to be appreciated in relation to the global flows of free-market exchanges, the yearning interest for new goods, the generation of media and Internet, and the creation and refashioning of new spiritual economies. For instance, emergent Pentecostal and evangelical pieties have problematized the desire for alien goods (which can be signs of Satan as well as of success) and have necessitated inventive strategies of exposure (Meyer 1999).

In Liberia the Aladura prophet became a new power broker of spiritual knowledge; for many Liberians his authority replaced that of the traditional zo. The prophet's work was grounded in the Faith Home praxis. The activity between prophet and patient became the focus of that praxis. Though the categories of distinction implicated principles of power and control, the Aladura household and relationships also revealed a process of identification. Due to his direct experience with affliction, the prophet empathized and identified with the patients he treated. Thus the Aladura self evoked identification as well as difference between prophet and patient.

Through the healing praxis, the subject "came to himself." This phrase underlined the dynamic but gradual understanding of being a person in the Aladura way. Within the evolving web of human relations and the healing praxis of the church, the idea of coming to oneself did not represent a static goal, a "thing" to be accomplished, but became a process that brought self-awareness about one's situation, the quality of one's relationship, and some handle on one's spiritual and material goals. It evoked what one needed to do in order "to take care of the self" (Foucault 1988, 19–22), which, in Liberian terms, also meant "taking care of the body." Csordas notes that among charismatic Catholics salvation and healing were "almost synonymous" (2002, 69). This assertion applies to Aladura soteriology as well. Becoming a Child of Salvation became embodied in the context of social and ritual relations. Taking this approach, self-knowledge went hand in hand with practice and fell within the ambit of ritual struggle. The varieties of self-presentation—such as patient, member, follower, cross bearer, and prophet—and the intricate relationships that evolved between these attained full meaning and expression through the ritual praxis and in the creation of ritual bodies.

The way of being a person also implicated metaphysical assumptions about the self's potential. Indeed the awareness of invisible activities, of what was "behind" the presentation of the self, created greater ambiguity about the person. This was especially the case regarding witchcraft accusations from within the community, such as those that happened in the conflict between senior and junior ministers, between ministers and cross bearers, between members and patients. What one saw was not always what one got. The interaction between persons inferred ambiguity. Geschiere's notion of the "circularity of power" (2006), or, what I have re-coined as the "circularity of signs," applies: the prophet-healers paradoxically presented themselves as strong candidates of subversion. The misuse of virtue was always a possibility. Indeed this circularity might characterize any person (myself included) who found him- or herself within the web of consociate Aladura ties. The Aladura assumed the divisibility of the self—between visible and invisible, waking and dreaming, body and soul. The "true prophet" sought consistency between the public persona and private self, but total transparency was impossible and not necessarily desired in every context. Some matters best remained hidden. The prophet then often played his cards close to his sleeve.

Aladura agency (and self-identity) was rarely understood apart from ritual transactions and communal expectations. In this context bodily praxis stands out as the cultural basis for constituting the self—indeed, for synthesizing Christian and Liberian selves. This bodily praxis evoked a mode of being in the world, a specific Aladura habitus, that connected mind and body, and, yet, the praxis of struggle always entailed some objectification of the self, some representation of its place in the world. Through ritual struggle, the self became juxtaposed with others, but as a body in movement (Csordas 2002, 72, 87) both expressing and reproducing the "ritualized agent" (Bell 1992, 100).

The social and economic exigencies of contemporary Liberia make the Aladura discourse about an alienated, isolated, aggressive self all the more meaningful. Aladura views about witchcraft and the evils of wanton self-interest should be viewed in relation to this dynamic. In light of events that unfolded after 1989, the Aladura commentaries on human malice appear all-too-prophetic. The Aladura churches, however, always coupled the images of despair with those of hope. The struggling subject sought membership in the "Household of God," for which the Faith Home—in van Binsbergen's terms, a kind of "virtual village" (2001)—offered an effective context (or emplacement) for its expression. The Faith Home ironically also mirrored the duality of self and the dialectic between well-being and fear. This "grounded image" provided a coping strategy that helped manage the tension between good and evil, between purity and impurity, strength and enervation, knowledge and delusion—the forces, elements, and conditions that played out in the interaction of the self with others.

In Fernandez's terms, the Faith Home facilitated a "return to the whole" (1982, 562). In its praxis as "an intimate controlled space . . . that provide[d] for bodily needs" (Tweed 2006, 105), it also unearthed fracture and lack, broken bodies and troubled spirits. The ritual struggles revealed (indeed, provided testimony to) the moral contradictions and indeterminacy of the self and its relations with others. This awareness became the condition for new understanding and genuine transformation. The Faith Home rituals and rhythms expressed contrasts between spiritual and material realities; and, most significant, managed their interaction for the creation of healed bodies and renewed souls.

Catherine Bell notes that ritual has a "critical circularity to the body's interaction with this environment: generating it, it is molded by it in turn" (1992, 99). Ritual, in effect, reproduces culture. The various bodily presentations (such as bowing, kneeling, wearing white, prostrating, dancing, and rolling) performed through rite and custom embedded Aladura doctrine into experience more powerfully than exegetical form. Even during those moments when the discursive appeared most pronounced (such as a prophet's sermon or narration of a vision), the gestures, declarations, and exchanges that occurred also expressed and reinforced the prophet cosmology.

Ritual authority reproduced bodily and spatial oppositions. The act of delivering a vision as the faithful knelt facing the speaker not only expressed the value of hierarchy but also created a world of contrastive (yet interdependent) identities. The fundamental social distinctions—senior prophet–junior prophet, minister–cross bearer, and member-dweller—obtained special meaning in the Aladura notion of covenant and referred ultimately to the model of divine-human interdependency. In this discourse one also finds rhetorical contrastive tropes— front-back, face-behind, left-right, hot-cold, light-dark, high-low, inside-outside, control-flow, and tied-loosed—embedded in ritual performances and narratives that powerfully expressed and connected the bodily, spatial, and diachronic dimensions of struggle.

As a grounded image, the Faith Home revealed idioms of movement, passage, directionality, and spatiality, which dwellers used in constructing self-identity (Parkin 1992, 18): how the body positioned itself, or was positioned, within the mapped space and in relation to others, represented one of the central features of Aladura ritual. Thus the body became the locus for the soul's journeys or passages. The Aladura prophet, through a specific bodily praxis and within the parameters of sacred space, traveled between worlds, seeking to create the "proper relationship" between heaven and earth (Engelke 2007). The holy place—the high altar, the Faith Home, and Mount Tabborrar—provided the appropriate space, or focusing lens, for this journey, which always involved contest with forces of subversion.

For the Aladura the rite of passage (the crossings and dwellings) necessitated constant watch for the contumely transgressions that might reside within oneself as well as among others. This watchfulness became articulated through the praxis of ritual struggle, not a once-and-for-all event but part of the sacred community's engagement with the drama of salvation. The sacred journey always evoked the physicality of the Aladura way, evidenced, for instance, in the perceived power of words, the prostrated bodies in worship, and the boundaries of sacred space. Such grounded praxis enabled a glimpse, even an embodiment, of a transformed reality. It imagined a place, often evoked in Aladura prayers and visions, where the Children of Salvation might meet face to face and keep nothing secret in their hearts.

NOTES

1. In the colonial context the acronym AIC stood for African Independent Church, which served to distinguish African churches or movements that chose to separate from mission groups. Though still useful, the postcolonial context requires a more expansive meaning of the acronym AIC. The letter *I* in the acronym stands variously for an Initiated, Instituted, Indigenous, or Independent church. As Afe Adogame notes, this designation implies a "religious phenomenon that benefits from an array of descriptive labels such as separatist, protest, syncretistic, prophetic, nativistic, neo-pagan, sects, cults, primal religions and so on" (2004, 494). More recently the acronym has been used to refer to African International Churches, giving greater weight to the global, diaspora forms of African Christianity (Harris 2006, 3–5).

2. The works of Paul Richards (2006a, 2006b), Preben Kaarsholm (2006), and Mats Utas (2006) have challenged the notion of the "irrationality" of the violence that engulfs the "failed state." In his discussion of the Sierra Leone Civil War Richards posits the "rationality" of violence that emerges in conflict between modern and traditional factions and between egalitarian values and those based on seniority. West and Sanders (2003, 6–10), following the lead of John and Jean Comaroff and Arun Appardurai, question the dichotomy between traditional and modern. It is more accurate, they argue, to speak of "multiple modernities" that impact and emerge from both non-Western and Western cultures.

3. For a helpful critique of the New Barbarism thesis, see Mary Moran's discussion in *Liberia: The Violence of Democracy* (2006, 17–26).

4. Adogame proposes three types of African Pentecostal-Charismatic Churches in the diaspora setting: first, the church "headquartered in Africa;" second, the church "founded by new immigrants in the United States and Europe"; and third, the "para-churches" developed by "freelance evangelists," contemporary versions of the circuit riders, who move across a global network (2007, 20). Though Adogame speaks mainly about Pentecostal-Charismatic Churches, his model is also applicable to AIC, which in many cases have morphed into Pentecostal groups.

5. Moran also recognizes the relevance of traditional or indigenous cosmological concepts, such as occult power, for understanding the contemporary Liberian crisis. However, she prefers to examine the latter primarily in terms of "an explicitly *political* discourse . . . which is recognized as such by those who participate in it" (Moran 2006, 7).

6. The Comaroffs describe performances sponsored by South African police that produce a "metaphysics of *disorder*": "the hyperreal conviction, rooted in everyday experience, that society hovers on the brink of dissolution" (2006, 293–94). While

the Comaroffs talk about this in terms of the political or social *imaginary*, the phrase works well in evoking a central focus of Aladura theology.

INTRODUCTION

1. I use the terms *informant* and *interlocutor* interchangeably.

2. Concerning the Aladura as Spirit-centered, the Yoruba theologian Caleb Oluremi Oladipo comments: "Most indigenous Christians who are associated with *Aladura* groups believe that they are capable of receiving the Holy Spirit, and are able to keep a moral fellowship with God through Jesus Christ. The *Aladuras* regard the Holy Spirit as a metaphysical principle in the same manner they conceive of ancestors. Translating the functional understanding of the ancestors, most Yoruba Christians believe that the Holy Spirit is a divine essence who communicates to believers through ecstasy, vision, and dreams" (1996, 113). About Aladura churches the historian of religions Afe Adogame also notes: "The bedrock of their belief system is the pre-eminence of benevolent powers—God, Jesus Christ, the Holy Spirit, the legion of angels. The bestowal, manifestation, and appropriation of *agbara emi mimo* (power of the Holy Spirit) form the nerve-centre of Aladura spirituality" (2004, 504).

3. When discussing the beginnings of the Aladura movement in Nigeria Olu always elevated the role of Moses Orimolade, the founder of the C&S, over that of Josiah Oshitelu, the founder of the CLA. In doctrine and practice St. Peter's closely resembled the Church of the Lord, but the link with the older Orimolade secured the seniority and authenticity of the new church. For a discussion of Orimolade's work and the growth of C&S, see Peel (1968, 71–83) and Harris (2006, 41–53).

4. In a later essay, Peel notes his approach in *Aladura* was "intellectualist" and "sought to explain Aladura belief and practice as intellectually cogent responses, given the cultural premises of young Yoruba Christians, to the problems and dilemmas they confronted at a time of midcolonial crisis" (2004, 20).

5. Probst focuses on the role of scriptural models in the early history of the Aladura movement, especially in relation to the emergence of Josiah Oshitelu's authority and his production of an original holy script. Olupona and Adogame analyze Yoruba themes of sacred space and ritual in the Celestial Church of Christ. In her body of work Crumbley offers a comparative analysis of the role of women and concepts of power and purity in the Christ Apostolic Church, the Celestial Church of Christ, and the CLA. She explores the dynamics of transformation involved with facing cultural and social challenges. Benjamin Ray investigates the specific Yoruba character of the Aladura movement, drawing mostly on materials from the CLA and the Celestial Church of Christ. He insists, as do the others noted above, on the creative role that the Aladura movement has played in shaping both Christian and Yoruba experience in Nigeria. Hackett discusses the strategies and adjustments that the Nigerian Celestial Church of Christ made following the founder's death. Finally, Hermoine Harris looks at Yoruba adaptive processes in the work of a London branch of the C&S and gives special attention to the notions of spiritual power and possession.

6. By saying that "Africa has no tradition of asceticism," Gifford (1993, 187) overlooks both historic Ethiopian and AIC that stress practices of fasting and spiritual retreats that require sexual abstinence. Of course, much depends on how we define the term *ascetic.* If we understand it as something that devalues material existence, idealizes permanent withdrawal from society, and sees celibacy as irreversible, then the Aladura do not embrace an ascetic value. But if by *ascetic* we refer to a value that conditions spiritual progress on one's periodic renunciation of physical comfort, fasting, and sexual abstinence, then we can say the Aladura have an ascetic tradition.

7. Keeler did fieldwork among "syncretist" Muslims in Java, who insisted that rewards and blessings required self sacrifice. This led to a paradox: in order to obtain what one desired, one must deny desire. As Keeler comments: "Asceticism . . . posits a homology between desire overcome and desire fulfilled. In either case, the object of desire becomes uninvested, with the result that the gap between desire and object falls away" (1987, 47).

8. Here I use the phrase *performative act* as defined by Thomas Csordas: "Performative *acts* in healing are discrete gestures or verbal formulae construed primarily as acts of empowerment, protection, revelation, and deliverance" (1996, 96).

9. As Simon Coleman indicates in his study of Swede Faith Pentecostals (2006), even Pentecostals treat words as objects and money (or gifts) as transactional items. This approach becomes an effective and relevant theological strategy that collapses the dichotomy between symbol and presence.

10. Recent ethnographies have challenged a common syncretistic paradigm that assumed an inside-outside dichotomy—that is, the new church was seen as having an outward Christian form with an inward African content. This dichotomy had also been couched in terms of an authentic-inauthentic paradigm—the AIC represents an authentic African church and the mainline church does not. The dichotomy has also been implicit in several outstanding studies that see AIC in terms of resistance toward missionary Christianity, colonial domination, and the world capitalist market. Such an approach, however, underrates the continuity with mainline theologies, short shrifts the claims of conversion experiences, and neglects the role of Christian tropes in the creation of meaning within AIC communities (see Meyer 2004).

11. Gifford's work prompted debate among Liberian churchmen about the church's complicity with Doe's regime and the relevance of a theology of liberation. The *Liberian Studies Journal* featured an important exchange between Professor Levi Zangai of Public Administration at the University of Liberia and the Reverend Levi Williams III, dean of Gbarnga School of Theology. The journal published Zangai's 1993 commencement address to the Liberia Baptist Theological Seminary, in which he criticized Liberian Christians for forsaking *"moral and social responsibilities"* and for *"cast*[ing] *a vote of confidence for the status quo."* He challenged seminaries and Bible colleges to make a theology of liberation part of their curriculum (1994, 67). In letters to Zangai, Williams took exception to this view. He claimed that both Gifford and Zangai overlooked the wide spectrum of social approaches in churches and overrated the effectiveness of a "confrontational" theology of liberation (1994, 72–76). In a later work Gifford himself notes that the hegemony between the Liberian state and church was never uniform (1998, 48).

12. Shaw makes a compelling case for seeing divination rites and practices among the Temne of Sierra Leone in terms of image memories of slaving terror and raiding. "By examining Temne divination through the lense of ritual memory, I seek to explore forms of coherence through which diviners, clients, and others both remember the terror of the slave trade *and* turn that terror into creative ritual forms." This traces "a history of moral imagination . . . told primarily in the language of practical memory through places and practices, images and visions, rituals and rumors" (2002, 22). Such image or ritual memories persist as well in Liberian experience. But, as Mary Moran notes, the encounter between African American settler and indigenous groups provided the primary "template" for the Liberian colonial narrative (2006, 63).

13. The name for this festival was written several ways—"Tabborrah," "Taborah," "Tabora," and "Tabieorar." The official spelling in the Nigerian-based Church of the Lord (Aladura) was "Tabieorar." Among Aladura churches in Liberia, however, "Tabborrar" was the most popular written form. Thus, for this monograph, I have adapted that spelling.

1. THE FIELD OF PROPHECY

1. William Wade Harris was born near Cape Palmas in the mid–nineteenth century. In 1909 he was imprisoned for protesting against the Liberian government. While in prison he received a vision from the Angel Gabriel commanding him to become a prophet. Once he was released from prison, he donned a white robe, obtained a Bible, made a staff-cross, and went about the country preaching. In Liberia he had little immediate success. In 1913, along with female companions, he left Liberia and began evangelizing villages along the coasts of present day Ivory Coast and Ghana, commanding people to give up their "fetishes" and receive baptism. It is estimated that in two years he made almost fifty thousand converts. For discussions of Harris's work and the beginnings of Harriste churches, see Gordon Haliburton (1971), Sheila Walker (1983), and David Shank (1997).

2. According to Scheffers, "Neor seems to have been the first Bassa man to speak in tongues, to tremble while praying, and to practice healing. He was also the first to introduce the holy water and oil which continue to be tokens of the Spirit's power in many of the Bassa Independent Churches today. Neor's effect on those to whom he ministered is still apparent today as prayers are offered by the elderly to the 'God of Rev. Neor' parallel to the 'God of Abraham, Isaac, and Jacob'" (1987, 68–69).

3. Since Oshitelu's death there have been three primates: Dr. Emmanuel Adejobi (1966–1991), the Most Reverend Gabriel Oshitelu (1991–1998), and the Reverend Dr. Rufus Oshitelu (1998–present).

4. Among Liberians the term *kwi* was commonly used to refer to the civilized/modern, Western/white world. In the Kru language *kwi* meant "the dead" or "an oracle." Among the Grebo the term was used to refer to white people. What appears to link these meanings is an idea of something "other" to the ordinary world of indigenous Liberians. In the late nineteenth century Liberians began using the term to refer to Americo-Liberians, since this group had come to embody the white person's lifestyle (Tonkin 1981, 318–19). Thus, "being white" had cultural as well as racial significance.

This idea was brought home to me when the Liberian leaders of an Aladura church referred to an African American Spiritual church it had recently become affiliated with as "white."

5. Several leading members traveled to Nigeria and appealed to the primate for Fyneah's removal. After reviewing the situation, the primate asked Fyneah to step down and appointed a Nigerian, Joseph Orebanjo, to serve in the interim. In 1970, then Bishop Lewis Thomas, a Ghanian, was appointed and remained the head of the Liberia See for the next twelve years, until the Ogere headquarters assigned him to Sierra Leone. In 1982 Moses Mayson, a man of Kru background, became the first native Liberian to head the church since Fyneah's demotion.

6. In 1984 Apostle Moses Mayson estimated that the Liberian See had fifty-five branches (not including "prayer groups") and about ten thousand members. He admitted it was difficult to be exact, since the numbers varied depending on how many churches participated in the annual conference. Churches that broke away one year rejoined the next and vice versa. The church had its strongest branches among Kpelle, Kru, and Grebo groups; in recent years its Kissi membership had notably increased. One leader claimed the Loma "were slow to respond, but they afterwards became strong members. The Gola and Dey were hard to get to; they pretended to be Muslims." According to Gifford, by the end of the Doe era the CLA would have 129 participating branches (1993, 219).

7. Here my interpretation benefits from Cynthia Hoehler-Fatton's study (1998) in which she argues that the idea that Roho churches in Kenya are "schismatic" or "breakaway" bespeaks an authoritarian, missionary perspective. This model glosses the "continuum of charismatic, grassroots Holy Spirit religion, well established by the time missionaries constituted any real presence in the region" (396).

8. Liberians often used the word *tarry* with reference to an evening service or a midnight struggle. In the American South people use the term to refer to the custom of putting aside personal interest in order to spend quality time with another person. Crumbley notes also how the term was used to refer to a form of worship in the African American "Sanctified Church" of her Philadelphia childhood (2008, 73). It is possible that the term was introduced to Liberians by African American missionaries.

9. As in the case of the CLA, it was difficult to get an accurate rendering of the branches and membership of St. Peter's. The leaders sometimes counted patients who were not members and also referred to prayer groups as branches. In 1984 I could ascertain about fifteen branches. But the number changed depending on how many branches attended, left, or rejoined the annual conference. The configuration was always shifting. St. Peter's authorities at that time gave me estimates of membership that ran from as few as seven hundred to as many as twenty thousand. Some churches were extremely remiss in documenting membership. The enrollment of established branches ranged from about thirty to one hundred fifty members; thus I estimate that St. Peter's membership in 1984 numbered about one thousand. This figure, however, does not include the many, many patients who outnumbered members.

10. The Church of Salvation was founded in 1946 by Prophet E. J. Fofana, a veteran of World War II. The church was based in Bo, Sierra Leone, and had been especially

successful among the Mende population. One of its strongest branches though was in Freetown, a branch that Bundu belonged to when he lived there in the early 1970s. According to one researcher (Avery 1982, 56), in the 1970s the church had about six thousand members. In the early 1980s, by church accounts, it had more than twenty-five thousand.

11. The church also required that new members sponsor a sin sacrifice, which mandated the immolation of a goat. Most AIC I encountered approved animal sacrifices. Sheep and chicken were the most frequent victims. Sacrifices were performed for a variety of purposes—as thanksgivings, for fulfillment of vows, for promoting peace and harmony in the home or in the church, as part of a healing treatment, or as a protective measure against witchcraft, among other reasons. But no church observed sacrifice more often than the United Church of Salvation. Many members were middle-class professionals (engineers, teachers, travel agents, gold brokers, and shop owners) who had sufficient means to buy a goat or sheep for sacrifice. See Britt 2008.

12. The Christian Community Churches of Christ established branches throughout the Carolinas, Virginia, and the mid-Atlantic region. Before its contact with St. Peter's, it had sponsored mission work in Ghana.

13. Thus it is no accident that Aladura prophets often have the names of Hebrew prophets, such as Moses, Amos, Daniel, Hezekiah, and, as in Olu's case, Samuel. Some received these names at birth, which would be explained as a sign of their calling. Others received biblical names when they converted or became ordained. Interestingly, Olu named his first son Oshitelu, after the CLA founder. He firmly believed his son was destined to become a prophet as well.

14. Evangelical groups have always referred to the conversion experience of accepting Jesus as "Personal Savior and Lord" concomitant with a "born again" experience. Here, however, *Born Agains* refers to a worldwide Christian movement with strong evangelical and Pentecostal links. In her work Harris (see 2006, 218–27) explores the influence of Nigerian-based Born Agains on C&S practice in London. Like Gifford (1993), she sees the recent rise of global Pentecostalism and Born Agains as strongly influenced by "interdenominational North American Pentecostal culture …, not only in their origins, but in their contemporary style" (224).

2. Person and Power in Liberia

1. The term *cosmology* or *cosmogony* has often been linked by scholars to doctrinal or mythic components of culture. Examples of this approach can be found in Mircea Eliade's *Myth of the Eternal Return* (1974) and in the collection *Myth and Cosmos* (1967), edited by John Middleton. Eliade relates cosmology to mythic repetitions and patterns. Middleton, though, sees myth and cosmology as "connected to symbolic and social systems. They illuminate aspects of human, natural and supernatural relationships" (x). In the posthumous work *On the Edge of the Bush: An Anthropology of Experience* (1985), Victor Turner also links cosmology to doctrine, systems, and ideology. He describes these as "static models" of culture that belie the dynamic, problematic aspect of human experience. Similarly, Helen Hardacre, in her work *Kurozumikyo and the New Religions of Japan* (1986), defines cosmology as a "set

image of the universe" (9). She employs the term *worldview*, suggesting the interplay between social patterns and personal actions. Hardacre seeks to study "the ways people approximate religious ideas . . . and use them to achieve a variety of ends." The word *cosmology* can be used effectively so long as we acknowledge its reference to the multiple dimensions of human experience and society. What J. P. Kiernan suggests concerning *worldview* can apply here: that it refer to political and economic aspects as well as mythic and mystical; that it account for time/space descriptions; that it "take cognizance of an expansion in the universe of social discourse"; and that it indicate the "multiplicity of voices" (1981, 10).

2. This phrasing was inspired by E. Valentine Daniel's work (1987). The phrase "being a person the Aladura way" highlights a synthesis of personal and cultural experiences.

3. It is important to note that both Tonkin (1981) and Moran (1990) did their research among southeastern Liberian groups, where the model of "civilization" was inspired more by mission Christianity than by the settler culture. As such, the civilized category was defined less by notions of class than by the nature of one's work. Moran did her work among the Glebo people of Harper County and focused on how their understanding of this model related to the role and expectations of women. As she notes, what characterized a woman as civilized was her relation to her civilized husband. Moran comments: "These women are, more or less, housewives; they do no agricultural work, with the exception of some kitchen gardening, and status considerations prevent them from going into business for themselves in the public marketplace. The primary duties are the care of the home and the raising and training of children and servants" (67).

4. Among groups that represented "society business," the most widespread in Liberia and Sierra Leone, and strongest among Kpelle, Gola, Loma, and Mende groups, were the Poro (men's group) and Sande (women's group). Poro and Sande chapters had in recent decades become established among the Bassa, Dei, and Vai, who lived in communities near Monrovia. As Christian K. Højbjerg notes, interpretations of Poro and Sande have been largely functional, seeing these "secret societies" as serving to consolidate factions and provide cohesion and solidarity among them. Still, one can never make sweeping generalizations about the geographical work of societies. For instance, Poro also created cohering links across cultural divides while it helped entrench local loyalties (2004, 174–76).

5. Despite the significance given to the Sande Society and to women's domain, the values of seniority and patrimony took precedence. In his study of the Gola, Warren d'Azevedo (1994) notes that Sande becomes "an instrument of male control over women" (345). This was deemed necessary in part because of the potentially subversive and dangerous power of women. Indeed, the aggressive independent woman represents "negations of the existing order" (359). Such women were accused of having liaisons with asocial spirits or of committing witchcraft. In the traditional Gola world, as in that of other ethnic groups, most of those accused of witchcraft were women.

6. There are obviously problems with the term *soul*. It glosses over a variety of indigenous concepts that assume, in Morton Klass's words, *"an incorporeal dimension to the living, observable, corporeal entity"* (1995, 100). But the terms *soul* and *spirit* were those most frequently used by Aladura informants to refer to this incorporeal

dimension. *Spirit* was mentioned in more somatic terms than *soul.* Thus it might be said that the spirit has weakened in a person who appears sick; and that it has returned in one who recovers. Though ethnography on Liberian groups indicates that ideas of the person refer to different invisible elements, Aladura doctrine tends to simplify this. A Kpelle or Bassa member may indeed distinguish between an "incorporeal entity," which moves through dreams, and one that survives death, but for the Aladura such distinctions were not as important.

7. Klass indicates that the term *supernatural* is problematic when applied cross-culturally; it premises a dichotomy between natural and supernatural that often misrepresents (1995, 25–34). This applies to the Aladura. In Liberia they did not draw a sharp line between the natural and supernatural realms, between this side and that side. Movement between the two was constant and real.

8. In her work on divination among the Temne of Sierra Leone, Rosalind Shaw notes the relation between secrecy and power. Secrecy produces boundaries between social groups and also enhances the power or prestige of certain individuals. Shaw stresses that the Temne relate knowing oneself to knowing one's "hidden knowledge" and that diviners use this to enhance authority in the community. Also, a Temne diviner has the ability to know what is deep and hidden in others, as well as to know himself. This talent becomes articulated especially in how the Temne understand dreams. Thus the diviner not only interprets dreams of others, "but during diagnosis diviners can also *ascribe* a dream to a client or accused party, of which the latter may have had no prior knowledge" (1992, 43–44).

9. In his article "Christ in African Folk Theology," Matthew Schoffeleers notes the ambiguity the Bantu peoples feel about the person known as *nganga,* the traditional healer or diviner. The *nganga*'s ability to detect witchcraft can be related to his ability to commit witchcraft. Schoffeleers notes, however, that perceptions concerning a Christian *nganga* aspire to remove this ambiguity (1994:79).

10. In his discussion about Mende notions of *halei,* "power," Anthony J. Gittins notes its relation to the idea of a "swear/curse." Indeed particular *halei* objects made of pouches, horns, cowry shells, red cloth and various secret substances were used in traditional court settings. Witnesses might be asked to take an oath with *sondu wa halei,* "the big swear/curse," like swearing on the Bible. This particular association between *halei* and "the swear" illustrates how *halei* became "an agent of social control" (1987, 121–22). The Aladura minister's idea of the swear certainly differed from that of the Mende, but the notion of virtue also implied the importance of corrective action.

11. Among Aladura informants, there was the strong tendency to use the words *Spirit* and *Holy Spirit* interchangeably. Oladipo sees this tendency among many West African Christians, not just Aladura, as an example of the Christianization of a previously generic concept (1996, 46–47).

12. Hermoine Harris also indicates that the electricity metaphor for spiritual power was commonplace among diaspora Aladura in London. It was also used in traditional Yoruba culture (2006:89–93).

13. Similarly, Ray interprets Aladura ritual words and names as having "peformative force" because they establish communication between God and believer. Ray relates

this aspect of Aladura words and names to the Yoruba concept of *oriki*, "praise names," which when used in ritual contexts bring contact with the spiritual world (1993, 281).

14. Though he recognizes the spiritual and moral value of Aladura praying with psalms, Harold Turner unfortunately tends to dismiss it as "pure occult magic" (1967, 2:74). He describes this application as "the corruption of the Psalter into a new spiritual magic, with a return to views of prayer that are pagan and selfish" (75). This categorization betrays a Western Protestant view of magic and religion that obfuscates an understanding of Aladura ritual. Stanley Tambiah questions the customary distinction between "magical" and "religious" acts. Magical acts have been categorized as manipulations of multiple spirits or forces, while "religious acts" represent intercessions with the deity. One approach uses spells, the other uses prayer. These categorizations, however, simply do not work in the Aladura example, nor are they necessarily instructive in understanding other traditions. Is the Aladura prophet praying with psalms, water, and candles over a sick patient any more magical than the chaplain whose prayers accompany modern prescriptions and treatments? Ray notes the relevance of Tambiah's criticism in considering the Weberian categories "this-worldly" and "other-worldly." The pragmatic interest of Aladura churches notwithstanding, to characterize them as simply "this-worldly" betrays an unfair "theological judgment" (1993, 278). It also fails to appreciate an Aladura cosmology in which visible and invisible realities constantly interact.

15. As Turner notes, the Aladura acknowledged the "inadequacy of ordinary language" in religious contexts (1967, 2:281). Thus, God has responded by giving humans holy names. One Aladura theologian, J. Ade Aina, claimed that humans spoke these words before the construction of the Tower of Babel but lost them when God dispersed the races. Other members claimed that at Pentecost God revealed these words through the speaking in tongues (281). In Liberia I observed many occasions when holy words or names were voiced during trance or possession, but rarely did these resemble Pentecostal glossolalia.

16. *Open mole* refers to a condition of softness on the crown of the head. Informants believed the condition made one vulnerable to the attack of an evil spirit or to witchcraft. The term was also used to describe the fontanel condition of infants, which healers also tried to treat.

17. Turner notes that in Nigeria the Aladura were sometimes called "those water people" because of the important role water had in their customs (1967, 2:12). Aladura theologians described the use of water in "sacramental" terms. J. Ade Aina and D. Olu Abimbola referred to it as a natural element that came to humans undefiled. Abimbola ingeniously contended that "water is uncorrupted by human sin and the consequences of the fall, for God cursed the soil because of Adam's sin, but not water." This "theology of water," claims Turner, can be seen as a natural theology, in which water, a natural element, "can mediate God's action to men" (147–49).

18. In her discussion about witchcraft ideas among the Harrist churches of the Ivory Coast, Sheila Walker notes that they also make an ethical distinction between European and African forms of power and technology: "In discussing the differences in the technological ability between Africans and Europeans, the Harrist

attribute this inequality to the different uses that the two groups make of their spiritual force rather than either its quality or its quantity. Whereas Europeans use their Spiritual force constructively, the Africans use their destructively. An example commonly offered is the following. If a European builds a nice house, his neighbor will express his envy of the other man's success by working to build an even nicer house for himself. If an African builds a nice house in his village, however, rather than trying to outdo him in a constructive manner by building a better house, his jealous neighbors will try to 'suppress' him 'as a devil.' Europeans do not have more or different spiritual force than Africans. They just use it for positive rather than negative ends, their envy of the acquisitions of others encouraging them to work harder and produce more" (1980:118).

19. Informants often mentioned bottles, boxes, trunks, pots, and cans being used for such purposes. Interestingly, this compares to Gittins's description of Mende *halei* objects. They were "the small tin trunk filled with stones, or the iron pot. Half buried next to the verandah or door of a dwelling, these are believed able to protect property and householders, by deterring any potential malefactor" (1987, 111). The Mende and the Aladura, however, gave different meanings to the use of such containers. In the Mende case, a resident used it to protect himself and his property; in the Aladura case, an enemy used it to harm his neighbor.

20. In speaking about the education of children in Sierra Leone, Caroline Bledsoe notes that the theme of struggle has been adapted as a model for children. For instance, Mende parents emphasize that a child develops and obtains success only through struggle. The term was used primarily in reference to seeking personal goals and was distinguished from *work*, which served others and more clearly embraced communal values (1990:77–78).

21. Turner briefly refers to the term's metaphoric use with the following description: "Christian endeavor is known as 'struggling,' and involves obedience to some six positive commands—to pray, fast, give alms, love, preach, and read the Bible—six main prohibitions—concerning magic and idolatry, sex, foods, alcohol, tobacco, and litigation. Observance of these 'keeps a Christian's lamp always burning bright' and enables him 'to practice all the good ways, wish, and works of Jesus'" (1967, 2:69).

22. John Searle makes the distinction between acts that represent something and those that communicate. The latter require an audience, whereas the former do not (Humphrey and Laidlaw 1994, 78). This distinction is problematic when applied to the Aladura. Even ritual acts performed in isolation, such as midnight prayers or fasting, implied an audience, even if it was an invisible one; furthermore, every ritual act was understood through its connection with community habitus.

23. In his work *Paths toward a Clearing* (1989), Michael Jackson stresses the importance that "knowledge of the body" had in the ordering of experience for the Kuranko of Sierra Leone. Jackson argues against symbolic interpretations that privilege exegetical meaning over body praxis. As he states, "my argument is against speaking of bodily behavior as symbolizing ideas conceived independently of it" (136). Jackson relates his theme of bodily praxis to Pierre Bourdieu's model of habitus, the "'transposible dispositions' (that) arise in an environment of everyday practical activities" (128).

3. The Prophet: Paragon of Struggle

1. Gerhardus Oosthuizen notes that in African churches the designation *prophet* "has become closely associated with healing." Because the prophet's capacity to heal is related to his ability to see the other side, Oosthuizen also stresses the comparison with the traditional diviner (1992, 19, 165–93).

2. Kiernan criticizes Weber for creating a strong distinction between "rational and enthusiastic types of action" (1990, 158). In Zionist churches the social framework or institution became the vehicle that mediated and managed charismatic power. The same was true of Aladura churches. We might even suggest that power in the sense of charisma was embedded in social structure.

3. Anthropologists have long noted that traditional diviners and folk healers become so through experiences of affliction and misfortune. One can observe that pattern as well among southern Protestant groups. Southern Baptists, for instance, frequently tell stories about how the experiences of misfortune and loss led to conversion and call.

4. Interestingly, this inverts the assumption anthropologists have often made in associating women with nature and men with culture. Carol MacCormack indicates how among the Shrebo in Sierra Leone such associations usually depend on situations and contexts (1980, 95–96).

5. Certain images in dreams or visions could be ambiguous. Goats offer one example. At the United Church of Salvation the goat image became a sign that a goat sacrifice needed to take place. The church observed sin sacrifices that always involved immolation of a goat, which stood for the subject's sin being washed away. Aladura churches, however, did not observe sin or goat sacrifices, so the goat image carried other meanings, such as the presence of witchcraft in their midst.

4. The Circularity of Signs

1. Like the Aladura, according to Beryl L. Bellman, the Sucromu Kpelle support "two worlds of reality … : the world of dreams and the waking world" (1975, 107).

2. Scholars have largely neglected the topic of witchcraft among mission churches, as well as among AIC. Ethnographies by Birgit Meyer (1992), George Bond (2001), and Todd M. Vanden Berg (2005) make clear that witchcraft beliefs in mission-based churches and among mainline Christians remain persistent. Both Meyer and Vanden Berg claim the topic has been neglected by missiologists because of a top-down approach that privileges the work of church authorities and theologians and by anthropologists who may harbor some disdain toward and discomfort about missionary and mainline forms of Christianity.

3. Geschiere cites in particular the work of Eric de Rosny, a French priest who became apprenticed to *nganga*, or healers, in Cameroon. Through his work with the healers, de Rosny came to accept the reality of the *sorciers*, which he sums up in the following passage: "I came to see that evil *sorciers* do exist in flesh and blood. No doubt they are infinitely less numerous than … my panicky spokesmen affirmed, but they are nonetheless all too real. They are either people who manipulate others' credulity

for their own profit (sometimes even using poison); or persons who are not conscious of their perversity" (Geschiere 1997, 20).

4. In another conversation with Flomo, I asked him about the heartmen, a notorious cult that committed acts of human sacrifice that Liberians called "ritual execution." The minister immediately lowered his voice, since children were playing nearby. He rarely did this when we talked about witchcraft. This approach suggested that on one level the heartmen presented a greater threat than witchcraft. The minister's description of this cult echoed what I heard from other Liberians: It offered a client special powers in exchange for the sacrifice of a close relative. The perpetrators created a concoction from the body parts of the victim—skin from the forehead, palms, armpits, genitals, and heart. The potion was placed in a bag and the client wore it for protection and personal gain. The minister said that politicians were tempted to seek heartmen services, especially during election time. The description of the heartmen bears some resemblance to witchcraft: it involves personal gain at another's expense. But the minister also insisted that the cult was not a form of witchcraft or African science. The heartmen denoted a clear form of sinister evil, while both witchcraft and African science suggested greater ambiguity. In his study *The Mask of Anarchy* (1999), Stephen Ellis notes that in recent decades "reports of ritual killings were associated less with the traditional secret societies, such as the human leopards, than with so-called 'heartmen.'" Liberians considered modern Heartmen to be "freelance killers who specialize in procuring corpses or human organs for those who require them, particularly business people and politicians in search of wealth and power" (253).

5. Al-Hassan Conteh notes concerning the Nege witch: "The Nege . . . is believed to be a secret society that is linked with deals in human parts and human sacrifice for the achievement of various mundane activities. And whenever there is a mysterious drowning case, people are observed as invoking Nege as an alternative cause" (1990, 149).

6. Aladura prophets also consecrated vehicles. Such consecrations were often prescribed in relation to prophecies about motor accidents. Members routinely had their cars consecrated as a precaution. For the consecration the car might be washed with holy water and fumigated inside and out with incense smoke. Along with this consecration, the owner might be asked to take a holy bath. In some cases, while the car itself was being fumigated, the prophets might ask its owner to sit inside. Car consecrations also happened spontaneously. Once when I was attending a Sunday morning service at an Aladura branch, the senior prophetess instructed the male minister to go outside and consecrate my car by praying over it and sprinkling it with holy water.

7. In his study of Mororccan Hamadsha fraternities, Vincent Crapanzano indicates that in cases of individuals who had "symbiotic relationships" with *jinn* (pl., *jnun*), a "race of spiritual beings" (1973, 138), the fraternity sometimes encouraged the further development of the liaison, but monitored through the Hamadsha's control. In such cases the treatment and cure involved an ongoing process and effectively initiated the person into the fraternity. In the case of individuals who were attacked by a *jinn*—usually an "unnamed *jinn*" over whom the cult had no control—the

Hamadsha attempted to "exorcise" the spirit from its victim. The cure, then, became a "one-shot affair" (1973, 159).

8. Gittins describes a bush spirit associated with a light source: "*Njaloi* is a cruel spirit whose light attracts and confuses fishermen or straying travelers . . . ; the general understanding is that *njaloi* needs fresh prey for its hungry offspring. It lights a lamp and attracts the unwary, presumably with empty promises, only to catch them in its net. It is quite likely that such spirits can assume the form of either sex, that they enter into a sexual compact with those they ensnare, and that their promises are variable to some degree" (1987, 78).

9. The report Gittins gives of certain Mende nonancestral spirit called *tingoi* compares with our account of Mami Wata. The Mende describe this spirit as a woman with a fish or snake body. This siren "usually sits on a rock combing its long hair and looking into a mirror. Should it see a passer-by, it will jump into the river. A person who sees *tingoi* may try to catch the mirror or comb, fatally attracted by the charms of *tingoi*. The *tingoi* holds the promise of great riches and wealth to anyone who surprises her in the river, but also the threat of servitude" (1987, 77).

10. Harris (2006) notes the popularity of other texts as well: *The Original Key to the Sixth and Seventh Books of Moses*, *The Greater Key of Solomon*, and *The Lesser Key of Solomon* (197). She comments that the "historical origins appear to be a jumble of Solomonic legend, Egypto-Hellenic magic, Christian-Jewish mythology, Cabbalistic tradition, Gnostic and Arabic folklore, European occultism, the Talmud, and the Bible plus apocrypha." She refers to the "flourishing trade in Nigeria" of such works, which "have undoubtedly influenced Aladura" (256).

5. The Faith Home: Focused Space

1. The CLA Faith Home on Center Street in Monrovia was the largest and most fully staffed in Liberia. The compound, which included a cathedral, Faith Home, and high school, was enclosed by a six-foot cement wall. The Faith Home itself was a two-story building with fifteen rooms that accommodated assigned ministers and patients. The office of Apostle Moses Mayson, head of the Liberian See, was located on the second floor. The office's lobby, usually full of members and patients awaiting audiences, also opened onto a balcony facing Center Street. Below the lobby was the Faith Home chapel, where scheduled healing clinics took place. The cathedral, with an impressive bell tower, was adjacent to the Faith Home. An open courtyard separated the two structures. The school was located in a smaller building at the back of the compound. A corridor connected it to both the Faith Home and the chapel. Nested within this corridor, in a dark recess lit only by candlelight, was the Mercy Ground.

2. Concerning the Celestial Church of Christ's Mercy Ground, Ray notes that it was "modeled upon Christ's retreat into the wilderness for forty days where he renounced Satan and received the ministrations of angels. Imitating Christ, the Celestials go to the Mercy Ground, where angels are in attendance, for as long as they need. Most go to seek spiritual powers, others go to present petitions, for example, for the conception of children, some desire healing, others go to pray for forgiveness of sins" (1993, 277–78).

3. Based on his study of the Celestial Church of Christ, Ray gives the following description of each guardian angel's function: "The angel Michael wields a spiritual sword that conquers malevolent supernatural forces; Gabriel helps to cure barrenness; Uriel is called upon during private devotional prayers to make them effective; Raphael helps to ward off sickness and health hazards. These angels are also associated with four cardinal directions, East, West, North, and South respectively" (1993, 276).

4. Sometimes the surest mark of one's identity as "civilized" or "uncivilized" was clothing, especially among women. According to Moran, among the Glebo a civilized woman should never wear a lappa cloth in public, though she might relax the rule at home. At the same time, wearing a tailored lappa suit had become increasingly acceptable for the civilized woman (1990, 68).

5. Buckley and Gottlieb reject what they see as reductionist theories about menstrual customs: that they are constructed to oppress women or are based on a social neurosis. They adopt Mary Douglas's (1966) model of "dirt is matter out of place." In itself menstrual blood is not impure or bad. It represents a power that must be controlled or used in a creative way (Strathern 1996, 66–68). Crumbley (2008) also appears to follow this approach.

6. Turner observed the importance of "churching a corpse" among historic churches in West Africa. He claimed that many pay church dues in order to be assured they will be properly buried (1967, 2:254). I found this to be the case in Liberia as well. Indeed, some Aladura members kept joint associate membership with a Baptist, Roman Catholic, or Methodist church for this reason. In conversation a lay informant once expressed dismay to me that the Aladura church did not church a corpse and believed it would have more dedicated members if it did so. In her discussion of one man's sudden death, Moran demonstrates how churching a corpse related to the Glebo model of civilization. When the man's family began taking care of his burial, they soon learned that the man, a confirmed Episcopalian, had not paid his church dues and had allowed his membership to lapse. The local church, therefore, could not church the corpse, but it did agree to help with organizing a wake at the family's home. Meanwhile, "country" relatives of the man explored options with a Pentecostal prophet church. At first the church hesitated, but eventually it agreed to perform a service. In the end, however, the "civilized" relatives prevailed as Episcopal lay members officiated over a wake service at the home, with members of the prophet church also attending. Interestingly, Moran uses the term *Pentecostal Prophet* to cover the various independent groups in Harper that emphasize healing and distinctive musical styles of worship, which presumably would include the Aladura congregations established there since the 1960s. If the prophet church in the anecdote above had Aladura ties, its hesitation in churching the corpse might have been due to concerns about impurity (Moran 1990, 141–43).

7. The Faith Home serves as the primary social unit in Aladura practice. In Bourdieu's terms, it is governed by set structures and "durable, transposable dispositions" that demonstrate harmony (and disharmony) between individual and communal interests, between a subject's mental awareness and physical praxis. Habitus, the "system of dispositions," is generated through embodiment, a specified bodily praxis (1977, 72). In the Faith Home habitus, specific ritual events—fasting, holy baths,

consecrations, scheduled services, and prayers—represent primary forms of embodiment.

8. The United Church of Salvation described holy baths as consecrations, calling them body consecrations. The church's handbook states: "The Church undertakes the consecration of people and elements." Some informants, however, did understand these consecrations as purifications. From time to time the church also observed what it called a creek consecration. It authorized this ritual for both individuals and groups. I participated in one creek consecration, which had been mandated for all members. An hour before an evening service, everyone met at the chapel and changed into white gowns. They formed a single file, with men leading and women following, and walked to a creek behind the church. While members stood on the bank, the senior prophet waded waist-deep into the water and began praying. As he prayed he dipped an altar bell into the water three times. When he finished praying he tossed water in four directions. He then signaled for the men to take baths. After they completed their bathing, they returned to the bank and the women began to wade into the creek.

9. Stone notes concerning the Kpelle idea of ritual: "The word for 'fence,' *korang*, happens also to be the word for 'ritual' and for 'year.' Thus ritual can be understood as that which encloses acts valuable to the Kpelle as a fence protects the rice crop. To speak ritual, the Kpelle say, is to *korang bo* (open the fence)" (394).

6. Mount Tabborrar: The Sacred Passage

1. For many African Initiated Churches in Liberia and Sierra Leone, the annual announcement of "Divine Revelations" by a church's founder or leading authority was a standard practice. In Sierra Leone, Primate Fofana of the Church of Salvation published revelations every September or October that prophesied events for the next year. In Paynesville, Primate Daniel Sesay of the Universal Faith Healing Church also made copies of divine revelations he received during the church's annual Mount Orraatat struggle.

2. In the early Christian tradition the Mount of Transfiguration in the New Testament, where Jesus's disciples see him transfigured and in the company of Moses and Elijah, came to be called Mount Tabor. Though it seems unlikely that Oshitelu had knowledge of this tradition, one cannot rule it out totally, especially in light of the analogy to Elijah that Oshitelu made in speaking of his own mission. CLA authorities indeed came to refer to Oshitelu as "the Last Elijah" (Turner 1967, 2:287–89).

3. The Kingdom Assembly Church of Africa, commonly known as the Never Die Church, was among the most intriguing and controversial Liberian AIC. Its leader Richard Sleboe claimed that one could obtain physical immortality through faith. He also referred to himself as the Holy Spirit. Among Aladura informants, mention of Sleboe's name invited dismissive, if bemused, comments. I knew a patient at St. Peter's whose mental problems were diagnosed as being caused by Never Die doctrines. For discussion of the Never Die Church, see Gifford 1992.

4. Turner notes that the litany involved thirteen requests: forgiveness, cleansing, mercy, blessing, good children, perfect peace, victory, salvation, healing, lasting joy, favor, the mighty power of the Spirit, and steadfastness (1967, 2:225–26). For future

Tabborrars, however, St. Peter's planned not to use the Thirteen Questions, since the litany included a vow to remain faithful to the Church of the Lord. Also, after Tabborrar, Olu announced the change of the ritual mount's name to Mount Olive. He considered this fair to the CLA, but the change also reinforced the separate identity of St. Peter's.

5. The doctrinal mode of religiosity was represented by "frequent repetition of religious doctrine in verbal form." It included set ritual routines and "habitual bodily movements" as well as didactic forms, such as sermons. The imagist mode was expressed in a more "dramatic" ways with "vivid, detailed, emotionally charged episodic memories" (Laidlaw 2004, 4–5).

SCHOLARLY WORKS

Adogame, Afe. 2000. "Aiye Loja, Orun Nile—the Appropriation of Ritual Time-Space in the Cosmology of the Celestial Church of Christ." *Journal of Religion in Africa* 30 (1): 3–29.

———. 2004. "Engaging the Rhetoric of Spiritual Warfare: The Public Face of the Aladura in Diaspora." *Journal of Religion in Africa* 34 (4): 493–522.

———. 2007. "Raising Champions, Taking Territories: African Churches and the Mapping of New Religious Landscapes in Diaspora." In *The African Diaspora and the Study of Religion,* edited by Theodore L. Trost, 17–34. New York: Palgrave Macmillian.

Asamoah-Gyadu, J. Kwabena. 2005. "'Christ Is the Answer: What Is the Question?' A Ghana Airways Prayer Vigil and Its Implications for Religion, Evil and Public Space." *Journal of Religion in Africa* 35 (1): 93–117.

Ashforth, Adam. 2000. *Madumo: A Man Bewitched.* Chicago: University of Chicago Press.

———. 2001. "On Living in a World with Witches: Everyday Epistemology and Spiritual Insecurity in a Modern African City (Soweto)." In *Magical Interpretations, Material Realities: Modernity, Witchcraft and the Occult in Postcolonial Africa,* edited by Henrietta Moore and Todd Sanders, 206–25. London: Routledge.

———. 2005. *Witchcraft, Violence, and Democracy in South Africa.* Chicago: University of Chicago Press.

Auge, Marc. 1994. *A Sense of the Other: Timeliness and Relevance in Anthropology.* Translated by Amy Jacobs. Stanford, Calif.: Stanford University Press.

Avery, W. Leslie. 1982. "The Church of Salvation in Sierra Leone: An Attempt to Indigenize Christianity." *Orita* 14 (1): 55–67.

Baeta, Christian. 1962. *Prophetism in Ghana: A Study of Some "Spiritual" Churches.* London: SCM Press.

Bähre, Erik. 2002. "Witchcraft and the Exchange of Sex, Blood, and Money among Africans in Cape Town, South Africa." *Journal of Religion in Africa* 32 (3): 300–334.

Bell, Catherine. 1992. *Ritual Theory, Ritual Practice.* New York: Oxford University Press.

Bellman, Beryl L. 1975. *Village of Curers and Assassins: On the Production of Fala Cosmological Categories.* The Hague: Mouton.

———. 1984. *The Language of Secrecy: Symbols and Metaphors of Poro Ritual.* New Brunswick, N.J.: Rutgers University Press.

Beulow, George. 1980. "Eve's Rib: Association Membership and Mental Health among Kru Women." *Liberian Studies Journal* 9 (1): 23–33.

Bledsoe, Caroline. 1980. *Women and Marriage in Kpelle Society.* Stanford, Calif.: Stanford University Press.

———. 1984. "The Political Use of Sande Ideology and Symbolism." *American Ethnologist* 2 (3): 455–72.

———. 1990. "'No Success without Struggle:' Social Mobility and Hardship for Foster Children in Sierra Leone." *Man* 25 (1): 70–87.

Bond, George Clement. 2001. "Ancestors and Witches: Explanation and the Ideology of Individual Power in Northern Zambia." In *Witchcraft Dialogues: Anthropological and Philosophical Exchanges,* edited by George Clement Bond and Diane M. Ciekawy, 131–57. Research in International Studies, Africa Series, no. 76. Athens: Ohio University Press.

Bongmba, Elias. 2001a. *African Witchcraft and Otherness.* Albany: SUNY Press.

———. 2001b. "African Witchcraft: From Ethnography to Critique." In *Witchcraft Dialogues: Anthropological and Philosophical Exchanges,* edited by George Clement Bond and Diane M. Ciekawy, 39–79, Research in International Studies, Africa Series, no. 76. Athens: Ohio University Press.

———. 2007. "Anger as a Metaphor of Witchcraft: The Relation between Magic, Witchcraft and Divination among the Mupun of Nigeria. In *Imagining Evil: Witchcraft Beliefs and Accusations in Contemporary Africa,* edited by Gerrie Ter Haar, 113–42. Trenton, N.J.: Africa World Press.

Bourdieu, Pierre. 1977. *Outline of a Theory of Practice.* Translated by Richard Nice. Cambridge: Cambridge University Press.

Britt, Samuel I. 1992. "The Children of Salvation: Struggle and Cosmology in Liberian Prophet Churches." 2 vols. Ph.D. dissertation, University of Virginia.

———. 2008. "'Sacrifice Honors God': Ritual Struggle in a Liberian Church." *Journal of the American Academy of Religion* 76 (1): 1–26.

Brown, Delwin. 2001. "Refashioning Self and Other: Theology, Academy, and the New Ethnography." In *Converging on Culture: Theologians in Dialogue with Culture Analysis and Criticism,* edited by Delwin Brown, Sheila G. Davaney, and Kathryn Tanner, 41–55. Oxford: Oxford University Press.

Buckley, Thomas, and Alma Gottlieb, eds. 1988. *Blood Magic: The Anthropology of Menstruation.* Berkeley: University of California Press.

Cannell, Fenella, ed. 2006. *The Anthropology of Christianity.* Durham, N.C.: Duke University Press.

Carter, Jeanette. 1970. "The Rural Loma and Monrovia: Ties with an Urban Center." *Liberian Studies Journal* 2 (2): 143–51.

Charsley, Simon R. 1973. "Dreams in an Independent African Church." *Africa* 43 (3): 244–57.

Chesnek, Chris. 2002. "Our Subject 'Over There?' Scrutinizing the Distance between Religion and Its Study." In *Religious Studies, Theology, and the University: Conflicting Maps, Changing Terrain,* edited by Linell Cady and Delwin Brown, 45–64. Albany: SUNY Press.

Chopp, Rebecca S. 2001. "Theology and the Poetics of Testimony." In *Converging on Culture: Theologians in Dialogue with Cultural Analysis and Criticism,* edited by Delwin Brown, Sheila Davaney, and Kathryn Tanner, 56–77. Oxford: Oxford University Press.

Coleman, Simon. 2006. "Materializing the Self: Words and Gifts in the Construction of Charismatic Pentecostal Christianity." In *The Anthropology of Christianity,* edited by Fenella Cannell, 163–84. Durham, N.C.: Duke University Press.

Comaroff, Jean. 1985. *Body of Power, Spirit of Resistance: The Culture and History of a South Africa People.* Chicago: University of Chicago Press.

Comaroff, John, and Jean Comaroff, eds. 1993. *Modernity and Its Malcontents.* Chicago: University of Chicago Press.

———. 2006. "Criminal Obsessions, after Foucault: Postcoloniality, Policing, and the Metaphysics of Disorder." In *Law and Disorder in the Postcolony,* edited by Jean Comaroff and John Comaroff, 273–98. Chicago: University of Chicago Press.

Conteh, Al-Hassan. 1990. "Reflections on Some Concepts of Religion and Medicine in Liberian Society." *Liberian Studies Journal* 15 (2): 145–47.

Countryman, L. William. 1999. "Asceticism in the Johannine Letters?." In *Asceticism and the New Testament,* edited by Leif E.Vaage and Vincent L. Wimbush, 383–91. New York: Routledge.

Crapanzano, Vincent. 1973. *The Hamadsha: A Study in Moroccan Ethnopsychiatry.* Berkeley: University of California Press.

Crumbley, Deidra Helen. 1992. "Impurity and Power: Women in Aladura Churches." *Africa* 62 (4): 505–22.

———. 2003. "Patriarchies, Prophets, and Procreation: Sources of Gender Practice in Three African Churches." *Africa* 73 (4): 584–605.

———. 2006. "Power in the Blood: Menstrual Taboos and Female Power in an African Instituted Church." In *Women and Religion in the African Diaspora: Knowledge Power, and Performance,* edited by R. Marie and Barbara Dianne Savage, 81–97. Baltimore: Johns Hopkins University Press.

———. 2008. *Spirit, Structure, and Flesh: Gendered Experiences in African Instituted Churches among the Yoruba of Nigeria.* Madison: University of Wisconsin Press.

Csordas, Thomas J. 1994. *The Sacred Self: A Cultural Phenomenology of Charismatic Healing.* Berkeley: University of California Press.

———. 1996. "Imaginal Performance and Memory in Ritual Healing." In *The Performance of Healing,* edited by Carol Laderman and Marina Roseman, 91–113. New York: Routledge.

———. 2002. *Body, Meaning, Healing.* New York: Palgrave Macmillan.

Curley, Richard T. 1992. "Private Dreams and Public Knowledge in a Camerounian Independent Church." In *Dreaming, Religion and Society in Africa,* edited by M. C. Jedrej and Rosalind Shaw, 135–52. Leiden: E. J. Brill.

Daniel, E. Valentine. 1987. *Fluid Signs: Being a Person the Tamil Way.* Berkeley: University of California Press.

Davaney, Sheila G. 2001. "Theology and the Turn to Cultural Analysis." In *Converging on Culture: Theologians in Dialogue with Cultural Analysis and Criticism,* edited by Delwin Brown, Sheila Davaney, and Kathryn Tanner, 3–16. Oxford: Oxford University Press.

Davies, Douglas J. 2002. *Anthropology and Theology.* Oxford: Berg.

Davies, Owen. 2009. "Five Best: Books on Magic" *Wall Street Journal,* August 16, W8.

D'Azevedo, Warren. 1966. *The Artist Archetype of Gola Culture.* Reno: University of Nevada.

———. 1994. "Gola Womanhood and the Limits of Masculine Omnipotence." In *Religion in Africa: Experience and Expression,* edited by Thomas Blakely, Walter E. A. Van Beek, and Dennis L. Thomson, 343–62. London: James Curry.

De Jong, Ferdinand. 2004. "The Social Life of Secrets." In *Situating Globality: African Agency in the Appropriation of Global Culture*, edited by Wim van Binsbergen and Rijk van Dijk. Leiden: E. J. Brill, 257–76.

Dennis, Ruth E., and Ira E. Harrison. 1979. "Traditional Healers in Liberia: A Review of the Literature with Implications for Further Research." In *African Therapeutic Systems*, edited by Z. A. Ademuwagun, John A. A. Ayode, Ira E. Harrison, and Dennis M. Warren, 81–84. Waltham, Mass.: Crossroads Press.

Dorjahn, Vernon. 1962. "Some Aspects of Temne Divination." *Sierra Leone Bulletin of Religion* 4 (1): 3–8.

———. 1970. "Some Aspects of Migration in Liberia." *Liberian Studies Journal* 2 (2): 139–42.

Douglas, Mary. 1966. *Purity and Danger: An Analysis of the Concepts of Pollution and Taboo*. London: Routledge and Kegan Paul.

———. 1973. *Natural Symbols: Explorations in Cosmology*. New York: Vintage Books.

Drewal, Henry John. 1988. "Mermaids, Mirrors, and Snake Charmers: Igbo Mami Wata Shrines." *African Arts* 21 (2): 38–45.

———, ed. 2008. *Sacred Waters: Arts for Mami Wata and Other Divinities in Africa and the Diaspora*. Bloomington: Indiana University Press.

Drewal, Henry John, et al. 2008. *Mami Wata: Arts for Water Spirits in Africa and Its Diasporas*. Los Angeles: Fowler Museum of UCLA.

Drewal, Henry John, and Margaret Thompson Drewal. 1990. *Gelede: Art and Female Power among the Yoruba*. Bloomington: Indiana University Press.

Drewal, Margaret Thompson. 1992. *Yoruba Ritual: Performers, Play, Agency*. Bloomington: Indiana University Press.

Driver, Thomas T. 1991. *The Magic of Ritual: Our Need for Liberating Rites That Transform Our Lives and Our Communities*. New York: HarperCollins.

Eisenbaum, Pamela. 1999. "The Virtue of Suffering, the Necessity of Discipline, and the Pursuit of Perfection in Hebrews." In *Asceticism and the New Testament*, edited by Leif E. Vaage and Vincent L. Wimbush, 331–53. New York: Routledge.

Eliade, Mircea. 1974. *The Myth of the Eternal Return*. Translated by Willard Trask. Princeton, N.J.: Princeton University Press.

Ellis, Stephen. 1995. "Liberia 1989–1994: A Study of Ethnic and Spiritual Violence." *African Affairs* 94 (375): 165–97.

———. 2001. "Mystical Weapons: Some Evidence from the Liberian War." *Journal of Religion in Africa* 31 (2): 222–36.

———. 2006 (1999). *The Mask of Anarchy: The Destruction of Liberia and the Religious Dimension of an African Civil War*. London: Hurst.

Engelke, Matthew. 2005. "Sticky Subjects and Sticky Objects: The Substance of African Christian Healing." In *Materiality*, edited by Daniel Miller, 118–39. Durham, N.C.: Duke University Press.

———. 2007. *A Problem of Presence: Beyond Scripture in an African Church*. Berkeley: University of California Press.

Erchak, Gerald. 1976. "Who Is a Zo? A Study of Kpelle Identical Twins." *Liberian Studies Journal* 7 (1): 23–25.

Fabian, Johannes. 2002. *Memory against Culture: Arguments and Reminders*. Durham, N.C.: Duke University Press.

Fernandez, James. 1978. "Modern Religious Movements." *Annual Review of Anthropology* 7 (1): 195–234.

———. 1982. *Bwiti: An Ethnography of the Religious Imagination in Africa.* Princeton, N.J.: Princeton University Press.

Field, Margaret. 1970. *Search for Security.* London: W. W. Norton.

Fisiy, Cyprian, and Peter Geschiere. 1996. "Witchcraft, Violence, and Identity: Different Trajectories in Postcolonial Cameroon." In *Postcolonial Identities in Africa,* edited by Richard Werbner and Terence Ranger, 193–221. London: Zed Books.

Foucault, Michel. 1988. *Technologies of the Self.* London: Tavistock.

Fox-Genovese, Elizabeth. 1988. *Within the Plantation Household: Black and White Women of the Old South.* Chapel Hill: University of North Carolina Press.

Fraenkel, Merran. 1964. *Tribe and Class in Monrovia.* London: Oxford University Press.

Frei, Hans. 1992. *Types of Christian Theology.* New Haven, Conn.: Yale University Press.

Geertz, Clifford. 1973. *The Interpretation of Cultures: Selected Essays.* New York: Basic Books.

Geschiere, Peter. 1997. *The Modernity of Witchcraft: The Politics and the Occult in Postcolonial Africa.* Charlottesville: University Press of Virginia.

———. 1999. "Globalization and the Power of Intermediate Meaning: Witchcraft and Spirit Cults in Africa and East Asia." In *Globalization and Identity: Dialectics of Flow and Closure,* edited by Birgit Meyer and Peter Geschiere, 211–36. Oxford: Blackwell.

———. 2006. "Witchcraft and the Limits of the Law: Cameroons and South Africa." In *Law and Disorder in the Postcolony,* edited by Jean Comaroff and John Comaroff, 219–46. Chicago: University of Chicago Press.

Gifford, Paul. 1992. "Liberia's Never-Die Christians." *Journal of Modern African Studies* 30 (2): 349–58.

———. 1993. *Christianity and Politics in Doe's Liberia.* Cambridge: Cambridge University Press.

———. 1998. *African Christianity: Its Public Role.* London: Hurst.

Gittins, Anthony J. 1987. *Mende Religion: Aspects of Belief and Thought in Sierra Leone.* Nettetal, Germany: Steyler Verlag/Wort und Werk.

Hackett, Rosalind. 1980. "Thirty Years of Growth and Change in a West African Independent Church—a Sociological Perspective." *Journal of Religion in Africa* 9 (3): 212–24.

———. 1998. "Charismatic/Pentecostal Appropriation of Media Technologies in Nigeria and Ghana." *Journal of Religion in Africa* 38 (3): 258–77.

Hahn, Robert A. 1995. *Sickness and Healing.* New Haven, Conn.: Yale University Press.

Haliburton, Gordon. 1971. *The Prophet Harris.* London: Longman.

Hammoudi, Abdella. 2009. "Textualism and Anthropology: On the Ethnographic Encounter, or an Experience in the Hajj." In *Being There: The Fieldwork Encounter and the Making of Truth,* edited by John Boneman and Abdella Hammoudi, 25–54. Berkeley: University of California Press.

Handock, I. 1970. "Some Aspects of English in Liberia." *Liberian Studies Journal* 3 (2): 207–13.

Handwerker, W. Penn. 1973a. "Kinship, Friendship, and Business Failure among Market Sellers in Monrovia, Liberia, 1970." *Africa* 43 (4): 288–301.

———. 1973b. "Technology and Household Configuration in Urban Africa: The Bassa of Monrovia." *American Sociological Review* 38 (2): 182–97.

———. 1979. "Food Consumption Patterns in Monrovia, 1970." In *Essays on Economic Anthropology of Liberia and Sierra Leone*, edited by Vernon Dorjahn and B. Isaac, 197–223. Philadelphia: Institute of Liberian Studies.

Hardacre, Helen. 1986. *Kurozumikyo and the New Religions of Japan*. Princeton, N.J.: Princeton University Press.

Harley, George W. 1941. *Native African Medicine*. Cambridge, Mass.: Harvard University Press.

Harris, Hermoine. 2006. *Yoruba in Diaspora: An African Church in London*. New York: Palgrave Macmillian.

Hasselman, Karl-Heinz. 1979. *Liberia: Geographical Mosaic of the Land and People*. Monrovia, Liberia: Ministry of Information, Cultural Affairs and Tourism.

Hauerwas, Stanley. 2004. *Performing the Faith: Bonhoeffer and the Practice of Nonviolence*. Grand Rapids, Mich.: Brazos Press.

Hendrix, Thomas. 1994. "A Half Century of Americo-Liberian Christianity: With Special Focus on Methodism, 1822–1872." *Liberian Studies Journal* 19 (2): 243–74.

Hlophe, Stephen S. 1979. *Class, Ethnicity and Politics in Liberia*. Washington, D.C.: University Press of America.

Hoehler-Fatton, Cynthia. 1996. *Women of Fire and Spirit: History, Faith, and Gender in Roho Religion in Western Kenya*. New York: Oxford University Press.

———. 1998. "Founders and Foundresses: Revising the History of a Kenyan Independent Church." *Religion* 28 (4): 393–404.

Højbjerg, Christian K. 2004. "Universalistic Orientations of an Imagistic Mode of Religiosity: The Case of the West African Poro Cult." In *Ritual and Memory: Toward a Comparative Anthropology of Religion*, edited by Harvey Whitehouse and James Laidlaw, 173–85. Walnut Creek, Calif.: Altamira Press.

Horton, Robin. 1993. *Patterns of Thought in Africa and the West: Essays on Magic, Religion and Science*. Cambridge: Cambridge University Press.

Humphrey, Carolina, and James Laidlaw. 1994. *The Archetypal Actions of Ritual: A Theory of Ritual Illustrated by the Jain Rite of Worship*. Oxford: Clarendon Press.

Isichei, Elizabeth. 1995. *A History of Christianity in Africa: From Aniquity to Present*. Lawrenceville, N.J.: William B. Eerdmans.

Jackson, Michael. 1977. *Kuranko: Dimensions of Social Reality in a West African Society*. London: Hurst.

———. 1989. *Paths toward a Clearing: Radical Empiricism and Ethnographic Inquiry*. Bloomington: Indiana University Press.

Jedrej, M. C. 1974. "An Analytical Note on the Land and Spirits of the Sewa Mende." *Africa* 44 (1): 38–45.

———. 1976. "Aspects of a West African Secret Society." *Journal of Anthropological Research* 32 (3): 234–43.

Jedrej, M. C., and Rosalind Shaw, eds. 1992. *Dreaming, Religion and Society in Africa*. Leiden: E. J. Brill.

Jules-Rosette, Bennetta. 1981. "Faith Healers and Folk Healers: Symbols of Practice of Indigenous Therapy in Urban Africa." *Religion* 11 (1): 127–49.

Kaarsholm, P. 2006. "Violence as Signifier: Politics and Generational Struggle in KwaZulu Natal." In *Violence, Political Culture and Development in Africa*, edited by Preben Kaarsholm, 139–60. Oxford: James Curry.

Keane, Web. 2005. "Signs Are Not the Garb of Meaning: On the Social Analysis of Material Things." In *Materiality*, edited by Dennis Miller, 182–205. Durham, N.C.: Duke University Press.

———. 2006. "Anxious Transcendence." In *The Anthropology of Christianity*, edited by Fenella Cannell, 308–23. Durham, N.C.: Duke University Press.

———. 2007. *Christian Moderns: Freedom and Fetish in the Mission Encounter*. Berkeley: University of California Press.

Keeler, Ward. 1987. *Javanese Shadow Plays, Javanese Selves*. Princeton, N.J.: Princeton University Press.

Kiernan, James P. 1981. "World View in Perspective: Towards the Reclamation of a Disused Concept." *African Studies* 40 (1): 3–10.

———. 1990. *The Production and Management of Therapeutic Power: Zionist Churches within a Zulu City*. Lewiston, N.Y.: Edwin Mellen Press.

———. 1994. "Variations on a Christian Theme: The Healing Synthesis of Zulu Zionism." In *Syncretism/Anti-Syncretism: The Politics of Religious Synthesis*, edited by C. Steward and Rosalind Shaw, 68–84. London: Routledge.

Klass, Morton. 1995. *Ordered Universes: Approaches to the Anthropology of Religion*. Oxford: Westview Press.

Kleinman, Arthur. 1995. *Writing at the Margin: Discourse between Anthropology and Medicine*. Berkeley: University of California Press.

Korte, Werner. 1971. "A Note on Independent Churches in Liberia." *Liberian Studies Journal* 4 (1): 81–87.

Laidlaw, James. 2004. Introduction to *Ritual and Memory: Toward a Comparative Anthropology of Religion*, edited by Harvey Whitehouse and James Laidlaw, 1–9. Walnut Creek, Calif.: Altamira Press.

Latour, Bruno. 1993. *We Have Never Been Modern*. Translated by Catherine Porter. Cambridge, Mass.: Harvard University Press.

Leopold, R. S. 1983. "The Shaping of Men and the Making of Metaphors." *Anthropology* 7 (1): 21–41.

Lewis, I. M. 1986. *Religion in Context: Cults and Charisma*. Cambridge: Cambridge University Press.

Liebenow, J. Gus. 1987. *Liberia: The Quest for Democracy*. Bloomington: Indiana University Press.

Little, Kenneth. 1951. *The Mende of Sierra Leone*. London: Routledge and Kegan Paul.

MacCormack, Carol. 1980. "Proto-Social to Adult: A Sherbo Transformation." In *Nature, Culture, and Gender*, edited by Carol MacCormack and M. Strathern, 95–118. Cambridge: Cambridge University Press.

Masquelier, Adeline. 2001. *Prayer Has Spoiled Everything: Possession, Power, and Identity in an Islamic Town of Niger*. Durham, N.C.: Duke University Press.

Mattingly, Cheryl. 1998. *Healing Dramas and Clinical Plots: The Narrative Structure of Experience*. Cambridge: Cambridge University Press.

McGovern, Mike. 2005. "Rebuilding a Failed State: Liberia." *Development in Practice* 15 (6): 760–66.

McKenzie, Peter. 1997. *Hail Orisha!: A Phenomenology of a West African Religion in the Mid–Nineteenth Century.* Leiden: E. J. Brill.

Meyer, Birgit. 1992. "'If You Are a Devil, You Are a Witch and, If You Are a Witch, You Are a Devil': The Integration of 'Pagan' Ideas into the Conceptual Universe of the Ewe Christians in Southeastern Ghana." *Journal of Religion in Africa* 22 (2): 98–132.

———. 1998. "'Make a Complete Break with the Past.' Memory and Post-Colonial Modernity in Ghanaian Pentecostal Discourse." *Journal of Religion in Africa* 38 (3): 316–49.

———. 1999. "Commodities and the Power of Prayer: Pentecostalist Attitudes towards Consumption in Contemporary Ghana." In *Globalization and Identity: Dialectics of Flow and Closure,* edited by Birgit Meyer and Peter Geschiere, 151–76. Oxford: Blackwell.

———. 2003. "Ghanaian Popular Cinema and the Magic in and of Film." In *Magic and Modernity: Interfaces of Revelation and Concealment,* edited by Birgit Meyer and Peter Pels, 200–222. Stanford, Calif.: Stanford University Press.

———. 2004. "Christianity in Africa: From African Independent to Pentecostal-Charismatic Churches." *Annual Review of Anthropology* 33: 447–74.

Meyer, Birgit, and Peter Geschiere, eds. 1999. *Globalization and Identity: Dialectics of Flow and Closure.* Oxford: Blackwell.

Middleton, John, ed. 1967. *Myth and Cosmos.* Austin: University of Texas Press.

Middleton, John, and Edward Winter, eds. 1963. *Witchcraft and Sorcery in East Africa.* London: Routledge and Kegan Paul.

Milbank, John. 1990. *Social Theory and Theology.* Oxford: Blackwell.

———. 2004. Foreword to *Introducing Radical Orthodoxy: Mapping a Post-secular Theology,* by James K. A. Smith. Grand Rapids, Mich.: Baker.

Moore, Henrietta L., and Todd Sanders, eds. 2001. *Magical Interpretations, Material Realities: Modernity, Witchcraft and the Occult in Postcolonial Africa.* London: Routledge.

Moran, Mary H. 1990. *Civilized Women: Gender and Prestige in Southeastern Liberia.* Ithaca, N.Y.: Cornell University Press.

———. 2000. "Gender and Aging: Are Women "Warriors" among the Glebo of Liberia?" *Liberian Studies Journal* 25 (2): 25–41.

———. 2005. "Time and Place in the Anthropology of Events: A Diaspora Perspective on the Liberian Transition." *Anthropological Quarterly* 78 (2): 457–64.

———. 2006. *Liberia: The Violence of Democracy.* Philadelphia: University of Pennsylvania Press.

Muller, Carol Ann. 1999. *Rituals of Fertility and the Sacrifice of Desire: Nazarite Women's Performance in South Africa.* Chicago: University of Chicago Press.

Murphy, William. 1980. "Secret Knowledge as Property and Power in Kpelle Society: Elders versus Youth." *Africa* 50 (2): 193–207.

———. 1981. "The Rhetorical Management of Dangerous Knowledge in Kpelle Brokerage." *American Ethnologist* 8 (4): 667–85.

Nimely, Anthony. 1977. *The Liberian Bureacracy: An Analysis and Evaluation of the Environment, Structure and Function.* Washington, D.C.: University Press of America.

Nunley, John. 2008. "Jolly Masquerades and Mammy Wata in Sierra Leone." In *Mami*

Wata: Arts for Water Spirits in Africa and Its Diasporas, edited by Henry John Drewel, 73–79. Los Angeles: Fowler Museum of UCLA.

Nyamnjoh, Francis B. 2001. "Delusions of Development and the Enrichment of Witchcraft Discourses in Cameroons." In *Magical Interpretations, Magical Realities: Modernity, Witchcraft and the Occult in Postcolonial Africa,* edited by Henrietta Moore and Todd Sanders, 28–49. London: Routledge.

Ogungbile, David O. 1997. "Water Symbolism in African Culture and Afro-Christian Churches." *Journal of Religious Thought* 53/54 (2/1): 21–38.

Oladipo, Caleb Oluremi. 1996. *The Development of the Doctrine of the Holy Spirit in the Yoruba (African) Indigenous Christian Movement.* New York: Peter Lang.

Olajubu, Oyeronke. 2001. "The Influence of Yoruba Command Language on Prayer, Music, and Worship in African Christianity." *Journal of African Cultural Studies* 14 (2): 173–80.

Olupona, Jacob. 1987. "Celestial Aladura Christianity in the Yoruba Religious-Cultural Matrix." In *New Religious Movements in Nigeria,* edited by Rosalind Hackett, 77–93. Lewiston, N.Y.: Edwin Mellen Press.

Omoyajowo, Akinyele. 1982. *Cherubim and Seraphim: The History of an African Independent Church.* New York: Nok Publishers.

Oosthuizen, Gerhardus C. 1992. *The Healer-Prophet in Afro-Christian Churches.* Leiden: E. J. Brill.

Orr, Kenneth. 1968. "Field Notes on Tribal Medical Practices in Central Liberia." *Liberian Studies Journal* 1 (1): 20–41.

Orsi, Robert. 2005. *Between Heaven and Earth: The Religious Worlds People Make and the Scholars Who Study Them.* Princeton, N.J.: Princeton University Press.

Ortner, Sherry. 2006. *Anthropology and Social Theory: Culture, Power, and the Acting Subject.* Durham, N.C.: Duke University Press.

Parkin, David. 1992. "Ritual as Spatial Direction and Bodily Division." In *Understanding Rituals,* edited by Daniel de Coppet, 11–25. London: Routledge.

Peel, J. D. Y. 1968. *Aladura: A Religious Movement among the Yoruba.* London: Oxford University Press.

———. 2003. *Religious Encounter and the Making of the Yoruba.* Bloomington: Indiana University Press.

———. 2004. "Divergent Modes of Religiosity in West Africa." In *Ritual and Memory toward a Comparative Anthropology of Religion,* edited by Harvey Whitehouse and James Laidlaw, 11–30. Walnut Creek, Calif.: Altamira Press.

Pham, John Peter. 2004. *Liberia: Portrait of a Failed State.* New York: Reed Press.

Piot, Charles. 1999. *Remotely Global: Village Modernity in West Africa.* Chicago: University of Chicago Press.

Probst, Peter. 1989. "The Letter and the Spirit: Literacy and Religious Authority in the History of the Aladura Movement in Western Nigeria." *Africa* 59 (4): 478–95.

Ramsey, F. J. 2001. *Africa.* Guilford, Conn.: McGraw-Hill/Dushkin.

Ray, Benjamin. 1976. (1999). *African Religions.* Engelwood Cliffs, N.J.: Prentice-Hall.

———. 1993. "Aladura Christianity: A Yoruba Religion." *Journal of Religion in Africa* 23 (3): 266–91.

Resnik, Saloman. 1987. *The Theatre of the Dream.* Translated by Alan Sheridan. London: Tavistok.

Richards, Paul. 2001. "'Witches,' 'Cannibals' and War in Liberia." *Journal of African History* 42 (1): 167–69.

———. 2006a. "An Accidental Sect: How War Made Belief in Sierra Leone." *Review of African Political Economy* 33 (110): 651–63.

———. 2006b. "Forced Labor and Civil War: Agrarian Underpinnings of the Sierra Leone Conflict." In *Violence, Political Culture and Development in Africa*, edited by Preben Kaarsholm, 181–98. Oxford: James Curry.

Robbins, Joel. 2004. *Becoming Sinners: Christianity and Moral Torment in a Papua New Guinea Society*. Berkeley: University of California Press.

———. 2006. "Anthropology and Theology: An Awkward Relationship." *Anthropological Quarterly* 79 (2): 285–94.

———. 2007. "Continuity Thinking and the Problem of Christian Culture: Belief, Time, and the Anthropology of Christianity." *Current Anthropology* 48 (1): 5–38.

Salmons, Jill. 1977. "Mammy Wata." *African Arts* 10 (3): 8–15, 87–88.

Sanders, Todd. 2003. "Invisible Hands and Visible Goods: Revealed and Concealed Economies in Millennial Tanzania." In *Transparency and Conspiracy: Ethnographies of Suspicion in the New World Order*, edited by Harry G. West and Todd Sanders, 148–74. Durham, N.C.: Duke University Press.

Sanders, Todd, and Harry G. West. 2003. "Power Revealed and Concealed in the New World Order." In *Transparency and Conspiracy: Ethnographies of Suspicion in the New World Order*, edited by Harry G. West and Todd Sanders, 1–37. Durham, N.C.: Duke University Press.

Sanford, Mei-Mei. 2001. "Living Water: Osun, Mami Wata, and Olokun in the Lives of Four Contemporary Nigerian Christian Women." In *Osun across the Waters: A Yoruba Goddess in Africa and the Americas*, edited by Joseph M. Murphy and Mei-Mei Sanford, 237–50. Bloomington: Indiana University Press.

Sanneh, Lamin. 1983. *West African Christianity: The Religious Impact*. London: Hurst.

———. 1994. "Translatability in Islam and in Christianity in Africa: A Thematic Approach." In *Religion in Africa: Experience and Expression*, edited by Thomas D. Blakely, Walter E. A. Van Beek, and Dennis L. Thomson, 237–50. London: James Curry.

Scheffers, Mark. 1987. "Schism in the Bassa Independent Churches." In *Ministry of Missions to African Independent Churches*, edited by D. A. Shank, 62–95. Elkart, Ind.: Mennonite Board of Missions.

Schimmel, Annemarie. 1993. *The Mystery of Numbers*. New York: Oxford University Press.

Schmoll, Pamela G. 1993. "Black Stomachs, Beautiful Stones: Soul-Eating among Hausa in Niger." In *Modernity and Its Malcontents: Ritual and Power in Postcolonial Africa*, edited by Jean Comaroff and John Comaroff, 193–220. Chicago: University of Chicago Press.

Schoffeleers, Matthew. 1994. "Christ in African Folk Theology." In *Religion in Africa: Experience and Expression*, edited by Thomas A. Blakely, Walter E. A. Van Beek, and Dennis L. Thomson, 72–88. London: James Curry.

Schwab, G. 1947. *Tribes of the Liberian Hinterland*. Cambridge, Mass.: Peabody Museum.

Shank, David A. 1997. "The Taming of Prophet Harris." *Journal of Religion in Africa* 27 (1): 59–95.

Shaw, Rosalind. 1985. "Gender in the Structuring of Reality in Temne Divination: An Interactive Study." *Africa* 55 (3): 286–303.

———. 1992. "Dreaming as Accomplishment: Power, the Individual and Temne Divination." In *Dreaming, Religion and Society in African*, edited by M. C. Jedrej and Rosalind Shaw, 36–51. Leiden: E. J. Brill.

———. 2001. "Cannibal Transformations: Colonialism and Commodification in Sierra Leone." In *Magical Interpretations, Material Realities: Modernity, Witchcraft and the Occult in Postcolonial Africa*, edited by Henrietta Moore and Todd Sanders, 50–70. London: Routledge.

———. 2002. *Memories of the Slave Trade: Ritual and Historical Imagination in Sierra Leone.* Chicago: University of Chicago Press.

———. 2003. "Robert Kaplan and 'Juju Journalism' in Sierra Leone's Rebel War: The Primitivizing of an African Conflict." In *Magic and Modernity: Interfaces of Revelation and Concealment*, edited by Birgit Meyer and Peter Pels, 81–102. Stanford, Calif.: Stanford University Press.

Simpson, George E. 1980. *Yoruba Religion and Medicine in Ibadan.* Ibadan, Nigeria: Ibadan University Press.

Singler, John. 1990. "Linguistics and Liberian Languages in the 1970s and 1980s: A Bibliography." *Liberian Studies Journal* 15 (1):108–26.

Smith, James K. A. 2004. *Introducing Radical Orthodoxy: Mapping a Post-secular Theology.* Grand Rapids, Mich.: Baker.

Smith, Jonathan Z. 1987. *To Take Place: Toward Theory in Ritual.* Chicago: University of Chicago Press.

Stakeman, Rudolph. 1986. *The Cultural Politics of Religious Change: A Study of the Sanoyea Kpelle in Liberia.* Lewiston, N.Y.: Edwin Mellon Press.

Stone, Ruth M. 1982. *Let the Inside Be Sweet: The Interpretation of Music Event among the Kpelle of Liberia.* Bloomington: Indiana University Press.

———. 1994. "Bringing the Extraordinary into the Ordinary: Music Performance among the Kpelle of Liberia." In *Religion in Africa: Experience and Expression*, edited by Thomas. D. Blakely, Walter E. A. Van Beek, and Dennis L. Thomson, 297–388. London: James Curry.

Strathern, Andrew. 1996. *Body Thoughts.* Ann Arbor: University of Michigan Press.

Tahmen, George W. 1974. "Death ('ga') in Dan Culture: Concepts, Ceremonies and Folklore Concerning Death in North East Liberia." *Ethnologische Zeitschrift* 2: 159–83.

Tambiah, Stanley. 1986. *Culture, Thought, and Social Action: An Anthropological Perspective.* Cambridge, Mass.: Harvard University Press.

Ter Haar, Gerrie, ed. 2007. *Imagining Evil: Witchcraft Beliefs and Accusations in Contemporary Africa.* Trenton, N.J.: Africa World Press.

Thomas, Linda E. 1999. *Under the Canopy: Ritual Process and Spiritual Resilience in South Africa.* Columbia: University of South Carolina Press.

Tonkin, Elizabeth. 1980. "Jealousy Names, Civilized Names: Anthropology of the Jlao Kru of Liberia." *Man* 15 (4): 653–64.

———. 1981. "Model and Ideology: Dimensions of Being Civilized in Liberia." In *The Structure of the Folk Model*, edited by Lasilaw Holy and M. Stuchlik, 305–30. London: Academic Press.

Turner, Harold. 1967. *History of an African Independent Church*. 2 vols. Oxford: Oxford University Press.

Turner, Victor. 1985. *On the Edge of the Bush: Anthropology of Experience*. Tucson: University of Arizona Press.

Twe, Boikai S. 1994. "A Perspective on Psychological Disorders of Liberia." *Liberian Studies Journal* 19 (1): 41–48.

Tweed, Thomas. 2006. *Crossing and Dwelling: A Theory of Religion*. Cambridge, Mass.: Harvard University Press.

Utas, Mats. 2006." Media and Localized Ideoscapes of the Liberian Civil War." In *Violence, Political Culture and Development in Africa*, edited by Preben Kaarsholm, 161–80. Oxford: James Curry.

Van Binsbergen, Wim. 2001. "Witchcraft in Modern Africa as Virtualized Boundary Conditions of the Kinship Order." In *Witchcraft Dialogues: Anthropological and Philosophical Exchanges*, edited by George C. Bond and Diane M. Ciekawy, 221–63. Research in International Studies, Africa Series, no. 76. Athens: Ohio University Press.

Vanden Berg, Todd M. 2005. "Culture, Christianity, and Witchcraft in a West African Context." In *The Change Face of Christianty*, edited by Lamin Sanneh and J. Carpenter, 45–62. Oxford: Oxford University Press.

Van Dijk, Rijk. 1997. "From Camp to Encompassment: Disourses of Transsubjectivity in Ghanain Pentecostal Diaspora." *Journal of Religion in Africa* 27 (2): 135–59.

———. 2001. "Witchcraft and Skepticism by Proxy: Pentecostalism and Laughter in Urban Malawi." In *Magical Interpretations, Material Realities: Modernity, Witchcraft and the Occult in Postcolonial Africa*, edited by Henrietta L. Moore and Todd Sanders, 97–117. London: Routledge.

———. 2004. "Beyond the Rivers of Ethiopia": Pentecostal Pan-Africanism and Ghanaian Identities in the Transnational Domain." In *Situating Globality: African Agency in the Appropriation of Global Culture*, edited by Wim van Binsbergen and Rijk van Dijk, 163–89. Leiden: E. J. Brill.

Walker, Sheila. 1980. "Young Men, Old Men, and Devils in Aeroplanes: The Harrist Church, the Witchcraft Complex and Social Change in Ivory Coast." *Journal of Religion in Africa* 11 (2): 107–23.

———. 1983. *The Religious Revolution in Ivory Coast: The Prophet Harris and the Harrist Church*. Chapel Hill: University of North Carolina Press.

Welmers, William E. 1949. "Secret Medicines, Magic, and Rites of the Kpelle Tribe in Liberia." *Southwestern Journal of Anthropology* 5 (3): 208–43.

Werbner, Richard P. 1989. *Ritual Passage, Sacred Journey: The Process and Organization of Religious Movement*. Washington, D.C.: Smithsonian Press.

West, Gerald O., and Musa W. Dube, eds. 2000. *The Bible in Africa: Transactions, Trajectories and Trends*. Leiden: Brill Academic Publishers.

West, Harry G., and Todd Sanders, eds. 2003. *Transparency and Conspiracy: Ethnographies of Suspicion in the New World Order*. Durham, N.C.: Duke University Press.

Whitehouse, Harvey. 2000. *Arguments and Icons: Divergent Modes of Religiosity*. Oxford: Oxford University Press.

Williams, Levi C., III. 1994. "Responses to Zangai." *Liberian Studies Journal* 9 (1): 72–76.

Winder, R. Bayly. 1962. "The Lebanese of West Africa." *Comparative Studies in Society and History* 4 (3): 296–333.

Wintrob, Ronald. 1968. "Sexual Guilt and Culturally Sanctioned Delusion in Liberia, West Africa." *American Journal of Psychiatry* 125 (1): 89–95.

———. 1970. "Mammy Water: Folk Beliefs and Psychotic Elaborations in Liberia." *Canadian Psychiatric Association Journal* 15 (2): 143–58.

Zangai, Levi. 1994. "The Socio-Political Role of the Church in the Post-Doe Liberia." *Liberian Studies Journal* 19 (1): 65–71.

ALADURA AND OTHER AFRICAN INITIATED CHURCH TEXTS

The following section includes pamphlets and tracts I found distributed among AIC in Liberia and Sierra Leone. Many were Church of the Lord Aladura texts that circulated among other Aladura churches, including St. Peter's. Most texts did not include full bibliographic information.

Adejobi, E. O. A. 1965. *Armies of Jesus. A Lecture Delivered at the 3rd Annual Anniversary Celebration Week of the Armies of Jesus.* Lagos, Nigeria.

———. 1965. *Selected Hymns for "Bringing Christ To the Nation."* Church of the Lord Aladura.

———. 1967. *The Form of Annual Appointment and Blessing and Holy Dedication of the Church Constituted Officers.* Church of the Lord Aladura. Ijebu-Remo, Nigeria: Ogere Headquarters.

———. 1970. *A Doctrinal and Administrative Charge.* Delivered at the 5th General Churches Assembly, Kumusi, Ghana.

———. 1974. *Facts about Faith, Psychic and Spiritual Healing. An Address Delivered to the Theological College at the Emmanuel College, Ibadan, in Commemoration of the 7th Year Anniversary as Primate of the Church of the Lord Aladura, 7th May 1967 to 7th May 1974.*

———. 1974. *How to Become a Member of the Church of the Lord Aladura.* In Commemoration of the 7th Year Anniversary as Primate, 7 May 1974.

———. 1974. *Three Historic Addresses.* In Commemoration of the 7th Anniversary as Primate, 7th May 1974.

———. 1977. *The Church of the Lord (Aladura): Prelates, Clergy, Male and Female Ministers.*

———. 1983. *Divine Revelations from the Holy Mount Tabborrar for the Year 1983. In Memory of the Respected Late Dr. J. O. Oshitelu.* At the Spiritual Headquarters of the Church of the Lord (Aladura), Nigeria and Overseas.

———. n.d. *Agbole-Lgbagbo.* Lagos, Nigeria: Church of the Lord Aladura.

———. n.d. *The Divine Order of Worship, Services and Ceremonies of the Church of the Lord.*

———. n.d. *An Exposition of the Faith Home: Its Rules, Regulations, and Special Faith Home Prayers of the Church of the Lord Aladura.* Oshogbo, Nigeria: Funde and Sons Press.

———. n.d. *The Observations and Practices of the Church of the Lord Aladura in the Light of the Old Testament and the New Testament.* Ibadan, Nigeria: People's Star Press.

———. 1983. *A Short Devotional Speech.* To the 5th General Assembly of the Church of the Lord Aladura. Freetown, Sierra Leone.

———. 1983. *Speech from the Throne.* An Address Delivered at the 6th General Churches Assembly of the Church of the Lord Aladura. Freetown, Sierra Leone.

Atsansuyi, H. Olu. 1978. *The Church of the Lord at a Glance and the Role of Prophets.* Lagos, Nigeria: Aladura Theological Seminary, Bestrade Nigeria.

The Bible Doctrine of the Church of Salvation. 1973.

A Brief Resume of the Life Course of Dr. J. O. Oshitelu, Psy. n.d. Ijebu-Remo, Nigeria: Ogere Headquarters.

Bundu, Alpha Omega. 1984. *My Biography.*

The Churchman's Calender. 1984. The Church of the Lord Aladura.

The Church of the Lord Aladura (Cathedral). The History of the Church of the Lord Aladura. n.d. Monrovia, Liberia: Headquarters.

The Church of the Lord Hymn Book. n.d. Lagos, Nigeria: Grace, Enterprises.

The Church of Salvation Handook. 1983. Sierra Leone Conference.

A Consise Review on the Episcopal Tour of Dr. J. O. Oshitelu unto the Branches of the Church of the Lord, Ghana. 1959. Ode Remo, Nigeria: Degosen Printing Works.

Constitution and By Laws of St. Peter's Church of the Lord. n.d. Paynesville City, Liberia.

The Constitution and By-Laws of the Universal Faith Healing Church. 1984. Paynesville City, Liberia.

Evande, Peter. 1984. *A Biography of Reverend Senior Apostle Olu.*

Fofana, E. J. n.d. *Training Pamphlet for Ministers and Members.* Bo, Sierra Leone: Church of Salvation.

The Ministerial Policy and Conditions of Service Passed. 1982. Bo, Sierra Leone: Church of Salvation.

Oduwole, Samuel O. n.d. *The Cross Bearer and Rules of the Cross.* Monrovia, Liberia: Headquarters.

The Ordering of Cross Bearers and Rules Governing the Cross. 1980. Church of Salvation, Sierra Leone Conference.

Oshitelu, J. O. 1971. *Catechism of the Church of the Lord Aladura throughout the World and Holy Litany with the Church Prayer Drill.* Ogere, Nigeria: Headquarters.

———. n.d. *The Book of Prayer with Uses and Power of Psalms and Previous Treasures Hidden Therein.* Ogere, Nigeria: Headquarters.

St. Peter's United Church of the Lord Booklet of Hymns. n.d. Hyattsville, Maryland.

A Short Historical Sketch of the Church of Salvation. Compiled by the Church Administration. n.d. Bo, Sierra Leone.

Souvenir of the Church of the Lord Aladura. 1967. Freetown, Sierra Leone.

Abimbola, D. Olu, 215n17
achan, 7
Adejobi, E.O.A., 150–51, 154–55, 165,
    210n3
Adogame, Afe, 4, 49, 56, 77, 110, 139, 147,
    148, 188–89, 207nn1, 4, 208nn2, 5
African Glory Pentecostal, 19, 143
African Initiated Churches (AIC):
    authenticity and identity, 29;
    compared with mainline churches,
    209n10; defined, ix, 207n1; network-
    ing with Pentecostals, 28–29, 44–45,
    202; in Paynesville, 26, 28–29; univer-
    sal mission of, 29. *See also* Aladura;
    Church of the Lord Aladura; United
    Church of Salvation; St. Peter's
African Methodist Episcopal, 19
African science/African signs: contrasted
    with heartmen cult, 218n4; and coun-
    try doctor, 121–22; in food, 90; and
    halei, 74; and jina liaisons, 75; as magic,
    74; meaning of, 73–76; migration of, 45;
    and occult power, 2; placing signs, 63,
    70; related to *Sixth and Seventh Books of
    Moses*, 134; and subversive images of
    the prophet, 75; and temptation, 107;
    and virtue, 75; and witchcraft, 73; and
    zo, 121–22. *See also* occult power;
    witchcraft
age: in AIC, 53–54; and gender, 50–54;
    90, 97, 155; in Liberian culture, 53; and
    occult power, 53; and seniority, 52–53,
    176, 207, 213
agency, 4, 11–12, 204
AIC. *See* African Initiated Churches
Aina, J. Ade, 215n15
ajogun, 109–10, 149
Aladura: argument of images, 40, 48;
    authority, 52–53; beginnings, 19–23;
    beginnings in Liberia, 20–21; definition

of, 3, 19; churches, 4–6; cosmology,
    6–7; as culture, 9–10; on jina liaisons,
    40; Liberianization, xii, 22–23, 50;
    mission or mainline churches, 52; as
    mother church, 22, 171; and Pente-
    costal-Charismatic churches, 29; as
    problem-solving, 48; social and politi-
    cal critique, 12–13; studies about 4–5,
    208n5; and the syncretist model,
    209n8. *See also* Church of the Lord
    Aladura; St. Peter's; United Church
    of the Lord
alligator peppers, 67
altar, 54, 94, 177, 179, 186, 198
American evangelists, 18
Americo-Liberians (settlers), 20, 50–55
ancestors, 56, 60, 111, 124, 128, 140,
    208n2
angels, 61, 106, 146, 149–50, 210n1,
    219n2, 220n3
animal sacrifice, 76, 104, 121, 147–48,
    212n11, 217n5
anthropology, 7–11
anxious transcendence, 9–10, 202
Appardurai, Arun, 207n2
Assemblies of God, 18, 172, 180
Asamoah-Gyadu, O. Kwabena, 78
asceticism, 6, 209n6
ase, 60
Ashforth, Adam, 111, 135–36
Auge, Marc, 112
authority and hierarchy, 52–54, 83,
    85–87, 94, 99, 155–57, 205
aye lajo, 6, 56

Babalola, Joseph, 69
Baeta, Christian, 78
Baha'i, 17
Bahre, Erik, 110, 135
Bakker, Jim, 18

Baptists, 16, 26, 112

Bassa, 17–18, 19, 25, 34, 82, 88–89, 114–15, 116, 122, 143,144

Bassa Community Church, 18

Bassa Independent churches, 16, 19, 88–89, 122, 210n2

battery metaphor, 168

beach struggles, 76–77, 161–64, 191. *See also* ritual struggle

Bell, Catherine, 38, 41, 77, 205

Bellman, Beryl, 51, 115, 124, 165, 196, 217n1

blanket incense treatment, 125–27

Blatch, Sister, 19

Bledsoe, Caroline, 76, 216n20

blue incense, 43, 66, 70

bodily praxis and embodiment: and beach struggle, 164; the cultural self, 204, 216n2; and Faith Home schedule, 139, 220n7; and knowledge of the body, 216n3; meaning of, 55, 204–5; related to movement and spatiality, 205; and place, 205; and rite of passage, 206; and self-denial, 6; struggle as, 76–77. *See also* ritual struggle

Bond, George Clement, 56, 217n2

Bongmba, Elias, 112

Book of Prayer with Uses and Power of Psalms and Previous Treasures Hidden Therein, The, 63, 133

Born Agains, 44, 212n14

bottles and boxes, 74, 119–22, 216n19. *See also* occult power

Bourdieu, Pierre, 157, 196, 216n23, 220n7

breakaway churches, 30, 168

Brown, Delwin, 8

Browne, 43

Buckley, Thomas, 154, 220n5

Bundu, Alpha Omega, 30, 34, 35

bush camps, 195–96

bush struggles, 31–32, 83, 147

calling, 40, 81–84

candles, 41–42, 65–66, 116, 118, 158–61, 176

Cannell, Fenella, 8

car consecrations, 218n6

Carter, Jeanette, 25

Catherine Mills Rehabilitation Center, 25, 131

Celestial Church of Christ, 3, 4, 139–40, 147, 208n5, 219n2, 220n3

Cherubim and Seraphim (C&S), 3, 4, 31, 32, 44, 60, 133, 208n3, 208n5, 212n14

Charsley, Simon R., 100

Christ Apostle Church, 29

Christ Apostolic Church, 3, 4, 208n5

Christian Community Churches of Christ, 36–37, 46; 212n12

Church of Salvation (CS), 34–35, 211n10. *See also* United Church of Salvation

Church of the Lord Aladura (CLA): and Adejobi, E.O.A.,150–51, 154–55, 165, 210n3; Beginnings, 20–21; branches and members in Liberia, 211n6; Center Street headquarters, 219n1; in Liberia, 20–23; Liberianization, 22–23, 50; Mercy Ground, 147; as mother church, 22, 71; and Oduwole, Samuel, 5–6, 20–23, 50, 61, 93, 94, 170; and Oshitelu, Josiah, 18, 19, 32, 63, 133–34, 147, 169, 170, 208n3, 210n3, 221n2; Paynesville branches, 27–28; and Samuel Olu's background in, 4, 31–34; succession, 210n3; Tabborrar, Mount, 169–70. *See also* Aladura; and Samuel Oduwole

Church of the Twelve Apostles, 18

circle symbolism, 159, 160; 164

civil war, 12–13, 37, 203

civilized/uncivilized model, 213n3; Aladura critique of, 20; and Christianity as mark of, 17; and clothing, 51–52, 152–53; meaning of kwi culture, 20, 51, 210n4; and prestige values, 17, 50–51, 53

CLA. *See* Church of the Lord Aladura

cleansing ceremony, 69, 85

clothing, 45, 51–52, 104, 152–53

colonial context, 138, 207n2

color symbolism, 69, 114, 158, 160

Coleman, Simon, 63, 209n9

Comaroff, Jean, 41, 111

Comaroff, John, 41, 207–8n6

Congo Town, 17

Congo, 25, 26, 34–35, 144

Constitution and By Laws of St. Peter's Church of the Lord, 81

Conteh, Al-Hassan, 218n3

cosmology: Aladura, 47–49; and culture, 48; definition of, 47; 212–13n1; the dream soul's navigation of, 56–58; emergent character of, 48; and Faith Home's ritual space, 141–50; and performative acts, 6–7; and ritual, 3, 6–7; "this side" and "that side" structure, 56; as worldview, 213n1

country doctor, 40, 57–58, 74, 121–22. *See also* zo

country spurs, 67

Countryman, L. William, 6

coup, military, 11, 33, 37, 51

Crapanzano, Vincent, 125, 218n7

creek consecration, 221n7

crosses, 92–94

cross bearer, 54

Cross Bearer and Rules of the Cross, The, 93–94

crossroads (juncture), xii, 23, 72–73, 141

Crumbley, Deidra Helen, 5, 44, 63, 197, 208n5, 211n8, 220n5

C&S. *See* Cherubim and Seraphim Church

Csordas, Thomas J, 63, 77, 203, 209n8

culture/nature paradigm, 89–90, 217n4

Curley, Richard T, 100

cyclops jina, 127–28

dance, 162, 164

Daniel, E. Valentine, 213n2

Davies, Owen, 132

D'Azevedo, Warren, 54, 57, 124, 165, 213n5

de Rosny, Eric, 217n3

death and funerary practice, 154, 220n6

Dey, 211n6

Dennis, Ruth E., 68

Devil's incense, 66–69, 116, 125–27. *See also* blanket incense treatment

diaspora church: 41–46; in Hyattsville, Maryland, 43–46; and Pentecostal Charismatic churches, 44–45;

Tabborrar, 198–201; and videos, 43, 45; in Washington D.C, 41–46

divine messages, 98–106. *See also* dreams and visions

divine revelations, 221n1

doctrinal and imagist modes of religiosity, 196, 222n5

Doe, Samuel K., 11–12, 18, 40–41

Dorjahn, Vernon, 124

doubling, 57

Douglas, Mary, 220n5

Dragon, 1, 3, 74, 87, 109, 116–18, 120

dream soul (or self), 56–58. *See also* dreams and visions

dreams and visions: auspicious and inauspicious images in, 103–6; as communicative meaning, 100; crosses, 92–94; definition of dreams and visions, 98–99, 102; as divine messages, 98–106; interpretation of, 99–102; Oduwole's interpretions, 92–94; in private and public worlds, 106–8; rods, 57, 191; as theater, 101; as virtue, 107; and witchcraft, 95–96

Drewel, Henry John, 60, 73, 130

Drewel, Margaret Thompson, 60, 73

Driver, Thomas T, 7

Druize, 16

drums, 64, 145, 199

Dwarf, 127–29

dweller, 144, 150–57, 181. *See also* Faith Home

eating, idioms of, 58; 113–14

ECOMOG (Economic Community of West African States Cease-fire Monitoring Group), 37

Eisenbaum, Pamela, 6

ELWA (Eternal Love Working in Africa), 23, 25. *See also* Sudan Interior Mission

electricity metaphor, 214n12

Eliade, Mircea, 212n1

Ellis, Stephen, 73, 114, 203, 218n4

Engelke, Matthew, 8, 66

Episcopal, 26

Erchak, Gerald, 115, 123

ethnic groups,17–18, 51–53

Exposition of the Faith Home: Its Rules, Regulations and Special Faith Home Prayers of the Church of the Lord Aladura, An, 150–51, 155–56

Faith Healing Church of God, 28
Faith Home: in Aladura, 138–65; as abode of angels, 149–50; and Bassa household conigurations, 143; behind the tent, 146–47; bundling images, 138; chapel, 145–47; as consuming unit, 157; and death, 153; dweller, 144, 150–57; dwelling, 138; ethnic backgrounds, 144; and faith, 140; as family, 139–41; 144–45; as focused space, 166–67; food and cooking, 155, 157; as grounded image, 138, 205; habitus, 157; holy bell, 147–48; as Household of God, 140–41; and ile, 140; lived space, 143–45; menstrual rules, 146–47; minister-patient relationship, 144; Mercy Ground, 147; prayer room, 148; prayers schedule, 156; in reconstituting selves, 139, 167; as refuge, 165; ritual struggle, 150; ritual tension, 166–67; rules and regulations, 150–57; St. Peter's, 141–43; and semiotic ideology, 138; seniority rules, 155–56; spiritual bathrooms, 149; during Tabborrar, 180–83; and town (village) and forest (bush) dialectic, 165–66; and Yoruba background, 139–40
fasting: and cooking, 89–90; and culture/nature paradigm, 89–90; and gender, 90–91; in relation to renunciation, 6; restrictions on women, 91; as ritual struggle, 88–94; during Tabborrar, 177, 179, 184; typology of, 88; and witchcraft, 90–91
Fatal Attraction (movie)
Fernandez, James, 138, 164, 205
field of prophecy, 38–40
Fields, Margaret, 133
fieldwork approach, xiv–xvii, 8
Fisiy, Cyprian, 110
Flomo, James (pseudonym), 1, 81–82, 94, 98, 113, 118, 123, 173–75, 176, 178, 180–83, 185, 188, 189, 218n4

Florida water, 43 66, 68, 121, 126, 158, 176
flow and prophetic healing, 23, 29, 37–41
Fofana, E.J., 211–12n10, 221n1. *See also* United Church of Salvation
follower, xiv, 83
food, 88–89, 155, 177
Foucault, Michel, 203
founder model, 4, 39–40, 196
Fox-Genovese, Elizabeth, 140–41
Fraenkel, Merran, 18, 19
Frei, Hans, 8, 227
Fyneah, David, 21–23, 35–36, 211n5

gatekeeper, 178, 186
Gbarnga School of Theology, 209n11
Ghanaians, 20, 44
Ghanaian Pentecostals, 15, 44
Geertz, Clifford, 8
gender and women, 25, 53–54, 90, 97, 155, 197
Geschiere, Peter, 59, 109, 110, 111, 204, 217n3, 218
Gifford, Paul, 6, 15, 16, 26, 29, 209nn6, 11, 211n6, 212n14, 221
Gittins, Anthony J, 71, 74, 114, 123, 214n10, 216n19, 219nn8, 9
Glebo, 53
glossolalia, 63, 215n15
Gola, 17, 25, 28, 54, 114, 124, 213nn4, 5
Gottlieb, Alma, 154
Grebo, 18, 22, 25, 50

habitus, 27, 220n7
Hackett, Rosalind, 5, 208n5
Hahn, Robert, 55
halei, 74, 214n10, 216n19
Haliburton, Gordon, 210n1, 227
Hamadsha fraternities, 218n7
Hammoudi, Abdella, 2
Handwerker, W. Penn., 26, 143, 157
Hardacre, Helen, 212–13n1
Harley, George Way, 74
Harris, Hermoine, 5, 44, 60, 133, 208nn3, 5, 214n12, 219n10
Harris, William Wade, 18, 210n1
Harrison, Ira E., 68
Hauerwas, Stanley, 8

head of the mount, 176, 168–69, 176–80, 184, 188, 194. *See also* Olu, Samuel; Mount Tabborrar
healing: and affliction as calling, 81–84; and Faith Home procedure, 150–52; and flow between churches, 33–41; and the healer/patient relation, 38–39; as initiation, 38, 55; and Mount Tabborrar, 169, 180–81, 184; revealing a body of conceptions, 48. *See also* ritual struggle
heartmen, 218n1
Hebrew names, 212n13
Hendrix, Thomas, 15
hierarchy and authority, 52–54; 176–80
Hindus, 17–18, 132
Hoehler-Fatton, Cynthia, 211n7
Hojbjerg, Christian K, 213n4
holy baths, 157–61
holy bell, 85
Holy Ghost Mount Zion, 19
Holy Ghost Movement, 19
holy materials, 62–71, 158–61, 176
holy names, 62–64; 186; 214–15n13
holy registration, 151
holy rod, 65–66, 91–92
Holy Spirit: afflictions, 34; in Aladura, 208n3; controlling shouts, 164, 182; creating rules for the Faith Home, 152; dreams and visions, 107; and falling in spirit, 91, 99, 162, 175; and jina, 75; as power, 61; revelations, 3; and ritual space, 146; and special requests during Tabborrar, 169; and spirit, 214n11; and witches, 96; and virtue, 60–61. *See also* virtue
holy water, 41–42, 69, 104, 157–61. *See also* holy baths
Horton, Robin, 135
house consecrations, 41–42, 120–21
household configurations, 26, 140–41
Household of God, 140–41, 204

Ida Isegan, 69–70
incense, 65–69, 125–27
Indira Gandhi, 17
intellectualist model of explanation, 208n3

Isaiah, Charles (pseudonym), 173–75; 180–84
Isichei, Elizabeth, 134
Israel Christian Church, 29

Jackson, Annie (pseudonym), 1–2, 135, 181
Jackson, Michael, 48, 216n23
January, Sister Leila, 19
Jedrej, M. C, 100
Jina, 123–32; and Arabic jinn, 124; bush spirits, 124; and cold jina treatment, 125–27; cyclops, 128; defined, 124–25; in dreams, 129–30; Dwarf, 128–29; as "hot" and "cold," 125; and light sources, 218n8; and Mami Wata, 130–32; and Mende nonancestral spirits, 218n9; Nightman/Nightwoman, 129–30; as strangers, 127–28; in urban settings, 75; and wulu wu, 124. *See also* witchcraft
Jonah the patient, 125–27
Jules-Rosette, Bennetta, 135
Jung, Carl, 12

Kaarsholm, P, 207n2
Kabre, 49
Keane, Web, 8, 9–10, 64, 138, 202
Keeler, Ward, 6, 209n7
Kiernan, James P, 56, 64, 79–80, 81, 100, 107, 213n1, 217n2
King Gray, 23
kinship, 139–40
Kissi, 17, 20, 22, 25, 50, 144
Klass, Morton, 213n6, 214n7
Kleinman, Arthur, 13
knowledge of the body, 216n23
Korte, Werner, 18
Kpelle, 17, 22, 25, 28, 32, 34, 50, 57, 68, 74, 81, 88, 89, 115, 116, 122–23, 124, 143, 144, 217n, 221n9
Kpelle Town, 34
Krahn, 17, 22
Kru, 18, 22, 25, 34, 114, 144
Kuranko, 48
kwi, 21, 51–52, 210n4. *See also* civilized/uncivilized model

lappa cloth, 153, 220n4

Latour, Bruno, 9
Lebanese, 16, 25, 66, 105, 141
Leopold, R. S, 90
Levinas, Emanuel, 112
Lewis, I. M., 113
Liberia Baptist Theological Seminary, 12, 26, 114, 209n11
Liebenow, J. Gus, 17, 51
Lighthouse Full Gospel, 18–19
Little Meggido, 19, 29
Little, Kenneth, 115
Logan Town Church, 21, 36–37
Loma, 17, 25
Lutherans, 17

MacCormack, Carol, 217n4
magic, 215n14
making market, 25–26, 72–73
Mama Wata, 45, 130–32, 218n10, 219n9
Mano, 25, 28, 34, 114, 144
Marionite Christians, 16
marketplace, 72
Masowe Christians, 66
Masquelier, Adeline, 150
materiality, 9–10, 202
Mattingly, Cheryl, 49, 81, 97–98
Mausian model of the individual, 49
Mayson, Moses, 27, 89, 211nn5, 6
Mende, 25, 28, 71, 115, 123
menstruation, 54, 91, 148, 154, 197, 220n5
Mercy Ground, 1–2, 70, 76, 92, 142, 147–48, 151, 158, 181, 219n2
metaphysics of disorder, xiv, 207–8n6
Methodists, 17, 26
Meyer, Birgit, 15, 45, 46, 108, 217n2
Middleton, John, 212n1
midnight struggles, 80, 139, 145, 156, 180, 182–83, 199–200
mid-runner, 176–80. See also Flomo, James
Milbank, John, 7, 10
Modee, David (pseudonym), 28, 82–83, 92, 100, 113, 114, 178, 184, 186, 191
Modee, Willis, 28
Monrovia Bible Training Center, 37
Moore, Henrietta L. 110. 111, 136
Moran, Mary H, 44, 51, 53, 74, 109, 207nn3, 5, 210n12, 213n3, 220nn4, 6

Morgan, Felicia (pseudonym), 94–98. See also Saydee, Edward
mount secretary, 177–78
Muller, Carol Ann, 52
Murphy, William, 57, 107
Muslims, 16, 34, 209n7, 211n6

Nege, 114–16, 218n5
Neor, Henry, 19, 210n2
Never Die Church, 180, 221n3
New Barbarism theorists, 207n3
New Jerusalem Faith Healing Church, 29
nganga, 214n9, 217n3
Nigerians, 20, 21, 25, 30, 33, 37, 40, 50, 60, 119, 211n5
Nightman/Nightwoman, 129–31
numbering, ritual, 62
Nunley, John, 130
Nyamnjoh, F. B, xiii, 111
nye, 74

occult power, 207n5: and African science/African signs, 2; the concepts, 109–10; and cosmology, xiii; in dualistic world, 109; European and African forms compared, 215–16n18; front/back, 57–58; and good and evil, 109–10; and Mende concepts, 214n10; placing African signs, meaning of, 2, 109; and postcolonial context, 76; and South African concepts, 135; and the struggle metaphor, 110; and witchcraft, 110
Oduwole, Samuel O., 37, 50, 61, 93, 94, 170; and Center Street headquarters, 21; church planting in Liberia, 20–23; challenging kwi culture, 20; death of, 21; and Liberianization of Aladura, 20–23; reputation, 5–6, 23
Ogere, 21, 22–23, 27–28
Ogungbile, David, 69
Oladipo, Caleb Oluremi, 61, 208n2, 214n11
Olajubu, Oyeronke, 231
Olive, Mount, 168, 222n3
olive oil, 70, 159
Olu (Shoniyin), Apostle Samuel, 30–37; and AIC, 39; appointments during

Tabborrar, 176–79; authorizing Sandy, 43; and Bundu, 34–35; bush struggle, 31–32; calling, 31–32, 81; as captain of the ship (Tabborrar), 186–89; during the civil war, 37; and CLA, 4, 31–34, 168, 171; death of, 37; dreams and visions, 173; and ethnic groups, 33–34; and Faith Home household, 139, 148, 149; and Fyneah, 35–37; 168–69; hagiographic model, 39; head of the mount (Tabborrar), 172–95; identifying jina, 127; among the Kpelle, 32; and Liberianization, xii; during the military coup, 33; on Mount Olive name, 168, 222n4; and Nigerian background, 23; opposing the zo, 39; on Orimolade, 32, 208n3; on naming his son Oshitelu, 212n13; in Paynesville, 32–37; and prayer groups, 32, 36; reputation as healer, 39, 145; secret struggle, 189–93
Olupona, Jacob, 4, 56, 110, 208n5
Omoyajowo, Akinyele, 4–5
Oosthuizen, G. C., 217n1
open mole, 67, 215n16
ordination, 84–85
Orimolade, Moses, 4, 208n3
oriki, 214–15n13
Orisha, 40
Orsi, Robert, 7
Ortner, Sherry, 4, 12
Oshitelu, Dr. J.O, 18, 19, 32, 63, 133, 134, 147, 158, 169, 170, 186, 188, 208nn3, 5, 210n3, 212n13, 221n2

Parkin, David, 201
Paynesville City:
AIC in, 27–29, 1037; during the civil war, 12–13; CLA branches, 27–28; economy and industries, 25; ethnic groups, 25–27; field of prophecy, 40; Lebanese, 25; as "little community," 14, 27; mainline and mission churches, 26; medical facilities, 25; Mount Tabborrar, 28, 171; and St. Peter's Faith Home, 141–47; social and religious aspects, 23–27
Peel, J. D. Y., 4, 196, 208n4
Pentecostal Charismatic Churches, 5, 81–85, 203, 207n4

performative acts, 209n7
performative utterances, 63, 169
Personal witch, 118–20
Piot, Charles, 49
Poro Society, 53, 196, 213n4
possession and trance, 85, 188, 190, 215n
prayer group, 23, 27, 42–43
prayer room, 148
Presbyterian, 16
problem-solving, 48, 54–55
Probst, Peter, 4, 208n5
prophet: allocating and constituting roles, 79–81; ambivalence about role of, 3; 107–8; 203; in the argument of images, 40; 59; biblical paradigm for, 40, 58–59, 108; the boundary person, 47; compared to nganga, 59; as conduit of flow, 14, 37–38; definition of, 3, 78–81, 217n1; discourse, 41; experiencing the call, 81–84, 217n3; and Faith Home, 78; founder, 4, 39–40, 196; as healer, 78–79; and the Holy Spirit, 3; performances, 58; public and private selves, 204; misusing power, 79; in the public order, 40–41; and seniority, 52; as soldiers of the Lord, 58–59; temptations, 79; and virtue, 59, 60–62; and zo, 59,107–8
Prosperity Gospel, 18
purification, work of, 9

Rachel the Mano Woman (pseudonym), 180, 192, 193
Ray, Benjamin, xviii, 4, 39, 49, 56, 110, 150, 208n5, 214n13, 215n14, 219n2, 220n3
Resnik, Saloman, 101
Richards, Paul, xiii, 207n2
Ricoeur, Paul, 8
ritual struggle: Aladura emphasis on, 6; beach struggle, 161–64; contrasts and oppositions, 77, 194, 206; creating self-awareness, 203; defined, 3, 6, 76–77; and the Faith Home; and fasting, 88–91; and entangled roles, 194; and healing, 203; and the Holy Spirit, ix; and midnight struggle, 182–83; and renewal, 40–41; 201;

ritual struggle (*continued*)
  as rite of passage, 206; and ritualized bodies, 38; and the ritualized environment, 77; and role of audience, 216n2; as root metaphor, 76–77; spatiality and movement, 201, 205; and Tabborrar, 193–97, 201; and facing temptation, 85–88
road image, 48–49
Roberts, Oral, 18
Robbins, Jerome, 8–9
rod holder, 27; 53–54. *See also* holy rod

sacrifice, 76; 217n5. *See also* animal sacrifice
St. Peter's United Church of the Lord Aladura (St. Peter's): and AIC, 4, 39; as an Aladura church, 4–5; beginnings, 4, 32–34; and Church of the Lord Aladura; constitution and by-laws, 81; diaspora, 41–46, 198–201; Faith Home list of rules and regulations, 151–15; and Fyneah, 21–22, 35–36, 168–69, 177; membership and branches, 211n9; and Orimolade, 4; Paynesville headquarters, 32–37, 141–43; and Pentecostal-Charismatic churches, 81–85; on prophetic call, 81–85
Sandy, Kennedy, 37–38, 41–45, 198–201
spiritual lineage, 4; and Mount Tabborrar, 168–69; 171–201; and United Church of the Lord Aladura (UCL). *See also* Olu, Samuel
Sahlins, Marshall, 72
Sande Society, 53, 213nn4, 5
Sanders, Todd, 2, 110, 111, 136
Sandy, Kennedy, 38, 41–46,198–201
Sanford, Mei-Mei, 131
Sanneh, Lamin, 9
sassawood bark, 67–68
Saydee, Edward (pseudonym), 94–98, 155
Scheffers, Mark, 19, 210n2
Schimmel, Annemarie, 62
Schmoll, Pamela G, 58
Schoffeleers, Matthew, 214n9
Searle, John, 216n22
secrecy, 59, 73–76, 79, 106–7, 196, 204

self or person: African and Christian synthesis, 40; as body and soul, 58; being a patient, 54–56; as Child of Salvation, 49, 55; and circularity of signs, 204; in the civilized/uncivilized paradigm, 50–52; as dream soul, 56–58; dualities of, 49, 54, 76; 204–5; as hybrid, 50; Liberian representations of, 49–56; role of the Faith Home, 55–56; 167; secrecy of, 57–58; supernatural capacities of, 56–57; and "tribal" identities, 50–53; Western representation of, 49; Yoruba influence on 49–50
senior prophet/senior prophetess, 52
settlers. *See* Americo-Liberians
Sesay, Daniel, 221n1
sex and sexuality, 125, 129–30, 131–32, 153–55, 156, 192, 209n6, 219n8
Shank, David, 210n1
Shaw, Rosalind, 73, 128, 133, 210n12, 214n8
Sherman, Mary Brown Antoinette, 12
ship metaphor, 188–89
Shi'ite, 16
shouts, 30, 88, 191
sickness and affliction, 54–55
Sikhs, 17–18
Simpson, George E., 67
Singler, John,17
Sixth and Seventh Books of Moses, 132–34
slave raiding, 210n12
Sleboe, Richard, 221n3
Smith, Jonathan Z, 150, 166–67
Society of Earth, 113–14
Solomon, Daniel (pseudonym), 163, 169, 189–95
soul, 213–14n6. *See also* dream soul
South, American, 15, 211n8
Southern Baptist, 217n3
special requests, 169, 184–89. *See also* Tabborror, Mount
spirit familiars and spirit friends, 57
spiritual exercises, 10, 54, 62, 77, 84, 102, 156, 161–62, 182–83, 198, 199
spiritual interview, 151
spiritual mother, 53
Stone, Ruth M., 164, 221n9
struggle, definitions of term, 76–77, 216nn20, 21

Swede Faith Pentecostals, 209n9
Swedenborg, Emmanuel, 132
Sudan Interior Mission (SIM), 23

Tabborrar, Mount: adaptations, 170; altar, 177, 186–88, 191; as battery, 168; biblical models, 169–70, 221n2; during the civil war, 171; in the diaspora church, 198–201; and Faith Homes, 180–83; fasting, 184; evoking the founder's originary acts, 196; and gender, 197; as "holy struggle," 169; in Liberian and Nigeria, 170; name, 210n13, 212n2; and Nigerian background, 169–70; the 1984; observance, 169; offices and roles, 176–78; preparations, 171–75; purpose of, 168–69; revealed and trained knowledge, 179; rite of passage, 195–96; sacred space and sacred time, 170–71; ship metaphor, 188–89; special requests, 169, 184–85; tangled states, 194–95; Thanksgiving service, 188–89
Tagoe, Miatta, 27–28, 145
Tambiah, Stanley, 47–48, 215n14
tarry, 29, 211n8
Taylor, Charles, 12, 37, 200
Temne, 124, 133, 214n8
temptation, 85–87
Thai healing, 47
theology: and anthropology, 7–11; and authenticity, 4; and Christian culture, 7–11; as data, 10; defined, 7; and theology of liberation, 136; 209n9; and "ontology of peace," 10; and social experience, 4–5; as story, 8; and testimony, 11; as "theography," 8, 202; and theology of water, 215n17; as "thick description," 8
Thirteen Requests, 221–22n4
Thomas, Apostle Lewis, 38, 211n5
Thomas, Linda E, 7
Tolbert, William, 18
town (village) and forest (bush): and bush struggle, 71–72; dialectic between, 40; 71–73; and Faith Home, 72, 165–66; in light of the culture/nature model, 217n4; Mende view of, 71; and place of spirits, 71; and Tabborrar, 195–96;

transformative reproduction, 72; as virtual reality, 15; and witchcraft concepts, 120
Tonkin, Elizabeth, 51, 213n3
translation of scripture, 9–10
translocal spiritual economies, 43–44;
Tubman, William, 17
Turner, Harold, 4–5, 20, 60, 69, 76, 92, 133, 139, 147, 169, 215nn14, 17, 216n21, 220n6, 221n4
Turner, Victor, 212n1
Tweed, Thomas, 167
twins, 58, 68, 122–23
two brains or four eyes, 57;

United Church of the Lord Aladura (UCL),21–22, 35–36, 38, 195, 172, 168–69, 177–78
United Church of Salvation (UCS), 34–35, 221n7; and animal sacrifice, 212n11; and Bundu, Alpha O., 30, 34–35; healing policy of, 35; and St. Peter's, 34–35, 38, 39, 212n10. on use of holy rods, 35. See also Church of Salvation
United Healing Temple of Christ, 28
United Listeners of Christ, 28
Universal Church of God, 43, 44
Universal Faith Healing Church, 28
University of Liberia massacre, 11, 12, 169, 185
Utas, Mats, 207n2

Van Binsbergen, Wim, 72, 204
Van Dijk, Rijk, 44, 111, 113
Vanden Berg, Todd M., 136, 217n2
victory leafs (palm leafs), 69–70, 85, 146, 186
videos, 43, 45, 185
village as "virtual reality," 15
virtue (spiritual power): and ambiguity of power, 169; battery metaphor for, 62; as disruptive of the cultural order, 39; as free and spontaneous, 38–39; and holy materials, 62–71; and Holy Spirit, 60, 61; and institutional frame, 217n2; meaning of, 60–62; as mystical power, 61; and place, 70–71;

virtue (spiritual power) (*continued*)
the prophet's use of, 59, 60–62; the punitive role of, 61; as swear or oath, 60–61, 214n10. *See also* Holy Spirit, occult power

Walker, Sheila, 210n1, 215n18
water divinities, 130
Welmers, William E, 68
Werbner, Richard, 14, 166
West, Harry, 2
Whitehouse, Harvey, 196
Williams, Hannah, 21
Williams, Levi C., III, 209n10
Wintrob, Ronald, 131
witchcraft: and ambiguity, 59; animal forms, 28, 79, 95, 114–15, 118; 191; anthropophagic images of, 113–14; contexts for descriptions , 110, 112; deeds of witchcraft, 113; discourse, 2, 59; and human frailty and imperfection, 136–37; and intermediate spaces, 76; the ludic dimension of, 113; in mission and mainline churches, 217n2; and occult power, 109–13; and reality, 114; signs, 190–92; theories about, 110–12; and the virtual village, 75. *See also* African science/African signs; occult power

Yombe, 56
Yoruba: ajogun, 109–10; ase, 60; beginnings of Aladura movement, 19–20; influence on Aladura cosmology, 56; model for the Faith Home, 139–40; Holy Spirit as power, 61; notions of power, 60; on Olodumare's role, 60; and Olu's background, 30–32; Orisha, 40, 65

Zangai, Levi, 209n11
Zionist churches, 51, 79, 100, 217n2
zo (zoes), 39, 40, 57–58, 106–7, 120–23

CPSIA information can be obtained at www.ICGtesting.com
Printed in the USA
LVOW080414111212

310836LV00007B/12/P